OUT OF THE
NUCLEAR SHADOW

OUT OF THE
NUCLEAR SHADOW

Edited by
Smitu Kothari
Zia Mian

Lokayan
Delhi
Rainbow Publishers
Delhi
Zed Books
London

Out of the Nuclear Shadow was published in India in 2001
by Lokayan and Rainbow Publishers Ltd., 13 Alipur Road, Delhi 110 054

Out of the Nuclear Shadow was first published outside South Asia in 2001
by Zed Books Ltd, 7 Cynthia Street, London N1 9JF, London, UK and
Room 400, 175 First Avenue, New York, NY 10010.

Distributed in the United States exclusively by Palgrave, a division of
St Martin's Press, LLC, 175 Fifth Avenue, New York, NY 10010.

Cataloguing-in-Publication Data is available from the British Library.

Library of Congress Cataloging-in-Publication Data
Out of the nuclear shadow / Smitu Kothari and Zia Mian (editors).
p. cm.
Includes bibliographical references and index.
ISBN 1-84277-058-6 (CASED) — ISBN 1-84277-059 4 (LIMP)
1. Nuclear disarmament—India. 2. Antinuclear movement—India.
3. Nuclear disarmament—Pakistan. I. Kothari, Smitu. II. Mian, Zia.

JZ5786.094 2001
327.1'747'0954—dc21   2001017615

ISBN 1 84277 058 6 (Hb) UK
ISBN 1 84277 059 4 (Pb) UK

ISBN 81-86962-25-5 (Hb) India
ISBN 81-86962-26-3 (Pb) India

Cover design: EyetoEye, New Delhi
Typeset by Tulika Print Communication Services, New Delhi
and printed at Pauls Press, New Delhi.

For *Eqbal Ahmad*

(1932, Irki, Bihar–May 1999, Islamabad)
an activist no border could keep out,
an intellectual who challenged injustice everywhere,
a scholar who knew the power of truth,
a friend and teacher to us all,
a leader of our tribe.

For *Hansaben Kothari*

(December 18, 1929–June 4, 1999)
for nurturing conscience, pacifism,
the quest for justice,
and the love of our shared musical heritage.

Contents

Acknowledgements

This book was made possible by countless acts of support and kindness. We are especially grateful to Harsh Kapoor, who has with amazing determination made and maintained a South Asian peace movement website which is an oasis of solidarity in cyberspace. Without Harsh having gathered together much of the early writing that poured out of the hearts and minds of South Asian activists and scholars, this book would have been a monumental task. It has been made even easier by the efforts, ideas, and arguments of M.V. Ramana and Sharon Weiner. We cannot but delight in C.F. John's enthusiastic acceptance to illustrate the book.

We are also grateful to Praful Bidwai and Sadanand Menon for going through the manuscript and making suggestions; and to Achin Vanaik, Surendra Gadekar, Beena Sarwar, Arundhati Roy, Karamat Ali, Amulya Reddy, Itty Abraham, Pervez Hoodbhoy, Larry Lifschultz, Zuli Ahmad, and A.H. Nayyar for the generous gifts of their work, time and encouragement.

We are happy to acknowledge *Anumukti, Frontline, Himal, The Hindu, The News,* and *Dawn* for the use of articles that they originally published and to the authors who enthusiastically agreed to revise them. It is these publications that have helped make the South Asian nuclear debate possible, where many others in the media would have preferred to ignore dissent.

For helping turn an idea into a book, we are beholden to the Lokayan group, to P.T. George and Birendra for painstakingly typing and correcting the manuscript, to Nomita Jain for editing and glossing the text, to S.P. Das for preparing the index, to Indu and Purnima at Tulika for turning a messy manuscript into its present elegant form, and to Dhruva Narayan of Rainbow Publishers for managing the production. Finally, to Emma, whose smile and presence gave us the strength to leave behind this small token of solidarity for her generation.

Our greatest debt is to the numerous activists who protested the bomb, who wrote and signed statements, organised and attended meetings and marches, who strive to educate and mobilise their fellow citizens in one of the most crucial struggles of our time.

Out of the Nuclear Shadow

Nothing that has happened in India and Pakistan in the last fifty or so years has potentially graver consequences for the future of the people of the two countries than the nuclear weapons tests of May 1998. The explosions and the determination of the respective governments to have a nuclear deterrent means that the capability and willingness to wage nuclear war have been established beyond question. There must be no illusions about what this means. From now on, the spectre of nuclear war shall cast its terrible shadow over South Asia.

While the governments of India and Pakistan present May 1998 as one of their nation's glorious moments, in effect celebrating the demonstration of a capacity and willingness to repeat Hiroshima, the essays offered here are a small part of the effort in both countries to confront this future. The hope is to make accessible in one place the diversity of voices, traditions, and approaches that are weaving themselves into an anti-nuclear movement in India and Pakistan. Written before, during, and after the May explosions, they are both analysis and action in their attempt to understand and challenge the causes and consequences of the nuclearisation of South Asia. On display are outraged conscience and careful argument showing the futility, the perversity, and jeopardy.

What is not to be found here is surprise. Unlike many people in both countries, the authors gathered here were in their own ways prepared for the nuclear explosions. It was not just because of recent developments in politics in India and Pakistan, with the coming to the fore of new, more militant and belligerent, religious nationalism in both countries. The lure of the capacity for destruction, to be like those the world saw as powerful, was evident before nuclear weapons were invented. The struggle against this path was evident even in the life of Mahatma Gandhi, in a story that offers a parable for the past fifty years of India's quest for nuclear weapons, and hope for the future.

In his autobiography, *My Experiments with Truth*, Mahatma Gandhi relates a common rhyme he shared with the other students growing up in Rajkot, Gujarat:

> Behold the mighty Englishman
> He rules the Indian small,
> Because being a meat-eater
> He is five cubits tall.

On these little verses Gandhi builds a larger story, in a chapter entitled 'Tragedy'. The story begins with a friend telling the young Mohandas that many of their schoolteachers were in fact 'secretly taking meat and wine,' along with 'many well-known people of Rajkot.' Gandhi asked the older boy why? His friend told him: 'We are a weak people because we do not eat meat. The English are able to rule over us, because they are meat-eaters. You know how hardy I am, and how great a runner too. It is because I am a meat-eater. Meat-eaters do not have boils or tumours, and even if they sometimes happen to have any, these heal quickly. Our teachers and other distinguished people who eat meat are no fools. They know its virtues. You should do likewise. There is nothing like trying. Try, and see what strength it gives.'

For the young Gandhi this must have come as an amazing explanation for the presence and pattern of power and powerlessness in his world: in meat was found the cause of British conquest and rule over India, the origin of individual prowess and well-being, the social distinction of the local Indian elite, the learning and personal authority of his teachers, and even the transition from childhood to maturity.

The young Gandhi was overwhelmed by this powerful talisman— a source of power that is constrained in its use only by the intention of its possessor, a power able both to produce injustice and to end it. He writes: 'I wished to be strong and daring and wanted my countrymen also to be such, so that we might defeat the English and make India free.' He made his choice: 'So the day came... We went in search of a lonely spot by the river, and there I saw, for the first time in my life, meat... I simply could not eat it. I was sick. I had a very bad night afterwards. A horrible nightmare haunted me. Every time I dropped off to sleep it would seem as though a live goat were bleating inside me and I would jump up full of remorse. But then I would remind myself that meat-eating was a duty and so become more cheerful.' Gandhi was suffering, but it was for India.

In time, the meat worked another magic. The young meat-eaters sought to make meat more palatable, to enjoy the experience, to make themselves respectable by further emulating the real meat-eaters. Gandhi describes how he and his friends 'began to cook various delicacies with meat, and dress them neatly. And for dining, no longer was the secluded spot on the river chosen, but a State House, with its dining hall and table and chairs ... [I], forswore my compassion for the goats, and became a relisher of meat-dishes, if not of meat itself.'

This story illustrates a larger observation, made with great clarity by Ashis Nandy in *The Intimate Enemy. Loss and Recovery of Self Under Colonialism*; 'a colonial system perpetuates itself by inducing the colonised through socio-economic and psychological rewards and punishments, to accept new social norms and cognitive categories ... the ultimate violence which colonialism does to its victims [is] that it creates a culture in which the ruled are constantly tempted to fight their rulers within the psychological limits set by the latter.'

The Mahatma made this realisation a key part of his political sensibility. It is apparent most notably in *Hind Swaraj*, his political manifesto written in 1909 in the form of a dialogue between himself as a newspaper editor and an unnamed reader representing the ideas and aspirations of the Indian nationalist elite. Gandhi as the Editor asks, 'why do we want to drive out the British?' The Reader replies 'Because India has become impoverished by their Government. We are kept in a state of slavery. They behave insolently towards us, and disregard our feelings.' Under Gandhi's probing for a more positive vision, the reader declares 'we must own our own navy, our army, and we must have our own splendour, and then will India's voice ring through the world.'

Gandhi, as the voice of the Editor, replies 'You have well drawn the picture. In effect it means this: that we want English rule without the Englishman. You want the tiger's nature, but not the tiger; that is to say, you would make India English, and, when it becomes English, it will be called not Hindustan but Englistan. This is not the swaraj I want.'

This is however the independence that India gained. In the shadow of Hiroshima and Nagasaki, and Gandhi's ashes barely cold, India's new political leaders began the pursuit of their nuclear 'meat'. India's option to make and use nuclear weapons can be traced back to the July 1948 appointment of nuclear physicist Homi Bhabha, K.S. Krishnan, and S.S. Bhatnagar, first as the Scientific Advisory Committee to the Ministry of Defence, and then, in August, also as the Atomic Energy Commission.

There was no shortage of those willing to take up the call to realise the scientific and technological potential that was being created by India's nuclear complex. From the early 1950s onwards, as hundreds of Indian scientists were trained in nuclear science and engineering in the United States (over 1,100 in all between 1955 and 1974) right wing politicians and political parties pushed for India to develop its nuclear weapons. Speaking after the nuclear tests that he had ordered, with a clear sense of being vindicated, Prime Minister Vajpayee declared 'I have been advocating the cause of India going nuclear for well over four decades.' In triumph were forgotten the careful, laboured explanations of the need for the bomb; there was no problem with the fact that four decades earlier China was seen as a special ally not threat, that China then had no nuclear weapons, that Pakistan was struggling to find its feet as a state.

It is important, however, not to forget that the May 1998 nuclear tests were not the first to have taken place here. Indira Gandhi took the first decision in 1972 to test nuclear weapons. This led to the 1974 nuclear explosion. She and subsequent Prime Ministers continued to fund the nuclear weapons programme and some of them have admitted to thinking about ordering tests. Prodded by the nuclear weapon scientists, few hesitated out of principle, most lacked any sense of restraint other than simple uncertainty about whether the nuclear calculus was in their favour at that particular moment or whether to wait for a more opportune one.

It is ironic given how nationalistic India's elite has been, how committed to a kind of independence at any cost, that it has followed so blindly. One is reminded of Lord Macaulay's famous 1835 Minute on Education. Writing about British rule in India, he said the aim should be to create 'a class of persons Indian in blood and colour, but English in taste and opinions, in morals and intellect.' The British succeeded to the extent that a hundred or so years later it was anglicised Indians like Nehru and Jinnah who took over from them. American strategic thinkers, who preside like demented priests over their own nuclear weapons, can now boast they have had the same effect in even less time. Despite all their differences, within fifty years of inventing nuclear weapons, destroying Hiroshima and Nagasaki, and claiming that nuclear weapons were for defence, the US has successfully created enclaves of Indians, and Pakistanis who share their 'opinions', 'morals' and 'intellect'.

In the case of Pakistan, the story started later. From the setting up of Pakistan's Atomic Energy Commission in 1954, as part of the US inspired Atoms for Peace Programme, it was a small step for Pakistan's nuclear scientists and politicians like Zulfikar Ali Bhutto to begin making comparisons with the directions India's nuclear programme was taking and demanding Pakistan follow suit. As the late Eqbal Ahmad argued, India's obsession became Pakistan's choice.

None of this explains why the tests were conducted. Many reasons have been offered. None of them matter. A reason is after all a justification offered on the basis that it makes sense within some shared system of values where cause and effect and linkages between them are already agreed upon. If it is accepted that testing nuclear weapons is nothing but a demonstration of a capability and a preparedness to use them (if one is not prepared to use nuclear weapons, why test them?) then there can be no justification possible for testing nuclear weapons, not for India, Pakistan, or anyone else, not now, not previously, nor at any other time. To accept even the possibility of a reason for testing is to accept that there may be a reason for using nuclear weapons.

The horror that is nuclear war is little known and little understood in South Asia. In part this is because the invention and subsequent use of nuclear weapons by the US against Hiroshima and Nagasaki occurred just as independence finally came within sight. There were few who could or did get a sense of how within seconds of the atom bomb's going off tens of thousands of people were burnt and blasted and poisoned, and how the immediate survivors suffered and died from the injuries and the radiation they received. There were even fewer who realised that death from nuclear weapons could take decades.

The use of nuclear weapons in South Asia means tearing out the heart of one or more of its teeming cities. The effects would be beyond description. Put simply, if Pakistan and India each used only five of the dozens of bombs they may well have and targeted each other's largest cities, almost 3 million deaths are predicted, with another 1.5 million people severely injured. Many of the injured would probably perish as hospitals along with much else for miles around would be blasted and burned by the bomb.

Speaking to Parliament, Prime Minister Vajpayee explained that for him nuclear weapons were 'India's due, the right of one-sixth of humanity.' This idea seems to inform much of the official explanation, which is typically couched in the language of India's right to have nuclear weapons as long as others have such weapons. There is no such right—do the crimes that have already been committed elsewhere legitimate the perpetration on new crimes? It is the wisdom of blinding yourselves because others cannot see. For Nawaz Sharif in Pakistan, the nuclear explosions were a demonstration that he had chosen 'independence' over 'slavery'. Independent of what and independent to do what, he did not say.

The people of India, and Pakistan, 'one-sixth of humanity' and more, do have rights, and seek freedom. They have the right to food, a good education, health, secure livelihoods with dignity, and all the other entitlements that people have as communities and individuals, most especially freedom to make their own choices about their lives. The reality violates these rights. South Asia now is the home to the majority of the world's poor, the hungry, the sick, the non-literate. The polarisation of wealth and power is staggering and, for a majority, the catalogue of suffering and woe becomes more unbearable with each passing day.

The bomb is little consolation. However, the prodigious costs involved in creating, maintaining and deploying even a small nuclear arsenal, currently estimated as at least Rs. 70,000 crore for India, which the government is so intent on spending, would go a long way to meeting the needs and entitlements to people's security, justice and freedom. As Rammanohar Reddy shows in his essay *The Wages of Armageddon*, the estimated cost of just one of India's Agni missiles is enough to pay for 13,000 primary health clinics for a year, while the annual cost of developing the nuclear weapons arsenal would be comparable to the total central government funding of primary education.

After carrying out their respective nuclear tests, the governments of India and Pakistan have more or less agreed to sign the Comprehensive Nuclear Test Ban Treaty (ironically postponed by the recent vote by lawmakers in the US) and to negotiations on a world-wide

Fissile Material Cutoff Treaty (banning the production of the special materials used for making nuclear weapons). While these are important and worthwhile goals, these agreements can only limit the scale of the devastation in the event of nuclear war in South Asia. The nuclear weapons that have already been tested will remain; the material for making such weapons that has already been stockpiled will still be there, as will the plans and means to use them.

The nuclear weapons states, US, Russia, Britain, France and China, have accepted the *fait accompli* of a nuclear South Asia. The US has sought to strengthen economic, political and strategic ties with India. It seeks only to limit the possible threat outside South Asia, which India's government assures them of, for now. How far India has come was evident in President Clinton's visit to South Asia in the spring of 2000. India's elite greeted the US Commander in Chief of several thousand deployed nuclear weapons with adulation. The streets were swept clean, the poor pushed out of sight. After his speech he was mobbed by the members of parliament, who according to reports climbed over their desks in their urge to shake his hand.

While the US thinks of its global interests, and the British tag along, France and Russia compete to sell arms to India, everything from aircraft that can deliver nuclear weapons, to attack submarines, submarine launched cruise missiles, and even help with India's nuclear submarine project. Pakistan for its part is struggling to keep its economy afloat, and is bailed out with one carefully timed International Monetary Fund loan after another. The fears of Pakistan's disintegration into nuclear-armed anarchy and of the increasingly militant Islamist groups that stalk the land seem to be enough to make the world look away from the overthrow of its elected government by yet another military coup, in October 1999. The people of South Asia are alone in the shadow of the bomb.

In their new role as citizens of nuclear states, the people of India and Pakistan would do well to learn some of the lessons from the US-Soviet nuclear arms race and Cold War. The first of these is that terror does not last. People get used to it and new and greater sources of terror are devised. This is clear from the arsenals of all five of the established nuclear weapons states, who claim like India and Pakistan to deter enemies with nuclear weapons. The nuclear weapons states have all increased their arsenals from a few nuclear weapons to hundreds of weapons, and for the US and USSR thousands, and they all rely on thermonuclear weapons that are tens if not hundreds or thousands of times more destructive than the 'simple' nuclear weapons they started with. There will always be pressure for more and bigger bombs, and for smaller bombs, tactical bombs, neutron bombs. And as bomb begets bomb, missiles spawn offspring with longer-range and greater accuracy, adding lethality with every generation.

The second lesson is that arms racing is destructive even if there is no war because of the cold and calculated planning and costly preparations for such war that underlie the declared strategy, on both sides, of nuclear deterrence. The enmity, fear, and resources needed to sustain a cold war themselves need to be maintained and in the process society becomes poisoned, the economy deformed and the space for democracy and tolerance shrivels. This has started to happen already, with efforts by the governments in both India and Pakistan to instil a siege mentality in their respective citizens. Fearful people are further battered by the diversion of scarce economic resources into military technology and military preparedness at the cost of critical social needs.

The third and final lesson is that nuclear weapons, and the system that creates them and gives them purpose, take on a life of their own. Throughout the Cold War, the US and the Soviet Union claimed that their nuclear weapons were part of what was required to confront an implacable and unremitting ideological enemy. The Cold War ended a decade ago and yet there remain tens of thousands of nuclear weapons. In the same way, while it is vital to find a just resolution to the disputes that afflict India-Pakistan relations, especially that of Kashmir, unless nuclear disarmament is frontally addressed, the weapons will not go away. As long as they remain, the danger that they will be used exists.

Nuclear weapons mean that every Pakistan-India tension will have a nuclear edge. This will be unchanged by any agreement that the two states sign short of renouncing their nuclear weapons. As long as they remain, nuclear weapons can be taken up as an issue by political leaders eager to ride to power on the back of enmity and fear. Even if Indian and Pakistani policy makers agree now to restrain their nuclear ambitions, such an agreement may well unravel with the next crisis.

For the moment, driven by ambition and fear, befuddled by crisis and confusion, both countries are heading towards the abyss. There is hope in that both countries have stopped short of actually deploying nuclear weapons. But there are many that wish to flaunt the bomb, or to worship it, while others desire their enemy to look into the face of the demon and tremble. Deployment brings new dangers, of nuclear weapons use by accident, by misadventure, by recklessness. It must not be allowed. This is the first battle.

There is reason for hope. The euphoria that greeted the nuclear tests faded quickly. It was, anyway, a localised, largely urban, at times orchestrated reaction. A post-election survey conducted by the Centre for the Study of Developing Societies in Delhi, in November 1999, showed that despite the intense media coverage, the majority of Indians had not heard about the nuclear tests. Still free of the mind-numbing arguments asserting the need for nuclear weapons, India's people may be again its greatest hope.

There is also a tradition of struggle. We are an insurgent if not insurrectionary people. There is a not so visible history of opposition to the nuclear future in South Asia. Far removed from the centres of political authority, at the sites where nuclear facilities have been and are being built, be it uranium mines or nuclear power plants, local communities are engaged in remarkable struggles. Their movements and mobilisations are often not couched in the language of big ideas of social change and protest, but in the small traditions of defending livelihoods, community rights, public health, the right to information. They have marched, fasted, blockaded, occupied, gone to court, they have protested to survive and highlight their concerns. As the statements against nuclear weapons from scientists, academics, journalists, writers and poets, doctors, former soldiers, civic groups, and social movements from India and Pakistan gathered in this volume show, there are now new forces joining the struggle.

There are also individuals and groups around the world with hard won insights and awareness of the nature of the nuclear state and how best to fight it. They shall be allies in this fight. To this end, we have gathered extensive lists of anti-nuclear organisations, books, films and websites as a resource and teaching guide both for peace groups and concerned people everywhere.

The tasks that confront the peace movements in India and Pakistan are unprecedented. Not only must they educate their fellow citizens in what it means to live with nuclear weapons in their midst, they must do so without immobilising people with fear. They must organise to abolish nuclear weapons but cannot concentrate simply on the technology, politics, economics and culture of nuclear weapons because nuclear weapons cannot be abolished from South Asia or globally while leaving everything else unchanged. The solution to the bomb does not lie only in the area of nuclear weapons, the bomb is not its own answer. To abolish nuclear weapons will require confronting and transforming the fundamental structures of injustice within and between states that are the causes of insecurity, conflict, and war. We dedicate this book to that struggle.

January 2001   ZIA MIAN
                                              SMITU KOTHARI

VOICES OF CONSCIENCE

The Atom Bomb and Ahimsa

MAHATMA GANDHI

It has been suggested by American friends that the atomic bomb will bring *Ahimsa* (nonviolence) into being as nothing else could. If they mean that the bomb's destructive power will so disgust the world that it will turn away from violence for the time being, then perhaps it will. But I think this is very much like a man glutting himself on delicacies to the point of nausea. He turns away from them only to return with redoubled zeal after the effect of nausea is over. Precisely in the same way will the world return to violence with renewed zeal after the effect of its disgust has worn off.

Often good does come out of evil. But that is God's not man's plan. Man knows that only evil can come out of evil as good comes out of good. Although atomic energy has been harnessed by American scientists and army men for destructive purposes, it is undoubtedly within the realm of possibility that it may be utilised by other scientists for humanitarian purposes. However, this is not what was meant by my American friends. They are not so simple as to pose a question which implies such an obvious truth. An arsonist uses fire for destructive and nefarious purpose. Yet, a mother makes daily use of fire to prepare nourishing food.

As far as I can see, the atomic bomb has deadened the finest feelings which have sustained mankind for ages. There used to be so-called laws of war which made it tolerable. Now we understand the naked truth. War knows no law except that of might. The atom bomb has brought an empty victory to the Allied armies. It has resulted for the time being in the soul of Japan being destroyed. What has happened to the soul of the destroying nation is yet too early to see. The forces of nature act in a mysterious manner. We can only solve the mystery by deducing the unknown result from the known results of similar events. A slave holder cannot hold a slave without putting himself or his deputy in the cage holding the slave.

Let no one run away with the idea that I wish to raise a defence of Japanese misdeeds which occurred in the pursuit of Japan's own unworthy ambitions. The difference was only are of degree. I may assume that Japan's greed was more unworthy. But greater unworthiness confers no right on the less unworthy to destroy without mercy men, women and children in particular areas of Japan. The only moral which can be legitimately drawn from the supreme tragedy of the bomb is that it shall not be destroyed by counter-bombs. Violence cannot be destroyed by counter-violence.

Mankind will only emerge out of violence through nonviolence. Hatred can only be overcome by love. Counter-hatred only increases the surface expression as well as the depth of hatred. I am aware that I am repeating what I have stated many times before—and practised to the best of my ability and capacity. What I originally said (about non-violence) was nothing new. It is as old as the mountains. While I would not recite any copybook maxim, I did announce what I believed in with every fibre of my being. Sixty years of practice in various walks of life has only enriched this belief and it has been fortified by the experience of friends. It is the central truth by which one can stand alone without flinching. I believe in what Max Muller said years ago, namely, that truth needs to be repeated as long as there are men who do not believe it.

This essay first appeared in *Hanju* (Pune), July 7, 1946.

India's Obsession, Our Choice

EQBAL AHMAD

Young people to whom the future belongs are often right when powerful old men in khadis and suits are not. The Japanese youth who stood holding a placard in Tokyo was absolutely right. 'Nuclear Test?', the placard asked after three tests by India, 'Are you crazy?' Then there were five. 'Gone berserk', was Pakistan Foreign Minister's apt description.

Power Does Not Grow Here ...
It is well known that Indian leaders generally and the BJP wallahs have long viewed nuclear weapons as a currency of power. They view nuclear weapons as a permit to the club in which India does not belong, and should not enter with a population of half a billion illiterate and four hundred million under-nourished citizens. Furthermore, it is illusory to search for power through nuclear weapons. The nature of power changes in accordance with shifts in modes of production, knowledge and communication. In our time these shifts have been revolutionary. Power has changed in ways least understood by those who formally hold the reins of power.

The currency of power minted by nuclear weapons is counterfeit. When first invented, it was viewed as a weapon of war, and wantonly dropped on Hiroshima and Nagasaki. Its development and possession coincided with the rise of the US as a global power, a coincidence which confirmed it as a modern component of power. Its use also

proved that it was a weapon of total annihilation, therefore not usable, notwithstanding crackpot realists like Henry Kissinger and Herman Kahn who were obsessed with making nuclear weapons usable.

After the USSR tested its hydrogen bomb, it became a weapon of terror and of deterrence against war between two giants in a bipolar world. It also served as an umbrella for covert, proxy warfare. Given these facts and its association with superpowers, in the 1950s the identification of nuclear weapons with power was total. It was in the interest of the United States and the USSR to perpetuate this perception. But change has its own inexorable logic. Three events helped devalue nuclear weapons as a component of power. First the cases of Cuba and Vietnam. Together, the liberation movements of these two small nations reduced the most awesome nuclear power, in the words of Senator J.W. Fulbright, to 'a crippled giant'. Castro's revolution succeeded and survives to this day despite American nuclear power; in fact the possession of nuclear weapons constricted American ability to destroy that revolution. The Vietnamese demonstrated that a nuclear giant can in fact be defeated, even militarily. France offered a negative example. It tested and inducted nuclear weapons as a means to challenge the paramountcy of the United States in Europe. It did not work.

A third, related reality dawned: for the first time in history, political economy took precedence over military might as a component of power. In Europe the influence of France, now a nuclear power, does not surpass that of non-nuclear Germany. Similarly, Japan exercises much greater influence in the world than does China or France. South Africa and Israel offer contrasting examples. South Africa's prestige and influence in world politics increased after it had renounced and dismantled its nuclear arsenal while Israel's considerable nuclear capability—so scandalously tolerated and augmented by the United States—has added not a bit to its influence or security in the Middle East or beyond. That in 1998 India's leaders still view the possession of nuclear weapons as a necessary element to gain recognition as a world power, speaks volumes about their intellectual poverty and mediocre, bureaucratic outlook.

... But It Can Shrivel
India's mindless right-wing leaders who started it all and then proceeded to goad Pakistan into baring its nuclear capabilities may never

acknowledge that they have committed a crime against India and its neighbours, and that not one good—strategic or tactical, political or economic—can accrue from their blunder. In effect, these five tests may set back India's ambitions. As any politician and gang leader knows, power grows from the neighbourhood. A country that does not command influence and authority in its own region cannot claim the status of a world power. India's standing with its neighbours, already low, will sink further.

Excepting a few interregnums, such as the short-lived government of I.K. Gujral, India's governments have not been very sensitive toward their neighbours. At regional and international conferences, a participant is often astonished at the antipathy delegates from Sri Lanka, Nepal, Maldives and Bangladesh express towards India's policies. But I believe nothing shocked and angered India's neighbours more than its unilateral and surprise decision to carry out its 3+2 nuclear tests, thus starting a nuclear arms race and opening the way to potential holocaust in South Asia. They have a right to anxiety and anger as nature has so willed that they are no more safe than Indians and Pakistanis from the nuclear fallout.

An Indian scientist, Dr. Vinod Mubayi, rightly says that the RSS has now killed Gandhi twice: his body in 1948, and his legacy 50 years later. India shall suffer for some time to come from the effects of these killings. It had enjoyed what the French call a *prejudge favourable* in world opinion, a mystique of being uniquely ancient and pluralistic, a land of Hindus and Muslims, Christians, Buddhists and Zoroastrians, the spiritual home of Albert Luthuli, Desmond Tutu, Father Daniel Berrigan, and Martin Luther King. In a single blow, the BJP government has destroyed India's greatest asset. And more.

After decades of bitter squabble, India's relations with China, the world's most populous country and a fast growing economic giant, had been improving for the last six years. India–China amity had reached a level significant enough for Chinese leaders to counsel Pakistan, their old ally, to resolve its disputes with India. In a conversation with me, former Prime Minister I.K. Gujral cited China–India cordiality as a model for relations. A high-level Chinese military delegation was in India when Prime Minister Atal Behari Vajpayee proudly announced his first three nuclear tests. These had preceded and followed anti-China rhetoric. India's greatest single foreign policy achievement of the last two decades was thus buried away like nuclear waste.

For nearly four decades, India's rate of growth remained low at around 4 per cent per annum. Economists the world over dubbed this mysterious consistency as the 'Hindu rate of growth'. Then a decade ago, the curve began to move upward reaching a whopping 7.5 per cent in 1998. Hope had never prevailed so widely in India since Independence, and international capital had begun to view it as a grand investment prospect. Economists expected that in the next decade India would maintain a 7 per cent rate of growth, just about wiping out the abject poverty that so assails its people. This expectation too has been interred in the Pokhran wasteland. Estimates of a decline in growth are based not on the effects of sanctions but on the adverse turn in the investment climate. Lastly, with these tests Delhi may have put India in the fast lane of the arms race. A third world country can crash more easily in such a race than the second world power did.

II

The leaders of India and Pakistan have now appropriated to themselves, as others had done before, the power that was God's alone—to kill mountains, make the earth quake, bring the sea to boil, and destroy humanity. I hope that when the muscle-flexing and cheering is over they will go on a retreat, and reflect on how they should bear this awesome responsibility.

History demands that it be noted that Prime Minister Nawaz Sharif's initial good instincts were overwhelmed by forces in and out of Pakistan. Our knowledge of the factors that led to Pakistan's decision to carry out the tests is not complete, but enough is known to identify the main factors: The most important was the provocations of BJP leaders.

How Indian Leaders Goaded Pakistan . . .

There were too many provocations by BJP leaders to recount here. These included a warning by L.K. Advani, India's home minister, that Pakistan should note a change in South Asia's 'strategic environment'; Prime Minister Vajpayee's statement that his government might forcibly take Kashmiri territory under Pakistan's control; the handing over of the Kashmir affairs portfolio to the hardline home minister who had so enthusiastically overseen the destruction of the Babri Mosque; and the actual heating up of a limited but live conflict along the Line of Control in Kashmir. Pakistan's chief of army staff returned

from the front line with an assessment that we may in fact be witnessing the slow beginning of a conventional war. To my knowledge,
Delhi did little to reassure Islamabad. These developments greatly
reinforced among Pakistani officials a sense of foreboding. This was
accentuated by what a decade of embargo under the Pressler Amendment had done to the weapons sustainability of Pakistan's armed forces.
During the decade of Mohammed Zia-ul Haq, our defence forces
reverted to heavy reliance on US arms. In the last decade, these have
suffered not merely from obsolescence but also from a paucity of reliable spare parts. Pakistan could find itself unable to sustain a war with
India without soon running into serious supply problems. In a military
environment such as this, army leaders are likely to put a high premium
on an assured deterrent capability. This much is known to interested
military analysts the world over.

It is astounding that under these circumstances, and after testing
their nuclear device, India's leaders would engage in provocations,
verbal and military. Officials and legislators in Washington might also
note that their anti-nuclear sanctions actually compelled a speedier
development and testing of nuclear arms.

In an environment so fraught, the government needed political
support. Instead, Pakistan's opposition leaders—all except Ghinwa
Bhutto, Air Marshal Asghar Khan, and Sardar Farooq Ahmed Khan
Leghari—were in the streets taunting Nawaz Sharif to 'explode' a
nuclear bomb. The pack was led first by Jamaat-i-Islami leaders
who were soon overtaken by Benazir Bhutto. She seems to have
sensed in this national crisis an opportunity to restore her flagging for-
tunes. I know of few gestures in the ugly repertoire of Pakistani politics
as revolting as her demagogic toss of bracelets at Nawaz Sharif.

The G–8 responded mildly and in a divided fashion to India's
tests, signalling a soft response to the menace at hand and enhancing
the Pakistani sense of isolation and risk. Finally, like the Indian tests,
Pakistan's response was a tribute to the hegemony of the nuclear
culture and notions of deterrence so assiduously promoted by the
West during the Cold War.

. . . And Pakistan Fell for It

What then should Pakistan have done? My advice at the time was: do
not panic, and do not react. This translates as: do not listen to people
like Qazi Husain Ahmad and Benazir Bhutto who, either out of

ignorance, or more likely crass opportunism, were advocating nuclear tests, here and now. The arguments for steadying the jerking knee were compelling. Consider these:

One, India was the focus of adverse world attention both governmental and popular, and was likely to remain so for a while. A Pakistani test would immediately relieve the pressure on India and shift it to Pakistan with consequences surely worse for us than for India. Rather than take Delhi's burden upon itself, it was time for Islamabad to mount diplomatic initiatives and international campaigns to put pressure on India both within SAARC and worldwide, and reap some benefits for Pakistan's statesman-like posture.

Two, Pakistan's objectives in developing nuclear weapons are different from India's. Delhi's nuclear programme has been linked to the quest, however misguided, for power. Islamabad's is related to security. What Pakistan has sought is a shield against India's nuclear power. That requires the achievement of sufficient deterrence which we possessed by all appearances. India's five tests did not change that reality, at least not from what I know of strategic weaponry from a life time of studying it. Scientists and their managers like to test; that is what they do. The question we needed to ask was: Are we less defence capable today than a week ago? I don't think any honest person could have answered in the affirmative.

Three, one major risk Pakistan ran was to get drawn into an arms race with India, a country with far superior resources than ours. There was evidence to suggest that India would like us to do just that. The development of strategic armaments is an expensive business that carries little Keynesian logic. In other words, while it costs a lot, the economic multiplier is negligible. The reasons are that the development and production of strategic weaponry is a capital intensive and largely secret activity, which rarely yields either the economic multiplier or the technological spin off. It is thus that the Soviet Union and its satellites such as Poland and Czechoslovakia became highly sophisticated arms producers, but remained very underdeveloped economically. As a consequence, their states and societies grew disorganically and eventually collapsed. For Pakistan to avoid that fate, it had to resist falling into the trap of seeking strategic equivalence with India. Our requirement has been effective deterrence not equivalence. Deterrence demands fewer shifts in strategic planning and weaponry, providing a more stable environment for economic growth.

Finally, the most basic problems facing Pakistan today are economic and social. It is not an exaggeration to say that our future depends on how well we confront the challenges of economic slow-down and social fragmentation. Both are expressions of fundamental structural crises in our state and society, and neither is susceptible to simple crisis-management. In an environment such as this, Pakistan is considerably more vulnerable to international sanctions than India which, whatever its other weaknesses, has been and remains less dependent on foreign aid, loans and technology transfers than we are. For these reasons and more, it would have been much better for Islamabad to stay cool and calculating, utilising the opportunities Delhi has presented. But reason did not prevail.

III

Each historical time has its own temper. But one factor has been common throughout history to the attainment of progress and greatness. Historians of culture describe this one factor variously as syncretism, openness, pluralism, and a spirit of tolerance. Where ideas do not clash, diverse influences, knowledge, viewpoints, and cultures do not converge, civilisation does not thrive and greatness eludes.

Nuclear Gains and the Losses
The rightist environment of religious chauvinism and intolerance that the BJP and its allies promote in India—it pervades Pakistan for other reasons—is deeply harmful to India's future. Nuclearisation of nationalism has further degraded this environment. The tests have worsened the xenophobia of Hindutva supporters. Reaction no less than a habit of emulation among fundamentalist adversaries, will undoubtedly reinforce right-wing sentiments and excesses in Pakistan. In the aftermath of the blasts BJP supporters stormed a meeting of anti-nuclear scientists, attacked artist M.F. Husain's home and destroyed his paintings, in retaliation of US sanctions assaulted trucks carrying Pepsi and Coca-Cola, disrupted a concert by Pakistani musician Ustad Ghulam Ali. 'The atmosphere of intolerance has been gaining ground recently', says an editorial in the *Hindustan Times*. 'Such actions will break up the very fabric of this country' warns Ambika Soni, a leader of the Indian National Congress.

Pakistan's nuclear tests are having an even more profound impact on the domestic environment than on its defence or foreign relations. The phenomenon was to be expected, but its scope is greater than one could have imagined. It is too early to examine the import of the prime minister's blockbusting speech on June 11, 1998. A so-called revolution has been inflicted upon the country, if only in outline. Moreover, there is as yet no indication as to how the government proposes to bridge the ever-widening national chasm between intent and implementation. Necessarily then, what follows can only be a tentative assessment of Pakistan's gains and losses since the nuclear tests.

Rhetorical flourishes and emotional highs notwithstanding, the change in Pakistan's security environment is not substantive. While the shape of what some politicians and analysts grandiosely call the 'strategic balance' between India and Pakistan has changed, the realities underlying it remain largely unchanged. There was for nearly a decade an implicit threat that conventional war between the two could result in the use of nuclear weapons, in particular by the conventionally weaker party. This presumption is now explicit. It is debatable whether Pakistan's security interests were best served by maintaining that ambiguity or by following India into rendering its capability overt. I still believe that, notwithstanding Delhi's provocative muscle-flexing, Pakistan's security interests have not been served by matching India show-for show-plus-one. There is no way now to prove or disprove that proposition. What can be said however, is that the older verities remain true.

One such truth is that there exists a balance of mutual destruction that renders irrational, and therefore unlikely, the pursuit by either adversary of a decisive conventional war. This fact has traditionally defined the parameters of Pakistan-India conflict in the following ways: (i) Both sides could decide—but didn't—that the new risks were much too great to continue with old disputes, and engage in creative diplomacy to resolve them. (ii) They might continue the conflict, as they have so far done, at a low level of intensity by proxy warfare, and by bleeding each other by violent and not-so-violent sabotage operations. (iii) Tensions resulting from the former may result in the threat or actuality of conventional warfare of limited scope and/or duration. The Indian mobilisation and Pakistani riposte in 1987 and 1990 are examples of such threats that did not materialise. (iv) All three options require a sophisticated system of management for the nuclear arsenal in each country until such time as the parties agree to mutual disarmament. There has also existed a certain concentration of international monitoring on whether or not the two adversaries are reaching a level of confrontation that risks becoming nuclear. It was this phenomenon that produced the forceful US diplomatic intervention in the summer of 1990.

This paradigm has not significantly changed since India and Pakistan both conducted multiple nuclear tests. The conflict remains. Neither side has shifted from its old positions so as to make possible a meaningful peace process. The struggle in Kashmir continues with Pakistan's help, and so does India's harsh military effort to suppress it. Since the nuclear tests, India has beefed up its military presence there. Covert warfare continues. Since the eleven nuclear tests, Pakistan has blamed India for two bloody acts of sabotage—a bomb explosion in a cinema hall and the blowing up of a railway train. There is no evidence to suggest that the covert warfare between the two countries can no longer bring them close on occasion to conventional confrontations such as those that occurred in 1987 and 1990. There is evidence, however, that the great powers are more cognisant than before of the risks inherent in the simmering conflict between the two neighbours.

Pakistani officials and several commentators have been emphasising this last to be a major gain from the nuclear tests. They say that the question of Kashmir has now been placed on the front burner of international politics. This is true. But we need to inquire into the practical value—political, economic or military—of this achievement. Obviously, the recognition by the United States, the P–5, the G–8 and the UN Secretary-General that Kashmir is a core issue that ought to be addressed has not led them to soften their sanctions against Pakistan, which welcomes their interest, or harden them against India, which spurns it.

In contrast to India, Pakistan exhibited a sophisticated diplomatic posture. The Foreign Office's submissions to the big powers' meeting in Geneva and to the Security Council were excellent, carefully worded and admirably nuanced drafts. Similarly, Islamabad's unilateral moratorium on nuclear testing is a wise, no-cost gesture that is liable to favourably impress international opinion. Yet these commendable initiatives are unlikely to bring about a meaningful change in great power behaviour. The reason is that no significant shift has occurred in the South Asian equation of power, and in the relative importance of India and Pakistan in the world economy and politics.

When a nuclear balance of terror—in the Pakistan–India contest, this ought to be distinguished from such concepts as 'strategic parity' and 'military balance'—exists between two adversaries, the focus of conflict is on the conventional capabilities of each. It is for this reason that during the Cold War, the United States and USSR maintained huge conventional forces and deployed them in each other's proximity in Western and Eastern Europe. This rule applies with even greater force to the unique situation of India and Pakistan, for never before have two enemies so proximate and so environmentally-integrated possessed nuclear arms.

The tests have not improved Pakistan's conventional capability, actually or potentially. On the contrary, in this respect at least the international sanctions are likely to hurt Pakistan much more than India, which has a much larger, broader and more diversified industrial base. It is a significant indicator that in its recent budget India augmented formal defence spending by 14 per cent while the informal increase—i.e. if one counts allocations to its R&D and military-industrial complex—amounts to an estimated 33 per cent. Pakistan, by contrast, has increased defence spending by 8 per cent which is barely enough to meet the costs of inflation. Also, its industrial base is considerably smaller. It is most likely that in the coming years, the military disparity between the two countries will continue to grow.

One aspect in which a substantive change may have occurred in Pakistan's favour is its standing in the Middle East. The region's governments and people are living under the frightening shadow of Israel's nuclear arms. And, make no mistake. Israel is not India. It is not, by any definition, a normal contemporary state. It is the only member of the UN that has yet to declare its international boundaries. It is still committed to the expansionist agenda of achieving Eretz Israel. It is still colonising what remains of Palestinian land in Arab possession. A significant portion of its political society still aims at destroying the holy Muslim sites of Jerusalem. It still occupies, in violation of the United Nations Charter, the territories of three sovereign Arab countries.

It is still diverting and draining the water so essential to the survival of millions of Arab people. And yet, it enjoys the wholehearted support and protection of the United States. It is only natural that the beleaguered Arabs should welcome the emergence of a potential nuclear balance in their vicinity. The change in Arab attitudes toward Pakistan has been reinforced by growing evidence of India-Israel nuclear collaboration.

Yet the truth is that Pakistan is not in a position to benefit significantly from this favourable Middle Eastern disposition. Pakistan's ruling establishment knows that at the slightest hint of such a move, the wrath of the United States will descend on it; only then will we know what real sanctions are like. It is a risk that Pakistan's government cannot take, and Islamabad has been vowing not to take it. So this, too, is an unrealisable gain.

Beyond the change in atmospherics, which rarely endure, Pakistan's passage from an ambiguous to an explicit nuclear power has not substantially changed its strategic position. In contrast, the fallout has so far been most considerable at home. There, a state of emergency was imposed almost simultaneously with the announcement of the tests in Chagai.

Fundamental rights granted by the Constitution were suspended. The President, read the proclamation which was later approved by Parliament, 'was pleased to declare that the right to move to any court, including a High Court and the Supreme Court, for the enforcement of all the fundamental rights conferred by chapter 1 of part 2 of the Constitution shall remain suspended for the period during which the said proclamation is in force.' Nothing, except the good will of the executive authority, now stood between the citizens' rights and their violation. It was an extreme, draconian measure which democracies rarely if ever employ, save in the exceptional circumstances of total war or complete anarchy.

Ironically, emergency was imposed in Pakistan just as the highest authorities in the land were claiming that Pakistan had achieved strategic balance with its adversary, and that national security was now firmly assured. Are we to assume, then, that citizens' rights will deteriorate in this country in inverse proportion to officially proclai-med improvements in its security environment and national might?

Foreign currency accounts held by citizens and expatriates were seized and converted into local currency, arbitrarily and in violation of pledges made by the prime minister himself. It is true that these accounts had to be frozen in order to prevent a panic flight of capital and hard currency. But what justification is there for converting them into rupees, thus hurting large numbers of middle class citizens, expatriates and investors, and ruining above all the credibility of the state? Unless the government rectifies this injustice soon, the consequences of this amoral opportunism will be felt by the state and society for a long time to come.

On June 11, the Prime Minister addressed the nation, and was promptly dubbed a 'revolutionary' in the official media for promising land reforms, strict collection of loans and taxes and a host of austerity measures. There is not enough room here to comment on his extraordinary speech.

Four simple reminders are in order. One, to date, revolutions from above have failed, everywhere and at all times. Two, what succeeds from above are reforms, provided they are seriously conceived and methodically enforced. Three, enforcement of reforms requires a streamlined, lean, efficient, cooperative and rule-based administrative mechanism. That mechanism is in shambles—obese, corrupt, insecure and sullen. Four, it is a cardinal rule of reform, revolution, warfare and all such enterprises, not to fight on too many fronts simultaneously, and not to make too many enemies at the same time. Will someone close to the Prime Minister examine his otherwise commendable agenda in the light of these principles, interrupt all the yes-men that surround him and tell him the truth? That one person would do Nawaz Sharif, and Pakistan (if the Prime Minister listens to him), a very great favour indeed.

This essay combines three articles by Eqbal Ahmad which were published as his weekly columns in the Pakistani newspaper *Dawn*. The first of these articles, 'India's Obsession, Our Choice' (May 17) was written as Pakistan was still uncertain about its response to the Indian tests. The second, 'When Mountains Die' (June 4) was written days after Pakistan conducted its own tests. 'Nuclear Gains and Losses' (June 14), analysed with remarkable prescience the consequences of these tests for the future of the subcontinent.

India's Nuclear Nemesis

RAJNI KOTHARI

The world seemed to be pulling back from the nuclear brink towards which it had been moving for almost 45 years. The Gorbachev initiative put the Soviet Union on a more normal course of development which would have satisfied the consumer needs of its citizens, little realising that it had for so long got so stuck by the Cold War logic that it only led to its 'collapse'. The American celebration of the same heralded both the end of ideology and the end of history. At this very time, one found two relatively minor powers, both internally fragile and deeply divided, first India and then Pakistan, decide to pick up the gauntlet left by the two 'superpowers'. Interestingly, both were found to use the same jargon of nuclear warfare (deterrence, draft nuclear doctrine, and the rest) and promise to the 'whole world' a utopia of denuclearisation while itself (particularly India) getting prepared to engage in a piling up of the nuclear arsenal and an aggressive diplomacy of putting the other side on the defensive. All this sounding all the more dangerous in the case of India and Pakistan given the fact that they were so adjacent to each other and each of them was facing a scenario of internal destabilisation, religious extremism and economic brinkmanship producing in their wake a politics of increasing turbulence and turmoil, with more and more power shifting in the hands of the military. There was clearly no other way the nuclear arms could be 'tested' (in the case of Pakistan producing a complete military takeover).

As for India, it could be argued that if the Cold War was brought to an end following the collapse of the Soviet Union, a similar scenario may be sought to be enacted in the case of Pakistan. Growing internal conflicts and institutional erosion precipitated a scenario for India mounting an aggressive nuclear posture towards which there had already taken place a gradual technological build-up throughout the 1980s, leading to an announcement of the country deciding to become a nuclear weapons state on May 13, 1998. The announcement proved more important than real testing which incidentally was not even adequately registered on the monitors of global intelligence agencies meant to oversee any incidence of nuclear proliferation.

The idea of emerging as a 'great power' in world affairs merely on the basis of this announcement and the country's getting ready to gate-crash into the nuclear club did, of course, overlook the likely reaction from Pakistan. Islamabad too had been stealthily importing the relevant technological know-how (unlike India's steady build-up for close to two decades) but somehow this was not expected to translate the same into a nuclear explosion so very soon after India's own. It also meant not adequately realising that once India and similar other powers were to join the non-proliferation race, they were likely to face more dangerous responses from neighbouring regions. The internal erosion of the democratic process in Pakistan indicated that it was not likely to behave in as restrained and responsible way as reflected in India's 'unilateral announcement of a moratorium on nuclear testing, no first-use policy and non-use against non-nuclear weapon countries' while seeking to work towards a 'universal comprehensive and non-discriminatory disarmament as a central feature of India's foreign policy.' The latter, of course, by no means depends on what India alone does and is more a part of the long standing rhetoric of denuclearising the world as a whole. Indeed in many ways, it amounts to passing the buck from what India would undertake to what the world as a whole was being asked to accept. This should be read alongside two contrary positions being adopted by the two countries. Pakistan has spelled out its nuclear strategy as being one of minimum nuclear deterrence which, however, will call for continuing review and reassessment in light of India's nuclear build-ups, including if necessary further build-up of its missile programme and 'matching warheads' all of which in effect means it will be a strategy that is India-centric. The Indian position as repeatedly spelled out by its external affairs minister Jaswant Singh is to be 'neither country-specific nor threat-specific' but aimed at acquiring 'strategic space and autonomy' as had all along been aimed at which only meant that it would 'give India additional strategic space and autonomy.'

The nuclear arena is in any case an increasingly complex framework of international affairs—getting more and more uncertain and ambivalent. Such a counterposing of two quite different strategic positions has been brought out in a major study entitled *India's Nuclear Bomb: The Impact on Global Proliferation* by George Perkovich. It brings out three major aspects of India developing a nuclear capability—starting with the early thinking of people like Jawaharlal Nehru and Homi Bhabha of building technological self-reliance including Indian scientists' ability to build and deliver nuclear fusion weapons while still keeping the military out of it and ending in the May 1998 announcement by Vajpayee which necessarily involved the role of the military in carrying out the tests. First, despite the ambitious overtones of the Nehrus and the Bhabhas—and those who followed them—they had to depend exclusively on foreign technology and know-how which in turn required considerable time before producing effective nuclear weapons. Second, once it was decided to move beyond the mere goal of deterring a nuclear attack from other powers and to develop its own nuclear weapon capability, this needed to be done in a continuous manner following a lull between 1975 and 1980 (the first Pokhran test was carried out in 1974). Throughout the 1980s, work was done to re-define calculations and designs, to test non-nuclear components of devices and generally to develop the capacity to build lighter, smaller explosive devices. This effort was further enhanced when 'Rajiv Gandhi authorised an acceleration of this work which continued under Narasimha Rao' so that while the 'short-lived BJP government in 1996 authorised a nuclear test' whatever devices were tested then had been developed under the Congress governments before it. And third, for a long time Indian scientific and political leadership had conceived of nuclear weapons as 'political instruments' than as 'militarily usable devices', clearly distancing themselves from the 'dangerous nuclear doctrines that were developed and adopted in the defence establishments of the US and the Soviet Union.' The Vajpayee–Fernandes approval under the BJP-led coalition clearly moved away from this position as it accepted the role of the military, given its resolve to test-fire the nuclear device which could not be done without the active involvement of the military. With this decision the country bid good-bye to the earlier thinking in which the politicians had been joined by the scientists who had no interest in losing their relative autonomy in the nuclear enterprise.

The implications of this about-turn in strategic thinking on the nuclear front are there for us to see (just as the changed approach to multinationals and stepped-up foreign investments under the new coalition pushed the country towards the new global-corporate model of capitalism). The overall implications of the new combination of strategic thinking on the one hand and the new political economy on the other indicate quite clearly the right-wing shift of the new government.

The net outcome of these contrary pulls of pursuing great power ambition and joining the corporate globalising worldview (on the part of India) and a merely negativist reaction thereto along with a defensive stance of following the way India went (on the part of Pakistan) has been poignantly depicted by Prof. Joseph Rotblat, the leading conscience of the Pugwash movement (at some of the meetings of which I had occasion to confer with him in the years gone by), in a leading interview he gave to the *Indian Express* in early November 1999 entitled 'The Tragic Flaw of a Nuclear South Asia'. After tracing his own involvement from the Manhattan Project and his discourse with Neils Bohr and other once leading exponents of the bomb who had then sharply moved away from that position, Rotblat turned to India's nuclear strategy following Pokhran-II and the nuclear doctrine released thereafter and brought out, with utmost modesty (aware of the dilemma that India faced as he in his time had himself faced) yet as firmly and clearly as he could, the dangers attendant upon pursuing a pro-active nuclear policy at the cost of neglecting more pressing concerns of both socio-economic and political types as India seemed to him to have decided to do, giving up on the Gandhian path that he had himself moved closer to over time. Instead, he found it committing itself to deploying a nuclear arsenal as some of its more hawkish 'security' advocates were arguing (particularly India) and to a nuclear doctrine described as one of 'minimum credible nuclear deterrence', the very concept that these very strategic thinkers used to decry when it was employed by the United States and its western allies during the Cold War with the Soviet Union.

Let me finally bring out the international dimension of this strategy and doctrine. For as is becoming clear, such a pro-active strategy may indeed be gaining wider international support. For one notices the growth of a gradual even if in part reluctant and ambivalent incorporation of India's nuclear position by countries as diverse as the US on the one hand and Japan on the other, and, of course, France. Both the US Congress and President Clinton moving towards a waiver of sanctions, shifting away from the Glenn amendment and further more (with Gary Ackerman declaring that India's nuclear tests had enhanced its profile in his country), and Japan indicating, following a visit by Jaswant Singh, India's external affairs minister, that it was 'thinking over' the sanctions earlier imposed after India had conducted the nuclear tests. As for the American approach in this whole affair, there seems to be a clear effort at becoming a both overt and covert participant-cum-mediator, forcing India to move out of its traditional bilateral posture vis-a-vis Pakistan and moving towards what a leading Indian commentator, V. Sudershan, has called the growth of a 'India–Pak–US dialogue'. This is very much in keeping with the American global strategy of at once incorporating emerging regional powers and engaging in fostering a variety of 'peace accords' round the world, somehow hoping that the more dangerous the world becomes, the greater will be the dominant position of the United States in it. It may be the end of the Cold War in a manner of speaking but it is certainly not the advent of peace. Indeed, if anything, it heralds even greater dangers to the survival capacities of peoples, nations and civilisations.

Nuclear proliferation of the kind that South Asia has experienced is likely to be further emulated—some of it taking off from Pakistan, others from South Korea, Israel being already on the brink. Dominant powers like the US are likely to make use of such proliferation—while still for the record announcing policies of non-proliferation, CTBT (which has already received a jolt) and the like on issues that go far beyond these strategic dangers. Let me end this chronicle of looming dangers by pointing to the deep moral chasm in which large segments of world population are likely to get engulfed.

We have already heard of the serious accident that took place in Tokaimura in Japan (in a uranium processing plant) in the very country that has not yet fully recovered from the horrors of nuclear radiation spurred by Hiroshima. But then Japan is not the only country where accidents of such gravity have occurred (incidentally this very town of Tokaimura had experienced a quite bad accident only two years ago). We have, of course, heard about Chernobyl, a disaster that shocked the world and about Three Mile Island, in the US, though few of us have taken due note of the series of disasters that occurred in the southern Ural mountains in Russia in an industrial complex that was built by the Soviet Union for producing nuclear weapons (near a place called Chelyabinsk, code name 'Mayak'). Each of these disasters being worse than the 1986 Chernobyl melt-down. All of it was shrouded in secrecy not just by the Russians but by the Americans as well. So much so that according to a study carried out by Mark Hertsguard who has brought out 'the striking case of Cold War duplicity and double think', not even the local residents 'who were all the time receiving an enormous amount of radiation' came to know of it till much later following the exposure of a large dump of nuclear waste as a result of a cyclone in 1967. We are told that 'the same iron curtain of deception would have entombed the Chernobyl disaster but for the fact that radiation meters in Sweden and other places had done their job efficiently and the Soviet authorities led by Mr. Mikhail Gorbachev, their President, could deceive no more.' The moot point is that no one has found an answer to the disposal of nuclear waste and there seem to be even fewer ways to detect and prevent nuclear accidents. This is even more the case with the series of accidents and failures in waste disposal that have taken place in India, all the way from the fire at Narora to the multiple heavy water leaks in Kalpakkam, the collapse at Kaiga and the flooding at Kakrapur, not to speak of the series of small and big leaks and break-downs in and near nuclear power plants, projects and 'experiments' causing physical and psychological harm to workers employed in them and the populations living in and around them. While our scientists continue to make a distinction between generating nuclear power for producing electricity and generating it for making nuclear warheads, between 'peaceful uses' and producing nuclear weapons, it would be a serious mistake to overlook the prospects of using the former as a cover for the latter.

For, in some ways, these seemingly innocuous and incidental out-comes of becoming part of the nuclear nemesis overtaking the world, including in nations and regions for long considered 'safe', hold out a more dangerous prospect for the well-being and survival of the human populace than even the dangers posed by nuclear weaponry. For while the latter pose a threat, the former is already becoming one. The wholly unethical secrecy enveloping the hundreds of accidents in such a large array of nuclear power plants and the incessant release of such a large mass of nuclear waste seem to have numbed our senses and made us ignore in an almost systematic manner the fact that we may be actually already standing on the brink of what I have earlier called the nuclear nemesis. It needed the deep insights and intuition of a great mind like that of C. Rajagopalachari, 'Rajaji' as we knew him, to have so clearly seen the possible inching of the coming generations towards what in his philosophical view looked like a loss of real freedom in the pursuit of what was called 'science', leading both to a deterioration in people's real freedom of knowledge and in consequence 'a disastrous development in civilisation'. So much so, that even in his old age and with declining health, he undertook to go round the world and lead a campaign against the nuclear virus. In the Western world, too, Bertrand Russell and Albert Einstein raised their voices and were found to be leading the campaign against nuclear arms as well as the proliferation of nuclear energy as such. Today, in India and in South Asia, and indeed in the world at large, we need to pick up the threads of these visionaries. We need to rekindle the global 'peace movement' (in which I had occasion to participate when it was in the main located in the West, including joining in the Olaf Palme Commission) which seems to have lost its passion in the Western world and needs to be pursued once again, perhaps this time starting in South Asia and then spreading worldwide. What some of us began as an anti-nuclear Convention in Delhi soon after the Vajpayee government came forward with that terrible announcement (for which Vajpayee said he was waiting all his life) and the impressive Peace March that followed soon after needs to be continued. Nothing short of that will enable us to pull back from the brink, the point at which I started this essay.

This essay on re-escalating the nuclear arms race—worldwide, regionally in South Asia and in the immediate Pakistan–India neighbourhood—makes a point that is best brought out by succinctly stating my main contentions. The primary responsibility for re-escalation lies with India, given its ambition of emerging as a world power of some consequence, a goal that it failed to fulfill through a steady pursuit of geopolitical, economic and cultural (despite 'Hindutva') objectives. Whereas in the domestic sphere the goal of gaining and retaining political power led Vajpayee to adopt a strategy of moderate statecraft, he seems to have practically wiped it all out by indulging in an adventurist foreign and strategic policy. It is the same Vajpayee who had in his earlier incarnation as foreign minister under Morarji Desai pursued a far more contained and constructive approach to peace and disarmament (he had asked me to organise an international conference on disarmament) as well as de-escalation of Pakistan–India enmity, and was about to pursue the same objective in India's relation with China, when it was the latter who let him down given its preoccupation with humbling Vietnam. It has been a most unfortunate volte face on the part of a statesman of Vajpayee's stature throwing away a major opportunity of picking up the thread of Nehru's foreign and regional policy for which he had said he had high regard, a policy that I.K. Gujral tried for a while to resume on the basis of what came to be known as the 'Gujral Doctrine'. This exaggerated self-importance on the part of Vajpayee both as a political gamesman and as a national leader is likely to prove most costly in the long run to India's standing in world affairs.

India's recent efforts to gain the support of America, Japan and some European countries (especially France) in its pursuit of great power ambition—in the process, of course, further heightening the globalising mission of the United States as I have argued in this essay—can only contribute to the declining prospects of peace and genuine disarmament, especially in the nuclear arena.

The world stands once again on the precipice of a dangerous course and to no small extent India should take part of the blame for this. Its formulation of a draft nuclear doctrine only serves to make a 'further hardening of India's nuclear posture since Pokhran II', a doctrine that marks 'a triumph of the maximalist or extreme stand point and expresses the dominance of the classical Cold War mindset within the country's nuclear lobby' as has been persuasively brought out in a recent publication of the Movement in India for Nuclear Disarmament (MIND). It goes on to warn us that 'it (the Draft Nuclear Doctrine) will, if implemented, *ignite a nuclear arms race in Asia, as well as grievously damage the prospects of global disarmament*' (emphasis in the original). What started as a policy of constructing a 'minimum nuclear deterrent' is only likely to drive the country towards what the MIND document describes as a 'maximalist' standpoint which too was brought out not as a result of informing the Indian people but rather as a result of the Prime Minister writing in a letter to the US President explaining the reasons for carrying out the test. Once again, we are found to not just ourselves engage in an adventurist policy but in the process become privy—as a matter of policy—to the continuing dominance of world affairs by what is claimed to be the only remaining superpower in the world. It is becoming evident that the unfolding relationship will bring this whole scenario of India's ambition of acquiring the status of a world power being co-opted by the dominant world power to final fruition.

C F Shm

The End of Imagination

ARUNDHATI ROY

"The desert shook", the Government of India informed us (its people).

"The whole mountain turned white", the Government of Pakistan replied.

By afternoon the wind had fallen silent over Pokhran. At 3.45 p.m., the timer detonated the three devices. Around 200 to 300 m deep in the earth, the heat generated was equivalent to a million degrees centigrade—as hot as temperatures on the sun. Instantly, rocks weighing around a thousand tons, a mini mountain underground, vapourised . . . shockwaves from the blast began to lift a mound of earth the size of a football field by several metres. One scientist on seeing it said, "I can now believe stories of Lord Krishna lifting a hill."

—*India Today*

May 1998. It'll go down in history books, provided, of course, we have history books to go down in. Provided, of course, we have a future.

There's nothing new or original left to be said about nuclear weapons. There can be nothing more humiliating for a writer of fiction to have to do than restate a case that has, over the years, already been made by other people in other parts of the world, and made passionately, eloquently and knowledgeably.

I am prepared to grovel. To humiliate myself abjectly, because, in the circumstances, silence would be indefensible. So those of you who are willing: let's pick our parts, put on these discarded costumes and speak our second-hand lines in this sad second-hand play. But let's not forget that the stakes we're playing for are huge. Our fatigue and our shame could mean the end of us. The end of our children and our children's children. Of everything we love. We have to reach within ourselves and find the strength to think. To fight.

Once again we are pitifully behind the times—not just scientifically and technologically (ignore the hollow claims), but more pertinently in our ability to grasp the true nature of nuclear weapons. Our Comprehension of the Horror Department is hopelessly obsolete. Here we are, all of us in India and in Pakistan, discussing the finer points of politics, and foreign policy, behaving for all the world as though our governments have just devised a newer, bigger bomb, a sort of immense hand grenade with which they will annihilate the enemy (each other) and protect us from all harm. How desperately we want to believe that. What wonderful, willing, well-behaved, gullible subjects we have turned out to be. The rest of humanity (Yes, yes, I know, I know, but let's ignore them for the moment. They forfeited their votes a long time ago), the rest of the rest of humanity may not forgive us, but then the rest of the rest of humanity, depending on who fashions its views, may not know what a tired, dejected heart-broken people we are. Perhaps it doesn't realise how urgently we need a miracle. How deeply we yearn for magic.

If only, if only, nuclear war was just another kind of war. If only it was about the usual things—nations and territories, gods and histories. If only those of us who dread it are just worthless moral cowards who are not prepared to die in defence of our beliefs. If only nuclear war was the kind of war in which countries battle countries and men battle men. But it isn't. If there is a nuclear war, our foes will not be China or America or even each other. Our foe will be the earth herself. The very elements—the sky, the air, the land, the wind and water—will all turn against us. Their wrath will be terrible.

Our cities and forests, our fields and villages will burn for days. Rivers will turn to poison. The air will become fire. The wind will spread the flames. When everything there is to burn has burned and the fires die, smoke will rise and shut out the sun. The earth will be enveloped in darkness.

There will be no day. Only interminable night. Temperatures will drop to far below freezing and nuclear winter will set in. Water will turn into toxic ice. Radioactive fallout will seep through the earth and contaminate groundwater. Most living things, animal and vegetable, fish and fowl, will die. Only rats and cockroaches will breed and multiply and compete with foraging, relict humans for what little food there is.

What shall we do then, those of us who are still alive? Burned and blind and bald and ill, carrying the cancerous carcasses of our children in our arms, where shall we go? What shall we eat? What shall we drink? What shall we breathe?

The Head of the Health, Environment and Safety Group of the Bhabha Atomic Research Centre in Bombay has a plan. He declared in an interview (*The Pioneer*, April 24, 1998) that India could survive nuclear war. His advice is that if there is a nuclear war, we take the same safety measures as the ones that scientists have recommended in the event of accidents at nuclear plants.

Take iodine pills, he suggests. And other steps such as remaining indoors, consuming only stored water and food and avoiding milk. Infants should be given powdered milk. 'People in the danger zone should immediately go to the ground floor and if possible to the basement.'

What do you do with these levels of lunacy? What do you do if you're trapped in an asylum and the doctors are all dangerously deranged?

Ignore it, it's just a novelist's naivete, they'll tell you, Doomsday Prophet hyperbole. It'll never come to that. There will be no war. Nuclear weapons are about peace, not war. 'Deterrence' is the buzz word of the people who like to think of themselves as hawks. (Nice birds, those. Cool. Stylish. Predatory. Pity there won't be many of them around after the war. Extinction is a word we must try and get used to.) Deterrence is an old thesis that has been resurrected and is being recycled with added local flavour. The Theory of Deterrence cornered the credit for having prevented the Cold War from turning into a Third World War. The only immutable fact about the Third World War is that if there's going to be one, it will be fought after the Second World War. In other words, there's no fixed schedule. In other words, we still have time. And perhaps the pun (the Third World War) is prescient. True, the Cold War is over, but let's not be hoodwinked by the ten-year lull in nuclear posturing. It was just a cruel joke. It was only in remission. It wasn't cured. It proves no theories. After all, what is ten years in the history of the world? Here it is again, the disease. More widespread and less amenable to any sort of treatment than ever. No, the Theory of Deterrence has some fundamental flaws.

Flaw Number One is that it presumes a complete, sophisticated understanding of the psychology of your enemy. It assumes that what deters you (the fear of annihilation) will deter them. What about those who are not deterred by that? The suicide bomber psyche—the 'We'll take you with us' school—is that an outlandish thought? How did Rajiv Gandhi die?

In any case who's the 'you' and who's the 'enemy'? Both are only governments. Governments change. They wear masks within masks. They moult and re-invent themselves all the time. The one we have at the moment, for instance, does not even have enough seats to last a full term in office, but demands that we trust it to do pirouettes and party tricks with nuclear bombs even as it scrabbles around for a foothold to maintain a simple majority in Parliament.

Flaw Number Two is that Deterrence is premised on fear. But fear is premised on knowledge. On an understanding of the true extent and scale of the devastation that nuclear war will wreak. It is not some inherent, mystical attribute of nuclear bombs that they automatically inspire thoughts of peace. On the contrary, it is the endless, tireless, confrontational work of people who have had the courage to openly denounce them, the marches, the demonstrations, the films, the outrage—that is what has averted, or perhaps only postponed, nuclear war. Deterrence will not and cannot work given the levels of ignorance and illiteracy that hang over our two countries like dense, impenetrable veils. (Witness the VHP wanting to distribute radioactive sand from the Pokhran desert as *prasad* all across India. A cancer yatra?) The Theory of Deterrence is nothing but a perilous joke in a world where iodine pills are prescribed as a prophylactic for nuclear irradiation.

India and Pakistan have nuclear bombs now and feel entirely justified in having them. Soon others will too. Israel, Iran, Iraq, Saudi Arabia, Norway, Nepal (I'm trying to be eclectic here), Denmark, Germany, Bhutan, Mexico, Lebanon, Sri Lanka, Burma, Bosnia, Singapore, North Korea, Sweden, South Korea, Vietnam, Cuba, Afghanistan, Uzbekistan . . . and why not? Every country in the world has a special case to make. Everybody has borders and beliefs. And when all our larders are bursting with shiny bombs and our bellies are empty (Deterrence is an exorbitant beast), we can trade bombs for food. And when nuclear technology goes on the market, when it gets truly competitive and prices fall, not just governments, but anybody who can afford it can have their own private arsenal—businessmen, terrorists, perhaps even the occasional rich writer (like myself). Our planet will bristle with beautiful missiles. There will be a new world order. The dictatorship of the pro-nuke elite. We can get our kicks by threatening each other. It'll be like bungee-jumping when you can't rely on the bungee cord, or playing Russian roulette all day long. An additional perk will be the thrill of Not Knowing What To Believe. We can be victims of the predatory imagination of every green card-seeking charlatan who surfaces in the West with concocted stories of imminent missile attacks. We can delight at the prospect of being held to ransom by every petty trouble-maker and rumour-monger, the more the merrier if truth be told, anything for an excuse to make more bombs. So you see, even without a war, we have a lot to look forward to.

But let us pause to give credit where it's due. Whom must we thank for all this?

The men who made it happen. The Masters of the Universe. Ladies and gentlemen, the United States of America! Come on up here folks, stand up and take a bow. Thank you for doing this to the world. Thank you for making a difference. Thank you for showing us the way. Thank you for altering the very meaning of life.

From now on it is not dying we must fear, but living.

It is such supreme folly to believe that nuclear weapons are deadly only if they're used. The fact that they exist at all, their very presence in our lives, will wreak more havoc than we can begin to fathom. Nuclear weapons pervade our thinking. Control our behaviour. Administer our societies. Inform our dreams. They bury themselves like meat hooks deep in the base of our brains. They are purveyors of madness. They are the ultimate coloniser. Whiter than any white man that ever lived. The very heart of whiteness.

All I can say to every man, woman and sentient child here in India, and over there, just a little way away in Pakistan, is: Take it personally. Whoever you are—Hindu, Muslim, urban, agrarian—it doesn't matter. The only good thing about nuclear war is that it is the single most egalitarian idea that man has ever had. On the day of reckoning, you will not be asked to present your credentials. The devastation will be indiscriminate. The bomb isn't in your backyard. It's in your body. And mine. Nobody, no nation, no government, no man, no god, has the right to put it there. We're radioactive already, and the war hasn't even begun. So stand up and say something. Never mind if it's been said before. Speak up on your own behalf. Take it very personally.

In early May (before the bomb), I left home for three weeks. I thought I would return. I had every intention of returning. Of course, things haven't worked out quite the way I had planned.

While I was away, I met a friend of mine whom I have always loved for, among other things, her ability to combine deep affection with a frankness that borders on savagery.

'I've been thinking about you,' she said, 'about The God of Small Things—what's in it, what's over it, under it, around it, above it...'

She fell silent for a while. I was uneasy and not at all sure that I wanted to hear the rest of what she had to say. She, however, was sure that she was going to say it. 'In this last year—less than a year actually—you've had too much of everything—fame, money, prizes, adulation, criticism, condemnation, ridicule, love, hate, anger, envy, generosity—everything. In some ways it's a perfect story. Perfectly baroque in its excess. The trouble is that it has, or can have, only one perfect ending.' Her eyes were on me, bright with a slanting, probing brilliance. She knew that I knew what she was going to say. She was insane.

She was going to say that nothing that happened to me in the future could ever match the buzz of this. That the whole of the rest of my life was going to be vaguely unsatisfying. And, therefore, the only perfect ending to the story would be death. My death.

The thought had occurred to me too. Of course it had. The fact that all this, this global dazzle—these lights in my eyes, the applause, the flowers, the photographers, the journalists feigning a deep interest in my life (yet struggling to get a single fact straight), the men in suits fawning over me, the shiny hotel bathrooms with endless towels—none of it was likely to happen again. Would I miss it? Had I grown to need it? Was I a fame-junkie? Would I have withdrawal symptoms?

The more I thought about it, the clearer it became to me that if fame was going to be my permanent condition it would kill me. Club me to death with its good manners and hygiene. I'll admit that I've enjoyed my own five minutes of it immensely, but primarily because it was just five minutes. Because I knew (or thought I knew) that I could go home when I was bored and giggle about it. Grow old and irresponsible. Eat mangoes in the moonlight. Maybe write a couple of failed books—worstsellers—to see what it felt like. For a whole year

I've cartwheeled across the world, anchored always to thoughts of home and the life I would go back to. Contrary to all the enquiries and predictions about my impending emigration, that was the well I dipped into. That was my sustenance. My strength.

I told my friend there was no such thing as a perfect story. I said in any case hers was an external view of things, this assumption that the trajectory of a person's happiness, or let's say fulfilment, had peaked (and now must trough) because she had accidentally stumbled upon 'success'. It was premised on the unimaginative belief that wealth and fame were the mandatory stuff of everybody's dreams.

You've lived too long in New York, I told her. There are other worlds. Other kinds of dreams. Dreams in which failure is feasible. Honourable. Sometimes even worth striving for. Worlds in which recognition is not the only barometer of brilliance or human worth. There are plenty of warriors that I know and love, people far more valuable than myself, who go to war each day, knowing in advance that they will fail. True, they are less 'successful' in the most vulgar sense of the word, but by no means less fulfilled.

The only dream worth having, I told her, is to dream that you will live while you're alive and die only when you're dead. (Prescience? Perhaps.)

'Which means exactly what?' (Arched eyebrows, a little annoyed.)

I tried to explain, but didn't do a very good job of it. Sometimes I need to write to think. So I wrote it down for her on a paper napkin. This is what I wrote: To love. To be loved. To never forget your own insignificance. To never get used to the unspeakable violence and the vulgar disparity of life around you. To seek joy in the saddest places. To pursue beauty to its lair. To never simplify what is complicated or complicate what is simple. To respect strength, never power. Above all, to watch. To try and understand. To never look away. And never, never to forget.

I've known her for many years, this friend of mine. She's an architect too.

She looked dubious, somewhat unconvinced by my paper napkin speech. I could tell that structurally, just in terms of the sleek, narrative symmetry of things, and because she loves me, her thrill at my 'success' was so keen, so generous, that it weighed in evenly with her (anticipated) horror at the idea of my death. I understood that it was nothing personal. Just a design thing.

Anyhow, two weeks after that conversation, I returned to India. To what I think/thought of as home. Something had died but it wasn't me. It was infinitely more precious. It was a world that has been ailing for a while, and has finally breathed its last. It's been cremated now. The air is thick with ugliness and there's the unmistakable stench of fascism on the breeze.

Day after day, in newspaper editorials, on the radio, on TV chat shows, on MTV for heaven's sake, people whose instincts one thought one could trust—writers, painters, journalists—make the crossing. The chill seeps into my bones as it becomes painfully apparent from the lessons of everyday life that what you read in history books is true. That fascism is indeed as much about people as about governments. That it begins at home. In drawing rooms. In bedrooms. In beds. 'Explosion of self-esteem', 'Road to Resurgence', 'A Moment of Pride', these were headlines in the papers in the days following the nuclear tests. 'We have proved that we are not eunuchs any more,' said Mr Thackeray of the Shiv Sena. (Whoever said we were? True, a good number of us are women, but that, as far as I know, isn't the same thing.) Reading the papers, it was often hard to tell when people were referring to Viagra (which was competing for second place on the front pages) and when they were talking about the bomb—'We have superior strength and potency.' (This was our Minister for Defence after Pakistan completed its tests.)

'These are not just nuclear tests, they are nationalism tests,' we were repeatedly told.

This has been hammered home, over and over again. The bomb is India. India is the bomb. Not just India, Hindu India. Therefore, be warned, any criticism of it is not just anti-national, but anti-Hindu. (Of course, in Pakistan the bomb is Islamic. Other than that, politically, the same physics applies.) This is one of the unexpected perks of having a nuclear bomb. Not only can the Government use it to threaten the Enemy, they can use it to declare war on their own people. Us.

In 1975, one year after India first dipped her toe into the nuclear sea, Indira Gandhi declared the Emergency. What will 1999 bring? There's talk of cells being set up to monitor anti-national activity. Talk of amending cable laws to ban networks 'harming national culture' (*The Indian Express*, July 3). Of churches being struck off the list of religious places because 'wine is served' (announced and retracted, *The Indian Express*, July 3, *The Times of India*, July 4). Artists, writers, actors, and singers are being harassed, threatened (and succumbing to the threats). Not just by goon squads, but by instruments of the government. And in courts of law. There are letters and articles circulating on the Net—creative interpretations of Nostradamus' predictions claiming that a mighty, all-conquering Hindu nation is about to emerge—a resurgent India that will 'burst forth upon its former oppressors and destroy them completely.' That 'the beginning of the terrible revenge (that will wipe out all Moslems) will be in the seventh month of 1999.' This may well be the work of some lone nut, or a bunch of arcane god-squadders. The trouble is that having a nuclear bomb makes thoughts like these seem feasible. It creates thoughts like these. It bestows on people these utterly misplaced, utterly deadly notions of their own power. It's happening. It's all happening. I wish I could say 'slowly but surely'—but I can't. Things are moving at a pretty fair clip.

Why does it all seem so familiar? Is it because, even as you watch, reality dissolves and seamlessly rushes forward into the silent, black and white images from old films—scenes of people being hounded out of their lives, rounded up and herded into camps. Of massacre, of mayhem, of endless columns of broken people making their way to nowhere? Why is there no sound-track? Why is the hall so quiet? Have I been seeing too many films? Am I mad? Or am I right? Could those images be the inevitable culmination of what we have set into motion? Could our future be rushing forward into our past? I think so. Unless, of course, nuclear war settles it once and for all.

When I told my friends that I was writing this piece, they cautioned me. 'Go ahead,' they said, 'but first make sure you're not vulnerable. Make sure your papers are in order. Make sure your taxes are paid.'

My papers are in order. My taxes are paid. But how can one not be vulnerable in a climate like this? Everyone is vulnerable. Accidents happen. There's safety only in acquiescence. As I write, I am filled with foreboding. In this country, I have truly known what it means for a writer to feel loved (and, to some degree, hated too). Last year I was one of the items being paraded in the media's end-of-the-year National Pride Parade. Among the others, much to my mortification, were a bomb-maker and an international beauty queen. Each time a beaming person stopped me on the street and said 'You have made India proud' (referring to the prize I won, not the book I wrote), I felt a little uneasy. It frightened me then and it terrifies me now, because I know how easily that swell, that tide of emotion, can turn against me. Perhaps the time for that has come. I'm going to step out from under the fairy lights and say what's on my mind.

It's this:

If protesting against having a nuclear bomb implanted in my brain is anti-Hindu and anti-national, then I secede. I hereby declare myself an independent, mobile republic. I am a citizen of the earth. I own no territory. I have no flag. I'm female, but have nothing against eunuchs. My policies are simple. I'm willing to sign any nuclear nonproliferation treaty or nuclear test ban treaty that's going. Immigrants are welcome. You can help me design our flag.

My world has died. And I write to mourn its passing.

Admittedly it was a flawed world. An unviable world. A scarred and wounded world. It was a world that I myself have criticised unsparingly, but only because I loved it. It didn't deserve to die. It didn't deserve to be dismembered. Forgive me, I realise that sentimentality is uncool— but what shall I do with my desolation?

I loved it simply because it offered humanity a choice. It was a rock out at sea. It was a stubborn chink of light that insisted that there was a different way of living. It was a functioning possibility. A real option. All that's gone now. India's nuclear tests, the manner in which they were conducted, the euphoria with which they have been greeted (by us) is indefensible. To me, it signifies dreadful things. The end of imagination. The end of freedom actually, because, after all, that's what freedom is. Choice.

On the 15th of August last year we celebrated the fiftieth anniversary of India's independence. Next May we can mark our first anniversary in nuclear bondage.

Why did they do it?

Political expediency is the obvious, cynical answer, except that it only raises another, more basic question: Why should it have been politically expedient?

The three Official Reasons given are: China, Pakistan and Exposing Western Hypocrisy.

Taken at face value, and examined individually, they're somewhat baffling. I'm not for a moment suggesting that these are not real issues. Merely that they aren't new. The only new thing on the old horizon is the Indian Government. In his appealingly cavalier letter to the US President (why bother to write at all if you're going to write like this?) our Prime Minister says India's decision to go ahead with the nuclear tests was due to a 'deteriorating security environment'. He goes on to mention the war with China in 1962 and the 'three aggressions we have suffered in the last fifty years (from Pakistan). And for the last ten years we have been the victim of unremitting terrorism and militancy sponsored by it . . . especially in Jammu and Kashmir.'

The war with China is thirty-five years old. Unless there's some vital state secret that we don't know about, it certainly seemed as though matters had improved slightly between us. Just a few days before the nuclear tests General Fu Quanyou, Chief of General Staff of the Chinese People's Liberation Army, was the guest of our Chief of Army Staff. We heard no words of war.

The most recent war with Pakistan was fought twenty-seven years ago. Admittedly Kashmir continues to be a deeply troubled region and no doubt Pakistan is gleefully fanning the flames. But surely there must be flames to fan in the first place? Surely the kindling is crackling and ready to burn? Can the Indian state with even a modicum of honesty absolve itself completely of having a hand in Kashmir's troubles? Kashmir, and for that matter, Assam, Tripura, Nagaland—virtually the whole of the Northeast—Jharkhand, Uttarakhand and all the trouble that's still to come—these are symptoms of a deeper malaise. It cannot and will not be solved by pointing nuclear missiles at Pakistan.

Even Pakistan can't be solved by pointing nuclear missiles at Pakistan. Though we are separate countries, we share skies, we share winds, we share water. Where radioactive fallout will land on any given day depends on the direction of the wind and rain. Lahore and Amritsar are thirty miles apart. If we bomb Lahore, Punjab will burn. If we bomb Karachi—then Gujarat and Rajasthan, perhaps even Bombay, will burn. Any nuclear war with Pakistan will be a war against ourselves.

As for the third Official Reason: Exposing Western Hypocrisy—how much more exposed can they be? Which decent human being on earth harbours any illusions about it? These are people whose histories are spongy with the blood of others. Colonialism, apartheid, slavery, ethnic cleansing, germ warfare, chemical weapons—they virtually invented it all. They have plundered nations, snuffed out civilisations, exterminated entire populations. They stand on the world's stage stark naked but entirely unembarrassed, because they know that they have more money, more food and bigger bombs than anybody else. They know they can wipe us out in the course of an ordinary working day. Personally, I'd say it is more arrogance than hypocrisy.

We have less money, less food and smaller bombs. However, we have, or had, all kinds of other wealth. Delightful, unquantifiable. What we've done with it is the opposite of what we think we've done. We've pawned it all. We've traded it in. For what? In order to enter into a contract with the very people we claim to despise. In the larger scheme of things, we've agreed to play their game and play it their way. We've accepted their terms and conditions unquestioningly. The CTBT ain't nothin' compared to this.

All in all, I think it is fair to say that we're the hypocrites. We're the ones who've abandoned what was arguably a moral position, i.e.: We have the technology, we can make bombs if we want to, but we won't. We don't believe in them.

We're the ones who have now set up this craven clamouring to be admitted into the club of superpowers. (If we are, we will no doubt gladly slam the door after us, and say to hell with principles about fighting Discriminatory World Orders.) For India to demand the status of a superpower is as ridiculous as demanding to play in the World Cup finals simply because we have a ball. Never mind that we haven't qualified, or that we don't play much soccer and haven't got a team.

Since we've chosen to enter the arena, it might be an idea to begin by learning the rules of the game. Rule number one is Acknowledge the Masters. Who are the best players? The ones with more money, more food, more bombs.

Rule number two is Locate Yourself in Relation to Them, i.e.: Make an honest assessment of your position and abilities. The honest assessment of ourselves (in quantifiable terms) reads as follows:

We are a nation of nearly a billion people. In development terms we rank No. 138 out of the 175 countries listed in the UNDP's Human Development Index. More than 400 million of our people are illiterate and live in absolute poverty, over 600 million lack even basic sanitation and over 200 million have no safe drinking water.

So the three Official Reasons, taken individually, don't hold much water. However, if you link them, a kind of twisted logic reveals itself. It has more to do with us than them.

The key words in our Prime Minister's letter to the US President were 'suffered' and 'victim'. That's the substance of it. That's our meat and drink. We need to feel like victims. We need to feel beleaguered. We need enemies. We have so little sense of ourselves as a nation and therefore constantly cast about for targets to define ourselves against.

Prevalent political wisdom suggests that to prevent the state from crumbling, we need a national cause, and other than our currency (and, of course, poverty, illiteracy and elections), we have none. This is the heart of the matter. This is the road that has led us to the bomb. This search for selfhood. If we are looking for a way out, we need some honest answers to some uncomfortable questions. Once again, it isn't as though these questions haven't been asked before. It's just that we prefer to mumble the answers and hope that no one's heard.

Is there such a thing as an Indian identity?

Do we really need one?

Who is an authentic Indian and who isn't?

Is India Indian?

Does it matter?

Whether or not there has ever been a single civilisation that could call itself 'Indian Civilisation', whether or not India was, is, or ever will become a cohesive cultural entity, depends on whether you dwell on the differences or the similarities in the cultures of the people who have inhabited the subcontinent for centuries. India, as a modern nation state, was marked out with precise geographical boundaries, in their precise geographical way, by a British Act of Parliament in 1899. Our country, as we know it, was forged on the anvil of the British Empire for the entirely unsentimental reasons of commerce and administration. But even as she was born, she began her struggle against her creators. So is India Indian? It's a tough question. Let's just say that we're an ancient people learning to live in a recent nation.

What is true is that India is an artificial state—a state that was created by a government, not a people. A State created from the top down, not the bottom up. The majority of India's citizens will not (to this day) be able to identify her boundaries on a map, or say which language is spoken where or which god is worshipped in what region. Most are too poor and too uneducated to have even an elementary idea of the extent and complexity of their own country. The impoverished, illiterate agrarian majority have no stake in the state. And indeed, why should they, how can they, when they don't even know what the state is? To them, India is, at best, a noisy slogan that comes around during the elections. Or a montage of people on Government TV programmes wearing regional costumes and saying Mera Bharat Mahan.

The people who have a vital stake (or, more to the point, a business interest) in India having a single, lucid, cohesive national identity are the politicians who constitute our national political parties. The reason isn't far to seek, it's simply because their struggle, their career goal, is—and must necessarily be—to become that identity. To be identified with that identity. If there isn't one, they have to manufacture one and persuade people to vote for it. It isn't their fault. It comes with the territory. It is inherent in the nature of our system of centralised government. A congenital defect in our particular brand of democracy. The greater the numbers of illiterate people, the poorer the country and the more morally bankrupt the politicians, the cruder the ideas of what that identity should be. In a situation like this, illiteracy is not just sad, it's downright dangerous. However, to be fair, cobbling together a viable pre-digested 'National Identity' for India would be a formidable challenge even for the wise and the visionary. Every single Indian citizen could, if he or she wants to, claim to belong to some minority or the other. The fissures, if you look for them, run vertically, horizontally, layered, whorled, circular, spiral, inside out and outside in. Fires when they're lit race along any one of these schisms, and in the process, release tremendous bursts of political energy. Not unlike what happens when you split an atom.

It is this energy that Gandhi sought to harness when he rubbed the magic lamp and invited Ram and Rahim to partake of human politics and India's war of independence against the British. It was a sophisticated, magnificent, imaginative struggle, but its objective was simple and lucid, the target highly visible, easy to identify and succulent with political sin. In the circumstances, the energy found an easy focus. The trouble is that the circumstances are entirely changed now, but the genie is out of its lamp, and won't go back in. (It could be sent back, but nobody wants it to go, it's proved itself too useful.) Yes, it won us freedom. But it also won us the carnage of Partition. And now, in the hands of lesser statesmen, it has won us the Hindu Nuclear Bomb.

To be fair to Gandhi and to other leaders of the National Movement, they did not have the benefit of hindsight, and could not possibly have known what the eventual, long-term consequences of their strategy would be. They could not have predicted how quickly the situation would career out of control. They could not have foreseen what would happen when they passed their flaming torches into the hands of their successors, or how venal those hands could be.

It was Indira Gandhi who started the real slide. It is she who made the genie a permanent State Guest. She injected the venom into our political veins. She invented our particularly vile local brand of political expediency. She showed us how to conjure enemies out of thin air, to fire at phantoms that she had carefully fashioned for that very purpose. It was she who discovered the benefits of never burying the dead, but preserving their putrid carcasses and trundling them out to worry old wounds when it suited her. Between herself and her sons she managed to bring the country to its knees. Our new government has just kicked us over and arranged our heads on the chopping block.

The BJP is, in some senses, a spectre that Indira Gandhi and the Congress created. Or, if you want to be less harsh, a spectre that fed and reared itself in the political spaces and communal suspicion that the Congress nourished and cultivated. It has put a new complexion on the politics of governance. While Indira Gandhi played hidden games with politicians and their parties, she reserved a shrill convent school rhetoric, replete with tired platitudes, to address the general public. The BJP, on the other hand, has chosen to light its fires directly on the streets and in the homes and hearts of people. It is prepared to do by day what the Congress would do only by night. To legitimise what was previously considered unacceptable (but done anyway). There is perhaps a fragile case to be made here in favour of hypocrisy. Could the hypocrisy of the Congress Party, the fact that they conduct their wretched affairs surreptitiously instead of openly, could that possibly mean there is a tiny glimmer of guilt somewhere? Some small fragment of remembered decency?

Actually, no.

No.

What am I doing? Why am I foraging for scraps of hope?

The way it has worked—in the case of the demolition of the Babri Masjid as well as in the making of the nuclear bomb—is that the Congress sowed the seeds, tended the crop, then the BJP stepped in and reaped the hideous harvest. They waltz together, locked in each other's arms. They're inseparable, despite their professed differences. Between them they have brought us here, to this dreadful, dreadful place.

The jeering, hooting young men who battered down the Babri Masjid are the same ones whose pictures appeared in the papers in the days that followed the nuclear tests. They were on the streets, celebrating India's nuclear bomb and simultaneously 'condemning Western Culture' by emptying crates of Coke and Pepsi into public drains. I'm a little baffled by their logic: Coke is Western Culture, but the nuclear bomb is an old Indian tradition?

Yes, I've heard—the bomb is in the Vedas. It might be, but if you look hard enough, you'll find Coke in the Vedas too. That's the great thing about all religious texts. You can find anything you want in them—as long as you know what you're looking for.

But returning to the subject of the non-vedic nineteen nineties: We storm the heart of whiteness, we embrace the most diabolical creation of western science and call it our own. But we protest against their music, their food, their clothes, their cinema and their literature. That's not hypocrisy. That's humour.

It's funny enough to make a skull smile.

We're back on the old ship. The S.S. Authenticity Indianness.

If there is going to be a pro-authenticity/anti-national drive, perhaps the government ought to get its history straight and its facts right. If they're going to do it, they may as well do it properly.

First of all, the original inhabitants of this land were not Hindu. Ancient though it is, there were human beings on earth before there was Hinduism. India's tribal people have a greater claim to being indigenous to this land than anybody else, and how are they treated by the state and its minions? Oppressed, cheated, robbed of their lands, shunted around like surplus goods. Perhaps a good place to start would be to restore to them the dignity that was once theirs. Perhaps the Government could make a public undertaking that more dams like the Sardar Sarovar on the Narmada will not be built, that more people will not be displaced.

But, of course, that would be inconceivable, wouldn't it? Why? Because it's impractical. Because tribal people don't really matter. Their histories, their customs, their deities are dispensable. They must learn to sacrifice these things for the greater good of the Nation (that has snatched from them everything they ever had).

Okay, so that's out.

For the rest, I could compile a practical list of things to ban and buildings to break. It'll need some research, but off the top of my head, here are a few suggestions.

They could begin by banning a number of ingredients from our cuisine: chillies (Mexico), tomatoes (Peru), potatoes (Bolivia), coffee (Morocco), tea, white sugar, cinnamon (China) . . . they could then move into recipes. Tea with milk and sugar, for instance (Britain).

Smoking will be out of the question. Tobacco came from North America.

Cricket, English and Democracy should be forbidden. Either kabaddi or kho-kho could replace cricket. I don't want to start a riot, so I hesitate to suggest a replacement for English (Italian. . .? It has found its way to us via a kinder route: Marriage, not Imperialism). We have already discussed (earlier in this essay) the emerging, apparently acceptable alternative to democracy.

All hospitals in which western medicine is practised or prescribed should be shut down. All national newspapers discontinued. The railways dismantled. Airports closed. And what about our newest toy—the mobile phone? Can we live without it, or shall I suggest that they make an exception there? They could put it down in the column marked 'Universal'? (Only essential commodities will be included here. No music, art or literature.)

Needless to say, sending your children to university in the US, and rushing there yourself to have your prostate operated upon will be a cognizable offence.

The building demolition drive could begin with the Rashtrapati Bhavan and gradually spread from cities to the countryside, culminating in the destruction of all monuments (mosques, churches, temples) that were built on what was once tribal or forest land.

It will be a long, long list. It would take years of work. I couldn't use a computer because that wouldn't be very authentic of me, would it?

I don't mean to be facetious, merely to point out that this is surely the shortcut to hell. There's no such thing as an Authentic India or a Real Indian. There is no Divine Committee that has the right to sanction one single, authorised version of what India is or should be. There is no one religion or language or caste or region or person or story or book that can claim to be its sole representative. There are, and can only be, visions of India, various ways of seeing it—honest, dishonest, wonderful, absurd, modern, traditional, male, female. They can be argued over, criticised, praised, scorned, but not banned or broken. Not hunted down.

Railing against the past will not heal us. History has happened. It's over and done with. All we can do is to change its course by encouraging what we love instead of destroying what we don't. There is beauty yet in this brutal, damaged world of ours. Hidden, fierce, immense. Beauty that is uniquely ours and beauty that we have received with grace from others, enhanced, re-invented and made our own. We have to seek it out, nurture it, love it. Making bombs will only destroy us. It doesn't matter whether we use them or not. They will destroy us either way.

India's nuclear bomb is the final act of betrayal by a ruling class that has failed its people.

However many garlands we heap on our scientists, however many medals we pin to their chests, the truth is that it's far easier to make a bomb than to educate four hundred million people.

According to opinion polls, we're expected to believe that there's a national consensus on the issue. It's official now. Everybody loves the bomb. (Therefore the bomb is good.)

Is it possible for a man who cannot write his own name to understand even the basic, elementary facts about the nature of nuclear weapons? Has anybody told him that nuclear war has nothing at all to do with his received notions of war? Nothing to do with honour, nothing to do with pride. Has anybody bothered to explain to him about thermal blasts, radioactive fallout and the nuclear winter? Are there even words in his language to describe the concepts of enriched uranium, fissile material and critical mass? Or has his language itself become obsolete? Is he trapped in a time capsule, watching the world pass him by, unable to understand or communicate with it because his language never took into account the horrors that the human race would dream up? Does he not matter at all, this man? Shall we just treat him like some kind of a cretin? If he asks any questions, ply him with iodine pills and parables about how Lord Krishna lifted a hill or how the destruction of Lanka by Hanuman was unavoidable in order to preserve Sita's virtue and Ram's reputation? Use his own beautiful stories as weapons against him? Shall we release him from his capsule only during elections, and once he's voted, shake him by the hand, flatter him with some bullshit about the Wisdom of the Common Man, and send him right back in?

I'm not talking about one man, of course, I'm talking about millions and millions of people who live in this country. This is their land too, you know. They have the right to make an informed decision about its fate and, as far as I can tell, nobody has informed them about anything. The tragedy is that nobody could, even if they wanted to. Truly, literally, there's no language to do it in. This is the real horror of India. The orbits of the powerful and the powerless spinning further and further apart from each other, never intersecting, sharing nothing. Not a language. Not even a country.

Who the hell conducted those opinion polls? Who the hell is the Prime Minister to decide whose finger will be on the nuclear button that could turn everything we love—our earth, our skies, our mountains, our plains, our rivers, our cities and villages—to ash in an instant? Who the hell is he to reassure us that there will be no accidents? How does he know? Why should we trust him? What has he ever done to make us trust him? What have any of them ever done to make us trust them?

The nuclear bomb is the most anti-democratic, anti-national, anti-human, outright evil thing that man has ever made.

If you are religious, then remember that this bomb is Man's challenge to God.

It's worded quite simply: We have the power to destroy everything that You have created.

If you're not (religious), then look at it this way. This world of ours is four thousand, six hundred million years old.

It could end in an afternoon.

This essay first appeared in *Frontline*, August 1–14, 1998.

A Pakistani in Hiroshima

BEENA SARWAR

Hiroshima, August 5, 1998

The day before the 53rd anniversary of the world's first atomic bombing that levelled the city of Hiroshima and killed thousands of innocent men, women and children, I am walking from the 15-storey high Sun Route Hotel across from the city's powerful Peace Museum near the hypocentre, marked by the famous A-bomb Dome, to cross the river. The water is low, exposing the sandy bank below. A crane stands serenely on one leg near the water's edge. Above, at the road level, is a monument to a school that was flattened on August 6, 1945.

One of several that dot the city, the monument features women in relief on a huge stone slab. Usually it is forlorn, flanked only by an iron pillar that proclaims in Japanese and English, 'Let peace prevail on earth' and the outline in iron of a folded paper crane perched atop another pillar, colourful garlands of tiny paper cranes draped below it. But today, the grassy patch in front of it is busy with high school students armed with brooms. An elderly Japanese woman adds to the fresh flower bouquets heaped in front of the monument. Smoke from incense sticks curls towards the sky.

'Six hundred students from our school died,' explains a shy school girl in halting English, gesturing to the stone monument. She seems a little older than Sadako Sasaki was when she died of leukemia in 1955, having been exposed to radiation from the atom bomb when she was two years old.

The iron crane playing solemn sentinel to this monument is a reminder of the Japanese tradition that cranes signify peace, happiness, long life—a symbol that has come to mean 'no more nukes'. It is said that anyone who folds a thousand paper cranes will get cured even of cancer.

It was this belief that led Sadako, once the fastest runner in her class, to fold 1,300 paper cranes as she lay critically ill in hospital, far from her friends and relatives, and schoolfriends. But the cranes did not help Sadako, and her brief life ended at 12 years after an eight-month struggle. Her grieving classmates contributed to building a children's peace monument in Hiroshima and her story has come to symbolise the tragedy of nuclear war.

Today, garlands of paper cranes are visible everywhere in the city along with flower bouquets, banners and placards as the momentum towards August 6 gathers force. There's no frenzy, no anger. Just intense determination of thousands to remember the past and make the future nuclear-free.

I am already late for the discussion I'm to attend on the Indian and Pakistani nuclear tests and the urgency of nuclear abolition, a part of the programme that comprises the 1998 World Conference Against Atomic and Hydrogen Bombs, organised by Gensuikyo (the Japan Council against A & H Bombs, which has strong links to the Japan Communist Party and a highly political agenda). South Asian unpunctuality won't do here, so I carry on, leaving the students to their grassy patch and make my way along the river bank to the venue of the discussion.

I love this walk on the mud track along the river, shaded from the intense sunlight by a canopy of leafy trees holding hands overhead, the orchestral, insistent hum of cicadas blocking out all other noise in this shady tunnel.

Hard to imagine the scene 53 years ago, when nothing was left alive in this area, the river gorged with dead bodies . . . people jumping in to escape their agony, their skin peeling off like rags exposing blood-dripping flesh, eyeballs and inner organs torn out, eardrums perforated from the supersonic shock wave resulting from the explosion and the intense heat (hotter than the sun, at 3000–4000 degrees Celcius on ground zero) of the fireball, the 440 m. per second winds (the fastest tornado is 70 m per second) flinging aside buildings, animals, human beings . . . men, women, toddlers, children, pregnant women, babies, old people . . . bloated, bleeding, many no longer bearing any resemblance to human beings. . . .

No wonder those who survived, the *hibakusha* (literally, 'witness-survivor of the A-bomb'), are so fiercely anti-nuclear. Many, initially fired by hatred and the desire for revenge, have since channelled their anger into the peace movement, centred around the idea that no one should have to suffer the way they or their loved ones did (and still do, with radiation-induced diseases striking them down even now).

This is the message that comes across in the privately-run 'Peace Museums' of Hiroshima and Nagasaki. Among the most moving exhibits are the personal effects of some of the 6,300 junior and senior high school students who were out in the open demolishing buildings when the bomb fell. Nothing was left of their bodies, all that remains are a few charred and twisted lunch boxes and summer uniforms, like the one stitched for herself by a 12-year old schoolgirl. More than half the people who died in Hiroshima that day were children.

No wonder the *hibakusha* refer to the A-bomb as a weapon of the devil and to the scenes they witnessed as being from hell. Today, human beings have amassed enough such weapons to create that hell hundreds of times over and have even come up with creative excuses to justify this—inane phrases like 'deterrence' and 'balance of power'. It's sheer bullying and terrorism, a precursor to mass murder of innocents by design or accident. No wonder Joseph Rotblat, the 1995 Nobel Peace Prize recipient, can't sleep at night without the aid of pills—he left the Manhattan Project that made the first bomb and has spent his life campaigning against it, but has never been able to forgive himself and his fellow scientists for their contribution to this madness.

The insistent hum of the cicadas fades as I emerge from the canopy of trees to cross the road and go through a neat concrete jungle of shops and apartments to enter another air-conditioned hotel bliss to escape the oppressive humidity.

Inside the musically named Kosei Ninken Kaikan Hall, on the panel sit anti-nuclear activists and organisers like Dr. Joseph Gerson of the Friends Society, USA, and the Edith Ballantyne, German-born former president of the International Women's League for Peace and Freedom, along with J.P. (N.D. Jayaprakash of the Delhi Science Forum) and Pakistan Socialist Party representative Nazar Ali Qasim from Rawalpindi.

The presence of Pakistanis and Indians at this conference has meant a lot to the Japanese participants. The conference, attended by over 10,000 people in Hiroshima and Nagasaki, has been an annual event since 1955 when radioactive fallout from the US nuclear tests at Bikini Atoll fell on a Japanese fishing boat, killing at least one person and causing illnessess to the others. Although Indians participate every year, this year they are here in force, some 20 of them, mostly from the left-wing trade unions.

This is the first time in twenty years that Pakistanis have attended (three of us); the Bangladesh delegates didn't arrive, and Nepal was represented by a lone participant, Uttam Lal Manadhar from the Kavre UNESCO Youth Club, and Sri Lanka by three Buddhist priests and a student union. 'We thought everyone in India and Pakistan was for the tests, but it is encouraging to learn that there are anti-nuclear movements in these countries,' is a thought commonly voiced both at public platforms and in personal meetings.

How does an anti-nuclear person, already saturated in anti-nuclear material, convey what it means to be in Hiroshima on these days? How the experience reinforces all those beliefs already held, not only that human beings cannot coexist with nuclear weapons but that what also needs to be changed is not just ridding the world of nuclear weapons—but that the peace philosophy prevails over the psyche that produces such weapons and then justifies them. 'We shall overcome,' said Admiral Ramdas in one of his e-mails, some time before we met for the first time over breakfast in Hiroshima on the 15th floor of the Sun Route, overlooking the A-Bomb Dome and the Peace Park; something symbolic about all this, a retired Indian naval officer and a Pakistani journalist, attending different peace conferences, and meeting not to justify each other's countries policies but to reaffirm a working relationship against the nuclear psyche. He is right. We shall, we must, overcome.

Besides the visits to the Peace Museums, it is the personal contacts that strengthen this resolve, people like Prof. Ikuro Anzai, the highly regarded director of the Kyoto Peace Museum, a Peace Studies professor, economist and political activist who pulls red silk handkerchiefs out of the air at drafting committee meetings just as everyone is falling down from exhaustion.

The courage of the *hibakusha*, not just the celebrated ones (celebrated because of their suffering—what a price to pay) like Senji Yamaguchi, who even today fights for his mental health, who tried to kill himself a few times before his resolve to convey the anti-nuclear message to the world prevailed. People like Hideko Matsuya, frail, crippled, confined to a wheelchair and fighting her own government in court for refusing to recognise and give her medical compensation as a *hibakusha* because the head injuries that paralysed her were caused by a flying roof tile and not by radiation. Her case, which has been taken up as a test case by the Nihon Hidankyo (the Japan Confederation of A & H-bomb sufferers) is pending in the courts.

Nihon Hidankyo has put together a powerful set of photo panels titled 'The A-Bomb and Humanity', with which they hope to tour South Asia. Shin Nishimoto, a school teacher like so many other anti-nuclear activists, was the moving force behind the trip to Sri Lanka and Pakistan in December 1998. No one who had seen those photographs or the paintings done by the *hibakusha* would have celebrated India and Pakistan's newly-acquired capacity to threaten a similar hell to each other.

You are asking for Nuclear bomb to bring peace in the region. Why don't you ask for peace itself.

The Hard Choice

A.H. NAYYAR

It is indeed a sad moment for peace lovers in Pakistan. Normally they would have advocated a unilateral renunciation of the nuclear option by Pakistan. Now they have retreated to a position from where they are only calling for restraint. They have come down to asking Pakistan to keep the nuclear ambiguity intact, the same ambiguity that they always regarded—and most certainly still do—as a destabilising factor in the region. This had to come, for many a threshold has been crossed in the past few days.

The Indian nuclear tests can be seen as an expected outcome of the general perceptions that have evolved in India over the last 50 years. Perceptions about themselves and about others. About being traditionally in the forefront of anti-imperialist struggle, defying the hegemonic superpower domination. About being destined to an important role in global affairs. About being at least as important as the five big powers. Pakistan occupies only a minor place in this perception. Perhaps a little more important than other neighbours, but certainly a dangerous irritant that is used by superpowers to tie India down. That this self-perception is deeply embedded in India was clearly shown in a survey conducted among the Indian elite in 1995 by the Joan B. Kroc Institute. It showed that the Indian nuclear programme was not perceived as Pakistan-specific and that the Indian elite sees it as aimed at achieving the above objectives. A similar poll conducted in Pakistan in 1996 by the same institution gave a different picture. For a vast majority, threat to the country comes mainly from India. The nuclear programme is justified only to counter Indian hegemonic designs in the region. For the Pakistani elite the cost of this pursuit is unimportant.

There is thus a very peculiar situation at hand. India is treading the nuclear path, with the ambition to match the nuclear weapons states, so as to carve out a global role for itself. Pakistan is being dragged along by its policy that is only reactive to India. Now the repeated Indian nuclear tests have posed a serious dilemma for Pakistan. As viewed by its policy makers, Pakistan is damned if it conducts its own nuclear test and damned also if it does not.

If it does not, then: one, it will be seen as a loss of face in the world which has been made to believe for years that Pakistan has only stopped short of the last screw and is ready to meet the challenge in no time. Policy makers regard it as a matter of pride that Pakistan is labelled as a nuclear threshold state and is a part of the global nuclear debates. It is a different matter that the Indians do not seem to believe this. They are already taunting Pakistan into a test duel. (See, for example, Manod Joshi's statement, *Jang*, May 13, 1998). Two, there will be loss of face inside the country also where a strong security hype has been created over the decades, with reassuring, and at times boastful, claims that there will be a certain tit-for-tat response. The Ghauri missile was a most recent exercise of this kind after which even the foreign minister lost his diplomatic veneer, claiming that the Ghauri gave Pakistan an edge over India. What worries the policy makers is that all that was 'gained' by Ghauri in this senseless race has simply evaporated with the Indian tests. Three, Pakistan has always struggled to achieve parity with India on defence matters, sometimes even deluding itself of having achieved it. The objective was to claim an equal status in geopolitics. The greatest fear facing Pakistani policy makers is that of losing that claim.

Against this, if it does test its own nuclear weapon, it faces several consequences. For one, there will be sanctions that can have devastating consequences for its fragile economy. Secondly, it will have to bargain away the ambiguity that has been the cornerstone of its supposed nuclear doctrine.

Thirdly, the ensuing nuclear arms race is definitely going to prove costlier than it has been so far. The veil of ambiguity had at least allowed an opportunity to put a hold on the nuclear race; the 'enemy' was left guessing on what the level of capability was. With the veil gone, it will be a weapon versus a weapon. The parity that Pakistan may seek to achieve by exploding a nuclear weapon will still elude it. The techno-logical leap that India has taken is most certainly far too big for Pakistan, at least for now and perhaps in the foreseeable future also. India has demonstrated two major advancements (if that is what these can be called) in the May 11 and 13 tests: first, constructing a thermonuclear weapon and second showing that they can make tactical weapons also.

These two will have to be matched by Pakistan if it aims at a credible deterrence. The race will also involve having efficient and reliable delivery systems. The Prithvis, Agnis, Ghauris and if our president has any say in the matter, then Ghaznavis and Babaris, will most definitely lead to missile defence systems which proved so destabilising even to the USA and the USSR that the ABM treaty was one of the early treaties entered into by the two. With India having already announced launch-ing a missile defence system production, Pakistan is not likely to opt out of this next step.

The race will go on. More fission weapons, more hydrogen bombs, more tactical weapons, larger and longer ranged missiles, missile defence systems and so on. Imagine the burden of this on the economies of the two countries. It is futile to doubt the technical capability of achieving the objective. It is now well-recognised that nuclear weapons and missiles can be developed by any nation that has a modest technical capability and a resolve to put necessary resources into it. It only requires putting textbook knowledge into practice. Or, even easier is to just reverse-engineer. Fourthly, a Pakistani test will heighten tension in the region. Covert wars will increase. It will, in fact, reinforce that false sense of security which has allowed Pakistan to support insur-gencies across the border.

An overt nuclearisation of South Asia with associated developments in delivery systems, etc., cannot be a 'better deterrent' than the non-weaponised one as the protest lobby would like us to believe. If anything, it will be much more unstable. The Ghauri missile took about 10 minutes to travel 1,100 km. The Prithvi and Hatf take less than five minutes to reach their targets 300 km away. What time do they leave for a rational response? The history of the USA–USSR Cold War is replete with incidences of false alarms and the world was spared of the Armageddon by: one, the longer flight time the ICBMs needed to cover the long distance between the two countries; two, by the excellent

command, control and intelligence systems; and three, by the permissive action links established in the command hierarchy that prevented pushing of buttons either accidentally or in panic. India and
Pakistan do not have the luxury of any of these. Pakistan's security
concern being solely tied to India, its 'nuclear doctrine' is based on the
awareness of the increasing disparity in conventional defence capabilities. The nuclear weapons are to be used in a war with India when
conventional defence systems fail to withstand Indian superiority.
The message too is very clear: 'If in any future conflagration we find
that our forces are losing ground, we shall not hesitate to use whatever
nuclear arsenal we have. It may be small, but it surely will cause a
damage that cannot be acceptable to you. We also know that you have
a much larger stock of nuclear weapons, and that you can indeed
inflict much worse damage onto us, but our level of desperation is
such that that is acceptable to us in comparison to a capitulation to
your hegemony.'

This 'doctrine', combined with the inevitability of the nuclear race
if Pakistan continues to follow its policy of being dragged behind India,
makes the situation extremely unstable. A little mistake here and a
panic there can easily lead to a havoc upon the peoples of the two
countries. Should this be allowed?

It is time that Pakistan for once makes a hard choice: that of a unilateral nuclear disarmament, rather than choosing to match the Indian
response with a test of its own, or even keeping a non-weaponised
nuclear option. For this, it will have to come out of the binds of its
security perceptions and to make a rational choice of putting all the
resources it has got into the economic development and welfare of its
people. That is the only way to make the country worth defending.

War and Peace

ANAND PATWARDHAN

Undeclared war rages on the Pakistan–India border and threatens to expand into full-fledged declared war with the ever-present danger of a nuclear holocaust. But, even if the unthinkable is averted and war is contained, untold damage has already been done to the peace process. What do we, on both sides of the man-made divide, who count ourselves amongst a vocal minority of peace advocates, do at this juncture, when all around is sound and fury? How do we begin to reach out to that silent majority on both sides that perhaps knows in its heart of hearts that only peace between neighbours can bring economic justice and political freedom?

Today in both countries, the very forces that caused the poor to become poorer by selling land, air, water and sovereignty have draped their ugliness in the flag. In India, the Bofors gun, hitherto the symbol of Congress corruption, is now a weapon of pride. And the BJP, whose hardline stand was totally discredited, has emerged as a direct beneficiary of the war. In Pakistan, a similar process of empowering hatred and rewarding corruption is taking place.

In this atmosphere, who can dare come out on the street and say 'stop this war now!' or 'begin unconditional dialogue for peace' when the media daily flashes a heart-rending story of a brave jawan's family that vows upon his body to send every available son to the front as soon as he comes of age? No TV channel or newspaper, private or public can afford to steer clear of the path of patriotic fervour. On the airwaves as the death toll rises Lata Mangeshkar's '*E mere watan ke logon, jara aankh me bhar lo paani*' replaces even the national anthem as the song of choice. Politicians rush to be photographed by the side of the bereaved, businessmen rush to publicly declare how much they are donating to the war effort and multinational corporations rush to advertise their products in tricolour or in green depending on their geography. Even the stock market rises to the occasion, demonstrating that for tumescence, confidence is more important than health.

Hundreds of young lives have been lost on the icy slopes of Kargil and the suffering caused to their families will last long after public memory fades. But if there is one victim that remains completely unmourned it is the peace process itself. Five years before Vajpayee set out for Lahore on his goodwill bus journey to meet Nawaz Sharif, peace activists from India and Pakistan had been crossing the border annually to hold large conventions, exchange ideas, literature, films and to make joint recommendations to their respective governments to restore trade, travel, and communications between the two countries,

to eschew the nuclear path and make phased, parallel cuts in defence expenditure and to resolve core issues, including Kashmir, across the table rather than await another war.

All those who made these trips across the border were struck by the overwhelming desire for peace that ordinary people in both countries spontaneously demonstrated. When Pakistanis visited India they were struck by the outpouring of love and affection that Indians showered on them and likewise it was when we visited Pakistan, all this in marked contrast to the hate politics that prevailed amongst certain political groups in both countries and the cautious, even suspicious tone adopted by sections of the media.

Many have argued that Vajpayee's visit to Pakistan and the fact that Nawaz Sharif met him there with open arms was not an event that either of them initiated out of personal conviction but an event that took place because in the wake of the nuclear misadventures of May 98, a groundswell of public opinion already felt that peace was no longer a luxury but a necessity.

What we failed to see was that peace in the hands of politicians is not a peace that can be relied upon. Vajpayee and Sharif are both products of hate politics and cannot themselves be the antidote of the very poison that brought them to power. Sadly, that poison is no longer the monopoly even of the parties that first began to use it. Other parties learned the power of poison (a Sonia Gandhi poster vows to make mincemeat of any intruder in Kargil) and the war hastened its spread into the brains of the urban middle class and the elite. The enemy has become an undifferentiated target of hate.

Afghan mercenary, ISI agent, Kashmiri militant, Pakistani soldier, all are equal, all are a sub-species deserving of extermination. As the poison makes its way further, soon the undifferentiated target will include all Pakistanis and all Indian Muslims who do not take a public and publicised patriotic stand and it will eventually include all those, Muslims and non-Muslims who do not bay for the blood of the enemy. Where then lies the hope for peace and sanity? Clichéd though this may sound, it undeniably lies in the very areas where our modern economy and its hand-maiden politics of hate have not fully penetrated, in our villages. Some weeks before Kargil hit the headlines, on May 11 (the anniversary of India's nuclear test) a peace march began from the village of Khetolai, near the nuclear test site. It wound its way slowly through the countryside of Rajasthan and Uttar Pradesh to conclude three months and 1,500 km later on August 6 (the day in 1945 when the US dropped its atomic bomb on Hiroshima) in Sarnath where Buddha once spread his message of peace and compassion. Having spent a few days with the marchers, I know from our interactions with local communities that humanity is alive and well—though this is a glimpse that is rarely visible any more in the urban jungle.

Those who have read this piece so far will doubtless be concerned why the rights and wrongs of Kargil and Kashmir are not its primary subject. For the record, I will say that the violation of the LOC by Pakistani or Pakistan supported intruders was both morally and politically wrong. The torture of soldiers and combatants is reprehensible. The loss of young lives on the border is tragic. I will also say that I believe that a long-term just and viable peace can be won in Kashmir and for that matter anywhere in the world, including Kosovo and Iraq, through democratic rather than military means. The battle of Kargil may end in diplomatic and military victory. But the war will be lost if we continue to believe that winning territory through the force of arms is more important than winning hearts and minds through the force of reason.

A Plea for a United Struggle for Peace

I.A. REHMAN

Let me begin with an anecdote. Some friends recently met in Lahore to rest their heels after having walked about a kilometre in a protest march. They complained that they were getting tired of trudging for the same causes year after year. They had done this in the 1960s, in the 1970s, in the 1980s, and now the 1990s were coming to an end. And with them the 20th century. But nothing changed.

Their complaint raises several distressing questions. Are we too fatigued to walk a few hundred yards to assert our dignity as conscious human beings? Have we been reduced to a crowd of mere mourners over our tragedies or passive protesters against what we believe is wrong or unjust? Are the matters confronting us in fact immutable or has something been lacking in our endeavours in respect of direction or diligence? I believe we have gathered here not only to find answers to these questions but also to offer, to the best of our ability, an alternative vision, alternative to whatever phantoms we have been chasing, to inspire nearly one-fifth of humankind.

The ordinary people in our part of the world have always enjoyed an advantage over the rulers. The latter condescend to ponder the objective reality only when they are out of power while we, their victims, cannot blink at it even for a moment. Not a day passes when we are not reminded of our plight—when we see our children begging in the streets or working like galley slaves in workshops, when we turn our face away from a woman ravaged by men blinded by lust, or when we hear of haris held captive by chain gangs. Every now and then, we are impelled to look back on our journey in time, especially during the five decades of so-called freedom. And what we recall is not reassuring at all.

True, wanton violence that accompanied our accession to independent statehood in August 1947 had made Faiz warn us of a night-smitten dawn and had persuaded Mahatma Gandhi to stay away from fireworks in Delhi. But we were not without hope because we could answer the call—'*chaley chalo keh woh manzil abhi nahin ayee.*' However, soon afterwards the states we thought we had founded started claiming what they asserted the people owed them and began erasing the pledges and commitments about what they owed to the people. All of you know and many better than me as to how we were cheated out of our right to govern ourselves and now there is no pretence even about the government being for the people. I will try to say something only on the principal tool the state has employed to subdue civil society—the bogey of national security.

Under the cover of national security, the state in Pakistan—and perhaps one could say this about the other states across the whole of South Asia too—has relegated the citizens to the status of subjects. We were persuaded to go hungry, to accept sickness as an unavoidable affliction and to remain unlettered because whatever resources we had were needed to buy weapons that were supposed to be essential for national security. We were ordered to forget about civil liberties for which we had fought against the alien rulers and to submit to draconian laws because this was a prize for security that we should have gladly paid. Our aspirations for social justice, egalitarianism and equality of opportunity were dismissed as utopian dreams that had to be sacrificed at the altar of national security. And we are told to thank God for our rulers, however ignorant and wicked and rapacious they were, because that was the demand of patriotic duty. The result is that our state, the state of Pakistan, has only one item on its agenda—how to get loans from foreign countries and how to avoid repaying them. Till some years ago, it pretended its inability to fulfill its responsibilities to the people for want of resources. Now it is denying such responsibilities altogether. Equipped with the borrowed rhetoric of globalisation our rulers appear determined to shed their benevolent functions and rely more and more on their coercive powers. Their mindless worship of the new tin-gods betrays not only their lack of comprehension but also a stunning contempt for the people.

Last May, our wayward states delivered a most foul blow to people's interests by raising the spectre of their extinction. I know there are people in India and Pakistan who believe that a balance of terror has been created and therefore the danger of war between them—between these two peoples who are closer to one another than to any other section of humanity—has disappeared. I have great respect for all such people and they include many I have admired and have learnt from, but I am unable to agree with them, for I am not prepared to credit the apparatuses governing us with the ability to break out of the suicide construct they have painstakingly created. We must not dismiss the danger of a nuclear holocaust especially in view of the lack of guarantees against human error, even if it is free of perfidy, to which our proneness is well established. Besides, nuclear weapons have nowhere created a balance in favour of sanity and rectitude, they have only unleashed a mad race for deadlier weapons of mass destruction. In any case, nuclear weapons are not such a nectar of wisdom that their owners start behaving like people of culture and compassion. Above all, nuclear weapons do not cause havoc only when they are used in war; their presence in a country itself causes grave harm to the state and civil society.

We are all aware of the follies on the global political scene committed by the major nuclear powers and we should not expect the new nuclear knights to behave differently. Notice the tone and tenor of official rhetoric in the sub-continent after May 1998. Even when nuclear weapons are not used in war their availability increases a state's capacity for mischief against its neighbours. The record of conflicts all over the world since 1945 amply demonstrates this. But far more devastating is the impact nuclear weapons have on a state's conduct in domestic affairs. The logic we apply in external relations cannot leave our conduct at home unaffected.

When a state, especially one that has a long tradition of exploiting national security to justify a variety of aberrations, comes into possession of nuclear armaments, its political structure, its economy and the outlook of its people are further distorted. The myth of invincibility the state acquires makes it more irresponsible in its treatment of the people and it begins to lose whatever respect for democratic principles it may have had. Pakistan offers a typical example of democracy losing out to the national security school. There should be no doubt in the people's mind that the more they hear of arguments derived from Pakistan's nuclear capacity, the less become the possibilities of establishing democratic institutions.

The strains that nuclearisation are going to impose on Pakistan's economy, and possibly on India's too, have unfortunately not become the subject of debate because of the sanctions imposed by the rich patrons. But as the effect of these sanctions wears off, the pressure for enhancement of nuclear capability will start coming into play and the people will see their share of the national cake getting smaller and smaller.

Governments in the underdeveloped world are notorious for using any increment in their armaments to justify more arbitrary rule. In our case, it will mean consolidation of the already strong authoritarian tendencies, greater freedom for the so-called law-enforcing agencies to play with citizen's lives, increased discrimination against the disadvantaged sections of society and further impoverishment of the masses.

Finally, in states obsessed with national security, the use of violence to suppress dissent becomes the norm. The result is a society that gets brutalised. Again, we should take a look at Pakistan's history. The partition riots, when people were killed for their belief or their name legitimised resort to violence when political argument failed. Our frequent use of violence against political dissidents has thoroughly brutalised society. We were brutalised when we answered Bengal's legitimate demands with cannon-fire and the same thing happened in Baluchistan and Frontier Province and Sindh. As a result, the Pakistan state has become increasingly majoritarian, the space for opposition parties has contracted, respect for rule of law and due process has declined, and ordinary people have started thirsting for their fellow-being's blood. When I see the police gloating over the number of people they kill in custody or when somebody appears in the street to demand extra-legal tribunals, I hang my head in shame for I do not know what should I tell the coming generation. If the present trend continues, we may not be able to smile at our children and beating wives and strangling daughters may be upheld as virtues. A brutalised human being becomes a predatory beast who will spare no one and will ultimately bring disaster to himself and his kith and kin.

The theory of rule by terror offers little room for civil society to play its due role. This is what we are now witnessing in Pakistan. One by one the institutions of civil society have been put on the block. After the 14th amendment, Parliament has been reduced to a pack of nodders and a democratic functioning of political parties has come under constitutional bar. The academic community by law is kept out of the national discourse. The media outside official control is being bullied into surrender. Trade unions have been divested of their functions in a sector where they had existed since before independence. And once the 15th amendment is passed, the federal government will not only totally eclipse Parliament and the judiciary, it will assume the power to tell me what to eat, what to wear and what to think.

That in this situation states and societies become extremely vulnerable to anti-democratic and anti-people forces is not only a lesson of history, it is also part of our recent experience. Rabid communalists, religious fundamentalists and sectarian militants are threatening to monopolise public politics. One hears ordinary citizens, alienated as they are from the facade of democracy, arguing for a chance to be given to fascists. As if something can be said in favour of taking chances with potassium cyanide.

This then is the bitter harvest we are reaping for our bondage to the national security state, for viewing armaments as the final arbiters of a nation's destiny, for allowing the state to suppress civil society.

And now we must ask ourselves: are we too tired to stand up and call a halt to the process of our degradation, to walk a mile and bring about a change and promise our children the joys of peace that two generations in Pakistan and India have been deprived of?

The very fact that we have been able to assemble here—all of us who represent scores of people's organisations in Pakistan and all our colleagues and partners from India—reinforces the hope that we shall resist and have the capacity to overcome. The presence of distinguished delegates from outside Asia assures us of the benefit of their experience of social revival.

But how are we going to go about the task we have accepted? One of the fundamental lessons humankind has learnt after centuries of trial and tribulation is that peace, democracy and human rights are indivisible and interdependent. If you do not respect human rights of all people, regardless of their belief or gender or social status, you will have neither democracy nor peace. It is only under the banner of peace, democracy and human rights that we can begin to restructure our states, to revive our egalitarian ideals and to re-establish the authority of civil society *versus* the state, as party to party, to use a phrase Jinnah could employ decades ago to question the conduct of imperialist rulers.

It would be presumptuous on my part to suggest what we should be doing during the two days of our deliberations, but allow me to say that the eyes of the long suffering millions of the sub-continent are on us. They no longer deserve to be treated as they have been by humpties and dumpties of different hues. Neither strength of rhetoric nor abstruse theories will move them. It will be necessary to look closely at everything that is of concern to them in Pakistan, in India, and in the region as a whole—whether it is Kashmir, or persecution of minorities, or negation of womanhood, or threat to security of life, or joblessness, or hunger, or corruption of the elite.

Fortunately there is a huge mass of people in our countries who have not yet come under the spell of the tiny minority that occupies commanding heights in politics and economy. If we are not prepared to mobilise them into a powerful movement for peace, if we are not capable of joining hands across national frontiers and across continents, we may go home to rest our heels. But if we are true to the sentiment that has brought us here, there is a promise of glorious fight and of rewards history will thank us for. Let us then pool our resources, forge links among the large number of activist groups, and underwrite peace and with it the future of life on this land of ours.

Based on a presentation made at the first Pakistan Peace Conference, February 18, 1999.

c.F.Dan

The Struggle for Nuclear Disarmament

PRAFUL BIDWAI

The principled, non-jingoistic response of a cross-section of society to India's nuclear tests indicates the beginnings of a powerful nuclear disarmament movement by citizens which is long overdue.

The tide has turned. The manufactured 'consensus' over the Bharatiya Janata Party-led government's decision to cross the nuclear threshold now stands exposed for what it was: flimsy, uninformed, reluctant acceptance of the *fait accompli* that a particular political party with a unique nuclear obsession had inflicted upon us all without the fig leaf of a security rationale or a strategic review. Today, there is sharp political polarisation on this issue. The Left has taken a principled stand opposing nuclearisation. Large chunks of the political centre have demarcated themselves from the BJP. At least three former Prime Ministers have questioned the decision, or expressed reservations about it.

Even the seemingly mandatory salutation to our scientists' 'achievement' has given way to a sharply critical debate on the ethics of developing weapons of mass destruction. Over 300 scientists have questioned this 'achievement'. The disclosure that the defence and nuclear scientific lobby had repeatedly demanded the tests (see former Prime Minister H.D. Deve Gowda's press statement) has drawn strong condemnation from ethically-minded scientists.

The signs on the street are encouraging. There have been over 30 demonstrations and meetings in at least eight Indian cities, involving diverse groups of people such as scholars, scientists, social activists,

human rights campaigners, feminists, trade unionists and environ-
mentalists, besides political activists. Highly regarded former Generals
and Admirals have joined this growing mobilisation. Those who have
taken a clear stand include former Chief of Naval Staff Admiral N.
Ramdas, Lt. Gen. Gurbir Mansingh, Air Marshal J. Zaheer and Lt.
Gen. V.R. Raghavan. Among nuclearisation's critics are former Atomic
Energy Commission Chairman M.R. Srinivasan, former Supreme
Court Judge V.R. Krishna Iyer, Gandhians such as Y.P. Anand (former
Chairman of the Railway Board) and Sidharaj Dhaddha, besides artists
and writers. No one dare accuse this movement as that of some kind of
a lunatic fringe of peaceniks unconcerned about India's security.

A movement devoted primarily to disarmament and peace has a
number of invaluable functions: conducting public education on the
evil of nuclear weapons, working as a clearing house of information
and ideas, cross-sectoral mobilisation of protest, organising public
agitations, providing a clear focus for unorganised groups and citizens,
and advocacy and lobbying. Such a movement must be broad-based
and inclusive, yet it must be lucidly clear about its goals lest it stray
from its main functions. It must recognise that people will come to
the disarmament platform out of a range of considerations and motives,
and from different social and ideological backgrounds. But at the same
time, it must carefully articulate principles and doctrines in such a
way as to retain its identity, integrity and effectiveness.

At least nine such premises and principles are essential.

The first premise is that nuclear weapons are uniquely evil instruments of mass destruction with the potential to exterminate all life
from this planet. They are incomparably more destructive than any
other weapon. Their use or threat of use violates all criteria of *jus in
bello* (justice in the conduct of war) because they kill massively, indiscriminately, without distinguishing between combatants and civilians,
and in barbaric ways. They are simply incompatible with the notion of
proportionate and legitimate use of force.

As the Government of India itself argued for 50 years, until May
11, not only the use of nuclear weapons, but even the threat of use,
must be declared unacceptable and illegal. In its submission before
the International Court of Justice in 1995, the government pleaded:
'Use of nuclear weapons in any armed conflict . . . even by way of
reprisal or retaliation . . . is unlawful.' More, even their manufacture

and possession 'cannot under any circumstances be considered as permitted.' India's classical position was that such manufacture and possession be declared a 'crime against humanity'. The BJP has committed just that crime.

The second premise is that nuclear weapons, no matter who possesses them, do not provide security. Indeed, as the government itself consistently argued, nuclear weapons degrade security, both for nations and internationally. Such weapons are strategically irrational. The celebrated December 1996 statement of 60 former Generals and Admirals, including Commanders of the North Atlantic Treaty Organisation and the Warsaw Pact, says: 'We, military professionals, who have devoted our lives to the national security of our countries and our peoples, are convinced that the continuing existence of nuclear weapons in the armouries of nuclear powers, and the ever present threat of acquisition of these weapons by others, constitute a peril to global peace and security and to the safety and survival of the people we are dedicated to protect . . . Long term international nuclear policy must be based on the declared principle of continuous, complete and irrevocable elimination of nuclear weapons.'

The third premise is that the concept of nuclear deterrence must be categorically rejected on moral, political, legal and strategic grounds. This has a powerful resonance in India's own past policy, which continued to oppose nuclear deterrence as an 'abhorrent' and 'repugnant' doctrine. Deterrence theory is a mere article of faith, an unfalsifiable, unverifiable dogma. It contradictorily assumes that states will simultaneously act both rationally (by making hard-nosed calculations) and out of fear simultaneously. It also assumes that those making decisions on nuclear weapons are accountable and hence act responsibly. This is demonstrably false in situations of conflict.

The 'theory' also assumes that non-nuclear weapons states will be deterred from militarily engaging nuclear weapons states and that nuclear weapons states will not fight conventional wars with one another. This had been repeatedly disproved: during the Korean and Vietnam wars, the Falklands war, in conflicts over the Ussuri between China and the former Soviet Union, the war between China and Vietnam in 1979, in Afghanistan in the 1980s. Deterrence is unstable and quickly degenerates into an arms race, which has a profoundly irrational character. That alone explains why the five permanent members of the Security Council (P–5) amassed an overkill-level arsenal of 69,000 weapons—enough to destroy the world 50 times over during the Cold War.

There is no such thing as 'minimal deterrence'. One man's 'minimum' is another's 'maximum'. Both could be ruinous. There is no significant period in the past 50 years when a nuclear weapons state did not stockpile weapons when others were also doing so. What was a 'minimum deterrent' for China in 1965 became unacceptable in less than seven years.

Equally important, deterrence is prone to breakdown. There were over 100 cases of false alerts, weapons activation and near-hits between NATO and Warsaw Pact members despite elaborate risk-reduction measures, PALs (permissive action links or codes for authorising use of weapons), hot lines and early warning systems. A Brookings Institution study says it was sheer luck, not deterrence, that prevented a nuclear conflict between the two blocs during the Cold War. The world came far, far closer to it during the 1962 Cuban missile crisis than imagined, indeed even known, by the two sides. Nuclear deterrence does not, cannot work reliably. It legitimises the possession and threat of use of nuclear weapons. It must be rejected.

The fourth premise is universal nuclear disarmament. True security lies only in a nuclear weapons-free world. The P–5 countries have resisted serious nuclear restraint and failed to fulfil their obligations under Article VI of the Nuclear Non-Proliferation Treaty. They have also tried to impose unequal treaties upon others. This won't do. The Nuclear Club is a group of hypocrites. India has now put in its application for joining this club, albeit as a junior member.

The fifth premise is that the present government's policy represents a radical, dangerous and unacceptable break with all the sane and sensible components of India's past nuclear doctrines, including opposition to deterrence. India opposed the premise that nuclear weapons provide security. Thus, even during the peak of the Comprehensive Test Ban Treaty (CTBT) debate, Foreign Secretary Salman Haidar told the Conference on Disarmament: 'We do not believe that the acquisition of nuclear weapons is essential for national security and we have followed a conscious decision in this regard. We are also convinced that the existence of nuclear weapons diminishes international security. We, therefore, seek their complete elimination.'

The sixth premise is that the BJP's nuclear policy is inseparably linked to a toxic, belligerent, male-supremacist, hate-driven beggar-thy-neighbour nationalism and a notion of nationhood that is anti-pluralist, communal and militaristic. Underlying it is opposition to disarmament and peace. The Sangh ideology castigated Gandhi's secularism and ahimsa for 'emasculating' Hindu 'manliness'. That is why Gandhi had to be eliminated.

Nuclearisation promotes secrecy and the militarisation of everyday life. National nuclear arming creates a false sense of pride and imposes continuing and rising economic, social and political costs. The social and economic costs of nuclearisation can be crippling. Nuclear weapons are incompatible with rational development goals.

The seventh premise is that the Indian bomb is neither 'anti-imperialist' nor meant to promote disarmament. As Prime Minister A.B. Vajpayee told US President Bill Clinton in his May 11 letter, India's intention is not to challenge the unequal global nuclear order but to join it, on the side of the biggest discriminator, the US. This government craves that India be recognised as a nuclear weapons state. Achieving that, not promoting nuclear disarmament, is its goal. Its actions with Pakistan reacting quickly with its own tests have set back the global disarmament agenda. You cannot blow a hole into the disarmament agenda and then say you only wanted peace. As Gandhi said: 'The moral to be drawn from the supreme tragedy of the bomb is that it will not be destroyed by counter-bombs...' It is futile to cite 'sovereignty' here. This Government talks of sovereignty only in respect of the 'right' (which no one has) to make weapons of mass destruction, while violating sovereignty in remedying the unequal international economic order in the interest of the people.

The eighth premise is that nuclearisation has created an unacceptably dangerous situation in South Asia. The chances of a nuclear attack/conflict breaking out in this region are far higher than they were at any point of time during the Cold War except perhaps during the Cuban missile crisis. This is so not because South Asian leaders and Generals are more irresponsible, but because South Asia is the only part of the world to have had a relentless hot-cold war for 50 years. It bristles with mutual hatred, suspicion and hostility on many counts. Any of them could turn into a flashpoint—Kashmir, the eastern border, military exercises getting out of hand, as in 1987.

The two states continue to sacrifice hundreds of men in fighting an insane war at Siachen, the world's highest-altitude conflict, where it costs Rs 1.5 lakh to deliver one chapati. Today, their politicians are actually talking about using nuclear weapons. Witness Jammu and Kashmir Chief Minister Farooq Abdullah's June 8 statement and Pakistan Foreign Minister Gohar Ayub Khan's on June 10. Equally worrisome, both are working on battlefield-level tactical nuclear weapons (hence the sub-kilotonne tests), which considerably lower the danger threshold.

At the height of the Cold War, the lag time for missiles between NATO and the Warsaw Pact group was never less than 30 minutes. In the case of India and Pakistan, the flight-time would be just two to three minutes—inadequate for war prevention. Given that virtually no interception of missiles is possible, a nuclear warhead could almost certainly be delivered across the border with devastating results. This devolves a particularly onerous responsibility upon those living in South Asia.

The ninth and final premise is that India must never test or make or deploy nuclear weapons again. It should declare it will never use nuclear weapons under any circumstances, regardless of the status of the adversary or nature of the threat. It must also seek similar assurances from others. This alone can redeem the horrible wrong India committed against its stated policy and its own people. It alone can help us return to the global disarmament agenda with a modicum of credibility. Or else no one will take India's protestations of peace seriously. Once you deceive the world and yourself so massively, you have to do more than just offer vague promises of 'responsible' conduct as a nuclear weapons state.

More, the government must clearly reiterate its sensible past doctrines opposing nuclear deterrence and revive the Rajiv Gandhi plan for step-by-step disarmament. This can help it reshape the disarmament agenda, with support from South Africa, Mexico, Egypt, Brazil, New Zealand, Australia, Canada, Japan and Sweden, and perhaps Pakistan.

Beyond these premises, a disarmament movement may have legitimate internal differences, for instance, on the relationship between nuclear power and nuclear weapons, on the policy transition from Jawaharlal Nehru to Lal Bahadur Shastri to Indira Gandhi and beyond, and on the CTBT. For instance, some members may believe that the only guarantee of a real freeze on weaponisation is a freeze on nuclear power. Some others might not. But they should still be able to work together. Again, some may have misgivings about the CTBT in keeping with the official posture of 1996. Others may believe that it is, unlike the NPT, non-discriminatory and imposes equal and fairly effective obligations on all states; under the circumstances, India should sign it while fighting for total disarmament. But it should still be possible to debate the issue dispassionately and in an informed way.

Historically, such differences have never prevented disarmament campaigns from becoming effective. What has crippled them is lack of clarity on the point that nuclear weapons are wholly evil, unacceptable and indefensible—that is, the failure to mobilise enough moral force internally. Moral force is all-important when you are rolling back an epochal injustice. Without it, India could not have achieved independence, nor South Africa liberation from apartheid. On such morality, there can be no compromise.

THE NUCLEAR BURDEN

Pakistan's Fateful Nuclear Option

ZIA MIAN

Pakistan has thought and done the unthinkable. With its nuclear weapons tests it has demonstrated to itself, as much as to the world, that it is now a murderous state. It is willing and now able to commit nuclear mass murder. This was not done with universal consent. There were brave voices who spoke the language of right and wrong, and not that of power.

There was a nuclear debate. But there should have been no need for one. Nuclear weapons have become the one great exception to the sense that here are some issues that a society should never debate because the issue itself is so unethical. A simple example is that few if any modern societies would feel it necessary or even acceptable, to have a debate on whether it is right to kill and eat children.

When it comes to nuclear weapons, however, the moral response has been dulled. What is at issue is whether it is right or wrong to want to have, and to want to use, the power to kill hundreds of thousands, perhaps millions of people in the blink of an eye, to maim many more and to poison them so they die slowly and painfully over years from cancers and other illnesses induced by radiation. The experience of Hiroshima should have been enough to convince anyone that nuclear weapons were an affront to humanity. Despite this there has been a worldwide debate about nuclear weapons for over fifty years.

This has happened in large part because nuclear weapons are usually not discussed in moral terms. From the very beginning of the nuclear age there has been a tendency to use language that hides the reality of what is being considered. But it is more than simple disguise. Language is used as an anaesthetic, as a way to kill feelings. Without feelings, morality dies. These are the first casualties of nuclear weapons.

Nowhere is this more evident than among those people whose job it is to deal with these weapons on a daily basis. The American scientists who build the first ever nuclear bomb simply called it 'the Gadget', as if it were just another strange invention rather than the most destructive weapon that had ever been made. When it came time to kill people with these weapons, the scientists and soldiers involved found the most innocuous names possible for the weapons: the bombs that destroyed the Japanese cities of Hiroshima and Nagasaki were called 'Little Boy' and 'Fat Man'.

This refusal to confront the reality of nuclear weapons is not confined to the United States. It has afflicted every state that has developed them. The Soviet Union named its first bomb, the 'article'. Britain called its first nuclear explosion 'Hurricane', France had the 'Blue Mouse', and China named its first nuclear weapon simply 'device 596'. The same escape can be found closer to home; India called its nuclear bomb test in 1974, 'Smiling Buddha' and more recently simply 'Shakti'. All of these illustrate what psychologist Robert Jay Lifton has called 'nuclear numbing', the process by which 'we domesticate these [nuclear] weapons in our language and attitudes. Rather than feel their malignant actuality, we render them benign.'

Pakistan has its way of talking about its nuclear weapons without really talking about them. For more than a decade while it lacked a nuclear bomb that it could name, the debate in Pakistan was only about a 'nuclear option', or a 'nuclear capability'. There was never a mention of what it was an option for. Pakistan's scientists are so used to a nameless bomb that they have not so far given a name to the nuclear tests.

If the nerve of moral outrage is dulled, there is hope that the sharp prick of knowledge can serve to revive it. Laying out the enormity of what is involved in Pakistan's nuclear tests can serve this purpose. Pakistan is believed to have tested a simple nuclear weapon of the kind that was used 52 years ago against Hiroshima. In Hiroshima, the atomic bomb killed between 210,00 and 270,000 people, and destroyed more than 90 per cent of the city. Pakistan's nuclear tests were a demonstration that it could do the same thing to one or more of India's major cities. The city could be Bombay, or Delhi, or any one of nearly half a dozen others. That any of these cities would be largely destroyed is obvious.

What needs to be faced is how many people would be killed. Estimates of the deaths that would result from such an attack vary, but each new estimate is larger than the one that came before. An early estimate was that an attack on Bombay would kill between 103,000 and 265,000 people, while 26,000–175,000 would die if Delhi was the target. Later estimates suggested there might be 136,000 deaths in Bombay, and more than 220,000 people injured, while in Delhi, the toll would be 40,700 deaths and 66,900 injured. The most recent estimate, based on the 1991 Indian Census, is that as many as 700,000 people would die in Bombay alone. It hardly needs to be added that since almost half the population of India, like that of Pakistan, is under the age of fifteen, about half of all these deaths would be the deaths of children.

In the final analysis, a nuclear test is about proving you have the power to do this. Becoming a nuclear weapons state, a status both India and Pakistan now claims, means keeping this power. Giving up nuclear weapons means accepting that there is nothing, nothing at all, that could ever justify wanting or having such terrible power.

Nuclear Weapons Need Enemies

Despite the moral argument against nuclear weapons, in the states that have built these weapons there has been public support for them. This has not been because all these people woke up one day and wanted nuclear weapons. Public support for them is built by creating a sense of crisis and fear. They are told that there is an 'enemy' and the bomb is the only defence. And that is all. In this atmosphere of absolute conflict, peace is ruled out.

There is no doubt about the overwhelming elite support for nuclear weapons in Pakistan, and that this is shared by large numbers of ordinary people. The nation-wide celebration of Pakistan's nuclear tests is sufficient to prove this. This level of support, according to opinion polls, has not changed for over a decade. This is remarkable. In one of the most tumultuous periods in Pakistan's history, where military dictatorship gave way to elected government, governments came and went, economic policies changed, the Cold War ended, the Soviet Union collapsed, and the United States imposed sanctions on Pakistan because of its nuclear weapons programme, nuclear weapons have remained beyond question.

There are two reasons behind this massive and enduring support for nuclear weapons. The first is that most people know little if anything about nuclear issues. This is an obvious inference from polling data showing that support for nuclear weapons in Pakistan is constant regardless of educational attainment. From the illiterate to those having only a basic education to those with degrees, about the same proportion of them support these weapons. There is rarely such unanimity except when based on a shared ignorance. In the absence of information, there is no incentive to change one's mind. There is indeed, no reason to even think about changing one's mind.

That the nuclear debate is starved of information is evident, one only has to look at newspapers, magazines and electronic media. There is never more than assertion that nuclear weapons are vital. This is the second reason for the strong and enduring support for nuclear weapons. For over a decade, Pakistan's people have had heard nothing but repeated public declarations by all of their Presidents, Prime Ministers and military leaders that Pakistan's nuclear weapons were vital for the 'national interest'. One former Chief of Army Staff, General Mirza Aslam Beg, went so far as to say that giving up Pakistan's 'nuclear capability' would amount to 'nuclear castration'. When things are presented in this way it is evident that many people will conclude nuclear weapons are Pakistan's last and only hope.

It is not just an abstract support for nuclear weapons that has been created. The weapons have been personified. They are now embodied in A.Q. Khan, who led the uranium enrichment project—to make the special nuclear material used in Pakistan's nuclear weapons and is now credited with having carried out the nuclear tests. He has for years been a national public figure, appearing on national television and making speeches at all kinds of public events. This is almost unprecedented, anywhere in the world, for the head of what is meant to be a secret military project.

But nuclear weapons need enemies to make them worthwhile. For decades, India has been projected as an absolute and unremittingly hostile enemy, without scruple, willing to exploit every opportunity. It is the source of everything that goes wrong in Pakistan. An Indian hand is identified behind every untoward event. Any challenge to the status quo is interpreted as an Indian conspiracy against national security. India cannot be talked to or reasoned with, it must be confronted. No one has summed this all up better than General Mirza Aslam Beg. He has declared that Pakistan faces an Indian threat 'emanating from the deeper recesses of the Hindu psyche.'

The final and darkest element in manufacturing a 'national consensus' in support of nuclear weapons is maintaining ignorance. That is at work can be seen in the deliberate orchestration of hate by sections of the media against individuals and groups who argue against nuclear weapons. Debate that might inform people about alternative ways of thinking is not only discouraged, it is not tolerated.

One example will suffice to show how the process works. There was a seminar organised by the Islamabad branch of the Pakistan–India People's Forum for Peace and Democracy in February 1996. This meeting was reported under banner headlines that said 'People's Forum Meeting: Ridiculous Speeches Poking Fun at Islam, Abusing Armed Forces'. The speakers were reported as having made 'provocative speeches against Islam, Pakistan and the armed forces.' For the record, the provocation was the speakers airing of their opinion that Pakistan should not become engaged in a nuclear or missile race against India.

Subsequent newspaper reports led with headlines such as 'Prime Minister has ordered an enquiry into speeches against Pakistan and Islam. Organisers of non-governmental dialogues between India and Pakistan are not patriots. Cases should be instituted against them.' Another blared out 'Prime Minister has ordered an enquiry into the slander against armed forces. This is treason against the country.' In both stories, senior politicians were quoted as having said that this was a case of treason. Others went further, arguing that if the government would not act to prosecute such traitors, people should take the law into their own hands.

Most of this reportage was confined to the Urdu press. The English press remained largely neutral, while the government controlled media was determinedly silent. The consequences of these actions are not surprising. For the majority of the people who can read, and who pass on their interpretation of the world to those who can't (the majority of people, lest it be forgotten). Even participation in the debate should not be allowed to those who think that Pakistan should give up its nuclear weapons.

This is the political environment within which the nuclear tests took place. Having created public opinion in favour of nuclear weapons, it was only too easy for Pakistan's leaders to claim that they had no choice and that it was public opinion that demanded the tests. It was easy and may have sounded convincing. It should not have. Public opinion in Pakistan has asked for many things, like an end to poverty, and no leader ever paid attention.

Nuclear Weapons Are No Defence

Having laid out the immoral nuclear destructiveness that is now available to Pakistan's armed forces, and the ignorance and hate that are required to bring nuclear weapons into being and help keep them, it is time to turn to why Pakistan has nuclear weapons at all. At one level the answer is easy: Pakistan has nuclear weapons because India has nuclear weapons.

This justification for Pakistan's nuclear weapons has taken root in a wider public because it is simple, direct, to the point and has no reason behind it to argue with. It has been put most clearly by General K.M. Arif, former Vice-Chief of the Army Staff. He has argued that Pakistan needs its nuclear weapons because 'to counter a threat you must possess the same capability as the opponent enjoys. We must have a nuclear device against a nuclear device, a missile against a missile, and a plane against a plane, and a tank against a tank.'

What General Arif did not explain is why Pakistan should get nuclear weapons if India has them. A nuclear threat to Pakistan is simply assumed. It is believed that somehow India will use nuclear weapons to threaten Pakistan in peacetime, or in a war. Supporters of nuclear weapons often use this idea of 'nuclear blackmail'. It was used by Pakistan's Prime Minister in justifying the tests, when he said that 'Bowing and submitting to others is not our wont.' Having nuclear weapons, he said, would mean Pakistan would not be 'subservient'.

There is a long history of how 'nuclear blackmail' has been tried. During the Cold War, both the US and the Soviet Union made nuclear threats numerous times, with the United States making around twenty such threats and the Soviet Union making five or six. This suggests that nuclear weapons are no protection against nuclear threats. If a state with nuclear weapons is going to make a threat, it will make it regardless of whether the state being threatened has nuclear weapons of its own.

The facts of the last fifty years also tell another story. Nuclear weapons states have elected to fight wars on many occasions. They have lost many of them. Britain fought and lost at Suez, even though it had already developed nuclear weapons. The United States suffered significant defeats during the Korean War and the war ended with stalemate. The French lost Algeria, even though they had their nuclear weapons. China's nuclear weapons did not help against Vietnam. The most famous examples are of course the defeat of the United States in Vietnam, and the Soviet Union in Afghanistan despite having enormous numbers of nuclear weapons. In all these cases, a non-nuclear state fought and won against a nuclear-armed state.

The only other argument made for nuclear weapons is that they are supposed to deter attacks by other nuclear weapons and so prevent war between nuclear-armed states. Pakistan's Prime Minister claimed in his speech announcing the nuclear tests that 'It is my opinion that had Japan possessed a nuclear bomb, Hiroshima and Nagasaki would never have been destroyed.' This is nuclear deterrence.

The proof of nuclear deterrence is supposed to be the absence of war between the superpowers during the Cold War. But this cannot be proven. All that can be said is that the absence of war coincided with both sides having nuclear weapons. It is not logical to deduce that nuclear weapons prevented a war that would otherwise have taken place. The absence of war between the United States and the Soviet Union may simply have been due to neither side wanting a war. The experience of total war in World War II was so terrible, more than 20 million Soviets were killed, that this may have been sufficient to prevent a major war. It should also be noted that the US and USSR fought numerous proxy wars across the third world.

To understand nuclear deterrence one has to start with realising that it is fundamentally an American idea used to justify US nuclear weapons. While many supported it during the Cold War, especially academics and strategic thinkers, it is significant that General George Lee Butler, who actually had command over all of the United States' strategic nuclear weapons has said the world 'survived the Cuban missile crisis no thanks to deterrence, but only by the grace of God.'

The nuclear arsenals of the nuclear weapons states show what happens when a state searches for deterrence. None of them has stopped at a few simply atom bombs. Each nuclear weapons state has build hydrogen bombs—this is why India is said to have tested one on May 11. But having a hydrogen bomb is not enough. The nuclear weapons states have built hundreds if not thousands of them, along with nuclear submarines, specially hardened silos, or mobile missiles.

The nuclear tests by India and Pakistan are only a beginning. The next steps will demand to see nuclear weapons being assembled, tested and then deployed, ready for use. Realising that deterrence does not exist, both sides will try to create it. The consequences of such a move are all too obvious. The history of the superpower arms race is there for all to see. A recent study has estimated the United States spent at least $4 trillion ($4,000 billion) to develop, produce, deploy, operate, support and control the nuclear forces of the United States over the past 50 years. The cost of the nuclear weapons alone is estimated at $375 billion.

This is what the pursuit of deterrence costs. Incidentally, since Pakistan's military spending is now about $3 billion a year, it would take Pakistan a thousand years to pay for such a nuclear deterrent.

Nuclear Weapons Start Nuclear Wars

Pakistan's leaders have found one more use for nuclear weapons. It is as a deterrent against Indian conventional forces. Air Chief Marshal (retired) Zulfikar Ali Khan has said that Pakistan's nuclear weapons would provide a deterrent against 'the overwhelming conventional military superiority that India has clearly achieved.' Nawaz Sharif reiterated this in his justification of the tests, saying 'These weapons are to deter aggression, be it nuclear or conventional.'

The use of nuclear weapons as a deterrent against conventional attack implies Pakistan is prepared to turn a conventional battle, like those fought by India and Pakistan in 1948, 1965 and 1971 into a nuclear war, a final war. Pakistan's refusal to agree to a no-first strike agreement with India, i.e. neither side will use nuclear weapons first, is suggestive that Pakistan's armed forces are prepared to do just this. What does it mean to even think of using nuclear weapons first in such a situation? It means that Pakistan is prepared to murder countless Indian civilians because of the failure of Pakistani politicians, diplomats and generals to prevent war.

Addressing the details of different nuclear war fighting scenarios may lead to some insight, but several factors will shape all these scenarios and suggest certain inescapable conclusions. According to Lt. General (retired) Mujib ur Rehman Khan, the first and obvious one is that Pakistan's first strike against India will bring the fury of India's atomic power on our heads and it will entail the devastation of Pakistan. . . . The world will pronounce Pakistan's doom.'

The reason, in part, is geography. Pakistan has a lack of 'strategic depth'. Everywhere is too close to India. This basically means that any Pakistani military offensive will only be able to reach at most a thousand kilometres or so into India. But everywhere in Pakistan lies within the reach of Indian military forces. If Pakistan uses nuclear weapons first, its choice of targets will be limited. With a few nuclear weapons it can wreck appalling devastation, but cannot hope to destroy India's ability to fight back. At the same time, by using nuclear weapons against India, it will have invited the complete nuclear destruction of Pakistan.

The second obvious and inescapable conclusion arises from asking when Pakistan would take a decision to use its nuclear weapons. Lt. General (retd.) Mujib ur Rehman Khan has asked 'will Pakistan resort to nuclear means at the fall of Lahore, or when a strategic area is about to be overrun? By the time we are in a position to take such a momentous decision, our present borders will have been pushed inwards towards the interior, putting us that much more at a disadvantage. At the same time, the Indians will have attained the necessary air superiority to have turned the scale of the conventional battle to their advantage. Under such adverse conditions, how do we launch this nuclear strike to stem India's military success?' He concludes there are no definite answers.

This presents a truly dreadful prospect. Under such 'adverse conditions' Pakistan's military leaders may use nuclear weapons because they feel their only alternative is to lose these weapons altogether. One way this could happen is that Indian conventional attacks on Pakistan's military airfields and troops, deliberately or accidentally, might undermine Pakistan's nuclear weapons arsenal. A hypothetical example is if India attacked the Sarghoda airfield, where Pakistan is supposed to keep its Chinese made M–11 missiles, or some place where the F–16s were waiting loaded with a nuclear weapon each. Pakistan's generals might be faced with the prospect of losing their nuclear weapons altogether, or having to use them even though the situation was not absolutely desperate.

Without anyone having planned it, there would be an instance of inadvertent escalation, conventional war would turn nuclear. The consequences would be devastating for India as well as for Pakistan.

It was just such fears that led both the United States and Soviet Union to rely on very large conventional armies facing each other in Europe, even though both had nuclear weapons. The fact is that amid all the talk of nuclear deterrence for much of the Cold War, in Europe where US and Soviet forces directly confronted each other, they relied on giant armies prepared for conventional battles. This is also why, even though it talks about its nuclear weapons deterring conventional attack, Pakistan keeps such a large army.

Even if there is no planned first strike with nuclear weapons that invites an even more terrible reply, and even if there is enough good luck that nuclear weapons are not used inadvertently, there is always the chance of their accidental use. This possibility has worried even former Pakistani Chief of Army Staff, General Beg. He has argued 'Pakistan and India may neither have the resources nor the capability to develop . . . a system for ensuring nuclear safeguards and security.' As a consequence, an attack, he says, could 'escalate to a nuclear level' where 'there can be a real danger of nuclear accident and unauthorised use of nuclear weapons due to the absence of a fail-safe system.' In other words, nuclear weapons could be used accidentally, or by some-one who was not supposed to be able to make the decision.

The possibility of using nuclear weapons as a response to a conven-tional conflict is so immoral and dangerous that it must be rejected. It is clear that any first use of nuclear weapons by Pakistan, whether as a planned first strike, inadvertently or accidentally, would surely invite a nuclear response. The only way to ensure against all these risks is to remove nuclear weapons from Pakistan's military planning. It is only by not having them that there can be certainty that they will not be used. Renouncing nuclear weapons means Pakistan has the double benefit that it cannot use them and that these weapons will not be used against it. It will be neither a nuclear murderer nor a nuclear victim.

The Price Of Nuclear Weapons

The cost of a nuclear weapons programme is far greater than simply the death of morality and the corruption of language and politics. The financial costs are great, this is why they are kept secret. In Pakistan even estimating the cost is hard. Part of the problem is that disentangling the money spent on the nuclear weapons programme from that of the money spent on the Pakistan Atomic Energy Commission (PAEC) is practically impossible. That they are tied together is indisputable. As he doled out the credit for the nuclear test, Prime Minister Nawaz Sharif said 'The entire nation takes justifiable pride in the accomplish-ments of the Pakistan Atomic Energy Commission, the Dr. A.Q. Khan

Research Laboratories and all affiliated organisations.' Incidentally, for PAEC, this was illegal. It is bound by its charter to work only on the peaceful uses of nuclear energy.

At a more material level, many of the nuclear scientists and engineers who work on the bomb programme must have received their training by the PAEC, and some may be seconded from it; there are apparently 'seven thousand highly skilled and professional people, including more than two thousand PhDs, M Phils, MSs, MScs, BEs at Kahuta. Similarly, the uranium that is mined and processed at Dera Ghazi Khan is used by both to make fuel for the KANUPP nuclear reactor in Karachi and to make nuclear weapons material at Kahuta. Since the nuclear power plant at Karachi is so dangerous, old, and has produced a fraction of the electricity it was supposed to, it is possible to imagine that it is kept open as no more than a fig-leaf for the nuclear weapons project. In which case a large share of the greater than six billion rupees budget of PAEC over the last two decades, may have directly or indirectly subsidised the nuclear weapons programme.

To these costs must be added the military spending in Pakistan which has driven the nuclear programme. For years this military spending has meant a reduction in development spending. Military spending in the 1996 budget was twice the military budget in 1990. The significance of 1990 is that in that year military spending was equal to the budget allocation for development, i.e. for building schools, hospitals, roads, etc. Since then military spending has increasingly overtaken development spending and now for exceeds it.

The effects of persistently lower-than-necessary development spending are cumulative. Each generation that is deprived of decent healthcare and housing, education and employment, is less able to provide these for the generation that comes after. There is a spiral of underdevelopment. That this is at work in Pakistan is evident from the fact that on the United Nations Development Programme's aggregated measure of the quality of people's lives in different countries, the Human Development Index, Pakistan has slipped from number 120 in 1992 to 128th place in 1995, and in 1999 it had fallen to 138.

To all this must now be added the cost of the sanctions imposed on Pakistan in response to its nuclear tests. This may amount to billions of dollars of aid and loans. Much of this would frankly have been squandered, and used to enrich the already wealthy and provide them with even greater comforts. But some at least would have gone to supply water, perhaps build a school, a hospital, a road, something that would have helped.

It is unclear how long sanctions will remain in force. But even when they are lifted, Pakistan will only be back to where it is now. The fact is that to begin creating the conditions within which real development can take place will need massive reductions in military spending. Such reductions cannot however take place as long as India is treated as a threat requiring nothing less than a willingness to use nuclear weapons against it, and the willingness to have nuclear weapons used against Pakistan in response. If national nuclear suicide is being offered as the only way to confront India, any reduction in military spending will be seen as subtracting from national military capability. It is only by engaging in nuclear disarmament, and so demonstrating that relations with India are not being interpreted as issues of life and death for the nation, that it becomes possible to debate military spending.

Making Nuclear Weapons Destroys People's Health And The Environment

The whole process of creating and maintaining even a nuclear weapons arsenal like Pakistan's exacts a terrible toll on people's health and on the environment. There is increasing evidence from around the world that from the moment uranium is dug out of the ground to the disposal of long lived radioactive waste that is dangerous for tens of thousands of years, the materials that form the essential ingredients for nuclear weapons bring with them the prospects of sickness and death.

The first public evidence of the human and environmental damage done by the nuclear programme has already emerged. It is to be found in Dera Ghazi Khan, the site of Pakistan's first, and for a long time its only, uranium mining and processing operation. Officially part of the Pakistan Atomic Energy Commission (PAEC), this is also where workers mined the uranium that went to Kahuta to make nuclear weapons. In 1996, the 500 or so workers at the plant went on strike, demanding 'payment of compensation to the heirs of the employees [who] died during their duty or became handicap[ped], provision of all necessary safety measures both at the plant and at the site, sacking of the doctor and lady doctor of the PAEC dispensary as due to their incompetence several employees lost their lives.' The government's response was draconian. Newspapers reported that 'Security guards of PAEC and other law enforcing agencies have besieged the colony and all installations. No one is being allowed to enter or come out of the area.'

That the first strike over health and safety issues in part of Pakistan's nuclear complex has broken out at Dera Ghazi Khan is not surprising at all. Uranium is both radioactive and poisonous, handling it in any form is fraught with risk. But, unlike in a laboratory where highly trained and careful scientists who know the risks may handle tiny amounts of such dangerous material with relative safety, the mining and processing of uranium ore is an industrial scale process. Its labour intensive character leads to large numbers of relatively unskilled workers, who know little about the short or long term risks that they are being subject to. The dangers to health are increased substantially in such a setting.

Briefly, the process of turning the tiny amounts of uranium found in some rocks into large amounts of pure uranium that can be used to make fuel for nuclear reactors or for nuclear weapons requires that huge amounts of rock need to be dug out of the earth, pulverised into dust and chemically processed. The uranium ore emits radiation and exposes anyone close to it even before it is taken out of the ground. Digging up the ore releases radioactive gases that were trapped inside the rock, adding to the risk. The ore has then to be crushed and the waste rock removed. The crushing produces a radioactive and poisonous dust that can be breathed in, that settles on clothes, in hair, and on the skin. Because it is so fine, it can be blown in the wind and settle in the surroundings, on grass, leaves, and water, contaminating everything.

Uranium mining, the first stage, leaves behind as waste over 99 per cent of the rock in which the uranium ore was located. This contains most of the radioactivity and many toxic heavy metals as well as the acids and alkalis used to extract the uranium. These can leach into the soil and groundwater. Because the processing is often done away from the site of the mining, the ore has to be transported to the processing plant. This is often done after the ore has been substantially crushed, and some of the waste rock removed, leaving less material that needs to be transported.

If the transport of the ore is done on open trucks, the uranium dust may well be blown around all along the route. Once at the processing plant, there is more crushing and grinding of the rock. But now even though the total amounts of material are smaller than at the mine, the risks of inhaling even small quantities of dust are larger. The impact on the uranium miners and the local environment of such waste is enormous.

The dangers do not end there, they just move to another site. The next step is transforming the uranium into a gaseous form that is suitable for enrichment at the Kahuta facility. This involves the use of highly corrosive and toxic chemicals that react violently with moisture in the air and are fatal if breathed in. Once the uranium has been enriched and can be used to make nuclear weapons, it leaves behind a radioactive, toxic and corrosive waste. This waste comprises almost all of the initial material, and needs to be disposed of safely. It is usually stored as cylinders of gas at the enrichment plant, but these will eventually degrade and lead to an environmental disaster.

There is no information about what has happened at the Kahuta plant with regard to health and safety issues or how the waste is dealt with. The US, which invented many of the processes and technologies used in making nuclear weapons, is still struggling to come to terms with this kind of waste from its nuclear weapons programme. A 1997 report claims the giant steel cylinders containing this waste gas are so radioactive that even the rust that forms and then falls off the outside is treated as 'dangerous waste'. The cylinders, despite being over one-third of an inch thick have corroded, and some leak, and 'every time one leaks, as some have, it releases puffs of toxic gas and uranium that can end up in the groundwater.'

Pakistan also has a new nuclear reactor, located on the banks of the Jhelum river, that uses uranium to produce plutonium, the other material used for making nuclear weapons. It is reported to have started operating. This adds new threats that the nuclear weapons programme poses to the environment. In particular, if this reactor has an accident it could pollute the river with radioactivity and thus poison irrigation and drinking water drawn from it. Further, the process of extracting plutonium produced by the reactor from the spent uranium fuel, known as reprocessing, generates the largest amounts and the most dangerous radioactive waste of a nuclear weapons programme. The US Department of Energy, responsible for making US nuclear weapons, has estimated that reprocessing accounts for 85 per cent of the radioactivity released in the nuclear weapons production process, 71 per cent of the contaminated water and 33 per cent of the contaminated solids. These wastes are so dangerous that they need to be stored safely for at least 1,000 years so that they do not get into the environment.

As long as Pakistan retains its nuclear weapons, it will need to keep at least some of these sites open. If, as seems possible, it starts to increase the size of its nuclear arsenal, more and more sites will become part of the nuclear weapons complex, and more communities exposed to the dangers of radioactive waste. These dangers and any accidents will most certainly be kept secret.

It is only by renouncing nuclear weapons that damage can be stopped. The sooner this is done, the less chance there is of more workers being exposed to radioactivity, and of further damaging the environment. Once this is done, there will be no need to keep these places secret, and the process of assessing the harm that has already been done, and cleaning up the mess can be started.

Giving Up Nuclear Weapons

A number of interconnected reasons have been given as to why Pakistan should renounce its nuclear weapons, and the way of thinking about national security and about India that goes with them. These can be loosely titled the moral or ethical, the social, the strategic, the political, the economic, and the environmental. Taken together they form a way of looking at the issue of Pakistan's nuclear weapons that leaves little choice but to disarm.

The final question is whether Pakistan should unilaterally renounce these weapons (as South Africa has done), or as part of a bilateral process with India (as has been done by Argentina and Brazil), or only as part of an international agreement on nuclear disarmament. In one sense this is beside the point. The need for Pakistan to disarm is so great that whichever of these is easiest should be adopted.

The best and easiest way for Pakistan to disarm is to do so unilaterally. Firstly, because it has the power to do it. Unilateral actions do not leave it dependent on the wishes, intentions or actions of other states. Unilateralism in this context is actually an act of self-empowerment. Secondly, unilateral disarmament would make it very difficult for India to use Pakistan as a justification for its own nuclear weapons. Pakistan would no longer be a nuclear target.

If the Indian state keeps its nuclear weapons, despite the fact all the arguments that apply to Pakistan apply even more so to India, then that is a matter for India's people and its peace movement. Right now Pakistan's policy only helps India's nuclear hawks increase the pressure for keeping India's nuclear programme. Atal Behari Vajpayee now claims India's nuclear tests were justified by Pakistan's subsequent nuclear tests. By opting out of a self-destructive arms race, Pakistan would for the first time strengthen the arguments of the Indian peace movement. They would be able to point to Pakistan and say if Pakistan can do this, why can't India.

To those who want to keep nuclear weapons, the political, economic, environmental and moral benefits of renouncing nuclear weapons are outweighed by the supposed strategic guarantee of national sovereignty that the bomb brings. They argue, as Nawaz Sharif has done, that everything pales besides the need of the nation to live with self-respect. The economic costs are bearable when the fate of the nation is at stake, the environmental dangers are insignificant because the nation is its people and their self-respect, not land. The same argument is made in India.

The question for all those who support nuclear weapons is where is the self-respect in thinking about and being willing to kill hundreds of thousands if not millions of people? What kind of self is it that needs such destruction as a mark of respect?

Earlier versions of this essay appeared in Samina Ahmad and David Cortright (eds.), *Pakistan and the Bomb*, University of Notre Dame Press, 1998, and in *Seminar*, No. 468, August 1998.

India and the Bomb

AMARTYA SEN

Weapons of mass destruction have a peculiar fascination. They can generate a warm glow of strength and power carefully divorced from the brutality and genocide on which the potency of the weapons depend. The great epics—from *Iliad* and *Ramayana* to *Kalevala* and *Nibelungenlied*—provide thrilling accounts of the might of special weapons, which not only are powerful in themselves, but also greatly empower their possessors. As India, along with Pakistan, goes down the route of cultivating nuclear weapons, the imagined radiance of perceived power is hard to miss.

The Moral and the Prudential
Perceptions can deceive. It has to be asked whether powerful weapons in general and nuclear armament in particular can be expected—invariably or even typically—to strengthen and empower their possessor. An important prudential issue is involved here. There is, of course, also the question of ethics, and in particular the rightness or wrongness of a nuclear policy. That important issue can be distinguished from the question of practical benefit or loss of a nation from a particular policy. We have good grounds to be interested in both the questions—the prudential and the ethical—but also reason enough not to see the two issues as disparate and totally delinked from each other. Our behaviour towards each other cannot be divorced from what we make of the ethics of one another's pursuits, and the reasons of morality have, as a

result, prudential importance as well.[1] It is in this light that I want to examine the challenges of nuclear policy in the subcontinent in general and in India in particular.

Whether, or to what extent, powerful weapons empower a nation is not a new question. Indeed, well before the age of nuclear armament began, Rabindranath Tagore had expressed a general doubt about the fortifying effects of military strength. If 'in his eagerness for power', Tagore had argued in 1917, a nation 'multiplies his weapons at the cost of his soul, then it is he who is in much greater danger than his enemies'.[2] Tagore was not as uncompromisingly a pacifist as Mahatma Gandhi was, and he is warning against the dangers of alleged strength through more and bigger weapons related to the need for ethically scrutinising the functions of these weapons and the exact uses to which they are to be put as well as the practical importance of the reactions and counteractions of others. The 'soul' to which Tagore referred includes, as he explained, the need for humanity and understanding in international relations.

Tagore was not merely making a moral point, but also one of pragmatic importance, taking into account the responses from others that would be generated by one's pursuit of military might. His immediate concern in the quoted statement was with Japan before the Second World War. Tagore was a great admirer of Japan and the Japanese, but felt very disturbed by its shift from economic and social development to aggressive militarisation. The heavy sacrifices that were forced on Japan later on, through military defeat and nuclear devastation, Tagore did not live to see (he died in 1941), but they would have only added to Tagore's intense sorrow. But the conundrum that he invoked, about the weakening effects of military power, has remained active in the writings of contemporary Japanese writers, perhaps most notably Kenzaburo Oe.[3]

Science, Politics and Nationalism

The leading architect of India's ballistic missile programme and a key figure in the development of nuclear weapons is Dr. Abdul Kalam. He comes from a Muslim family, is a scientist of great distinction, and has a very strong commitment to Indian nationalism. Abdul Kalam is also a very amiable person (as I had discovered when I had been closeted with him at an honorary degree ceremony in Calcutta in 1990, many years before the blasts). Kalam's philanthropic concerns are strong, and he has a record of helping in welfare-related causes, such as charitable work for mentally impaired children in India.

Kalam recorded his proud reaction as he watched the Indian nuclear explosions in Pokhran, on the edge of the Thar desert in Rajasthan, in May 1998: 'I heard the earth thundering below our feet and rising ahead of us in terror. It was a beautiful sight.'[4] It is rather remarkable that the admiration for sheer power should be so strong in the reactions of even so kind-hearted a person, but perhaps the force of nationalism played a role here, along with the general fascination that powerful weapons seem to generate. The intensity of Kalam's nationalism may be well concealed by the mildness of his manners, but it was evident enough in his statements after the blasts ('for 2,500 years India has never invaded anybody'), no less than his joy at India's achievement ('a triumph of Indian science and technology').

This was, in fact, the second round of nuclear explosions in the same site, in Pokhran; the first was under Indira Gandhi's prime ministership in 1974. But at that time the whole event was kept under a shroud of secrecy, partly in line with the government's ambiguity about the correctness of the nuclear weaponisation of India. While China's nuclearisation clearly had a strong influence in the decision of the (Indira) Gandhi government to develop its own nuclear potential (between 1964 and 1974 China had conducted 15 nuclear explosions), the official government position was that the 1974 explosion in Pokhran was strictly for 'peaceful purposes', and that India remained committed to doing without nuclear weapons. The first Pokhran tests were, thus, followed by numerous affirmations of India's rejection of the nuclear path, rather than any explicit savouring of the destructive power of nuclear energy.

It was very different in the summer of 1998 following the events that have come to be called Pokhran-II. By then there was strong support from various quarters. This included, of course, the Bharatiya Janata Party, or the BJP, which had included the development of nuclear weapons in its electoral manifesto, and led the political coalition that came to office after the February elections in 1998. While previous Indian governments had considered following up the 1974 blast by new ones, they had stopped short of doing it, but with the new—more intensely nationalist—government the lid was lifted, and the blasts of Pokhran-II occurred within three months of its coming to power. The BJP, which has built up its base in recent years by capturing and to a great extent fanning Hindu nationalism, received in the elections only a minority of Hindu votes, and *a fortiori* a minority of total votes in the multireligious country. (India has nearly as many Muslims as Pakistan and many more Muslims than in Bangladesh, and also of course Sikhs, Christians, Jains, Parsees, and other communities.) But even with a minority of parliamentary seats (182 out of 545), the BJP could head an alliance—a fairly ad hoc alliance—of many different political factions, varying from strictly regional parties (such as the AIADMK, the DMK and the MDMK of Tamil Nadu, the Haryana Lok Dal and the Haryana Vikas Party of Haryana, the Biju Janata Dal of Orissa, the Trinamul Congress of West Bengal) to specific community-based parties (including the Akali Dal, the party of Sikh nationalism), and some breakaway factions of other parties. As the largest group within the coalition, the BJP was the dominant force in the 1998 Indian government (as it is in the present coalition government since the new elections called in late 1999), which gives it much more authority than a minority party could otherwise expect in Indian politics.

The BJP's interest in following up the 1974 blast by further tests and by actually developing nuclear weapons received strong support from an active pro-nuclear lobby, which includes many Indian scientists.[5] The advocacy by scientists and defence experts was quite important in making the idea of a nuclear India at least plausible to many, if not quite fully acceptable yet as a part of a reflective equilibrium of Indian thinking. As Praful Bidwai and Achin Vanaik put it in their well-researched and well-argued book, 'The most ardent advocates of nuclear weapons have constantly sought to invest these weapons with a religious-like authority and importance—to emphasise the awe and wonder rather than the revulsion and horror—to give them an accepted and respectable place in the mass popular culture of our times.'[6]

The Thrill of Power

Kalam's excitement at the power of nuclear explosions was not, of course, unusual as a reaction to the might of weapons. The excitement generated by destructive power, dissociated from any hint of potential genocide, has been a well-observed psychological state in the history of the world. Even the normally unruffled J. Robert Oppenheimer, the principal architect of the world's first nuclear explosion, was moved to quote the two-millennia-old *Bhagavad Gita* (Oppenheimer knew Sanskrit well enough to get his *Gita* right) as he watched the atmospheric explosion of the first atom bomb in a US desert near the village of Oscuro on July 16, 1945: 'the radiance of a thousand suns . . . burst into the sky'.[7]

Oppenheimer went on to quote further from the *Bhagavad Gita*: 'I am become Death, the shatterer of worlds.' That image of death would show its naked and ruthless face next month in Hiroshima and Nagasaki (what Kenzaburo Oe has called 'the most terrifying monster lurking in the darkness of Hiroshima'[8]). But in the experimental station in the US desert, code-named 'Jornala del Muerto' (translatable as 'Death Tract'), there was only sanitised abstractness firmly detached from any actual killing.[9] The thousand suns have now come home to the subcontinent to roost. The five Indian nuclear explosions in Pokhran on May 11 and May 13, 1998 were quickly followed by six Pakistani blasts in the Chagai hills. 'The whole mountain turned white', was the Pakistan government's charmed response. The subcontinent was by now caught in an overt nuclear confrontation, masquerading as further empowerment of each country.

These developments have received fairly uniform condemnation abroad, but also considerable favour inside India and Pakistan, though we must be careful not to exaggerate the actual extent of domestic support. Pankaj Mishra did have reason enough to conclude, two weeks after the blasts, that 'the nuclear tests have been extremely popular, particularly among the urban middle class'.[10] But that was too soon to see the long-run effects on Indian public opinion. Furthermore, the enthusiasm of the celebrators is more easily pictured on the television than the deep doubts of the sceptics. Indeed, the euphoria that the television pictures captured on the Indian streets immediately following the blasts concentrated on the reaction of those who did celebrate and chose to come out and rejoice. It was accompanied by doubts and reproach of a great many people who took no part in the festivities, who did not figure in the early television pictures, and whose doubts and opposition found increasingly vocal expression over time. As Amitav Ghosh, the novelist, noted in his extensive review of Indian public reactions to the bomb for *The New Yorker*, 'the tests have divided the country more deeply than ever'.[11]

It is also clear that the main political party that chose to escalate India's nuclear adventure, namely the BJP, did not get any substantial electoral benefit from the Pokhran blasts. In fact quite the contrary, as the analyses of local voting since the 1998 blasts tend to show. By the time India went to the polls again, in September 1999, the BJP had learned the lesson sufficiently to barely mention the nuclear tests in their campaign with the voters. And yet, as N. Ram (the political commentator and the editor of *Frontline*) has cogently argued in his anti-nuclear book *Riding the Nuclear Tiger*, we 'must not make the mistake of assuming that since the Hindu Right has done badly out of Pokhran-II, the issue has been decisively won'.[12]

Indian attitudes towards nuclear weaponisation are characterised not only by ambiguity and moral doubts, but also by some uncertainty as to what is involved in making gainful use of these weapons. It may be the case, as several opinion polls have indicated, that public opinion in India has a much smaller inclination, compared with Pakistani public opinion, to assume that nuclear weapons will ever be actually used in a subcontinental war.[13] But since the effectiveness of these weapons depends ultimately on the willingness to use them in some situations, there is an issue of coherence of thought that has to be addressed here. Implicitly or explicitly an eventuality of actual use has to be a part of the possible alternative scenarios that must be contemplated, if some benefit is to be obtained from the possession and deployment of nuclear weapons. To hold the belief that nuclear weapons are useful but must never be used lacks cogency and can indeed be seen to be a result of the odd phenomenon that Arundhati Roy (the author of the wonderful novel *The God of Small Things*) has called 'the end of imagination'.[14]

As Roy has also brought out with much clarity, the nature and results of an actual all-out nuclear war are almost impossible to imagine in a really informed way. Arundhati Roy describes a likely scenario thus: 'Our cities and forests, our fields and villages will burn for days. Rivers will turn to poison. The air will become fire. The wind will spread the flames. When everything there is to burn has burned and the fires die, smoke will rise and shut out the sun.'[15]

It is hard to think that the possibility of such an eventuality can be a part of a wise policy of national self-defence.

Established Nuclear Powers and Subcontinental Grumbles
One of the problems in getting things right arises from a perceived sense of inadequacy, prevalent in India, of any alternative policy that would be entirely satisfactory and would thus help to firm up a rejection of nuclear weapons through the transparent virtues of a resolutely

non-nuclear path (as opposed to the horrors of the nuclear route). This is perhaps where the gap in perceptions is strongest between the discontent and disgust with which the subcontinental nuclear adventures are viewed in the West and the ambiguity that exists on this subject within India (not to mention the support of the nuclear route that comes from the government, the BJP, and India's pro-nuclear lobby). It is difficult to understand what is going on in the subcontinent without placing it solidly in a global context.

Nuclear strategists in South Asia tend to resent deeply the international condemnation of Indian and Pakistani policies and decisions that do not take note of the nuclear situation in the world as a whole. They are surely justified in this resentment, and also right to question the censoriousness of Western critics of subcontinental nuclear adventures without adequately examining the ethics of their own nuclear policies, including the preservation of an established and deeply unequal nuclear hegemony, with very little attempt to achieve global denuclearisation. The Defence Minister of India, George Fernandes, told Amitav Ghosh: 'Why should the five nations that have nuclear weapons tell us how to behave and what weapons we should have?' This was matched by the remark of Qazi Hussain Ahmed, the leader of Jamaat-e-Islami (Pakistan's principal religious party), to Ghosh: '. . . we don't accept that five nations should have nuclear weapons and others shouldn't. We say, "Let the five also disarm".'[16]

The inquiry into the global context is indeed justified, but what we have to examine is whether the placing of the subcontinental substory within a general frame of a bigger global story really changes the assessment that we can reasonably make of what is going on in India and Pakistan. In particular, to argue that their nuclear policies are deeply mistaken does not require us to dismiss the widespread resentment in the subcontinent of the smugness of the dominant global order. These complaints, even if entirely justified and extremely momentous, do not establish the sagacity of a nuclear policy that dramatically increases uncertainties within the subcontinent without achieving anything to make each country more secure. Indeed, Bangladesh is now probably the safest country in the subcontinent to live in.

Moral Resentment and Prudential Blunder
There are, I think, two distinct issues, which need to be carefully separated. First, the world nuclear order is extremely unbalanced and there

are excellent reasons to complain about the military policies of the major powers, particularly the five that have a monopoly over official nuclear status as well as over permanent membership in the Security Council of the United Nations. The second issue concerns the choices that other countries—other than the Big Five—face, and this has to be properly scrutinised, rather than being hijacked by resentment of the oligopoly of the power to terrorise. The fact that other countries, including India and Pakistan, have ground enough for grumbling about the nature of the world order, sponsored and supported by the established nuclear powers without any serious commitment to denuclearisation, does not give them any reason to pursue a nuclear policy that worsens their own security and adds to the possibility of a dreadful holocaust. Moral resentment cannot justify a prudential blunder.

I have so far not commented on the economic and social costs of nuclearisation and the general problem of allocation of resources. That issue is important, even though it is hard to find out exactly what the costs of the nuclear programmes are. The expenses on this are carefully hidden in both the countries. Even though it is perhaps easier to estimate the necessary information in India (given the greater need for disclosure in Indian polity), the estimates are bound to be rough.

Recently, C. Rammanohar Reddy, a distinguished journalist at the major daily *The Hindu,* has estimated that the cost of nuclearisation is something around half a percentage of the gross domestic product per year.[17] This might not sound like much, but it is large enough if we consider the alternative uses of these resources. For example, it has been estimated that the additional costs of providing elementary education for every child with neighbourhood schools at every location in the country would cost roughly the same amount of money.[18] The proportion of illiteracy in the Indian adult population is still about 40 per cent, and it is about 55 per cent in Pakistan. Furthermore, there are other costs and losses as well, such as the deflection of India's scientific talents to military-related research away from more productive lines of research, and also from actual economic production. The prevalence of secretive military activities also restrains open discussions in Parliament and tends to subvert traditions of democracy and free speech. However, ultimately the argument against nuclearisation is not primarily an economic one. It is rather the increased insecurity of human lives that constitutes the biggest penalty of the subcontinental nuclear adventures. That issue needs further scrutiny.

Does Nuclear Deterrence Work?

What of the argument that nuclear deterrence makes war between India and Pakistan less likely? Why would not the allegedly proven ability of nuclear balance, which is supposed to have kept peace in the world, be effective also in the subcontinent? I believe that this question can be answered from four different perspectives.

First, even if it were the case that the nuclearisation of India and Pakistan reduces the probability of war between the two, there would be a trade-off here between a lower chance of conventional war against some chance of a nuclear holocaust. No sensible decision-making can concentrate only on the probability of war without taking note of the size of the penalties of war should it occur. Indeed, any significant probability of the scenario captured by Arundhati Roy's description of 'the end of imagination' can hardly fail to outweigh the greater probability, if any, of the comparatively milder penalties of conventional war.

Second, there is nothing to indicate that the likelihood of conventional war is, in fact, reduced by the nuclearisation of India and Pakistan. Indeed, hot on the heels of the nuclear blasts, the two countries did undergo a major military confrontation in the Kargil district in Kashmir.

The Kargil conflict, which occurred within a year of the nuclear blasts of India and Pakistan, was in fact the first military conflict between the two in nearly 30 years. Many Indian commentators have argued that the confrontation, which was provoked by separatist guerrillas coming across the Line of Control from Pakistan (in their view, joined by Army regulars), was helped by Pakistan's understanding that India would not be able to use its massive superiority in conventional forces to launch a bigger war in retaliation, precisely because it would fear a nuclear holocaust. Whether or not this analysis is right, there is clearly substance in the general reasoning that the enemy's fear of nuclear annihilation can be an argument in favour of military adventurism without expectation of a fuller retaliation from the enemy. Be that as it may, the proof of the pudding is in the eating, and no matter what the explanation, nuclearisation evidently has not prevented non-nuclear conflicts between India and Pakistan.

Third, the danger of accidental nuclear war is much greater in the subcontinent than it was in the Cold War itself. This is not only because the checks and controls are much looser, but also because the distances involved are so small between India and Pakistan—that there is little time for any conversation when a crisis might occur and a first strike were feared. Also, the much-discussed hold of fundamentalist jihadists within the Pakistan military and the absence of democratic control add to the fear of a sudden flashpoint.

Fourth, there is a need also to assess whether the peace that the world enjoyed with nuclear deterrence during the global Cold War was, in fact, predictable and causally robust. The argument for the balance of terror has been clear enough for a long time, and was most eloquently put by Winston Churchill in his last speech to the House of Commons on March 1, 1955. His ringing words on this ('safety will be the sturdy child of terror, and survival the twin brother of annihilation') has a mesmerising effect, but Churchill himself did make exceptions to his rule, when he said that the logic of deterrence 'does not cover the case of lunatics or dictators in the mood of Hitler when he found himself in his final dug-out.'[19]

Dictators are not unknown in the world (even in the subcontinent), and at least part-lunatics can be found with some frequency in both the countries, judging by what some eloquent commentators seem to be able to write on the nuclear issue itself. But perhaps more importantly, we have reason to note that risks have been taken also by people with impeccable credentials on sanity and lucidity. To give just one example (a rather prominent one), in choosing the path of confrontation in what has come to be called the Cuban Missile Crisis, President Kennedy evidently took some significant risks of annihilation on behalf of humanity. Indeed, Theodore C. Sorenson, Special Counsel to President Kennedy, put the facts thus (in a generally admiring passage): 'John Kennedy never lost sight of what either war or surrender would do to the whole human race. His UN Mission was preparing for a negotiated peace and his Joint Chiefs of Staff were preparing for war, and he intended to keep both on rein. . . . He could not afford to be hasty or hesitant, reckless or afraid. The odds that the Soviets would go all the way to war, he later said, seemed to him then "somewhere between one out of three and even".'[20]

Well, a chance of annihilation between one-third and one-half is not an easy decision to be taken on behalf of the human race. I think we have to recognise that the peace of nuclear confrontation in the Cold War partly resulted from luck, and may not have been pre-ordained. To take *post hoc* to be *propter hoc* is a luxury that can be quite costly for charting out future policies in nuclear—or indeed any other—field. We have to take account not only of the fact that circumstances are rather different in the subcontinent compared with what obtained during the nuclear confrontation in the global Cold War, but also the world was actually rather fortunate to escape annihilation even in the Cold War itself. And the dangers of extermination did not come only from lunatics or dictators.

So, to conclude this section, the nuclearisation of the subcontinental confrontations need not reduce the risk of war (either in theory or in practice), and it escalates the penalty of war in a dramatic way. The unjust nature of world military balance does not change this crucial prudential recognition.

Were the Indian Government's Goals Well Served?

I come now to a question of rather limited interest, but which is asked often enough, addressed particularly to India. Even if it is accepted that the subcontinent is less secure as a result of the tit-for-tat nuclear tests, it could be the case that India's own self-interest has been well served by the BJP-led government's nuclear policy. India has reason to grumble, it is argued, for not being taken as seriously as one of the largest countries in the world should be. There is unhappiness also in the attempt by some countries, certainly the United States in the past, to achieve some kind of a 'balance' between India and Pakistan, whereas India is nearly seven times as large as Pakistan and must not be taken to be at par with it. Rather the comparison should be with China, and for this—along with other causes such as getting India a permanent seat in the Security Council—India's nuclear might could be expected to make a contribution. The subcontinent may be less secure as a result of the nuclear developments, but, it is argued, India did get some benefit. How sound is this line of argument?

I have some difficulty in pursuing this exercise. Even though I am a citizen of India, I don't really think I can legitimately inquire only into the advantages that India alone may have received from a certain policy, excluding the interests of others whose interests were also affected. However, it is possible to scrutinise the effects of a certain policy in terms of the given goals of the Indian government (including strategic advantages over Pakistan as well as enhancement of India's international standing), and ask the rather coldly 'scientific' question whether those goals have been well served by India's recent nuclear policy. We do not have to endorse these goals to examine whether they have actually been better promoted.

There are good reasons to doubt that these goals have indeed been better served by the sequence of events at Pokhran and Chagai. First, India had—and has—massive superiority over Pakistan in conventional military strength. That strategic advantage has become far less significant as a result of the new nuclear balance. Indeed, since Pakistan has explicitly refused to accept a 'no first use' agreement, India's ability to count on conventional superiority is now, to a great extent, less effective (along with increasing the level of insecurity in both countries).

In the Kargil confrontation, India could not even make use of its ability to cross into the Pakistani administered Kashmir to attack the intruders from the rear, which military tacticians seem to think would have made much more sense than trying to encounter the intruders by climbing steeply up a high mountain from the Indian side to battle the occupants at the top. This not only made the Indian response less effective and rapid, it also led to more loss of Indian soldiers (1,300 lives according to the Government of India's estimate and 1,750 according to Pakistan's estimate) and added greatly to the expenses of the war conducted from an unfavoured position ($2.5 billion in direct expenses).[21] With the danger of a nuclear outburst, the Indian government's decision not to countercross the Line of Control in retaliation was clearly right, but it had no real option in this respect, given the strategic bind which it had itself helped to create.

Second, the fact that India can make nuclear weapons was well established before the present tit-for-tat nuclear tests were conducted. Pokhran-I in 1974 had already established the point, even though the Indian official statements tried to play down the military uses of that blast a quarter of a century ago. After the recent set of tests, India's and Pakistan's position seem to be much more even, at least in international public perception. As it happens, Pakistan was quite modest in its response. I remember thinking in the middle of May 1998, following the Indian tests, that surely Pakistan would now blast a larger number of bombs than India's five. I was agreeably impressed by Pakistan's moderation in blasting only six, which is the smallest whole number larger than five. The Government of India may deeply dislike any perception of parity with Pakistan, but did its best, in effect, to alter a situation of acknowledged asymmetry into one of perceived parity.

Third, aside from perceptions, in terms of the scientific requirement for testing, Pakistan clearly had a greater case for testing, never having conducted a nuclear test before 1998. This contrasted with India's experience of Pokhran-I in 1974. Also, with a much smaller community of nuclear scientists and a less extensive development of the possibilities of computerised simulation, the scientific need for an actual test may be much greater in Pakistan than in India. While Pakistan was concerned about the condemnation of the world community by testing on its own, the Indian blasts in May 1998 created a situation in which Pakistan could go in that direction without being blamed for starting any nuclear adventure. Eric Arnett puts the issue thus: 'In contrast to its Indian counterparts, Pakistan's political elite is less abashed about the need for nuclear deterrence. Military fears that the Pakistani nuclear capability was not taken seriously in India combined with a feeling of growing military inferiority after being abandoned by the USA after the Cold War create an imperative to test that was resisted before May 1998 only because of the threat of sanctions. The Indian tests created a situation in which the Pakistani leadership saw an even greater need to test and a possible opening to justify the test as a response that was both politically and strategically under-standable.'[22]

The thesis, often articulated by India's pro-nuclear lobby, that India was in greater danger of a first strike from Pakistan before the summer of 1998 lacks scientific as well as political credibility.

Fourth, nor was there much success in getting recognition for India as being in the same league as China, or for its grumble that inadequate attention is internationally paid to the dangers India is supposed to face from China. Spokesmen of the Indian government were vocal on these issues. A week before the Pokhran tests in 1998, Indian Defence Minister George Fernandes said in a much-quoted television interview, 'China is potential threat number one. . . . The potential threat from China is greater than that from Pakistan.'[23] In between the tests on May 11 and May 13, Indian Prime Minister Vajpayee wrote to President Clinton to point to China as being related to the motivation for the tests. This letter, which was published in *The New York Times* (after being leaked) on May 13, did not name China, but referred to it in very explicit terms: 'We have an overt nuclear weapons state on our borders, a state which committed armed aggression against India in 1962. Although our relations with that country have improved in the last decade or so, an atmosphere of distrust persists mainly due to the unresolved border problem. To add to the distrust that country has materially helped another neighbour of ours to become a covert nuclear weapons state.'[24]

However, as a result of the tit-for-tat nuclear tests by India and Pakistan, China could stand well above India's little grumbles, gently admonishing it for its criticism of China, and placing itself in the position of being a subcontinental peace-maker. When President Clinton visited China in June 1998, China and the United States released a joint statement declaring that the two countries would cooperate in non-proliferation efforts in the subcontinent.

Mark Frazier's assessment of the gap between Government of India's attempts and its achievement in this field captures the essence of this policy failure: 'Had it been India's intention to alert the world to its security concerns about China as a dangerous rising power, the tests managed to do just the opposite—they gave the Chinese officials the opportunity to present China as a cooperative member of the international community seeking to curb nuclear weapons proliferation. Far from looking like a revisionist state, China played the role of a status quo power, and a rather assertive one at that.'[25]

Fifth, nor did the blasts advance the cause of India's putative elevation to a permanent membership of the Security Council. If a country could blast its way into the Security Council, this would give an incentive to other countries to do the same. Furthermore, the new parity established between India and Pakistan after Pokhran-II and Chagai Hills also militates against the plausibility of that route to permanency in the Security Council, and this too could have been well predicted. I personally don't see why it is so important for India to be permanently on the Security Council (it may be in the interest of others for this to happen, given India's size and growing economic strength, but that is a different issue altogether). However, for the Government of India which clearly attaches importance to this possibility, it would surely have been wiser to emphasise its restraint in not developing nuclear weapons despite its proven ability to do so since 1974, and also use the pre-1998 asymmetry with Pakistan, in contrast with the symmetry that developed—following the Indian government's own initiative—after Pokhran-II and Chagai.

One of the interesting sidelights that emerge from a scrutiny of Indian official perceptions is the extent to which the government underestimates India's importance as a major country, a democratic polity, a rich multireligious civilisation, with a well-established tradition in science and technology (including the cutting edge of information technology), and with a fast-growing economy that could grow, with a little effort, even faster. The overestimation of the persuasive power of the bomb goes with an underestimation of the political, cultural, scientific and economic strengths of the country. There may be pleasure in the official circles at the success of President Clinton's visit to India and the asymmetrically favoured treatment it got in that visit vis-à-vis Pakistan, but the tendency to attribute that asymmetry to Indian nuclear adventure, rather than to India's large size, democratic politics, and its growing economy and technology is difficult to understand.

On Separating the Issues
To conclude, it is extremely important to distinguish the two distinct problems, both of which have a bearing on subcontinental nuclear policies. First, the world order on weapons needs a change and in particular requires an effective and rapid disarmament, particularly in the nuclear arsenal. Second, the nuclear adventures of India and Pakistan cannot be justified on the ground of the unjustness of the world order, since the people whose lives are made insecure as a result of these adventures are primarily the residents of the subcontinent themselves. Resenting the obtuseness of others is not a good ground for shooting oneself in the foot.

This does not, of course, imply that India or Pakistan has reason to feel happy about the international balance of power that the world establishment seems keen on maintaining, with or without further developments, such as an attempted 'nuclear shield' for the United States. Indeed, it must also be said that there is an inadequate appreciation in the West of the extent to which the role of the Big Five arouses suspicion and resentment in the Third World, including the subcontinent. This applies not only to the monopoly over nuclear armament, but also, on the other side, to the 'pushing' of conventional, non-nuclear armaments in the world market for weapons. For example, as the *Human Development Report 1994*, prepared under the leadership of that visionary Pakistani economist Mahbub ul Haq, pointed out, not only were the top five arms-exporting countries in the world precisely the five permanent members of the Security Council of the United Nations, but also they were, together, responsible for 86 per cent of all the conventional weapons exported during 1988–92.[26] Not surprisingly, the Security Council has not been able to take any serious initiative that would really restrain the merchants of death. It is not hard to understand the scepticism in India and Pakistan—and elsewhere—about the responsibility and leadership of the established nuclear powers.

As far as India is concerned, the two policies—of nuclear abstinence and demanding a change of world order—can be pursued simultaneously. Nuclear restraint strengthens rather than weakens India's voice. To demand that the Comprehensive Test Ban Treaty be redefined to include a dated programme of denuclearisation may well be among the discussable alternatives. But making nuclear bombs, not to mention deploying them, and spending scarce resource on missiles and what is euphemistically called 'delivery', can hardly be seen as sensible policy. The claim that subcontinental nuclearisation would somehow help to bring about world nuclear disarmament is a wild dream that can only precede a nightmare. The moral folly in these policies is substantial, but what is also clear and decisive is the prudential mistake that has been committed. The moral and the prudential are, in fact, rather close in a world of interrelated interactions, for reasons that Rabindranath Tagore had discussed nearly a hundred years ago.

Finally, on a more specific point, no country has as much stake as India in having a prosperous and civilian democracy in Pakistan. Even though the Nawaz Sharif government was clearly corrupt in specific ways, India had no particular advantage in undermining civilian rule in Pakistan, to be replaced by activist military leaders. Also, the encouragement of across-border terrorism, which India accuses Pakistan of, is likely to be dampened rather than encouraged by Pakistan's economic prosperity and civilian politics. It is particularly important in this context to point to the dangerousness of the argument, often heard in India, that the burden of public expenditure would be more unbearable for Pakistan, given its smaller size and relatively stagnant economy, than it is for India. This may well be the case, but the penalty that can visit India from an impoverished and desperate Pakistan in the present situation of increased insecurity is hard to contemplate. Enhancement of Pakistan's stability and well-being has prudential importance for India, in addition to its obvious ethical significance. That central connection—between the moral and the prudential—is important to seize.

Based on the first Dorothy Hodgkin Lecture at the Annual Pugwash Conference in Cambridge, U.K., on August 8, 2000. For helpful comments, I am grateful to Jean Dreze, Ayesha Jalal, V.K. Ramachandran and Emma Rothschild.

Notes

[1] I have tried to explore the connections between the two sets of questions in the analysis of economic problems in 'Rational Fools: A Critique of the Behavioural Foundations of Economic Theory', *Philosophy and Public Affairs*, 6 (1977), and *On Ethics and Economics* (Oxford: Blackwell, 1987).

[2] Rabindranath Tagore, *Nationalism* (London: Macmillan, 1917; new edition with an introduction by E.P. Thompson, 1991).

[3] Kenzaburo Oe, *Japan, the Ambiguous, and Myself* (Tokyo and New York: Kodansha International, 1995).

[4] *The Times of India*, June 28, 1998.

[5] On this see George Perkovich, *India's Nuclear Bomb: The Impact on Global Proliferation* (Berkeley, CA: University of California Press, 1999). See also T. Jayaraman, 'Science, Politics and the Indian Bomb: Some Preliminary Considerations', mimeographed, The Institute of Mathematical Sciences, C.I.T. Campus, Chennai, 2000.

[6] Praful Bidwai and Achin Vanaik, *New Nukes: India, Pakistan and Global Nuclear Disarmament* (Oxford: Signal Books, 2000, p. 1).

[7] For a graphic account of this episode and the chain of events related to it, see Robert Jungk, *Brighter Than a Thousand Suns: A Personal History of Atomic Scientists* (New York: Penguin Books, 1960).

[8] Kenzaburo Oe, *Hiroshima Notes*, translated by David L. Swain and Toshi Yonezawa (New York: Grove Press, 1996, p. 182).

[9] As the consequences of nuclearisation became clearer to Oppenheimer, he went on to campaign against nuclear arms, and in particular opposed the development of the hydrogen bomb.

[10] Pankaj Mishra, 'A New, Nuclear India?' in *India: A Mosaic*, eds. Robert B. Silvers and Barbara Epstein (New York: New York Review of Books, 2000), p. 230. The essay is dated May 28, 1998.

[11] Amitav Ghosh, 'Countdown: Why Can't Every Country Have the Bomb?' *The New Yorker*, October 26 & November 2, 1998, p. 190. See also his later book, *Countdown* (Delhi: Ravi Dayal, 1999), which further develops some of his arguments.

[12] N. Ram, *Riding the Nuclear Tiger* (New Delhi: Left Word Books, 1999), p. 106. See also his 'Preface' to *India: A Mosaic*, eds. Silvers and Epstein (New York: New York Review of Books, 2000).

[13] See Amitav Ghosh, *Countdown* (1999).

[14] Arundhati Roy, 'The End of Imagination'. See also her 'Introduction' to *India: A Mosaic*, eds. Silvers and Epstein (New York: New York Review of Books, 2000).

[15] Arundhati Roy, 'The End of Imagination', p. 52 this volume.

[16] Ghosh, 'Countdown', *The New Yorker*, 1998, pp. 190 and 197.

[17] C. Rammanohar Reddy, 'Estimating the Cost of Nuclear Weaponisation in India', mimeographed, *The Hindu*, Chennai, 1999.

[18] The so-called PROBE report cites two distinct estimates made by two government committees, which came to roughly the same figure; see *Public Report on Basic Education* (New Delhi: Oxford University Press, 1999).

[19] Robert Rhodes James, *Winston S. Churchill: His Complete Speeches 1897–1963* (New York: R.R. Bowker, 1974), pp. 8629–30.

[20] Theodore C. Sorenson, *Kennedy* (London: Hodder and Stoughton, 1965), p. 705. '*The Kennedy Tapes*' too bring out how close the world came to a nuclear annihilation.

[21] Bidwai and Vanaik, *New Nukes*, pp. xiii, xv.

[22] Eric Arnett, 'Nuclear Tests by India and Pakistan', *SIPRI Yearbook 1999* (Oxford: Oxford University Press, 1999, p. 377).

[23] Even though it is not clear whether Fernandes knew about the dates of the impending tests, he would certainly have seen—and in part been in charge of—the connection between Indian defence postures and its international pronouncements.

[24] 'Nuclear Anxiety: India's Letter to Clinton on the Nuclear Testing', *The New York Times*, May 13, 1998, p. 4.

[25] Mark W. Frazier, 'China–India Relations since Pokhran II: Assessing Sources of Conflict and Cooperation', *Access Asia Review*, 3 (July 2000), National Bureau of Asian Research, p. 10.

[26] *UNDP, Human Development Report 1994* (New York: United Nations, 1994, pp. 54–55, and Table 3.6).

The Immorality of Nuclear Weapons

AMULYA REDDY

Nuclear weapons are not just another class of weapons in the long history of development of weapons. Nuclear weapons are unique—their impacts are primarily on innocent civilian non-combatants, particularly women and children; their radiation effects persist for generations after their detonation; they are intrinsically indiscriminate; they are largely uncontrollable; and above all, they are instruments of mass murder on a scale unparalleled in human history. This uniqueness of nuclear weapons is now clearly affirmed in an Advisory Opinion of the International Court of Justice rendered in the month of July 1996.

Nuclear weapons have security, political and economic implications. In the ultimate analysis, however, the issue of nuclear weapons is a *moral* question. It is a question of right and wrong, good and evil, ethics. It is this ethical aspect of nuclear weapons,[1] especially as it applies to the designing and manufacture of nuclear weapons, that is the focus of my presentation.

The only actual uses of nuclear weapons against civilian populations during a war were by the US in Hiroshima and Nagasaki in 1945. The mentality that went behind ordering and executing the bombardment of Hiroshima and Nagasaki cannot really be understood without the context of the large-scale violence of World War II. Apart from the sheer magnitude of the numbers of casualties caused during the entire war, there are two other important thresholds that were crossed during the war. The first was the fire bombing carried out by the Allies of cities like Dresden, Hamburg and Tokyo. These resulted in an unprecedented scale of destruction and were the first really major attacks against civilian populations during the war. The second, and perhaps equally important, was the Holocaust.

After Pokhran II, there was a distressingly and disappointingly small minority of Indian scientists who spoke up against the nuclear tests. Though I was one of them, my attitude intensified after a visit to Poland in September 1999. There, a World Energy Assessment meeting in Cracow enabled me to visit the infamous Nazi concentration camps Auschwitz and Birkenau now preserved as museums.

During World War II, about 1.5 million innocent victims from all over Nazi-occupied Europe, overwhelmingly Jews, either went directly to the gas chambers and the crematoria at Auschwitz and Birkenau, or indirectly via the camps where they were held prisoners until they were too weak to labour.

Primo Levi in his powerful account *Survival in Auschwitz* of his personal experience has described life in the camps.[2] The tour of the camps left me with a completely unexpected feeling. The scale of human extermination was so enormous that I had to remind myself, particularly because the camps have been unpopulated since 1944, that there used to be human beings there. Human belongings— toothbrushes, shoes and suitcases—were piled from floor to ceiling in huge rooms, a separate room for each item, but the aggregate was more reminiscent of factory inputs. Even the room full of human hair looked like raw material for an industry, in the Auschwitz case, the manufacture of tailor's lining cloth.

If Auschwitz was unbelievable, its neighbour Birkenau located three kilometres away, beggared the imagination. Birkenau was spread over 175 hectares with 300 buildings each capable of housing 1000 inmates. Birkenau was a scale-up from the pilot plant demo at Auschwitz with a peak of 20,000 prisoners to full-scale commercialisation of mass-murder technology at Birkenau with 100,000 prisoners in August 1944.

The powerful impression that persisted was of detailed engineering resulting in '. . . the immense technological complex created . . . for the purpose of killing human beings.' The meticulous organisation and rigorous management were characteristic of mega-industries, 'gigantic and horrific factories of death.' The main gate of Auschwitz displayed the inscription 'Arbeit macht frei' ('Work brings freedom').

Perhaps a more apt announcement would have been 'Technology completely decoupled from values.'

As the scale of killing increases, the technology often (but not always) becomes more and more sophisticated—from knives to guns to machine guns to bombs to gas chambers and crematoria to atomic bombs. Also, with increasing scale, not only does the distance from victims become greater, but also the complexion becomes more and more technical. Burial is sufficient for one body, but for hundreds or thousands of bodies, one thinks in terms of 'throughput', 'air/fuel ratios' and 'burning capacity'.

In Auschwitz, it is obvious that nothing happened spontaneously. Everything was designed and planned. A Nobel Prize winner, Fritz Haber, developed the poison Cyclon B. One of Germany's top chemical industries, IG Farben, produced the poison for exterminating people in the gas chambers. Careful experiments were done to determine the time that it would take for a person to be poisoned. An engineering firm designed the crematoria furnaces to process 350 bodies per day in Auschwitz I. So, there must have been engineers preoccupied with the technical problems. Perhaps, like Oppenheimer talking about nuclear weapons, some even thought that the problem was 'technically sweet'. Or, like the Department of Atomic Energy scientist at the Bangalore Kaiga debate in 1989 who said: 'Hiroshima provided us with a fortunate opportunity to study radiation effects!'

Once the problem was defined as eliminating hundreds and thousands of people per day, the Auschwitz solution was inevitable. But, who defined the problem and promulgated the order? By and large, it was political decision-makers that defined the problem. There was a conference at Wannsee, a suburb of Berlin, on January 20, 1942, at which the Nazi leadership decided in less than two hours (before lunch!) on the 'final solution' to exterminate the Jews. Ethnic superiority, racial/religious hatreds and fundamentalist views are well-known bases for decisions with far reaching destructive impacts on human beings.

Why was this definition of the problem so widely accepted? There could be several reasons. The population had been innoculated against moral judgements so that there was a pervasive moral indifference. The informed were silenced and the articulate dissidents became the first inputs to the camps. The media and journals were not allowed to reveal the truth. As a result, many citizens genuinely claimed ignorance as an excuse. [*The New York Times Magazine of Sunday*, February 13, 2000, has an article entitled: 'The Good Germans' by Peter Schneider which shows that there were many Germans who protected Jews in the midst of Nazi terror, thus challenging 'the theory of mass guilt and deepening the culpability of the collaborators.']

The most serious problem is the plea of duty and the obligation to carry out orders. Recall the movie 'Judgement at Nuremberg' with Spencer Tracy as the judge trying the Nazi judges for furthering the extermination of Jews. These judges defended themselves by submitting that they were just carrying out orders. The judgement at Nuremberg was that a human being has to take full responsibility for the consequences of his/her actions and that the excuse of obeying orders is inadmissible.

Apart from the above factors that operate in the case of officials and technical personnel, there is the additional device of taking a top-down macro view (e.g., national security, geopolitical compulsions, etc.). In such a macro view, numbers and statistics displace human beings. New proxy words dominate the discussions—'burning capacity' replaces 'the number of corpses burnt', 'kilotonnes yield' replaces 'kilodeaths', etc.

Functionaries, however, cannot avoid contact with the prisoners and victims to keep the system going. A recent book *Ordinary Men: Reserve Battalion 101 and the Final Solution in Poland* by Christopher Browning deals with the whole question of how ordinary men become genocidal killers.[3] What is overwhelming and astounding in Auschwitz and Birkenau is the unbelievable cold-bloodedness of the operation. It appears that the guards treated inmates inhumanly because they believed that the victims were sub-human and 'things' rather than people. Once this belief is propagated and accepted, anything goes—as in the growing number of examples of ethnic cleansing and genocide (native Americans, Hindus and Muslims in Partition, Rwanda, Bosnia, Kosovo, and East Timor).

Walking through Auschwitz, I began to wonder how the development of the atomic bombs at Los Alamos, the test at Alamogordo and the bombing of Hiroshima and Nagasaki differed from the Nazi concentration camps. Of course the Allies in World War II were not driven by the racism of the Nazis, and they were not pursuing a final solution of extermination of any particular religious group. But with regard to the scale of killing, the recruitment of capable minds, the harnessing of science and technology (some perhaps hoping that the weapons would never be used and others even opposing the use of the weapons after they were developed), the extent of organisation, the resort to effective management, and the choice of targets to maximise annihilation of Japanese civilians, the Manhattan project was like the concentration camps, in fact, even more horrendous in its impact.

I started agonising over what all this meant for India. Since May 1998, the country has witnessed the scientist–politician nexus underlying the nuclear tests at Pokhran, the use of national security arguments to advance party agendas and the self-serving jingoism of the scientists. Of even greater importance has been the silence of its journals with a few notable exceptions, the obfuscation of ugly reality and the virtual absence of intellectual dissent.

After an initial silence on the subject (as if it never happened), the journal *Current Science* publicised the official/government version of the 'kilotonnes yield' of the test bombs but rejected/suppressed M.V. Ramana's estimates of the hundreds of thousands of innocent non-combatants who would be killed if even a primitive atomic bomb were exploded on Mumbai/Karachi.[4]

Other questions bothered me. Are the institutions on the Indian subcontinent necessarily more robust and moral than those in the Germany of the 1930s and 1940s? Are Indian politicians and parties less prone to exploit religious animosities? Are Indian scientists and engineers less eager to get political support for their next ego trip or power play (e.g., neutron bombs because they kill but don't destroy). Once the nuclear-tipped missiles are deployed, are there guarantees against 'some crazy guy doing some crazy thing?' Are we sure that Pokhran will not lead as inevitably to Lahore and/or Chagai to Mumbai as Alamogordo led to Hiroshima?

Scientists escape responsibility for the horrors that have sprung or can spring from science by the clever excuse of the amorality of science. For example, the well-known statement of the otherwise saintly, sincere and dedicated Kalam that 'he is only an engineer' and that 'his missile can also be used for delivering flowers'.

The amorality emerges from two conventional prescriptions for the relationship between the scientist (the subject) and the object of scientific study. Firstly, the scientist is urged to separate and distance himself/herself from the object of study even when the object is living. Secondly, it is recommended that the study must be devoid of emotion and values. It must be a cerebral objective activity devoid of feelings. The amorality of science stems from the isolation of the subject from the object and the removal or absence of emotions and feelings and values. And when the object of the study includes human beings, then the perception of people as 'things', lead inevitably to science becoming the instrument of violence, oppression and evil.

I submit that there is a way out of this moral crisis. The relationship between the scientist (the subject) and the object of scientific study must be such that initial separation (and distance) ends in subsequent unification (and embrace). The suppression of emotion during analysis must give way to emotion after analysis. The functioning of scientists as individuals, groups and institutions must be constrained and limited by moral strictures and taboos. Science, therefore, must not be neutral. It must be encoded with life affirming values.[5] The link between science and morality must be re-established.

A crucial safeguard is to insist that, quite apart from the top-down macro view of security, yields, kill-ratios, etc., there must be a bottom-up micro view based on human beings. We must see beyond the numbers and the statistics, we must see children and parents and grandparents, lovers and married couples, siblings, friends and comrades.

We must never forget the Gandhi talisman: 'Recall the face of the poorest and most helpless person. . . and ask yourself if the step you contemplate is going to be of any use to him. Will he be able to gain anything from it? Will it restore to him control over his life and destiny?'

Based on the Keynote Address to the *National Convention on Disarmament and Peace*, November 11, 2000, at New Delhi.

Notes

[1] J. Bronowski, *Science and Human Values* (Harper Collins, revised 1990) was a major contribution to discussion on the ethical aspects of nuclear weapons.

[2] Primo Levi, *Survival in Auschwitz*, (New York: A Touchstone Book, Simon & Schuster, 1996).

[3] Christopher R. Browning, *Ordinary Men: Reserve Battalion 101 and the Final Solution in Poland* (New York: Harper Perennial, 1998).

[4] This was subsequently published as M.V. Ramana, *Bombing Bombay* (Cambridge, USA: International Physicians for the Prevention of Nuclear War, 1999).

[5] Thanks are due to Shiv Visvanathan for this insight.

The Wages of Armageddon

C. RAMMANOHAR REDDY

Two of the world's poorest countries—India and Pakistan—are insistent on assembling a nuclear arsenal. Their polity seems not a bit perturbed about this. Indeed, in India at least, the message being conveyed by the state is that nuclear weaponisation will not be a burden on the economy.

Nuclear weapon programmes have always been shrouded in secrecy, so no one really knows what the five nuclear powers have spent on their arsenals. But the first secrets have begun to emerge, to reveal the gigantic outlays. *Atomic Audit*, the result of a four-year study by the Washington-based Brookings Institution, recently estimated that between 1940 and 1996 the US spent as much as $5.5 trillion (1996 prices) on nuclearisation. This outlay is equivalent to 20 times the gross domestic product (GDP) of India in 1997–98. Even for the richest country, $5.5 trillion was not a small amount. The expenditure on nuclear weapons was more than what the US government spent in the same period on six sectors that included education, environment, space research and law enforcement.

In their search for superiority over each other, the US and the erstwhile Soviet Union acquired enough weapons to destroy the world many times over. The size of either the US or the Soviet programme is therefore not relevant for estimating the potential costs of an Indian programme. But what could be of relevance to India is the distribution of costs in the US. The Brookings study found that the expenditure on

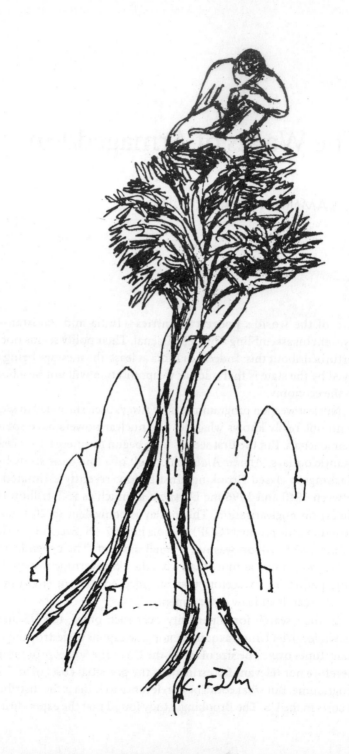

bombs itself constituted only 7 per cent of the total costs and another 7 per cent went towards dealing with the effects of tests, storing radio-active wastes and cleaning up the environment. A high 86 per cent went on on building delivery systems and a command, control, communications and intelligence system (C3I). In other words, it is the delivery and the C3I systems and not the costs of the bombs themselves that could form the most expensive part of an Indian weaponisation programme.

The programmes of Britain, France and China—the smaller nuclear powers—which may be closer to an Indian one also do not suggest that these weapons of mass destruction can be acquired cheaply. Camille Grand has pointed out that France's nuclear effort was extremely costly in financial terms, even for an industrialised country.[1] The cost ran between 0.4 and 1.2 per cent of the GDP between 1964 and 1992. At its high point, the French weaponisation programme imposed a burden of $1.9 billion (1987 prices) on the government in just one year, 1967. A full accounting of the British programme is yet to be done. But according to the authors of the Brookings study, between 1981 and 1997 Britain spent $8 billion on just the operating cost of its Polaris fleet of four submarines which carried nuclear-tipped missiles.

Perhaps the one country whose economic conditions when it embarked on a nuclear programme would come the closest to those of contemporary India is China. However, very little is known about the Chinese costs. But according to the most authoritative study of the Chinese programme, the government of the day did its best to control expenses through a variety of measures. Yet, the estimate is that in the decade 1955–64, China spent as much as 10.7 billion yuan (1957 prices) on weaponisation.[2] The burden was so large that the programme consumed more than a third of the state budget in 1957 and exceeded the defence budget in 1957 and 1958. The total cost in 1955–64 has been estimated as the equivalent of $28 billion at 1996 prices. And that was just the first decade of China's weapons programme.[2]

It could be argued that the experience of none of the five nuclear powers is applicable to an Indian programme of the late 1990s and the first decade of the 21st century. This is true to a certain extent. The US and the Soviet Union were 'pioneers' who engaged themselves in bizarre and expensive adventures in an attempt to 'win' a nuclear war. India, on the other hand, says it is only going to acquire a minimum deterrent capability. In theory, it will not also have to spend anywhere near what

China spent on nuclear weaponisation. The fifth nuclear power had to, after all, work in complete isolation and at a time when nuclear weapons and delivery systems were just a decade old. India, on the other hand, now has the 'benefit' of being able to draw on half a century of accumulated international knowledge on nuclear weapons as well as advances in material sciences and microelectronics which should hold down costs.

The most important factor that should, again in theory, keep Indian costs low is that a substantial part of the costs of developing a bomb and the missile delivery systems as well as the costs of some of the plutonium required for an Indian arsenal have already been incurred. In retrospect, it is clear that a good part of the space and nuclear energy programmes over the past 30 years has been directed towards developing and delivering nuclear weapons. This is true as well of a large component of the outlay on the Integrated Guided Missile Development Programme, which has yielded the Prithvi missile and will yield Agni and Agni-II and eventually the intercontinental ballistic missile, Surya. All these are sunk costs, which is one reason for the dominant view that the future costs of completing nuclear weaponisation will be low.

In the three months since the Pokhran tests, a number of independent estimates have been made of the total costs of an Indian weaponisation programme. These range from Rs 5,000 crore to Rs 20,000 crore over the next decade. But none of them has any meaning since they have either been arrived at by inflating past estimates to present-day prices or are the sum total of the cost of a list of components that has been arbitrarily drawn up without reference to any nuclear doctrine or to the likely composition of an Indian nuclear arsenal.

In 1985 a committee of senior defence personnel and representatives from defence and nuclear energy research establishments prepared an estimate of a weapons programme. According to one recent (unofficial) recollection, the group projected that a minimum deterrent comprising aircraft, the Agni and Prithvi missiles and a nuclear arsenal in the 'low three digit figures' would come to Rs 7,000 crore at 1985 prices.[3]

Significantly, this group does not appear to have included nuclear-powered submarines in its plan for an Indian minimum deterrent; nor did it make any provision for a C3I system. The estimate was also apparently drawn up over just a fortnight.

There have been two more coherent and plausible estimates of a weaponisation programme, both prepared by retired defence personnel. One was a 'broad brush calculation' made by the former Chief of the Army Staff, Gen. K. Sundarji[4] and the other by Brig. Vijai K. Nair[5] in 1992.

Gen. Sundarji's notion of a minimum deterrent was an arsenal of 150 bombs that could be delivered by aircraft and a missile force comprising the Prithvi and Agni missiles. His cost estimate was a very 'affordable' Rs 2,760 crore (1996 prices). With the required aircraft already with the IAF, the only expenses to be incurred were the costs of the bombs and the missiles.

For an arsenal of roughly the same size, Brig. Nair in 1992 projected a total cost of Rs 6,835 crore over a 10-year period. While Gen. Sundarji made no provision for C3I (on the implausible ground that 'such costs are common to conventional force requirements and are not to be taken as incremental costs'). Brig. Nair's estimate included about Rs 3,500 crore for C3I, testing and maintenance.

The relevance of these two estimates to an Indian programme is not so much their numbers as both assume a doctrine that is referred to in the jargon as second-strike capability. That is, in Gen. Sundarji's words, 'for minimum deterrence to be effective we have to ensure that in a second strike we can do unacceptable damage to our adversary'.

A second-strike capability is the other side of a policy of 'no-first use' which Prime Minister Atal Behari Vajpayee, announced during the last session of Parliament. In other words, the government policy is to acquire a nuclear capability which even if partly destroyed in a first strike from across the borders will remain large enough to devastate urban settlements in the adversary country.

In retrospect, while the 1998 tests by India and Pakistan have brought their nuclear ambitions into the open, it does appear that both countries have possessed for some time the capacity to carry out a nuclear strike at short, if not immediate, notice. Though India and Pakistan would like each other to believe this, the fabrication of a few bombs and (possibly) the equipping of the air force to deliver them do not mean that either country is now weaponised.

Nuclearisation would involve assembling an arsenal of a certain size and acquiring a certain kind of delivery system. This, in turn, would depend on the threat perceptions of the country. There is also the matter of building the associated C3I system. A C3I system would be necessary to monitor the nuclear build-up in the adversary countries, develop a foolproof chain of command to authorise and carry out a nuclear strike in an eventuality, protect the arsenal from unauthorised use and build a defence communication system that will withstand the effects of a first strike from the adversary and can then be used for a counter-attack.

There is no information in the public domain on where India is at in any of these components of a weaponisation programme. All that we do have are statements by Defence Minister George Fernandes, that the government is working on plans for a command and control system, while Prime Minister Atal Behari Vajpayee has said India does not plan to replicate the C3I systems of the Western nuclear powers. But building on Vajpayee's recent announcement of a no-first use policy combined with the development of a minimum deterrent, it is possible to construct what an Indian nuclear force would look like and therefore what a weaponisation programme would cost.

It is now clear as daylight that an Indian nuclear force would be designed to cover not only Pakistan but China as well. What was unstated for long has come into the open not just with the frequent remarks of the Defence Minister about China but also as revealed by the contents of Vajpayee's letter to US President Bill Clinton after the Pokhran tests, in which there was a reference to 'a big neighbour' with nuclear weapons. Moreover, even earlier the more substantive discussions on an Indian nuclear force as contained in the writings of Gen. K. Sundarji and Brig. Vijai Nair were based on the need to target both countries. If these are the threat perceptions that have been identified, then there are obvious implications for both the size of the arsenal and the sophistication of the delivery systems.

Number of Nuclear Bombs

The projections made outside the government are for an arsenal of 125–150 bombs. Each would be of just 15–20 kilotonne (KT) capacity, of the kind dropped on Hiroshima and Nagasaki. Gen. Sundarji, for instance, arrived at a figure of 150 based on the assumption that deterrence would require the ability to devastate five cities in Pakistan and 10 in China, each with three bombs. After taking into account losses in a first strike from an adversary, an Indian second-strike capability would require an arsenal of closer to 150 warheads. Brig. Nair also arrived at approximately the same number. This figure has also been talked about for decades. A recently declassified US State Department telegram to the US Embassy in New Delhi in 1966 refers to '(the former AEC official) Sethna's own figure of 150 bombs for a credible deterrent'.

Delivery Systems

Strategists have always talked about an Indian triad of delivery systems aircraft, land-based ballistic missiles and submarine-based ballistic missiles. India has the aircraft to deliver bombs, though they have to be equipped for the purpose. Land-based missiles would complement the air force. India already has the short-range Prithvi, though there is some controversy over whether it is suited for nuclear delivery. The intermediate-range, 1,600-km Agni is now going to be fully developed and will surely carry nuclear warheads. Further, the Defence Minister announced earlier this month the decision to go ahead with developing Agni-II, which will presumably be capable of traversing up to 2,500–3,000 km—well into China. And waiting on the drawing board of the Defence Research and Development Organisation is the inter-continental ballistic missile, Surya. We do not know when Surya will be ready or how much it will cost.

However, neither the aircraft nor the land-based ballistic missiles will within the logic of a nuclear deterrent give the protection of the submarine-launched ballistic missiles. Out at sea and under water, they cannot be destroyed quite as easily as aircraft or land-based missiles. But the big disadvantage is their cost. Gen. Sundarji in his estimates did not include subs, while Brig. Nair does. According to Admiral L. Ramdas, former Chief of the Navy, a 'second-strike capability can only be ensured with a submarine.' Similarly, Lt. Gen. V.R. Raghavan, former Director-General of Military Operations, says 'If Indian nuclear deterrence is to remain immune to a first strike by the adver-saries, a submarine-based capability is absolutely essential.' The general view is that the Indian triad would need five nuclear-powered submarines.

But such submarines are extremely expensive. According to some estimates, India has spent Rs 3,500 crore over the past 20 years in an as yet incomplete effort at building a submarine. The target date now is 2004.

C3I Systems

The most complicated, costly, controversial and critically important elements of weaponisation are the C3I systems. The US and the erstwhile USSR spent hundreds of billions of dollars on satellites to monitor an impending attack, command structures from where the political and military leadership could operate during a war and on what the two countries thought was a foolproof system to communicate orders from the highest political authority. But they did not succeed.

In a recent article, Dr. M.V. Ramana of MIT in the US writes that the US system gave 20,000 false alarms of a missile attack between 1977 and 1984. Mr. Stephen Schwartz, Director of the Brookings study of the US nuclear programme, says that in spite of spending more than $700 billion on the C3I systems, 'the US was never able to solve the problem of designing a system robust enough to survive a nuclear attack and coordinate a retaliatory launch'.

There is substance in Brig. Nair's view that there is no need for India to replicate the expensive systems of the nuclear powers of the West, which were trying to develop structures to 'win' a nuclear war. According to Brig. Nair, while some more money has certainly to be spent in India, the ongoing process of modernisation of the conventional forces is going to provide command shelters and satellite communication that can be integrated into a nuclear force. And that the incremental outlay needed will not be very large.

However, saving on a C3I system could be suicidal. With a no-first use policy, the Indian communication systems have to be hardened to withstand the electromagnetic pulses generated by an adversarial nuclear first strike. Otherwise, no one will be fooled by the Indian deterrent. There may also be no getting away from putting into space high-resolution satellites that will (try to) track a nuclear build-up on the other side. For, as Admiral Ramdas says, in a second strike, 'the riposte will have to be accurate to knock out launch stations, otherwise the exchange will give the adversary yet another opportunity to strike'.

In the end, an Indian weaponisation programme may well force on the country an expensive C3I system which itself, Lt. Gen. Raghavan, states, may cost 'as much as a good medium-sized army'. The costs will be huge because, according to him, a missile launch capability spread from Kutch in the west to Kashmir and then on the Ladakh–HP–UP–Arunachal frontier 'would need to be linked to an equally widely spread early warning, surveillance and C3I system, plus to the Capital,' all of which would require a massive 'state-of-the-art and technically manned infrastructure'.

A decision on what an Indian C3I should comprise is very much a choice between Scylla and Charybdis. If the government chooses to be economical, no adversary will believe that India has an effective second-strike capability. However, if it opts for an elaborate system, the outcome will be an extremely costly programme, which would compel the neighbours to make their systems more sophisticated and so the spiral will grow.

If India's nuclear weaponisation programme is defined as acquiring a second-strike capability comprising a triad delivery of 150 bombs, then certain costs will follow.

It is assumed that weaponisation will be carried out over a decade. All costs are at current prices. No account is taken of sunk costs since the attempt is only to estimate the future costs of nuclearisation. The unit cost figures have been drawn from what little has been published and from discussions with former defence personnel, independent security experts and researchers of nuclear issues.

Cost of plutonium: At best, India's current stocks of weapons grade plutonium are likely to suffice for no more than 50 bombs. To equip an additional 100 warheads each of 15 to 20 KT, about 800 kg of plutonium has to be produced. Neither the power nor the research reactors can yield so much plutonium in a decade. Hence, a new reactor is required. Of course, it will be a different matter if the Fissile Material Cut-off Treaty is negotiated over the next few years and India becomes a signatory. Capital cost: Rs 700 crore.

Cost of a missile production facility: A separate establishment has to be set up to produce the 120+ Prithvis, Agnis, Agni-IIs and Sagarikas. Capital cost: Rs 500 crore.

Cost of bombs: Estimates of a nuclear bomb of 15–20 KT vary from Rs 1 crore to Rs 15 crore. According to Mr. Stephen Schwartz of the Brookings Institution, a no-frills 15–20 KT bomb should cost between only $1 million and $2 million. On the assumption that the lower end of this estimate is a more realistic one, the cost per bomb will be Rs 4 crore.

Delivery systems—aircraft: The IAF's existing fleet of Mirage 2000s, Jaguars and Sukhoi-30s can be used for delivery. However, the aircraft have to be specially fitted for carrying the nuclear bombs. It is assumed that one squadron of 24 aircraft will be equipped for a nuclear strike. The cost of equipping each aircraft is Rs 2 crore to Rs 5 crore.

Delivery Systems—nuclear submarines: The general view is that India needs five nuclear-powered submarines for its nuclear force. However, according to Admiral L. Ramdas, it will be impossible to build five subs in a decade; at best three can be built. But how does one treat the costs of these subs? Brig. Nair, in his exercise, assumed that they were in any case going to be acquired by the Navy, so there was no need to cost them for a nuclear programme. This seems to be an unrealistic assumption. Hence, the cost of three submarines has been taken into account, with another two to be built later. The capital cost per submarine is Rs 4,000 crore.

Delivery system—missiles: If from an arsenal of 150 bombs one IAF squadron is equipped to carry out a nuclear strike, that will leave 126 missiles to be tipped with warheads. A certain hypothetical mix of the missiles is assumed.

Neither the Agni-II nor the Sagarika has been developed as yet. The present indication is that the Sagarika will be a 300-km distance cruise and not a submarine-launched ballistic missile. Since Agni-II will be a longer range version of the Agni, it has been assumed that it will cost about 20 per cent more than the latter. And that the Sagarika will cost 20 per cent less. Cost of each Prithvi: Rs 7 crore, cost of each Agni: Rs 50 crore, cost of each Agni-II: Rs 60 crore and cost of each Sagarika: Rs 40 crore.

The C3I systems: The shape of a likely C3I system is not known nor is any information available about the cost of individual components. As a first approximation it is assumed that at the very least the expenditure will be of the magnitude suggested by Brig. Nair in 1992. After adjusting for inflation, this comes to about Rs 3,525 crore. However, the actual expenditure will be higher since Brig. Nair assumed that much of the cost required for a reliable C3I system would be borne by the ongoing process of modernisation of the defence forces.

One additional item that has been costed here is that of two high-resolution satellites to track developments in China and Pakistan. This is a bare minimum. It is sometimes argued that such systems are meant to 'win' a nuclear war and are not required for an Indian second-strike capability. This may not be a tenable assumption since without any kind of monitoring or protection, the chances are that the Indian nuclear arsenal will almost be completely destroyed in the first strike itself. Hence, the cost of a C3I system: Rs 3,525+ crore; the cost of two satellites: Rs 1,000 crore each.

Defence systems: It has been argued that the process of modernisation is in any case strengthening the radar and defence systems. Yet, it does not stand to reason that special defences for the nuclear force are unnecessary. Experts such as Lt. Gen. Raghavan argue that to safeguard the nuclear submarine fleet, 'we shall also need a small protective surface naval and aircraft carrier-based capability to ensure the survival of (the) subs.' No estimates are available of the costs of such a fleet. However, account here is taken of phased array radars and anti-missile batteries to protect four or five missile sites and air bases. Cost: Rs 5,000 crore.

The total future costs of weaponisation come to Rs 28,000+ crore at current prices. And this without taking into account all C3I capital costs. However, for a number of other reasons as well, this is a large underestimate of the full burden of weaponisation.

First, the estimate is only of capital costs. The costs of annual operation and maintenance are not available. Second, future R&D costs have not been included. There are certain important components of both the delivery and C3I systems exclusively meant for the nuclear programme which are yet to be developed and whose R&D costs will be substantial. Third, it is assumed that there are no cost or time over-runs. This is an unrealistic assumption since not only in India but the world over, such over-runs are characteristic of all defence programmes. Fourth, there is the capital cost of an additional two submarines (Rs 8,000 crore) that has been excluded. Finally, if bigger and more powerful bombs like the ones tested in May are built, the costs will be higher.

Once all these costs are added on—as they must be—the total financial demands of nuclear weaponisation will be closer to a minimum of Rs 40,000 crore to Rs 50,000 crore over a 10-year period, or Rs 4,000–5,000 crore a year.

This is no small amount. Going by current figures, such annual costs will be equivalent to about 0.5 per cent of the GDP for 10 years running. They will consume 5 per cent of the Central government's tax revenue every year and increase the total annual defence expenditure by at least 10 per cent. The investment costs of weaponisation Rs 3,000 crore to 4,000 crore a year will increase the annual defence capital outlay by about 30 per cent.

There is another way of viewing the financial burden of weaponisation. The cost of each bomb is the same as that of 3,200 houses under the Indira Awas Yojana. The cost of one Agni missile can finance the annual operations of 13,000 primary health centres. The cost of an arsenal of 150 bombs is the same as the Central government funding of all public health programmes in 1998–99. The annual investment costs of weaponisation are the same as the Central government funding of elementary education in 1998–99.

The funds required for the true total cost of weaponisation (Rs 40,000–50,000 crore) are large enough to finance the incremental costs of universal primary education for two years. Alternatively, the annual demands of weaponisation will finance 25 per cent of the yearly incremental costs of sending every Indian child to school. These are the true opportunity costs of nuclear weaponisation.

The choice before the country could not be starker.

Notes

[1] *Strategic Analysis*, July 1998.

[2] John W. Lewis and Xue Litai, *China Builds the Bomb* (Stanford: Stanford University Press, 1988).

[3] 'Indian Nuclear Policy' in *Nuclear India*, IDSA, 1998.

[4] 'Imperatives of Indian Minimum Deterrence', *Agni*, Vol. 2, No.1.

[5] Vijai K. Nair, *Nuclear India* (Lancet, 1992).

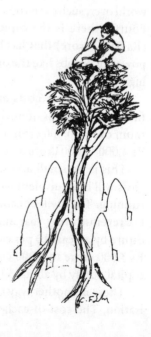

Why Women Must Reject Nuclearisation

KUMKUM SANGARI, NEERAJ MALIK, SHEBA CHHACHHI AND TANIKA SARKAR

A bomb does not discriminate, nuclearisation does. A nuclear bomb when dropped on any population does not distinguish between Hindus or Muslims, poor or rich, civilian or military, child or adult, men or women. However, nuclearisation—developing, manufacturing and maintaining nuclear weapons—affects specific social groups in particular ways.

India's decision to become a nuclear weapons state has a profoundly negative impact on women's lives. Women, being already disadvantaged within existing social and familial structures, will bear a larger part of the social cost of nuclearisation. This means:

- A decrease in access to resources, education, employment, services —a reduction in both physical and social mobility—and an increase in violence, fear and sexual oppression, and valorisation of ideologies that justify and maintain the existing status of women in society.
- The economic sanctions against India have given the government an opportunity to proceed with detrimental economic liberalisation in the name of 'survival'.
- The secrecy, disinformation and lack of public accountability that accompany nuclearisation are a recipe for anti-democratic and authoritarian regimes. They exclude the majority of citizens, and of course women from any policy and decision-making.

- Nuclearisation produces social consent for increasing levels of violence. It legitimises male aggression, and breeds the idea that nuclear explosions give a 'virility' to the nation that men as individuals can somehow also share.
- In the present political situation, the masculinist rhetoric of nuclearisation has been combined with a false patriotism and Hindutva ideologies. This effects all women in so far as it gives new militaristic meanings to national identity and demands 'othering' and animosity towards our neighbours.
- It effects women from the minorities even more since they become the implicit or explicit targets of this chauvinism.

Social Costs and Distribution of Resources

The social costs of nuclear weaponisation in a country where the basic needs of shelter, food and water, electricity, health and education have not been met are obvious. What should also be obvious is that the major brunt of this burden will have to be borne by the most vulnerable sections of society among which are the lower classes and women.

The high costs of keeping up with the nuclear arms race, together with the threatened sanctions by the powerful nations, will exacerbate an already grim economic situation. While the inevitable cutbacks in social security and welfare will hurt and damage all poor people, the proportion of the poor who are steadfastly denied a fair share of even the scarce resources will undoubtedly become larger.

The state of female health, nutrition and literacy is abysmally low, lower even than that of poor deprived men. Moreover, since patriarchal family norms place the task of looking after the daily needs of the family mainly upon women, scarcity of resources always hits women the hardest. Less food for the family inevitably means an even smaller share for women and female children, just as water shortages mean an increase in labour for women, who have to spend more time and energy in fetching water from distant places at odd hours of the day.

Crimes against women, including domestic violence, are often linked to deprivation, economic pressures and unemployment. For instance, female infanticide often occurs in very deprived households. And if a selection is made about which hungry mouths to feed, social and cultural values ensure that the girl is found more dispensable. These trends will now intensify; and the prospects of reversing them will weaken.

Despite the BJP leadership's claims to the contrary, we can expect a steep cutback in several sectors rendered 'insignificant' in the face of their macho assertion of national pride and self-esteem. We really need to question these false notions of national pride—does it rest on proving the capacity to destroy the planet or on providing basic life-sustaining amenities to its citizens?

In the field of education, though the recent budget boasts an increased outlay, together with the claim that the government will aim to provide free and compulsory education for girls up to college level, the real picture is sharply different. New policies and cutbacks will hit girls and poorer students hardest, at the level of both primary and higher education. For instance, the University Grants Commission, which finances the universities, has been progressively cutting back maintenance and other grants to institutions. In a recent move, it has even directed colleges and universities to raise their own resources to meet 20 per cent of the additional costs of increase in staff salaries and has unilaterally cut back its grants accordingly. As a result most colleges of Delhi University have decided to raise students' fees by Rs 3,000–4,000 annually. So much for the government's commitment to education, specially women's education!

Similarly, the areas of health and welfare are bound to suffer. Safe contraception has still not become a major priority of scientific research and public spending. Instead the present government has chosen to exploit the frequently-expressed middle class fear about the pressure on resources created by an increasing population, in which there is often a subconscious balancing of the dread of a population explosion with the means of annihilating ever-larger numbers of people.

Since women carry most of the burden of care of the sick, family health, etc., the health hazards that are directly caused by nuclearisation will also affect them more severely, both in terms of increased labour and in terms of social attitudes that tend to blame women for genetic malformations.

Lack of information is also a health-related issue. In keeping with India's goal, till now of promoting universal disarmanent, education about the consequences of nuclear experiments, explosions, and manufacture of nuclear missiles on civilian populations, public health and the environment should, in fact, be a priority expenditure. Instead, it is shrouded in secrecy. The Department of Atomic Energy in India has not made public any report on the health effects of radiation in its atomic plants. Though there have been several accidents at nuclear installations, affecting the health of workers and the people in the areas, no data has been disclosed. And the Atomic Energy Act (1962) ensures its non-availability to the public as all information related to nuclear technology is classified data. There have been reports from Pokhran that since the nuclear test in 1974, there has been an abnormal ratio of cases of polio, mental retardation and Down's Syndrome. The government has not bothered to investigate these. Instead, it has glibly announced that the present Pokhran tests are 'safe'.

In fact, there are 32 million radiation victims all over the world—workers in nuclear plants, the peoples of Hiroshima and Nagasaki where bombs have been dropped, people in the Pacific islands where several tests have been conducted, the uranium miners as well as the victims of nuclear weapons testing, waste dumping and the accidents that have happened all over the world.

Nuclearisation, then, will involve decisions about the disposal of very large sums of money and resources that could have had innumerable constructive uses in our poor, under-educated country. One might say that, in any case, there was very little spending on social welfare even before May 11, 1998. However, the possibility was far more real; all governments were accountable for ignoring such vital priorities. Now, with increasing tension on all sides, it will be far easier for this government to side step the issues altogether and to constantly cite the need for national security to undermine any demand for social welfare.

Conventional Weapons and Nuclear Weapons

The option of nuclear weaponisation means embarking on a self destructive and never-ending race for more and more lethal and costly weapons. The argument that it is cheaper to make a bomb than invest in conventional weapons is not convincing. Nuclearisation will not eliminate the necessity for conventional weapons. On the contrary, provoking neighbouring countries has made the prospect of conventional warfare far more imminent and has stepped up military investment. So, investment in non-nuclear weapons will increase and on top of that the cost of the arms race will have to be met. All this will come out of the strained resources of a country, where nearly half the people live below the poverty line. If militarism distorts the economy and polity so that no goals of social justice can be met, nuclearisation distorts it even more.

In sum, we will have to carry the double burden of conventional militarisation and nuclearisation. And this burden is both material and ideological. Nuclearisation, even more than militarisation, is breeding a new language of scientism.

Militarisation has been tied to global processes corresponding to Cold War policies, the arms race and deployment of new missiles. It tends to produce a more self-assertive policing of societies, new nationalisms, alongside new avenues of consumption. Toys, games, computer games, popular films and television programmes have already naturalised an inordinate degree of militarisation through representation and simulation of warfare and the values associated with it. These values range from the glorification of motherhood to social constructions of masculinity and feminity; it is after all necessary to control women in order to militarise men. The de-personalisation of technological warfare, as in the Gulf War, masks human suffering and casualties involved, and produces a tolerance for very high levels of violence.

All of these are intensified with nuclearisation which is, in addition, far more committed to secrecy and notions of expertise and is controlled by a tiny bureaucratic and scientific elite. Secrecy and lack of information, in fact, assists in creating media hypes that can project a false consensus around the issue. And public ignorance in turn is one of the keystones of this so-called consensus. For example, few people are aware that the costs that have been acknowledged are only the tip of the iceberg. The massive cost of maintaining and upgrading nuclear weapons remains hidden.

Secrecy also feeds the myth of scientific and bureaucratic expertise. Women, for whom even primary literacy is hard to come by, often have a common-sensical gut reaction against nuclearisation but since they are educationally the most deprived, they are less able to monitor and sift the information they get. What is more, the strange character of nuclear policy-making not only sidelines moral and ethical questions but engenders them. This elite gets to be represented as rational, scientific, modern and of course masculine, while ethical questions, questions about the social and environmental costs are made to seem emotional, effeminate, regressive and not modern.

This rather dangerous way of thinking which makes out that questions about human life and welfare are somehow neither modern nor properly masculine questions, or that men have no capacity and concern for peace and morality, can have disastrous consequences for both men and women. It trivialises human suffering. It pejoratively casts human caring as a sign of weakness or effeminacy, as the concern of the oppressed, as irrelevant to modern life. It carelessly rejects the histories of such caring in our own country or callously reverses them, as in the misuse of Buddhist symbolism. It downgrades non-nuclear countries as 'backward' and as unequipped to step into the twenty-first century. In short, it breeds a politics based on relegation of the weak and a neo-Darwinian survival of the fittest. What is more, the type of nationalism that accompanies nuclearisation demands obedience and conformity. It is repressive, silences dissent and dubs all humane and democratic protest as anti-national. In short, it makes it more difficult to imagine and work towards a better existence.

Increase in Aggression

Nuclearisation, then, is not a matter of military and technological decision or activities alone. A nuclearised India will construct for itself a cultural and educational environment that promotes a preference for aggression, violence and revenge. There will be a systematic deployment of technologies and scientific training that are geared to this at the cost of their peaceful, constructive or welfare deployment. In order to justify these priorities, people will be fed with more images of militaristic heroism, of brutality, of relentless pursuit of aggrandisement. Against this, images that grow out of peaceability, of tolerence and universal goodwill, will have to be systematically denigrated. Even the possibility of drawing upon human values and perceptions, traditionally asssociated with women to develop life-affirming and sustaining attitudes and methods for the entire social body, will be reduced.

Such new cultural activity and new education will promote a mind-set that enhances what are conventionally known as masculine values; to be a man is to be violent, eager to retaliate, to welcome brutality. The difference, of course, will be that now, such inclination towards violence will no longer be restricted to men alone. They will embrace the entire population. In fact, women will have to be included in the new values since mothers conventionally are socialising agents and are the first to teach children about the world.

Under the auspices of the BJP-led government, this in effect will mean a wider proliferation of the values that the RSS has already been trying to establish and propagate. Of all the political formations, the

Sangh had been the only one to develop a systematic training programme to teach their women how to hate single-mindedly, and how
to translate that hate into martial action. Since 1936 their women's
'shakhas' have worshipped the icon of the armed Goddess, recited
incantations invoking war and taught women how to handle weapons.
In their 'boudhik' or daily ideological training sessions, they have
explained how every Hindu woman must hate Muslims. They have
gone beyond glorifying women as mothers of soldiers. They have
perfected a formidable machine for producing an ideal-type woman
who is herself a fully militarised being. And she is further exhorted, in
their training schedule, to pass all this on to her children.

Since the RSS provides the basic ideology of the BJP, there is a real
danger of the multiplication of this ideology. It will assist their aim of
filling the country with clones of the women of the Sangh Parivar.
Their aggression and demand for violence against Muslims within the
country is already showing signs of extending to a country deemed to
be Islamic. The dangers are more acute given state control over the
educational and media apparatus, and the fact that the BJP is now in a
position to overhaul it in order to extend the values and training of the
'shakhas' into schools and homes. So far the qualities of preservation,
peace and forbearance have been associated with women alone. A just
and human social perspective surely needs to try and spread these
values among both men and women. However, the presence of the
bomb and the new culture that it will engender, will not allow this. The
Sangh Parivar will try to detach not simply men but also women from
these values and teach them to turn to beliefs that actively desire death,
destruction and extinction.

Nuclearisation, more than conventional militarisation, creates an
atmosphere of tension, insecurity, fear, even panic. It gains consent
for weapons of mass destruction by spreading the utterly false premise
that economic pressures and social problems can be redressed through
an accumulation of the capacity for violence. This sense of an increased
capacity for violence against so-called enemies translates into and
justifies everyday aggression against women, minorities and other
underprivileged sections. Consequently, women's fear of sexual
violence, used even otherwise as a form of containment, increases
with the celebration of masculinist violence. They are left with only
two options: either to accept greater containment of their activity and

mobility, or to militarise themselves, either retreat from public spaces, or allow themselves to be pulled into the language of violence against 'others'.

There can, however, be no development without peace, without eliminating the different, inter-related types of violence to which women are subjected—in the military and political sphere, in homes, neighbourhoods and workplaces.

Conclusion

We need to reject nuclearisation because of its social cost, new patriarchalism, danger of state authoritarianism, damage to the environment, and erosion of our rights as citizens. And we need to reject it from the standpoint of democratic and ethical principles, from a defence of citizen's rights.

Demands:

• Nuclearisation must stop.
• There should be no further tests and no weaponisation.
• There has to be a full democratisation of nuclear decision-making through:
  1. transparency and honouring the right of citizens to information;
  2. open and informed debate across the political spectrum;
  3. strict and open monitoring of the environment;
  4. increase in education on the implications and effects of nuclear experiments even for peaceful purposes.

• The government must undertake to spread information about their consequences: depletion of the ozone layer, destruction of forests, the results of radioactive fallout, the contamination of water resources, changes in the climate, damage to unborn foetuses, and the long list of diseases caused by radiation, from cataract and mental diseases to cancer.
• The state must provide genuine security for citizens through expansion of health, education and housing services.

The Smile that Makes Generations Sick

SURENDRA GADEKAR

The afterglow of Operation Shakti lingers on. Yes, India has done it. Our scientist and engineers and even our politicians are second to none. Recalls to mind those famous lines coined during the Russo-Turkish War of 1877–78 which gave the English language a word which describes rather well the mood in middle class India today: 'We don't want to fight, yet by jingo, if we do, We got the ships, we got the men, And we got the money, too!'

Achievement at What Cost

A nuclear test involves the release into the environment of large quantities of radioactive poisons. Poisons that shall linger on and on; long after the afterglow fades; long after the applause and the mutual back-patting fades; long after all the scientists, engineers, and even the evergreen politicians fade; long after historical constructs such as Pakistan, China and even beloved India fade. This deliberate poisoning of our soil and that most precious of all things in a desert, water, shall continue to extract an inevitable toll. Till now five other nations have conducted approximately 1,900 nuclear tests. Of these, 518 have been in the atmosphere, under water, or in space. Approximately 1,400 tests have been conducted underground in scores of places around the globe.

Obtaining complete and accurate data on the health and environmental effects of nuclear weapons testing is difficult. In large part this is because countries that have tested nuclear weapons give the principal responsibility of assessing the health and environmental effects of testing to the very agencies that make and test the weapons. These agencies have therefore found themselves with essentially contradictory missions. On the one hand, the reality of widespread fallout requires that people be carefully informed about the nature of fallout and the dangers of radiation. It requires openness and free discussion. On the other hand, there is the overwhelming desire for secrecy and the perceived need to build up nuclear arsenals come what may.

In this mindset, it is no wonder that the health and security of one's own citizens is sacrificed at the alter of geo-political considerations. Henry Wasserman very aptly named his book describing the US experience with the effects of ionising radiation as 'Killing Our Own'.

Except for at very high doses, radiation damage is not immediately apparent. Considerable damage is done to health and the environment before the public becomes aware.

A 1 KT explosion (explosive force equal to 1,000 tonnes of TNT) will typically produce 11 billion curies of radioactive fission products one minute after detonation and this will be reduced to 10 million curies in 12 hours, as the short-lived radionuclides decay. Most bombs have four to five kg of plutonium of which one can safely assume that more than half is left behind. Plutonium is one of the most toxic substances known. It has a half life of 24,000 years and would thus remain in the environment of Pokhran essentially for ever. Strontium-90 and Cesium-137, two other long lived radionuclides (half lives around 30 years each) are produced at the rate of 0.1 and 0.16 kilocuries per KT respectively.

Sometimes underground tests result in quick, massive releases into the atmosphere called ventings. Releases which take place slowly over a period of months or years are called seeps. The Des Moines test of 1962 vented 11 million curies while the Bainberry test of 1970 vented 6.7 million curies into the atmosphere. Mercifully operation Shakti hasn't resulted in ventings. Seeps are another matter and would require careful monitoring of the site.

The long-term dangers arising from wastes under the earth's surface have not yet been carefully assessed anywhere in the world. However, there is evidence quoted by the now dismantled Office of Technology Assessment of the US Congress which shows that soil and groundwater at the Nevada Test Site has been contaminated. This is not surprising since radioactive testing results in the drastic fracture of rock structures.

Of one thing we can be sure. If it is found that operation Shakti has resulted in radioactive contamination threatening to human health, the villagers living in the vicinity are unlikely to be told anything or asked to take precautions that might reduce their risks. In our pursuit of geo-political might, some have to pay the price of development. Modern versions of the ancient custom of human sacrifice for the sake of power and glory can be played to thunderous applause from a nation thirsty for international recognition.

On this World Environment Day, June 5, 1998 it is well to ponder over the fact that environment is not just trees and tigers.

Some have to sacrifice themselves for progress, so they say,
but who is to decide who sacrifices and for whom.

Reaping the Whirlwind

KALPANA SHARMA

Exactly six months after the nuclear tests were conducted in 1998 at a site just five kilometres away from their village, the people of Khetolai in Jaisalmer district are an unhappy lot. Young and old, men and women, complain that they have been virtually ignored since the tests brought their village into the limelight.

Khetolai is unaware that at this very moment, a study of the health impact of the test is being planned in Jodhpur. According to reliable sources in Jodhpur, the government is worried that rain might have led to some contamination of the underground aquifers around the nuclear test site. As a result, discussions are under way to set up a secret study of the area to test whether radioactivity can be detected in the soil, water, grass or animal milk.

'The Prime Minister said that some people should be prepared to sacrifice. In that case, they might as well as line us all up and shoot us,' says Jagmalram Bishnoi, one of a group of old men who sit in the village square taking in the morning sun. What do they feel six months after the tests? 'Our houses have cracks, the rain has further weakened them and some of our people are complaining of unusual health problems, particularly khujali (itching),' says Dharmaram Bishnoi. As we talk, another man walks up and shows his scalp which is flaking. Another shows his fingers, which are covered with rashes. Both say the doctors prescribe ointments which give no relief.

Others complain about animals being sick. But none are able to show an animal that is sick. 'The authorities have allowed us to graze our animals near the boundary of the test site as of the last 15 to 20 days,' says 79-year-old Mr. Shurtaram Bishnoi. With the recent rain, that area is now covered with grass.

The villagers recall May 11 when army personnel came to them in the morning and told them to remain outside their homes. They were given no explanation of why they were asked to do this. From 11 in the morning until after the test, they stood outside in the blazing May sun. The older men say they remember 1974, when the first nuclear test was conducted, and therefore guessed that something similar was going to occur. But some of the youngsters say that they thought their village was going to be attacked.

Bhanwari Bai says that she remembers that the ground shook and 'we saw a cloud of smoke which seemed yellow in colour.' She does not yet understand fully what happened but she also says that in the last six months many people are complaining of itching.

Asked if any government doctors have come to take any kind of health survey since the tests, the villagers say that nothing of the kind has happened yet. One of their demands to Prime Minister Vajpayee when he visited the test site was that a health monitoring centre be set up in the village.

'We are really upset that the Prime Minister never came to our village,' says the headmaster of the local school, Sohan Ram Bishnoi. He recalls, as do others, how they had made a banner supporting the test in the hope that the Prime Minister would come up to them and listen to their demands. But, they waited in vain. Later, when some of them tried to go to Pokhran for his public meeting, the level crossing on the road to Pokhran was shut and thorns were placed before it so that they could not go across.

'We have wept in front of the media and told everyone of our problems. People think we are shamming. We realise now that there is no point in that,' says Sohan Ram Bishnoi. 'Our fight is with the government and we will fight directly with them.'

This anger has manifest itself directly in the decision of the village to support the Congress (I) in the coming assembly elections. They echo the feelings of Madanlal Vyas, a chowkidar at the old fort in the centre of the city of Pokhran, sub-divisional head quarters of Jaisalmer district which is 24 km away from Khetolai. It also felt the tremors after the test. 'I am a BJP-wallah,' he says, 'but this time I am going to vote for the Congress (I).' Why? 'Because we have gained nothing from them,' he says. 'When we say to the authorities that we want to see the nuclear test site, they say you cannot. When we ask why, they say you will get sick. But if we will get sick, why did they do this,' asks Madanlal Vyas. '*Yeh to parmanu aur pyaz ka election hai aur jeetega pyaz* (This is an election between the nuclear test and the onion and it is the onion that will win),' claims Manohar Joshi, a local journalist and Congress (I) activist. He says that in previous elections, the BJP had coined the slogan: *Congress ke sashan mein, namuk milega ration mein* (During the Congress reign, salt will be sold in the ration shop), but instead this is precisely what is happening under the BJP. People, he says, see the price rise as the main issue and are unimpressed by the nuclear tests, particularly in Pokhran and the areas around the test site.

This essay first appeared in *The Hindu,* November 13, 1998.

Atomic Error

BITTU SAHGAL

> Deluded by modern western civilization, we have forgotten our ancient
> civilisation and worship the might of arms.
>
> Mohandas Karamchand Gandhi (*Collected Works*, 13:521)

Each year on June 5, World Environment Day rolls along and each
year many of us whose lives are focussed on defending the earth find
ourselves contemplating our purpose and effectiveness. At lead-up
meetings (to World Environment Day) this year across India, a variety
of issues featured in animated discussions that included the fate of the
almost defunct Narmada Project, Indian Aluminium Co. Ltd.'s
destructions of the Radhanagari Wildlife Sanctuary, Sanghi Cement's
manoeuverings in Narayan Sarovar, the Malik Makhbuja timber scams
in Madhya Pradesh's Bastar area, the abuse of human rights of adivasis
by several World Bank-funded projects, the threats to Periyar's ele-
phants from plans to raise the height of the dam wall and the fate of the
tiger.

   Though some scientists predict that the loss of biodiversity will
actually have more long-lasting and serious implications for the world
than the problems being presented by the nuclear industry, discussions
inevitably veered around the issue of the five nuclear tests our cowboy
government conducted. A sort of quiet descended in the room whenever
the subject of the tests came up. Everyone agreed that the hypocrisy of
the US and the UK on the issue of nuclear weapons was condemnable.

Nevertheless, social activists, environmentalists, teachers, students and even many businessmen seemed stunned by two key developments: First the tests themselves and the manner in which they were used to garner political advantage and then the chauvinistic response of the most unlikely sections of society. Opposition parties were, of course, outplayed by the BJP. They had no option but to cheer sullenly in unison as the Hindutva brigade sat in the glare of publicity brought on by delusions of grandeur. Thousands of NRIs overseas, on the other hand, smarting under the unspoken guilt of abandoning their country of origin for better financial prospects, tried to be more loyal than the queen. They flooded the Internet and fax machines in India with their support for the bomb, which they believe will make us as powerful as the US, UK, France, China and Russia. Votaries of the 'Hindu Bomb' of course, were the loudest of all—distributing sweets and blaring trumpets literal and figurative. As for the clutch of nucleocrats in India, this was their moment in the sun. Smarting under criticism in report after report of nuclear accidents in reactors, non-performance of atomic power plants and disfigurement of populations thanks to radiation poisoning, they positively glowed with pride.

To my mind, however, the most appalling of all responses was that of the frail Dr. Usha Mehta, symbol of living Gandhianism. Though she had been a participant in past meetings condemning the attacks on Hiroshima and Nagasaki, she nevertheless welcomed the Indian tests. Unfortunately she never once elaborated her rationale. Nor did she, or any of the other khadi-clad nationalists, opine on the inconsistency of their stand on India's nuclear tests vis a vis Mahatma Gandhi's lifetime teachings.

This is a good time to explore the track record of the global nuclear industry and the risks at which they place us all. And what better place to start than the very beginning of the nightmare? Hiroshima and Nagasaki seem to have been forgotten by those in whom new-sprung nuclear ambitions have emerged. A small reminder then:

'A bright light filled the plane,' wrote Lt. Col. Paul Tibbets, the pilot of the Enola Gay, the B–29 that dropped the first atomic bomb. 'We turned back to look at Hiroshima. The city was hidden by that awful cloud . . . boiling up, mushrooming.' For a moment, no one spoke. Then everyone was talking. 'Look at that! Look at that! Look at that!' exclaimed the co-pilot, Robert Lewis, pounding on Tibbets's shoulder. Lewis said he could taste atomic fission; it tasted like lead. Then he turned away to write in his journal. 'My God,' he asked himself, 'what have we done?'[1]

What indeed? When the heat wave reached ground level it burnt all before it including people. The strong wind generated by the bomb destroyed most of the houses and buildings within a 1.5 mile radius. When the wind reached the mountains, it was reflected and again hit the people in the city centre. The wind generated by Little Boy caused the most serious damage to the city and people. More than 200,000 people are known to have died because of the nuclear attack on Japan. No one knows how many more died unrecorded and unmourned.[2]

But all this is in the past, bomb votaries would have us believe. 'We only want to defend ourselves,' they add. Well then lets take a look at the way they would defend us by going down memory lane to take a second look at another major nuclear gift. Remember Chernobyl? Stated to be nothing more than a power plant, this devilish man-made monster revealed the cold hard truth about what is in store for everyone if a future Indian or Pakistani Prime Minister's patience runs thin. Or for that matter what could happen if the hundreds of small nuclear accidents that have taken place in India go really wrong.

At 1.23 a.m. on Saturday April 26, 1986, a powerful explosion took place inside the number four reactor at the Chernobyl nuclear power station in the Ukraine. It blew aside a 1,000 tonne, 60 cm-thick steel lid and blasted through the surrounding concrete structure. Only two people died immediately, though 30 others, mainly firemen, died subsequently of radiation burns following exposure to gamma and beta radiation. Initially some 135,000 people (and livestock) were evacuated from within a 30 km radius of the plant.

Later, as the true extent of radiation became known, 100,000 more people had to be evacuated. Gross deformities are now commonplace in the area and cancers are rampant. The long-term genetic devastation, many times more crushing than the original injuries, has only just begun to be tabulated. Ukraine and Byelorussia were the worst affected. Thyroid disorders are expected to run into millions across the radiation trail from Chernobyl. Though it was believed by the rest of the world to be one of the safest plants on earth, documents now reveal that Soviet scientists had known all along that the design was unsafe. Every nuclear power plant is a potential bomb and every one of them helps fuel the atomic arms race. Additionally, every one of them indulges in the ultimate colonisation adventure—intergenerational colonisation—by condemning yet-to-be-born citizens to the task of looking after the 'hot' wastes created by today's shortsighted scientists and politicians.

India used to lean heavily on the Soviet Union for its nuclear programme. It is now common knowledge that it turned out to be the world's most negligent nuclear power. Today, vast portions of the erstwhile Soviet Union have been reduced to nuclear graveyards. Nuclear submarines have been intentionally dumped in the sea; these now threaten Scandinavian fisheries and may prove to be a greater disaster than Chernobyl itself. Despite the abysmal record of the Soviet Union on the nuclear safety front, as Dr. Surendra Gadekar, editor of *Anumukti*, one of India's few newsletters that monitors things nuclear, laments, we have decided to put our atomic eggs in the Russian basket at Koodankulam. When you consider that vast numbers of Russian workers have not been paid their wages for months and are a hopelessly disgruntled lot, how are they ever to be trusted to put in their meticulous best while welding reactor parts and other such critical tasks at Koodankulam? Besides, for all the Russian postulations of having been 'betrayed' by India, we have heard not one peep out of them regarding sanctions against the white elephant we are setting up at Koodankulam.

On the issue of safety, despite hush-up attempts, revelations of leaks at BARC in Bombay and of accidents in other reactors such as RAPS (Rajasthan Atomic Power Station) in Rajasthan confirm such a view. It goes without saying of course, that the erstwhile Soviet Union, the UK, US, France and Japan are primarily responsible for the bulk of the globe's nuclear pollution. This has enhanced cancer rates globally and has led to a host of problems such as birth abnormalities, Down's Syndrome, auto-immune deficiencies and a host of future cancers that medicine has not even begun to deal with. But this takes nothing away from our own culpability as a nation. Dhirendra Sharma, who used to teach at the Jawaharlal Nehru University in Delhi, informs us that 'in India, an estimated 300 incidents of a serious nature have occurred causing radiation leaks and physical damage to workers.' These have so far remained official secrets. The Tarapur Atomic Power Station (TAPS), for instance, has suffered many serious mishaps, posing a great threat to the workers and the environment. A major mishap in Tarapur in 1979 resulted in thousands of litres of irradiated water gushing out from the reactor. But the Chairman of the Atomic Energy Commission (AEC) reluctantly acknowledged only a 'pin-hole leak'. A few years earlier in another serious incident, a reprocessing plant at

Tarapur was closed down due to contamination. It is reported that at least three persons died in the 'inert' chamber inside Tarapur and more than 3,000 workers have been exposed to non-permissible doses of radiation. The Madras Atomic Power Station (MAPS) Unit-I at Kalpakkam, was reported to have suffered an explosion soon after it was commissioned by the Prime Minister in July 1984. It therefore had to be shut down for an extended period of time. The RAPS Unit-I was damaged and had to be shut down on March 4, 1981. More than 2,000 workers were exposed to excess radiation that year and 300 had to be hospitalised. Ultimately RAPS-I was refurbished and started operations in 1997 after functioning sporadically for over a decade. But the shadow of inefficiency and risk still hangs heavy over this unit.

Alarmingly, attempts are now being made to brand anti-nuclear groups in India as anti-national. An emerging brand of fascism even prompted death threats against protestors in New Delhi who met to discuss and demonstrate their opposition to the tests and the nuclearisation of the subcontinent. Make no mistake, we are creeping towards a self-inflicted nuclear armageddon. It might, therefore, do us well to pause and consider the myth of cheap atomic power, which must be recognised as the handmaiden of nuclear weapons. Not one of our many nuclear reactors has been able to fulfil its promise in terms of either safety, or electricity generation. We have no assurance that the wastes will remain safe from natural disasters such as earthquakes. Yet, our government presses on, ostrich-like, pretending that nuclear plants can free India from chronic power shortages.

The fact is that our nuclear industry is sick and dying. Gadekar points out, for instance, that the nuclear dream is really a nightmare. 'The scientists and bureaucrats in charge of our nuclear programme are above accountability,' he laments. He and his doctor wife, Sangamitra, investigated the condition of villagers at Rawatbhatta in Rajasthan, where they discovered that gross radiation-related deformities are the order of the day. In Kerala, at Kollam and Alapuza, both the Indian Rare Earths and Kerala Minerals and Metals Limited are causing untold misery to communities who suffer from an exotic cocktail of ailments from Down's Syndrome to immunity impairments. Fishermen are now being told to move away so that the commerce in radioactive monazite ore can continue undisturbed. In Mumbai, the atomic arrogance of the Nuclear Power Corporation prompts them to flog the Tarapur unit for another decade, probably because they do not have the money to decommission what has come to be known as one of the world's leakiest nuclear reactors.

The birth and death of the nuclear fantasy, which once promised that electricity will be too cheap to meter, has taken place within one human life time. Unlike other environmental damage, however, the problems will not go away even if we stop building reactors, because existing wastes will stay hot for thousands of years. In fact, if the centralised bureaucracy of the Maurya kings such as Ashoka had discovered nuclear power, we in India and Pakistan would probably be spending half our current national budget storing and caring for or repairing the damage done by atomic wastes from Kandahar and Taxila in the north-west, to Pataliputra in the east and Shravana-Belgola in the south!

As for the five tests our nation conducted, in its futile attempt to show that it is now a super power, perhaps someone should remind our leaders of Mahatma Gandhi's advice—an eye for an eye would only make the whole world blind. To my mind only megalomaniacs would seriously defend the nuclear deterrent. Having gone nuclear, however, I for one feel less secure when I sleep than I did before 3.45 p.m on Monday, May 11, 1998 (the time of the blast).

Notes

[1] Hiroshima: August 6, 1945, *Newsweek*, July 24, 1995.

[2] http://www.csi.ad.jp/ABomB/index.html

The Patriot Games

SHIV VISVANATHAN

Antonin Artaud could not have done better. The timing was so immaculate and surreal.

Celebrating the 50th year of our independence, Atal Behari Vajpayee erased in one stroke the legacy of the national movement and its modernist aftermath: Panchshila, non-alignment, non-violence and the dream of a world of alternatives. It was a killing of the fathers that Freud would have been intrigued about.

The props were simple. A man pretending to be prime minister. The national flag as backdrop. Vajpayee announced that 'India today carried out three underground nuclear tests at Pokhran at 3.45 p.m.' A quick terse announcement. A political statement to be followed by a technical briefing. One correspondent even felt it was like an American press conference. As American as apple pie and Hiroshima.

The obscenity lay at several levels. It was not just the presence of Pramod Mahajan with a fascist bully boy smile standing at the back, playing Pierre Salinger in pyjamas. It was the timing.

On Buddh Purnima, India exploded three nuclear bombs. The era of the pseudo-secularists has actually arrived. Only a civilisation illiterate about itself would knit the bomb and Buddha together. Yet strangely, Buddha was the signifier of continuity for both nuclear events. When Pokhran took place in 1974, the news of the blast was conveyed to Mrs. Gandhi as 'Lord Buddha has smiled.' History repeats itself, first

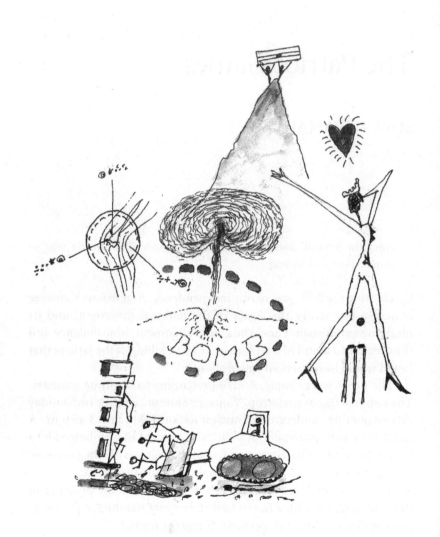

time as a tragedy and the second time as illiteracy. Gandhi was once asked what do you think of western civilisation? And he said 'It would be a good idea.' If he were to return today and had been asked 'What do you think of Indian civilisation,' he might remark 'that would also be a good idea.' In fact, the first thing that went out of the window was the ideal of a civilisation with its notions of myth, religion, morals, good conduct and tradition. We abandoned it all for history and the Nation State. Welcome to the moralism of the patriot games.

The patriot games are played on a subtle chequer board. Let us state its moves. Step one: It enacts the national movement as a simulation. There is a new sense of imperial oppression and there are new liberators. First, there is George Fernandes, the eternal adolescent and the army as chorus complaining about China. There is a touch of caring here. When George talks of snowmobiles for our jawans, I love him for it. Then there is the drumbeat of middle class machismo overthrowing Babar, Clive and Churchill in cafes and the internet. Militarise. Muscularise. Masculinise goes the modernist litany from Mambalam to Matunga. It is a plea for technology as a sign of toughness. If only we would get our act together, we would be taken seriously. We have the fourth largest army in the world. We have the third largest pool of scien-tific talent. Beware. We are one of the six in the nuclear club.

Beating the drums are two kinds of shakas; the RSS and the scientists in designer khakhis. The Ramannas and the Iyengars and the Brahmin hawks like K. Subramaniam. Hearing Raja Ramanna say 'Our boys have done a wonderful job' reminded me of an old Groucho Marx joke.

Groucho is pretending to be a scientist. He gets up and says 'I am going to make a great contribution to science. I am planning to retire.' I am reminded of the old men of Indian science, the Menons, the Swaminathans, the Ramannas. I wish they would retire. They have done enough damage to the idea of peace, sustainable development and the transfer of technology. This generation of scientists are not like the Ramans, Sahas or Kosambis. It is a generation of clerks salivating at every bell ring from the state. The Nation State. Sorry, the National Security State, which is against democracy and peer review, and which will not even allow a simple economic audit of the Indian nuclear programme. Scientific connivance and political illiteracy make perfect bedfellows.

Step two: Stage a spectacle. Carry out a controlled experiment with all its grandeur and secrecy. A circus no one saw but everyone has heard about. Did you hear that India exploded three bombs at 3.45 in the morning? A state secret to be shared by all. What more could a democracy want?

The first three experiments encapsulate the history of the bomb from Pokhran 1974 to Pokhran 1998. There is progress for you. India has joined the nuclear club. Club is the key word. Not community. Not movement. Club. Suddenly, a whole nation feels upwardly mobile. We have arrived, after a long pregnancy. Look at the way we read our history. The early efforts at nuclearism were shrouded in ambiguity and hypocrisy, with weakness. Remember how Narasimha Rao back-tracked under US pressure. But now we have moved from ambiguity to clarity. Clarity. A bully is clear. So are the stupid. Truth is more complex. But we have outgrown truth as we become a National Security State.

Step Three: Declare a holiday. Create a festival. Tell the people the bomb is for them. Fernandes is already claiming people should be involved in security. Involvement. Participation. The lovely language of World Bank governance. Now we know his sibling. Wonder what his German socialist friends think of Fernandes. Hello Petra Kelly. Didn't know your Judas friend, did you? When Petra died, George and Jaya Jaitley shed crocodile tears over her 'suicide' at Gandhi Peace Foundation. Wonder how Petra would have reacted to this green Judas had she lived? Khadi and nuclear bombs can only exist in complementarity in a mind like George Fernandes. The radio-active Gandhian.

There is a tremendous sense of euphoria, of achievement. Of competence. Of David against the Goliaths. Every—almost every—Indian stands proud at being nuclear, of becoming Goliaths. Look at the long lines waiting with flowers to congratulate Vajpayee. The Prime Minister stands bedecked and bewildered like the bridegroom of the year. Our tryst with destiny is complete. Everyone feels nationalistic. Pass out the *barfis*. It could be a hockey match. A Tendulkar century. A riot or a nuclear blast. We are happy with all four spectacles. Our scientific Tendulkars have struck effortlessly five times in a row. The crowd is berserk with joy. Yet there is a sadness when everything is a spectacle. A match. A riot. A blast. When there is little difference between these events. Worse. People forget that the worst kind of consumerism is the unquestioning consumption of science.

The BJP got it right. It knows that nationalism is tough to beat as a populist idea. After all, caste is fragmentary and class is divisive but the

Nation represents the whole. Look at the way dissent is silenced. Every political group wants to be implicated, get a lick of the nuclear ice-cream. The Congress insists that it was Rajiv and Indira who made the ice stick. The UF insists it is a three-in-one ice-cream. The first layer belongs to Indira, second to Gujral and the third to BJP. A truly coalitional ice-cream. A national nuclear ice-cream. Even communists are salivating, wondering if there is a Soviet component they could lay claim to. What is worse, they know you can't criticise nationalism. When Vajpayee fights the US imperial bully, Bardhan and Basu will clap. Dissenters sound silly. Praful Bidwai on BBC sounds as if he has got up from a hangover and murmurs the first thing that comes into his head, that 'It is a BJP plot to look decisive.' He is right but when he mouths it, the message has all the inanity of 'the butler did it'. The audience orchestration is superb. Gujral loves it. And Ramanna. And K. Subramaniam. And Jasjit Singh. Throw in a touch of Raja Mohan and Bharath Karnad. It is an orgy of agreement. Prim and proper. All the newspapers quote IAEA as saying 'it was not illegal'. The Patriot Games of Vajpayee beats any Asiad spectacle of Indira and Rajiv.

Even luck favours the BJP. Abdul Kalam is the ideal citizen and scientist. Ascetic as P.C. Ray. As nationalist as Meghnad Saha. A bachelor wedded only to science. You don't get them better. It is as if Aslam Sher Khan were to score the winning hockey goal against Pakistan. All of India seems to be celebrating. We have beaten China, Pakistan, USA, Germany and Britain. We have gatecrashed into history. Every Indian feels proud. We have won the Battle of Plassey, the Swadeshi struggle, the 1962 China war, all at one go. It is victory as virtual reality. *Saare jahan se accha, ye nuclear India hamara.*

There is truth in the lie. A convincing truth. A fragment of history. The nuclear club has been a coercive and hypocritical one. It is a search for monopoly. A demand of good behaviour by the one nation that has used the bomb twice on a people. The amoralism is stunning. Whether it is Thatcher, Blair, Bush or Clinton, you can't get lower than that. Third rate moralism dished out with equal ladles of Dale Carnegie and Ron Reagan. The Original Sin pretending to be the Immaculate Conception.

The Indians were brilliant in their counter response. Not since Krishna Menon played Chanakya in English were Indians so pleased with their own performance. It was the debate on CTBT that convinced India that it was on the right track. Arundhati Ghosh was superb as

Rani of Jhansi. Translate that as Joan of Arc for First World illiterates. It showed us as powerful dissenters of the global world. That set the stage for our moral crusade. But we were not just heroic. We were realists. It is this transition from Nehruvian idealism to global pragmatism that needs to be emphasised. It is like switching from the old Ambassador car to the new Maruti. Morality is now more slick, mobile and profitable.

Implied in this is a sense that mere goodness is weak, that good guys are dead guys. What one needs are good guys with nuclear sharp shooters. Acquire the nuclear colt, look the enemy dead in the eye and talk of a nuclear free world. Peace is what tough guys understand. Suddenly every Indian feels a nuclear bulge in his biceps. The akhada langurs show it to the world. The Mani Dixits play it down. To see this in operation one had to watch his performance in Aap ka Faisala, Aap ki Adalat. It was a debate between Dixit and Kanti Bajpai, professor of International Relations at JNU. Bajpai is the peacenik as scholar. Quiet. Quietly courageous. Full of questionmarks and footnotes. Bajpai understands peace. He knows it is a slow bumbling process and Indians have played a great role in its evolution. He is honest, ready to cite chapter and verse when Indians have sinned. Ironically he appears shy, hesitant, ectomorphic. A Ph.D., still fresh behind his ears.

Mani Dixit is like an old bear, amiable with a pot of honey inside, oozing the experience of power. The foreign secretary as hero. Talking to his IIC group. He exposes the hypocrisy of USA, the nukespeak of China. He underlines the Indian efforts to be moral. The struggles with complexity and ambiguity; of how Nehruvian idealism was whipped into muscular pragmatism. It is time to tell the world we are tough like you, that we are high calorie nuclear heroes.

Kanti Bajpai is sincere, persistent but Dixit is tough, clipped, amiably dismissive. A politician who smells a crowd. History is about tough guys. No more subaltern pap, old chap. We are pragmatists now. Love me, love my bomb.

The crowd loves it, applauds, happy to be a part of history. Even compere Manoj Raghuvanshi's moustache quivers like a weathervane in the right direction. How many Agni missiles did Gandhi have?

To the potent nationalist gin, the BJP adds the right twist, a touch of swadeshi lime. The bomb is Indian. Conceived by Indian science. Executed by Indian technologists. We don't smuggle technology like Dr. Khan. No nuclear Dawoods please, we are Indian. Our nuclear bomb is as home grown as Abdul Kalam. The MIT in his bio data stands for Madras Institute of Technology. Between Kalam, K. Subramaniam, Dixit, Ramanna the swadeshi *'Hum kissi se kum nahin* (I am lesser than no one)' is echoed clearly.

There is a hijacking and distortion of discourse that we must challenge. The new Dandi march must begin at the villages of Pokhran by challenging the trustees of this new official morality. We have to state that the above cast of characters cannot define our moral universe, anymore than ethical mutants like Clinton or Thatcher. We have to apply to the bomb, the Gandhian model of technology as one enhancing innovation, community, debate, trusteeship and love.

Let me put it tersely and personally. The current ideas of the bomb, of the Nation State, of the new Indian self violates:

—My sense of security
—My feelings of community
—My theory of democracy
—My celebration of science
—My idea of foreign policy
—My sense of history
—My legacy of Swadeshi
—My emotion of being Indian, very, very Indian

The nuclear rath yatra has to be halted. I appeal to our scientists to stand up and be counted. Say no to the bomb but do it openly and in conversation.

I request the People's Union for Civil Liberties and the People's Union for Democratic Rights to accept Indian and even Pakistani dissenting scientists as prisoners of conscience.

I appeal to our people and those in Pakistan to start a people-to-people foreign policy. Our states have run out of ideas for peace.

I ask every community to say no to the bomb from the Panchayat to the Internet.

I request our human rights activists, our Gandhians, our feminists, our ecologists, our Dalits, our housewives, tribals, trade unionists to stop this closing of the Indian mind.

India is and has to be a clearing house for ideas on peace, alternatives, non-violence for the global world. The future is now. We owe it to our children. Withdraw from the Patriot Games. Its noise as music covers the jackboots of a coming totalitarian era.

The Risks and Consequences of Nuclear War in South Asia

MATTHEW MCKINZIE, ZIA MIAN, A.H. NAYYAR AND M.V. RAMANA

The nuclear tests by India and Pakistan in 1998 created a grave new danger for the people of the two countries. Having tested nuclear weapons and ballistic missiles, the two states have announced that henceforth the threat of use of nuclear weapons shall be a key part of their national security policy. In this they follow the example of the United States and former Soviet Union, and the other nuclear weapons states. While it is possible that South Asia will now see its own version of a nuclear armed stand-off, there are so many differences—with respect to history, technology and geography—between the India–Pakistan and the United States–Soviet Union conflicts that the relatively peaceful end of the Cold War cannot be a sound indicator for what will happen in South Asia. This gives particular relevance to an examination of what nuclear weapons and nuclear war could mean in a South Asian context.

The Risks of War

There is a history of war in South Asia. India and Pakistan fought in 1948, 1965, and 1971 and in 1999. There is good evidence that in no case was there the expectation of a war on the scale and of the kind that ensued. Rather war followed misadventure, driven by profound errors of policy, political and military judgement, and public sentiment. Nuclear weapons do nothing to lessen such possibilities. There is even reason to believe they may make them worse in South Asia. One lesson of the 1999 Kargil war is that Pakistan saw its newly acquired nuclear weapons as a shield from behind which it can fuel and stoke the conflict in Kashmir, safe from any possible Indian retaliation. During this war, nuclear threats were made publicly by leaders on both sides. It took international intervention to stop the slide to a larger, more destructive war.

Pakistan's leaders have made clear they are prepared to use nuclear weapons first in any conflict, they hope by threatening to do so they will prevent war, and in the event of war they fear being overwhelmed by India's conventional military superiority. While India has offered an agreement for no-first use of nuclear weapons, its armed forces seem prepared to try to destroy Pakistan's nuclear capability before it is used, and seek their own capability to launch a nuclear attack if they believe that enemy nuclear missiles are armed and ready for launch. Pakistan, in turn, may seek to preempt such a situation by using its nuclear weapons even earlier in a conflict rather than risk losing them.

When it comes to picking targets for nuclear weapons there are really only two options. One option is to indiscriminately destroy cities in the hope of either forcing an end to hostilities or eliciting unconditional surrender. The second option is to try to use nuclear weapons to destroy military command structures and war fighting capabilities. Pakistan cannot hope to prevail in a drawn out war and its leaders have made clear they intend to follow the first option. Should India seek to try the second option and attack only military targets, the results may not be that different from deliberately using nuclear weapons against cities. This is because nearly all of Pakistan's significant military centres are either in or located close to cities. For instance, Karachi, Hyderabad, Bahawalpur, Multan, Lahore, Gujranwala, Rawalpindi, Peshawar and Quetta are all army corps headquarters. Islamabad has the air force and naval headquarters. These are obvious targets. Nuclear weapons cause destruction over such large distances that even if nuclear weapons were targeted specifically at military installations the cities would not escape.

Early Warning

The destructive power of nuclear weapons means the nuclear superpowers live in perpetual fear of a surprise attack. These fears are worsened by the deployment of ballistic missiles, which reduce the time it would take to mount a nuclear attack. During the Cold War, the superpowers addressed their fears by building complex early warning systems that would let each of them know they were about to be attacked and give them time to launch their nuclear weapons before they were destroyed. These systems also sought to limit the possibility of a war starting by accident or miscalculation by creating time during which policy makers and military planners could make decisions using real information about what was actually happening rather than responding simply on the basis of fear about what might happen.

The US and the Soviet Union, now Russia, relied on satellites and early warning radar systems to give them information within about one and a half minutes of the possible launch of a missile. They took about two and a half minutes to work out what was happening from this information. Advisors could be called and a threat determined a few minutes after this. In other words within about six or seven minutes, it was possible to decide if a nuclear attack may have started. Since the missiles would have taken about 25 minutes to travel from the US to the Soviet Union or in the other direction, there was still time for a final confirmation that the missiles were real. There was even time left to find out if there had been an accidental launch of the missiles, and to decide what to do.

The Failures of Early Warning

The United States has invested enormous financial and technical resources in setting up its early warning system. It has tried hard but without success to make it foolproof. There is no real history of all the failures. It is known, however, that between 1977 and 1984 there were over 20,000 false alarms of a missile attack on the US. Over 1000 of these were considered serious enough for bombers and missiles to be placed on alert.

Some of these incidents give terrifying insights into how easily even the most carefully designed and technologically advanced warning systems can go wrong. Two instances will suffice. In November 1979, the US missile warning system showed that a massive attack had suddenly been launched. A nuclear alert was declared. There was no attack. There were no missiles. The warning was due to a computer that had been used to test the warning system to see how it would behave if there were an attack. Somebody had forgotten to turn off the computer after the exercise.

A second example was even more dramatic. In June 1980, the early warning systems showed that two missiles had been launched towards the US. This was followed by signals that there were more missiles following the first two. The situation was considered to be sufficiently serious that the President's special airplane was prepared for take-off. Again there was no attack, nor any missiles. The reasons for the mistaken signals, and interpretations, were eventually traced to a computer chip that was not working properly.

The repeated failures of the US early warning system led at one time to an official enquiry that reported that the system 'had been mismanaged . . . by the Air Force, the Joint Chiefs of Staff, and the Department of Defence.' In other words, every institution assigned to make sure the system worked failed in its task.

It was not just the US early warning system that had problems. While there is little information yet on how the Soviet Union managed its nuclear weapons warning systems, there is at least one example from recent years that suggests it may not have worked any better than the US system. On January 25, 1995, a Norwegian rocket was launched to take scientific measurements. The Norwegian government told the Russian government in advance that this would happen. Nevertheless, when the rocket was picked up by Russian radar it was treated as a possible missile attack. It seems a warning was sent to the Russian defence minister's headquarters, the Russian military leadership, and to the commanders of Russian missiles that an attack may be underway. A message was then sent to Boris Yeltsin, the Russian President, and an emergency conference called with nuclear commanders over the telephone. Boris Yeltsin has confirmed that such an emergency conference did take place.

South Asia

There is some evidence that early warning systems in South Asia are limited in their scope and capabilities. For instance, in August 1998 the United States launched a major cruise missile attack against Afghanistan from its ships in the Arabian Sea. To reach the targets, scores of missiles flew long distances over Pakistan. Concerned about the possibility that Pakistan may detect these missiles and misinterpret the evidence as indicating that they were coming from India, the United States sent a very senior general to Pakistan in advance of the attack. His job was apparently to reassure Pakistan that it was not the target. It seems that Pakistan did not even detect the missiles.

Even if Pakistan and India had the technology for early warning, and even if it worked reliably, they could not use it against each other, geography has made sure of that. Instead of the twenty-five minutes or so warning time that the US and the Soviet Union had, it would take an Indian Prithvi missile somewhere between three and five minutes to reach almost anywhere in Pakistan. It would take Pakistan's Ghauri missile about five minutes to reach Delhi. An early warning system could give a warning of what was happening, advisors could be called, and then time would run out. There would be no time to decide whether the warning was real, or a mistake. The decision on how to respond, including possible nuclear retaliation, would have to be made regardless.

The Effects of Nuclear Weapons

Approximately 5,000 km east of New Delhi and 55 years ago two nuclear weapons were used by the United States to kill over 190,000 people in Japan. Agonising deaths took place for approximately a month after the explosions—indeed deaths continued for weeks after Japan surrendered. The impacts on that country and the world from these atomic bombings have been enormous, and continue to the present. Can one predict the effects of the use of nuclear weapons against cities in India or Pakistan today? In some ways 'yes' and in many important ways 'no'.

The effects of a nuclear weapon explosion are so immense and so different from those of conventional weapons that it is useful to present, as a case study, a familiar hypothetical 'target'. The nuclear weapon used by the United States to attack Hiroshima had a yield equivalent to 15 thousand tonnes of TNT and was detonated at 580 metres above the surface of the earth. This yield is comparable to the yields of the nuclear weapons that India and Pakistan claimed they tested in May 1998. We describe therefore the effects of a single explosion of a Hiroshima-sized nuclear bomb at an elevation of 600 metres over Bombay (Mumbai), India. The consequences of such an explosion for any other large, densely populated, South Asian city would be similar.

The short-term effects of a nuclear explosion—those that occur within the first few weeks—can be classified as either prompt or delayed effects. In addition there are long term effects, primarily related to radiation from fallout, that can develop over years.

Prompt Effects

Any person or object exposed to the explosion would first experience an extremely intense flash of heat and light, brighter than a thousand suns. Even looking at the flash could cause blindness. For 1.6-3.2 kilometres around the point of explosion (the epicentre, or ground zero), everything that could burn—wood, paper, clothes, vegetation, and all other combustible materials—would catch fire.

Exposure to neutron and gamma radiation, resulting from the nuclear reactions responsible for the explosion, would occur almost simultaneously. Radiation exposure could lead to a variety of symptoms such as nausea, bloody diarrhoea, and hemorrhages within a few days (other consequences of radiation could appear years later). These health effects are often fatal and include leukaemia, thyroid cancer, breast cancer, and lung cancer, as well as non-fatal diseases such as birth defects, cataracts, and mental retardation in young children, keloids, and others.

The third effect is the shock or blast wave, which would result in a forceful blow to any person or object in its path. The winds accompanying the shock wave would reach velocities of more than 110 kilometres per hour to a distance of 2.4 kilometres or more. The shock wave would destroy everything within a circle with a radius of 1.1 kilometres.

Up to 1.7 kilometres from the point of explosion, all houses not built with concrete would be destroyed. Many of the buildings in Bombay, especially older ones, are either badly designed or constructed with raw materials that are of poor quality (such as adulterated cement or improperly baked bricks). Every year several hundred buildings collapse by themselves, especially during the rainy season. Faced with the shock wave and these hurricane-force winds, buildings may collapse at significantly greater distances than those estimated here.

Delayed Effects

A few minutes after the explosion, the delayed effects would begin. The first of these is the firestorm that would result from the coalescing of individual fires started by the initial flash of light and heat. In the case of a Hiroshima-sized explosion over a city like Bombay, the radius of the region set on fire would be 1.7 to 2 kilometres. Due to the large area of the fire, the fire zone would act as a huge pump, sucking in air from the surrounding areas and driving heated air upwards. This pumping action would create winds with velocities as high as 50–80 kilometres/hour. The temperature in the fire zone would reach several hundred degrees, making it almost certain that there would be no survivors. Furthermore, fire-fighting would be almost impossible due to the combination of hurricane-force winds, thick smoke, the destruction of water mains and tanks by the shock wave, and the presence of debris from the blast blocking roads and access routes.

Other factors would lead to a probability of small explosions in the fire region and, therefore, to a greater chance that people would be injured as well as burned. In Bombay, for example, many houses contain gas cylinders (containing liquid petroleum gas) that are used for cooking. These are known to explode when exposed to fires. In addition, compared to cities in Japan and Germany during World War II, Bombay and other modern cities have much greater concentrations of motorised vehicles such as cars, scooters, and buses that use petroleum-based fuels. The corresponding storage and dispensing facilities for such highly inflammable and explosive fuels would only increase the numbers of casualties.

The second delayed effect is radioactive fallout. When a nuclear bomb explodes at low altitudes, a large amount of material is vaporised and carried aloft into the mushroom cloud. This material then mixes with the fireball's radioactive materials, which results in a cloud of highly radioactive dust. This radioactive fallout can travel large distances on the winds created by the explosion, as well as in the atmosphere, before ultimately falling back to earth. If, instead of assuming that the weapon is detonated at a height of 600 metres, we assume that the explosion happens at the surface with a wind velocity of 25 kilometres per hour, the area subject to levels of fallout that have a high likelihood of being fatal would be about 25–100 square kilometres. The wind direction during the period that the fallout is aloft (which could be fluctuating) would determine which areas would be subject to these levels of radioactivity. The regions subject to high levels of fallout would have high levels of casualties and radiation sickness. Further, Bombay, being close to the sea, has high levels of water vapour in the atmosphere. Water droplets would likely condense around radioactive particles and descend as rain, as was the case in Hiroshima and Nagasaki.

Even people who live in areas subject to lower levels of radiation, unless they are immediately evacuated, would be susceptible to radiation sickness. Given the large population of Bombay, the public panic that would follow a nuclear attack, and the likely damage to all forms of transportation infrastructure, such train stations and tracks, roads, petrol stations, dockyards, airports, etc., evacuation of survivors would be nearly impossible.

Casualty Estimates
The most recent Indian census data (from 1991) gives the population of Greater Bombay as 9,910,000; if the neighboring town of Thane is also included, the population is 12,572,000. Since the decadal growth rate for Bombay during the decade preceding this census was 20.21 per cent, these numbers may understate the current population significantly. Furthermore, there is also some evidence of undercounting in the 1991 census. The average population density of Bombay is about 23,000 people per square kilometre. There are regions, however, where the population density exceeds 100,000 people per square kilometre.

Since a nuclear explosion and its effects are complicated physical phenomena, with different types of effects occurring around the same time, it is impossible to predict numbers of casualties or injuries accurately. There are three ways to estimate the number of casualties from prompt effects. All of these are based on empirical data from Hiroshima when the casualties were expressed as a function of different variables— radius, overpressure, and thermal fluence, respectively. Using these three models and assuming the above population densities, we can calculate that there will be somewhere between 150,000 and 800,000 deaths in Bombay within a few weeks of the explosion. These would be the result from just the blast and fire effects of a Hiroshima-sized) nuclear weapon, and assuming that fallout effects are negligible (assumptions that lead to a very conservative casualty estimate).

For comparison, in the case of a weapon exploding at ground level, the areas damaged by fire and blast are somewhat less but radioactive fallout would be a more significant cause of deaths and sickness. Assuming that all the fallout is deposited in inhabited areas (and assuming they have a population density of 23,000, the average for Bombay) the number of people dying of all causes could be as high as 350,000 to 400,000 for a 15-kilotonne weapon. Many more people would be subject to lower doses of radiation, which in the case of already sick people, the old and the young, could well be lethal in the absence of medical care.

The above numbers include only the 'prompt' casualties, those who are injured or die right away or within a few weeks of the explosion. Many more people will certainly die from long term effects, especially radiation-related causes. Studies involving survivors of the atomic bombing of Hiroshima and Nagasaki reveal that the mortality rates for all diseases, leukaemia, and malignancies other than leukaemia, are all significantly higher than among people not exposed to radiation. Increases in the cancer rates of survivors of an atomic bombing of Bombay may be comparable to, if not greater than, those among Hiroshima and Nagasaki survivors.

There are a number of other reasons to believe that the casualty numbers cited above would be an underestimate in a city like Bombay. First, the assumed population densities are lower than the actual densities. Apart from undercounting and variations among regions, a substantial number of people come in every day from places as far away as Pune (four hours by train) to work in Bombay. The census does not take such commuters into account. Since an attack from the air is quite likely to take place during the day in order to maximise visibility, many commuters will also be killed or injured. Second, casualties from fallout have not been included in the estimates. Since fallout, even if present only in small quantities, can spread out to large regions and cause local hot spots, this is an important omission. Third, conservative figures for blast damage and regions affected by fire have been deliberately chosen. The actual areas are likely to be higher, implying a greater number of casualties.

There is another significant uncertainty in the estimates offered here, one that is likely to increase the casualties. There are a large number of industrial facilities in Bombay and its vicinity. India's highest concentration of chemical plants is in the Trans-Thane creek area, which has more than 2,000 factories. Central Bombay is home to several mills, which could cause additional fires and explosions, and which could spread toxic substances. The Union Carbide accident in Bhopal is an example of the kinds of effects that are possible due to escape of toxic chemicals. In addition to chemical industries, the largest nuclear laboratory in India—the Bhabha Atomic Research Centre—is in Trombay, just outside Bombay. A nuclear explosion in the vicinity of either reactor at the Centre (CIRUS and Dhruva) or near the reprocessing plant or the facilities storing radioactive waste and/or spent fuel could lead to the release of large amounts of radioactivity in addition to the quantities resulting from the explosion itself. This would increase the amounts of fallout significantly.

Hospitals and medical care in an overcrowded city such as Bombay are limited to begin with, and facilities within the affected area would be destroyed or damaged during the attack. The injured would be unlikely to find medical treatment.

The Effects of Nuclear War

We have described in some detail the effect of the use of one relatively small nuclear weapon on a large South Asia city. It is hard to imagine that if this dreadful event were ever to take place as the result of an attack there would be no response from the other side. Both Pakistan and India have sufficient nuclear weapons and the missiles and aircraft to destroy several, perhaps many, of the other's cities.

To illustrate the terrible consequences of a large-scale nuclear war in South Asia, we estimate the numbers of deaths and injuries from nuclear attacks on ten major Indian and Pakistani cities. To arrive at

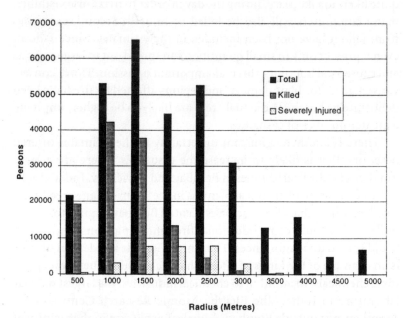

Figure 1 Total population and casualty data for the August 6, 1945 attack on Hiroshima in 500-metre rings around ground zero. Reference: Hiroshima Shiyakusho [Hiroshima City Office], *Hiroshima Genbaku Sensaishi* [Record of the Hiroshima A-bomb War Disaster], Hiroshima, 1971, vol. I.

consistent estimates for all of these cities we use a different, simpler, methodology than was used earlier for the detailed case study of the consequences of a nuclear attack on Bombay. We transpose onto each city the characteristics and consequences of the August 6, 1945 Hiroshima bombing with its mass fires, radiation sicknesses, severe burns, deaths in buildings collapsed by the shock wave, hurricane-force winds propelling missiles through the air, and blindness (Figure 1 plots the zones of death and injury experienced at Hiroshima).

This historical data from Hiroshima on the fraction of the population killed and injured in concentric five hundred metre wide rings out to a distance of five kilometres from the explosion is applied to a database that gives population distribution information for each of ten cities in South Asia. The 'LandScan' world population database was used for these calculations. It uses the best available census information and assigns them to grid cells of roughly 1 km by 1 km size by creating a probability distribution based on factors such proximity to roads, environmental characteristics such as climate and terrain slope, and night-time lights as seen by satellites.

Table 1 below shows the numbers of dead, severely injured and slightly injured persons after a nuclear attack on each of ten large South Asian cities. A total of 2.9 million deaths is predicted for these cities in India and Pakistan with an additional 1.5 million severely injured.

Table 1: Estimated nuclear casualties for 10 large Indian and Pakistani cities

City Name	Total Population within 5 kilometres of Ground Zero	Killed	Severely Injured	Slightly Injured
India				
Bangalore	3,077,937	314,978	175,136	411,336
Bombay	3,143,284	477,713	228,648	476,633
Calcutta	3,520,344	357,202	198,218	466,336
Madras	3,252,628	364,291	196,226	448,948
New Delhi	1,638,744	176,518	94,231	217,853
Pakistan				
Faisalabad	2,376,478	336,239	174,351	373,967
Islamabad	798,583	154,067	66,744	129,935
Karachi	1,962,458	239,643	126,810	283,290
Lahore	2,682,092	258,139	149,649	354,095
Rawalpindi	1,589,828	183,791	96,846	220,585

It should be appreciated that this exercise of predicting the casualties from nuclear attacks on cities in India and Pakistan based on the historical record at Hiroshima just scratches the surface of what would play out if nuclear weapons were used. There is also the loss of key social and physical networks that make daily life possible: families and neighbourhoods would be devastated, factories, shops, electricity and water systems demolished, hospitals and schools, and other government offices destroyed. The flood of refugees would carry the physical effects far beyond the cities.

The ultimate impact on both societies would extend well beyond the bombed areas in highly unpredictable ways. Nuclear attacks would provoke profound and enduring responses from citizens of India and Pakistan and of the world. Nothing would ever be the same again.

LIVING THE NUCLEAR LIFE

The Epidemic of Nuclearism

ASHIS NANDY

Nuclearism is the ideology of nuclear weaponry and nuclear arms-based security. It is the most depraved, shameless and costly pornography of our times. Such an ideology cannot be judged only by the canons of international relations, geopolitics, political sociology, or ethics. It is also a well known, identifiable, psycho-pathological syndrome. The following is a brief introduction to its clinical picture, epidemiology and prognosis.

Nuclearism does not reside in institutions, though it may set up, symbolise, or find expression in social and political institutions. It is an individual pathology and has clear identifiers. Many years ago, Brian Easlea argued in his book, *Fathering the Unthinkable*, that nuclearism went with strong masculinity strivings. Eastea was no psychologist, but the works of Carol Cohn and others have endorsed the broad contours of Easlea's analysis. They show that not only the language and ideology, but the entire culture of nuclear weaponry is infiltrated by hard, masculine imageries and those participating in that culture usually suffer from deep fears of emasculation or impotency. Indeed, that is the reason they participate in that culture with enthusiasm.

Such masculinity strivings or drive for potency usually goes with various forms of authoritarianism. Even people ideologically committed to democratic governance may vicariously participate in subtler forms of authoritarianism associated with nuclearism. There is support for this relationship outside psychology, too. Robert Jungk's work on the nuclear state shows that secrecy, security, surveillance and police state methods invariably accompany the nuclear establishment in every country. In that sense, the culture of nuclearism is one of the true universals of our time. Like Coca-Cola and blue jeans, it does not permit cultural adaptation or edited versions. It is the same in Paris and Pokhran, Lahore and Los Alamos.

Nuclearism is framed by a genocidal mentality. Eric Markusen and Robert J. Lifton have systematically studied the links. In their book, *The Genocidal Mentality*, Markusen and Lifton make a comparative study of the psychology of mass murderers, in Nazi Germany, in Hiroshima and Nagasaki, and among the ideologies of nuclearism today and find remarkable continuities.

In the genocidal person, there is, first of all, a state of mind called psychic numbing—a diminished capacity, or inclination to feel and a general sense of meaninglessness. One so numbs one's sensitivities that normal emotions and moral considerations cannot penetrate one any more. Numbing closes off a person and leads to a constriction of self process. To him or her, the death or the possibility of the death of millions begins to look like an abstract, bureaucratic detail, involving the calculation of military gains or losses, geopolitics or mere statistics. Such numbing can be considered to be the final culmination of the separation of affect and cognition, that is feelings and thinking, that the European enlightenment sanctioned and celebrated as the first step towards greater objectivity and scientific rationality.

The genocidal mentality also tends to create an area protected from public responsibility or democratic accountability. Usually, such responsibility is avoided by re-conceptualising oneself as only a cog in the wheel, advancing one's own bureaucratic or scientific career like everybody else, by taking and obeying orders from superior authorities faithfully, mechanically and without thinking about the moral implications of the orders. All the Nazi war criminals tried at Nuremberg at the end of World War II ventured the defence that they were under orders to kill innocent people, including women, children and the elderly, and could do nothing about it.

The other way of avoiding accountability is to remove it from individuals and vest it in institutions and aggregates. As if institutions by themselves could run a death machine without the intervention of individuals! After a while, even terms like the military-industrial complex, fascism, imperialism, Stalinism, ruling class, or American hegemony become ways of freeing actual, real-life persons from their culpability for recommending, ordering, or committing mass murders. In a society where genocidal mentality spreads, intellectuals also find such impersonal analyses soothing; they contribute to the creation of a business-as-usual ambience in which institutions are ritually blamed and the psychopathic scientists, bureaucrats and politicians who work towards genocides move around scot-free.

In acute cases, the genocidal mentality turns into necrophilia, a clinical state in which the patient is in love with death. Indeed, he or she wants to sleep with the dead, in fantasy and, in extreme cases, in life. Saadat Hassan Manto's famous story, 'Cold Meat' or 'Thanda Gosht' is, unknown to the author, the story of an 'ordinary' murderer and rapist who, while trying to satiate his sexual greed during a communal conflict, confronts his own with necrophilia and is devastated by that. Those interested in more authoritative case studies can look up Erich Fromm's *The Anatomy of Human Destructiveness*.

Nuclearism does not remain confined to the nuclear establishment or the nuclear community. It introduces other psychopathologies in a society. For instance, as it seeps into public consciousness, it creates a new awareness of the transience of life. It forces people to live with the constant fear that, one day, a sudden war or accident might kill not only them, but also their children and grandchildren, and everybody they love. This awareness gradually creates a sense of the hollowness of life. For many, life is denuded of substantive meaning. The psychological numbing I have mentioned completes the picture. While the ordinary citizen leads an apparently normal life, he or she is constantly aware of the transience of such life and the risk of mega-death for the entire society. Often this finds expression in unnecessary or inexplicable violence in social life or in a more general, high state of anxiety and a variety of psycho-somatic ailments. In other words, nuclearism begins to brutalise ordinary people and vitiates everyday life.

Studies by the likes of William Beardslee, J.E. Mach and Eleonora Masini show that these traits express themselves even in adolescents and children. Even children barely eight or ten years old begin to live in what they consider to be a world without a future; they are fearful and anxious about their life, but unable to express that fear and anxiety directly, because in a nuclearised society the fear of nuclear death is made to look like an abnormal psycho-neurotic state.

Many neurotics and psychotics at first look like charming eccentrics. To start with, nuclearism may appear a smart game and the partisans of nuclear weaponry may look like normal politicians, scholars, or defence experts. After all, the Nazi killers, too, were usually loving fathers, connoisseurs of good music and honest citizens. However, beneath that facade lies a personality that is insecure, doubtful about one's masculinity, fearful of the interpersonal world and unable to love. The mindless violence such a personality anticipates or plans is a pathetic attempt to fight these inner feelings of emptiness and the suspicion and the fear that one's moral self might already be dead within. You father the unthinkable because you have already psychologically orphaned yourself. You make contingency plans to kill millions because you fear that your inner-most core has already been cauterised against all normal feelings and human relations. Acquiring the power to inflict the death on millions and by living with the fantasy of that power, you pathetically try to get some confirmation that you are still alive. However, that confirmation never comes. For in the process of acquiring that power, you may not be not dead physically, but you are already dead morally, socially and psychologically.

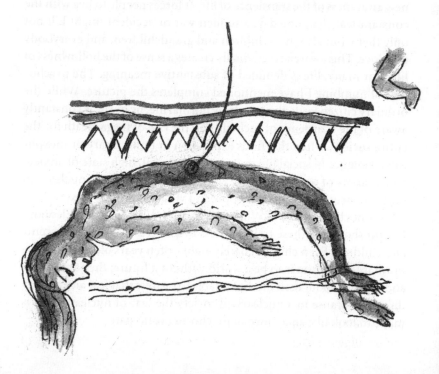

The Hindutva Weapon

AIJAZ AHMAD

The Pokhran explosions have brought independent India to a watershed comparable, in its long-term political significance, to the Sino-Indian War, the Emergency, and the destruction of the Babri Masjid. The national equation as well as India's international relations have been altered for the foreseeable future.

From the opening of the propaganda offensive by Defence Minister George Fernandes in early April to Prime Minister A.B. Vajpayee's letter to US President Bill Clinton after the explosions, the BJP government has maintained its focus on China as the strategic adversary that threatens India's security directly and as the main culprit behind Pakistan's nuclear capability, not to speak of the threat it is said to pose through Myanmar. This focus on China is deliberate, as the beginning of a methodical red-baiting offensive within the country, as the inauguration of an arms race on the Asian continent, and as an appeal to long-term US goals in Asia. What we are witnessing is the staging of a short-term Indo–US tension as a prelude to a long-term, comprehensive strategic alliance.

It is possible that there was an 'intelligence failure' on the part of the Central Intelligence Agency and that the US government was caught unawares, as is being claimed in some US circles. That is possible but not probable, given the American capabilities of global surveil-lance. Nor would it be the first time in recent history that the US would claim an 'intelligence failure' when it was necessary for it to pretend lack of advance information with regard to developments that it con-dones but is formally committed to opposing. The US is also bound by its own laws to impose sanctions against countries that undertake such tests. A degree of tension in the short run is inevitable. But the sanctions are likely to be imposed indifferently and shall be gradually relaxed, in the not-too-distant future. Multilateral agencies such as the World Bank, and some countries such as Japan, are likely to follow the US lead in the imposition as well as circumvention of these sanctions.

Meanwhile, the immediate reaction from various Western capitals shows that while the tests are being condemned all around, there is no consensus behind the sanctions and the Bhartiya Janata Party govern-ment shall be able to ride them out easily. The fact that key countries such as Russia, France and Britain—three members out of five in the nuclear club—have not imposed sanctions is as significant as the fact that the US has done so. This fact will also be cited within the US for relaxing the sanctions, in view of non-cooperation from 'allies' and because American sanctions in the context of this non-cooperation shall be portrayed as favourable to European capital and detrimental to American business interests. This argument shall gain further strength from the breakneck liberalisation and privatisation that the BJP government is now bound to undertake.

Aside from a possible short-term irritation, the long-term prospect is for a closer anti-China axis between the US and India. This possibility gains greater credence in the overall context in which these tests have been undertaken. We are witnessing immense intensification of an international campaign on the issue of Tibet. Key members of the Clinton administration, including high officials from the Pentagon, have visited India immediately after the BJP take-over, explicitly endor-sing the regime. This occasion was used to announce, with deliberate high visibility, the impending Indo–US joint exercises in high altitude combat.

The crash of economies in East and South-East Asia, from which the advanced capitalist countries have benefited enormously, is a key aspect of the changing international and regional environments. In this economic warfare, China is the next target, and the US shall greatly welcome military pressure on China. Americans know from long experience that many distortions and the eventual collapse of the Soviet economy ensued, at least substantially, from the unbearable pressure which that economy had to endure as the Soviet Union sought to retain some degree of military parity with the North Atlantic Treaty Organisation (NATO). Today, the US would like nothing as much as similar diversion of Chinese resources toward military expenditures in an Asian arms race. Behind the BJP's bogus anti-imperialism and the American sanctions lies this prospect of a far-reaching alliance in a new Cold War.

The deliberate demonstration of multiple technologies through five different tests—especially the thermonuclear explosion and the latter two tests with the objective of collecting data for further computer simulations—leaves no doubt that this is a step toward actual weaponisation, in keeping with the BJP's repeated promises to make the 'bomb'. Although these tests do not yet make India a nuclear power in the definitional sense, the BJP has nevertheless signalled that India will now become a nuclear power in the same sense in which Israel is. In this context, the distinction between testing and weaponisation becomes more or less a scholastic eyewash.

The terms of the discussion about the Comprehensive Test Ban Treaty (CTBT) have been changed drastically. Refusing to sign the CTBT on grounds of its discriminatory character when India was not a nuclear power could be reasonably construed as an act of resistance to unreasonable foreign pressure. By contrast, conducting actual tests, becoming a de facto nuclear power and then offering to consider accepting some portions of that treaty shall now be presented by the BJP-controlled media as an act of responsible statesmanship in the international arena. The BJP will try to take credit not on one count, but on three: for not signing the CTBT, for signing it, and for signing it only partially to the extent that Indian national interests are safeguarded.

This is a sophisticated approach with great propaganda value, and an alternative approach needs to be developed that is somewhat different from the alternatives being posed, even after these tests, by advocates and opponents of the CTBT. A call to sign it now converges alarmingly with what Clinton is demanding and the BJP itself is proposing. A call not to sign it amounts to pious nostalgia for the way the world was before these tests. The BJP can in fact live with either of these options. By not signing it, it keeps open the option for further tests and open weaponisation. By signing it, all of it or parts of it, the BJP manages to diffuse international condemnation, appeases the CTBT activists, carries on perfecting technology for weaponisation in laboratories, and paves the way for the Indo–US axis sooner, rather than later.

In practice, the BJP will act precisely the way it acted on the Ayodhya issue and the way it has been acting on the nuclear issue until now. It said openly that it was going to do in Ayodhya what others would shudder even to think. Then, it did what it said it would do, in contravention of all legality, human decency and its own bogus promises. With that design accomplished, it restrained its allies from immediately going on to similar vandalism in Kashi and Mathura, so as to project for itself an image of relative moderation while keeping that issue alive but simmering only very slowly, for another time, even as the situation on the ground in both those places has been changing imperceptibly but fundamentally. The issue of the Ram Mandir itself was largely taken out of public debate while the most meticulous preparations have been made, right under the noses of all the official guardians of Indian secularism, for the building of the Mandir at an opportune time, exactly in the place where the Masjid once stood.

The BJP has acted in the same fashion on the nuclear issue. It, and the Bharatiya Jana Sangh before it, have repeatedly promised weaponisation. Upon taking power, it assigned the highest priority to carrying out these tests, without informing either friend or foe, with exactly the kind of covert preparation and lightning strike that it had practiced at Ayodhya. Having demonstrated its hawkishness, it will now offer to sign the CTBT, but only partially, knowing that the alternative pressures, to sign all of it or sign none of it, will only grow in the coming weeks and months, and that it must allow time for the sense of horror to get routinised and for the passions to subside. Then it will strike again, with yet another surprise, just as it will one day undoubtedly launch the building of the Mandir in the most dramatic way possible.

The CTBT is going to remain an issue in public debate. So a position has to be taken and the only possible position is that decisions of such far-reaching importance ought not be used, cynically, as bargaining counters and that the situation, therefore, must be frozen until the nation has sorted out the very basic parameters of its governance. The point needs to be made that India has to have the capability but also has to refrain from tests and deployments. The more crucial point, however, is that, having acted like thieves in a night of long knives, this government has lost the right to rule and must resign so that a more responsible government can take over.

That a party which commands merely a quarter of the national vote could take an action of this magnitude so secretly and unilaterally, without a national debate, without consultation with senior leaders of the Opposition, without a strategic review it had promised, without informing its own allies in government, raises questions not only about the competence of the BJP to rule but also about the kind of powers that are concentrated in the Prime Minister's Office (PMO). What this event demonstrates most dramatically is not that we need a presidential form of government but that far-reaching reforms are needed to prevent the PMO from acting in so presidential a manner. Moreover, when the PMO itself has been taken over by the semi-secret organisation of the Rashtriya Swayamsevak Sangh (RSS), which then brings its own mode of functioning to this high office, the question arises whether or not the PMO alone should continue to have sole authority over decision-making on the nuclear issue. Should there not be an autonomous agency for this critical area of decision-making that is equally answerable to the executive, the legislature and the judiciary? There needs to be a debate, in Parliament and outside Parliament, as to the kind of mechanisms we require which guarantee operational secrecy but decision-making transparency on issues of basic national policy?

Nor can the argument be made that such precipitate action was necessary in view of some immediate foreign provocation. China had taken no steps in recent years and even decades that posed any threat to Indian security. Pakistan had not carried out any nuclear tests, and its 'conventional' intervention in Indian domestic affairs, as in Kashmir and Punjab, should be dealt with through 'conventional' and political means. Meanwhile, India already has enough technology, as the BJP government itself said, to match Pakistan's recent missile test, so that 'Pokhran' simply cannot be presented as a response to 'Ghauri'.

Nor have these tests any element of anti-imperialist nationalism. The BJP has not said that these were designed against the US nuclear threat in the Pacific–Indian Ocean zones. It has targeted neighbours, instead. Far from securing us against imperialist threats, this action will lead to an unnecessary, expensive, dangerous and unethical arms race in Asia, will sabotage the South Asian Association for Regional Cooperation (SAARC) within South Asia, and will negate the process of normalisation with China. In so doing, the tests indeed play into the hands of imperialists who are keen to keep Asia divided and have all of us squander our resources on weapons of destruction instead of mutual, regional cooperation that can free us from imperialist pressure.

In this sense, of making the people of Asia fight each other, the BJP is acting today in imperialist interest as the RSS, through its communalism, used to undermine the national struggle against British colonialism.

The crucial reason why the BJP government needs to be confronted has to do, however, not so much with external relations as with what these explosions have wrought inside the country. The combination of (a) the show of Indian might and independence in decision-making, (b) the inviting and defying of US sanctions, and (c) the ability to act decisively despite coalition constraints, has enabled the BJP to pick up the mantle of anti-imperialism in the tradition of the National Movement. This is a crucial moment in our history because the issue of anti-imperialism has hounded the RSS throughout its existence. Everyone knows—and therefore the BJP and the US also know—that defiance of imperialism is a basic ingredient in Indian nationalism. For the BJP to graduate from 'Hindu' nationalism to 'Indian' nationalism, and thus to become a nationally hegemonic power, it too must go through this baptism of fire. The real fire it will not go through, but such fires as can be simulated by organising mass frenzy and on the electronic media. For this to happen, spectacles must be organised, just as the destruction of the Babri Masjid was orchestrated essentially as a fascist spectacle.

If that spectacle paved the way for the BJP to emerge as an all-India party and eventually the ruling party, these nuclear fireworks help it cut across the Hindu/secular divide and reach out to claim the mantle of Indian nationalism as such. This will unite very broad sections of the Indian middle classes—and not only the middle classes—whatever the immediate behaviour of the stock market might be. The impression will gain ground that the BJP is the only party capable of providing India with a coherent, assertive, visionary leadership. This effect is not going to wear off in days, or weeks, or months. Only a sustained counteroffensive can prevent it from still being there 20 years from now.

The BJP had so far established its leading role in defining Indian culture and Hindu religion. Now it has made its first massive attempt to capture the high ground of anti-imperialism. In both cases, the appeal is made to atavistic feelings of aggression, in the form of a promise to redeem honour. Meanwhile, if the Ayodhya movement redefined the role of Ram in Indian belief systems as an all-India deity and warrior-prince, the Pokhran explosions were deliberately scheduled on Buddha Purnima and were nicknamed 'Buddha Smiles Again'; if Ambedkarites have their anti-caste Buddha, Hindutva will have its own Buddha who will bless nuclear weapons for the greater glory of Bharat Mata. These fantastic re-writings of the Indian past must not be dismissed simply as ludicrous, which of course they are. It is precisely the evocative power of this irrationality that is the most frightening, the most dangerous part; such are the raw materials of which fascist victories are made.

So powerful, in fact, is the lure of this mob psychology that the Congress as well as much of what remains of the United Front have already fallen in line. A story is doing the rounds that what Vajpayee accomplished was only what P.V. Narasimha Rao had attempted. In his TV appearance, Jaipal Reddy tried hard to make out that the BJP was only taking credit for an event that had been prepared by the U.F. Former Prime Minister Deve Gowda has pronounced that the explosions are 'necessary' for Indian security. Arjun Singh, the chief custodian of Congress secularism, has declared that the tests were not at all designed to enhance the political prestige of the BJP. Many more statements of this kind can be expected as time goes by.

In a quick poll of 1,007 adults in six metropolitan cities conducted in the wake of the explosions, the IMRB found support for them among 91 per cent of the respondents. The cynics of the Congress and the U.F. are responding to this jingoistic consensus that BJP has crafted. In the process, we are witnessing a sea-change in public discourse. The BJP has, in reality, departed from the national consensus on nuclear policy as it was first formulated in Nehru's days and was then adjusted in the early 1970s. But the indecent haste of the Congress and U.F. stalwarts to take credit for what the BJP has wrought is creating the impression that the Vajpayee government has only implemented what has been Indian policy all along.

These are the most dangerous of times. The whole process of coalition-making that brought the BJP to power has shown that not only is Congress secularism merely pragmatic, but so has been the secularism of majority of the non-Left political formations in the country. Most of them can easily move into an equally pragmatic communalism, as the Trinamul Congress is now showing. Even in that arena, the Left is in reality rather isolated but secularism itself has been such a fundamental value in India that most of these pragmatic communalists dare not confess to their ideological shifts even as they join up with the BJP. Thanks to this ambiguity, the Left has a relatively wider area of manoeuvre in anti-communal politics.

In the wake of these hawkish tests, the extent of collaboration among virtually all the non-Left parties is far greater and much more openly professed. The Left, therefore, has a much narrower room for mano-euvre, much more squarely in danger of being called 'anti-national' and being made, in the foreseeable future, an object of full-scale repression on the charge that it has 'extra-territorial loyalty'. The spectre of the repressions that took place in the wake of the Sino-Indian War of 1962 now haunts the land, less than two months into the BJP government. And yet, the Left will lose its very raison d'être if it does not differentiate itself from the kind of national chauvinism that is represented by the BJP's designs in the nuclear arena, and if it does not define for itself and the nation, a nationalism different, more compre-hensive, more fundamentally anti-imperialist than the kind that the BJP will predictably unleash on the question of US sanctions. The Left has to move with the greatest of caution but move it must. On the nuclear issue itself, three things need to be done.

Firstly, all the secular, anti-communal and anti-fascist forces should come together on the platform that in acting in a unilateral, irresponsible and chauvinist manner which threatens regional peace, the Vajpayee government has lost the right to rule and must therefore resign.

Secondly, on the question of sanctions, all patriotic forces have to take the position that no foreigner has the right to threaten us with economic strangulation. But this point has to be made alongside the equally fundamental points that (a) the BJP's irresponsible behaviour has brought upon us not only American sanctions but also ridicule from peace-loving peoples worldwide, and (b) the American sanctions are themselves a bargaining position and a prelude in the formation of a long-term Indo–US axis in Asia.

Thirdly, public discussions and hearings should be organised in as many places as possible, involving eminent scientists, the more sane military experts, some sensible politicians, social scientists, philo-sophers, jurists, economists and political activists of various kinds, to consider various issues of nuclear power in the drastically altered situa-tion that now exists. The arbitrary nature of the PMO's powers should be part of this discussion. Similarly, we need a nationwide discussion and perhaps even an independent commission, to investigate issues of nuclear safety and the environmental and ecological costs involved in adopting this nuclear road. After all, Indian citizens do live even in Pokhran. In the process, the Reds may learn to be a little more Green and the Greens a bit more Red. Initiatives of this kind can help break the initial isolation that is inevitable in opposing the BJP's jingoism.

But isolation on the nuclear issue can be broken most effectively only if this issue, for all the gravity it has, is not addressed in isolation. The connection must be made with the communal agenda, with the fact that a step of this magnitude has been taken purely for the greater glory of the RSS, and that the consensus behind Vajpayee's nuclear policy amounts to a consensus behind Hindutva. Equally strongly, the point needs to be made that this act of bogus anti-imperialism is designed to facilitate the ability of the Hindutva forces to implement a programme of liberalisation and privatisation far more drastic than anything P. Chidambaram was able to implement or even envision. If the consensus built on nuclear sabre-rattling is not broken, public properties shall be sold to private capital more or less in the style of Russia, because after a swadeshi nuclear bomb there need be no other swadeshi.

This essay first appeared in *Frontline*, May 23–June 5, 1998.

The Climber's Case

J. SRI RAMAN

What happened on May 11, 1998, was more than a series of Indian nuclear blasts in a desert test range. Pokhran was a package. It was an explosion with a range of extra-radioactive fallouts: political, economic, and socio-cultural. Consequently, every response to the event, too, was an integrated whole. Especially those that sought to convey a message. The response of the media was no exception. A response that, by its approval or disapproval of the tests, sought to mould public opinion.

There is little need for any but the ludicrously over-academic to ascertain who won the media vote: the ayes loudly and clearly outnumbered the nays. It would be more interesting and instructive to see how exactly the response performed its role, how the media helped manage or manipulate opinion in favour of Pokhran and all that it stood for, to bring out the method behind the media-Pokhran that has been blasting away since that mid-summer newsbreak.

It would be especially useful to examine the response from within the elite section of the English-language press, or what are known as national newspapers. And, for two reasons. In the first place, these newspapers continue to hold a pre-eminent place among the media, including the electronic, as opinion-setters. Directly or derivatively, they wield considerable influence over not only public opinion but also opinion-makers, and not only opinion-makers but policy makers as well.

Second, they do it with a significant difference. Their pro-bomb response was free from the crudities of the fellow-campaigners in the plebian sections of the print media. It illustrated a new strategy to market an old, even stale message.

It was not the unabashed jingoism of the majoritarian kind. It, actually, took pains to take an ostensibly anti-jingoist stance. It did not greet the blasts, for example, with screaming headlines of 'Jai Shri Ram', once a pious chant and now a communal war-cry heard in hundreds of streets in the wake of the tests. It even went out of its way to warn against such expressions of euphoria. It spoke to, and for, those who shared the sentiment but shied away from the slogans.

It spoke to, and for, a broadened constituency of a conglomerate of political forces associated with the idea of an Indian, if not a Hindu, bomb. Especially the recent addition to the following, the section that tried to see the original base as the lunatic fringe of a larger camp. The urban segment, particularly from the new generation, of an ultra-nationalist camp.

The audience made for a particular pro-bomb argument. For a package to answer the package that was Pokhran. The argument began by claiming legitimacy for the tests and what they entailed. And, it went on to question not just the logic but the legitimacy of any opposition to them.

It claimed legitimacy for Pokhran and the policy it announced by claiming a national consensus in its favour. It did so despite known facts to the contrary: the coalition in power had not sought and secured a vote on the issue; there was no post-Pokhran verdict of a consensual kind, either electoral or parliamentary, on the question; the blasts only implemented an item on the National Agenda of Governance adopted by the coalition partners post elections. There, certainly, had been no national debate on the subject. At the same time, however, the argument claimed also that the blasts were a departure from the past. The claim was that courage had been found at last to act upon a consensus that was already and always there. Pokhran was projected as a symbol of a brave new political order, a brave new leadership, and a brave new India. This, even as it was equated with patriotism of a stale stereotype.

An equally, if not even more, unarmed part of the argument was that Pokhran represented a triumph of Indian science. Official claims in this regard—of the government in general and specifically the science establishment were unquestioningly accepted and enthusiastically endorsed as soon as they were publicised by a media that has specially prided itself on its scepticism and even cynicism. It remained eloquently silent, by and large, over an important scientific aspect of the issue—the mass-destructive character of a nuclear weapon in its diabolical dimensions that make it a concern of not pure pacifists alone. The claimed success of Indian science was equated, above all, with a nationalism that was no different from nuclear militarism.

The claim of a pro-bomb consensus traced it back to Pokhran I of Indira Gandhi. The much-vaunted 'bold departure' was claimed to have been made, however, from an older, Nehruvian foreign policy consensus. As for the departure from India's position hitherto on the nuclear issue in the international arena, it was hailed as an abandonment of hypocrisy, ambiguity, etc. It was a no-nonsense nationalism, of which the blasts were supposed to have given the world notice.

The theme was enlarged and embellished by dwelling on the departure with respect to one particular detail: India vis-à-vis the Third World. Of the many strands woven into the pro-Pokhran fabric, none testified more to skill of a cynical kind. It was a two-phased tactic: first, damn the Third World; second, damn the anti-nuclear-weapon campaign by identifying it with the Third World. Opponents of Pokhran thus became pleaders for perpetuating India's place among the wretched of the earth writhing under despots and its membership of the club of the world's poor.

Conversely, Pokhran was projected as a passport to a higher world status. It spelt something like an upward national mobility. Join the nuclear club, and you will jump straight out of the Third World—that was the mantra of this media. Never mind about the state of the nation's economy, especially the majority of its people. And, who cared about the fate of the erstwhile fraternity of the destitute, with whom we ceased to have anything in common that historic moment of May?

Similar was the strand of the argument related to the Left. Here, too, it was a two-step tactic: Damn the Left, first, for double standards on the issue; and, then, damn the anti-nuclear-weapon campaign by identifying it with the Left and the Left alone. What about the Chinese bomb; how about the Soviet bomb, they would chortle, and the prosecution rested the case as though the opponents of Pokhran were not opposed to nuclear weaponisation elsewhere and everywhere.

The media was divided on the next step of nuclear diplomacy. A section was, loudly and clearly, for India signing the Comprehensive

Test Ban Treaty unconditionally to press and preserve the advantage gained with Pokhran; another was for conditional signing of the CTBT; and a third was undecided about how to justify an abrupt about-turn on the treaty, considering that the political camp of Pokhran, too, had till recently opposed it as discriminatory. But, all of them were agreed on one point (or one and a half points!): that the blasts and the emergence of India as a nuclear-weapon state somehow bettered the prospect of global nuclear disarmament (and that the CTBT would not stall its further development as such a state).

It is not as if even individual members of this media spoke in one voice. Each one of them, in fact, allowed space for other opinions, but little doubt was left that these represented the 'other' viewpoint. The apparently liberal indulgence of dissent made the main argument more acceptable and thus added to the legitimisation of Pokhran.

This broad review is based on a representative sample of such opinion in this section of the media—*Indian Express* (mainly) and *The Pioneer* among daily newspapers and *India Today* among the periodicals. Following are illustrations, which speak for themselves and will need comment only to reinforce the above points about a specially influential media response.

Indian Express of May 12, on the morrow of Pokhran, greeted its readers with a frontpage editorial, signed by Chief Editor Shekhar Gupta, headlined 'Road to Resurgence'. Outlining the argument to be pursued in the coming days, it opened with an unequivocal accolade: 'The triple test at Pokhran ends three decades of nuclear debate, self-denial and fence-sitting. Several times in recent years Indian leadership—irrespective of party affiliation in an era of shifting coalitions—came close to taking the plunge. It is just as well that this momentous step has been taken by leaders who have always believed in unabashed and unambiguous nuclearisation. More reassuring, even for those who have been arguing for restraint and ambiguity, is the fact that these leaders also enjoy an impeccable reputation in terms of personal integrity and national commitment. It is, therefore, reasonable to presume that they have chosen to make so bold a departure from the past after a great deal of deliberation as to what is best for India's interests. The scientific wherewithal has been there for several years now. The only thing that lacked was the trigger device of political will and the kind of supreme confidence that enables leaders to move away from the familiar, well-trodden path and thereby find themselves a place in history.'

Clearly recognisable are quite a few of the ingredients of the recipe of nuclear weaponisation offered as the media response to Pokharan. More than lightly touched upon was the theme of a tacit consensus as also of the bold departure. Not only the bravery of the new leadership but the other qualities it was believed to possess were presented as an incontestable line of argument. Asserted was the no-frill character of a pro-Pokhran nationalism that was no admirer of 'ambiguity' and no respecter of restraint.

The editorial pursued the theme by recalling and ridiculing the claim made after Pokhran I that it was a 'peaceful nuclear explosion'. 'The world saw it, by and large, as an expression of weakness and hypocrisy.' With apparently unconscious irony, it added: 'India is prepared with a diplomatic wet blanket to contain the fallout by offering to be a willing and active player in the international nuclear arms control regime. The difference now is that India seeks to play the game as a nuclear weapon power. This is the end of ambiguity and hypocrisy.' The postulate here was India's post-Pokhran preparedness to sign the CTBT. The exercise was not intended as 'an end of ambiguity and hypocrisy', as we shall see.

Followed the 'scientific-triumph' strand, with a special bravo for a bureaucracy's supposed success in keeping an official secret: 'This is a time for popular euphoria and celebration. And celebrate we must as this success demonstrates to the world a remarkable scientific capability built during a quarter century of international technology transfer restrictions. It is also a cause for reassurance that even in these cynical times when we tend to believe so easily that any fellow-Indian's loyalties are purchaseable for a few dollars, a scholarship or a green card the establishment has managed to keep such a major move a secret despite the snooping that extends from the Capital's cocktail circuit to outer space.' (Whether the US non-detection of the tests, so alluded to, was due to the alleged negligibility of the yield or any other factor was a matter that the media did not choose to investigate.)

The editorial added: 'But this is also a time for reflecting where we go from here . . . Pokhran II is like a jump start to India's dormant, frozen spirit. But, it won't, by itself, be a short-cut to the place India wishes, and desires to have on the international stage. It is now up to Vajpayee and Advani to moderate the euphoria, contain the diplomatic fallout and exploit the advantage they have given themselves, and India by creating this new mood of resurgence.' With certain other steps, it was implied, Pokhran would indeed be a short-cut to a higher world status for the country.

In the same issue, on the editorial page, was carried a regular editorial as well on the event, under a double-decker headline: 'End of uncertainty: Now the world must react realistically to Pokhran.' It started by reiterating that Pokhran represented at once a consensus and a radical break: '. . .Twenty-four years ago, it (India) had shown a similar resolve with the first tests of a fission device. No Indian is complaining now—no institutional voice can be heard, at least. It was the same story in Indira Gandhi's day. No wing of ruling power structure, from the legislatures to the corporate sector, voiced serious objections to the test. In the intervening years, there has been a wide-ranging debate in legislatures, talk-shops and the media, and an unequivocal, institutional consensus has emerged. The government has merely used this consensus to initiate a change in policy direction, to break with traditional patterns of thought which were created by the ghost of Congress past.' The conclusion about no Indian complaint was reached within twelve hours of the tests.

The editorial then warmed to what was to become a favourite theme with the entire pro-Pokhran fraternity of these high echelons—the tests as something that finally set India apart from the Third World identified in turn with some widely unloved members: '. . .the tests should not be seen as the expression of a single despot's will . . . (like) . . . the belligerent initiatives of Libya and Iraq. Neither can it be dealt with by an air-strike on a presidential palace.' This was addressed, evidently, to the West.

Interestingly, the editorial added: '. . .The immediate objective of the tests is obvious: daring Pakistan to show whether it has comparable capability and end the uncertainty of the last few weeks. But, the long-term objective is to tell the world that the time for unqualified restraint is over. India is no longer satisfied with its subaltern role of being a lonely, unsung campaigner against the CTBT . . .' Pakistan was to answer the question soon, and the paper to take up a campaign for the CTBT.

It did so the very next day. In an article under the double-decker headline, 'Burdens of the nuclear state: The morning after' in his column National Interest, Shekhar Gupta insisted: 'The signals that go out from India now need to reflect the mind of a mature, self-assured and powerful nation and not the reaction of a defensive, jingoistic and shaky establishment.' The reaction, that is, to the idea of signing the CTBT. The column wanted a break with the national consensus hitherto on this issue. Unconscious irony made its appearance again in the subsequent observation: 'The applause for the induction (in Sri Lanka) of the IPKF (Indian Peace-Keeping Force), to begin with, was unanimous and chorus-like, as has by now become the norm when it comes to national security issues.' With the column urging a departure from the beaten track, the opportunity for Third World-bashing of a specific style was not allowed to go unused: 'The world by and large is not pleased with us. Today, there isn't even the old Third World lobby of drumbeaters unless a Castro, Gaddafi or Saddam decides to embarrass us by rising in our support.' (Nelson Mandela did not exactly rise in India's support at the latest non-aligned summit, but that did appear to distinctly embarrass the government and its leadership.)

The editorial of the day was even more explicit. Its headline urged: 'Seize the day Forget national ego, move on to CTBT'. Only a day after the event, the paper said: 'Now that the self-congratulatory euphoria occasioned by the nuclear tests has begun to fade, the government must immediately get down to the job of dealing with the fallout.' The editorial euphoria, however, lingered on: '. . .the tests have raised India to a new level where it can look upon these nations (of the West) as its peers, and so see that its point of view gets a decent hearing.'

Noting that the government had 'announced its willingness to subscribe to certain elements of the treaty', the editorial said: 'So far, no signatory has chosen to treat the CTBT as a negotiable instrument. . . . India should follow the example set by China and France and sign unconditionally.' Reason? 'The test explosions have given it (India) a database that should preclude the need for further testing, except in computer stimulations.' The claim was to become a key element of the argument.

Two further tests took place on May 13. The editorial of May 14 said: 'It seems almost certain that the government wants to go ahead and sign the Comprehensive Test Ban Treaty—when it is good and ready. That is, after completing its test programme, which it says now is the case. . .'

An editorial on May 19 was devoted to the theme of 'scientific triumph' alone. It deserves to be quoted at length for its unquestioning acceptance of official claims and for its equation of nuclear science with nuclear militarism. Under the headline 'Scientific breakthrough:

In complete nuclear weaponisation', it said: 'Dr. A.P.J. Abdul Kalam's statement that 'nuclear weaponisation is complete' is supported by the other assertions made by him and his colleagues at a press conference. ... There can be no doubt ... that India's scientists have the capability to produce (the) hydrogen bomb with destructive forces several fold higher than the fission bomb which laid Hiroshima and Nagasaki waste.

'. . . the Prithvi and Agni missiles can be armed with nuclear warheads ... critical data have been obtained to enable the scientists to continue working on refining various types and sizes of nuclear weapons in the laboratory and on computers.

'. . . India's nuclear chiefs chose on one of their rare days in the sun to reassure the world that the fearsome power at their fingertips is intended only to secure India from threat, not to threaten anyone.

'Dr. Kalam . . . said the command and control system was being given a new direction . . . In furtherance of this, the Defence Ministry took charge over the weekend of the Bhabha Atomic Research Centre and the Defence Research and Development Organisation of another key nuclear research and development establishment. . .'

There was a return to the 'Third World' theme on May 27. The article in the National Interest column of the day, headlined 'Self-pity of the nuclear state: Stop eating enriched grass', warned against the folly of seeking support in these quarters. Upward national mobility was stated as the objective of the tests: '... only to an inferiorly complexed mind steeped in Nehruvian hypocrisy would a Third World bomb sound like a sexy new idea. Poor nations acquire nukes to find a short-cut out of the Third World. At least that's what we have been told over the decades by the pro-bomb lobby. Here we want to use ours to confirm our status as the leader of the world's wretched.'

On May 28, Pakistan responded with its own nuclear tests in the Chagai range. The paper's response was subdued. 'If May 11 was the test of India's will', it said in the next day's editorial, 'this is now a test of its wisdom'. The event did not affect the argument significantly: especially since the official claim that the Pakistani tests were a less complete series than India's was accepted.

The position on the CTBT was modified as days passed, with the government showing no readiness to sign it immediately and uncondi-tionally. The headline of an editorial of July 7 said it: 'Get subtle: Don't use a sledgehammer on the CTBT.' Followed a rephrasing of the position, with its own kind of ambiguity and, yes, hypocrisy: 'As far as accepting treaty constraints on testing are concerned, there need be no hesitation on technical grounds. Scientists from the Atomic Energy Commission and the Defence Research and Development Organisation have said they are confident about the results of the five tests in May and the option now available of sub-critical and computer testing which the CTBT permits. Some experts like Arundhati Ghosh, India's former chief negotiator at Geneva, have expressed qualms about the CTBT verification process. That should be re-examined for possible problems. Politically, it is a more complex matter. The government is going to have to work hard at carrying public opinion along with it. Most people have been led to believe that the treaty is discriminatory and flawed. The government will have to explain why the discriminatory aspects no longer hold after India acquired the capabilities of nuclear powers.' Arundhati Ghosh's objection to the continuing discriminatory character of the treaty against countries that remain non-nuclear was ignored.

The fact, actually, did not matter, according to the argument. This was made clear again in an article headlined, 'India's dilemma: CTBT vs ignorance' by Manvendra Singh in a column named Strategic Stance. The article carried the 'Third World'-bashing to a new level of crudity: '. . .why should the country continue to cry itself hoarse that the CTBT is discriminatory? The treaty certainly does not enable, say Togo, to conduct nuclear experiments, so in that sense it does discriminate against that paragon of non-alignment. But then Togo has not conducted nuclear experiments, and so it does not have the wherewithal to continue the testing programme using supercomputers and micronukes. Is that something with which India should be exercised to an order so as to label probably the most comprehensive international nuclear arrangement as discriminatory?. . . On this score, India has always been isolated by this delightful club of the destitute.' It is only a climber of a country that can affect such contempt for, and a suddenly higher status than, its economic peers just because it has made a bomb.

But, one had to wait till August 24 (after the first post-Pokhran Hiroshima anniversary) for the most unashamed statement of the argument in all its mind-boggling mindlessness. Under the headline 'Left out of history: Think of national interest', the day's main editorial declaimed: 'See what has happened? The tears of the golden jubilee celebrations (sic) of Nagasaki have not yet dried on third-world cheeks. And the children of Baghdad have not yet got their third meal or vitamin

C tablets, despite good brother Saddam's best humanitarian efforts. Not to speak of the proletarian struggle of the beloved comrades of Havana and Pyongyang. Now see, he has struck again—the imperialist. So impeach him—right now. Professional third-worldists and rusted anti-imperialists are out in the marketplace of dead ideas, wailing over the American aerial atrocities against humanity . . . they are not talking about Osama Bin Laden, who is, after all, a defender of faith and a campaigner against white horror. Their subject of complaint is the American President, who, symbolically, is a living negation of everything that is third-worldist or moral. . .'

The editorial went on to deliver the coup de grace: 'The imperialist knows quite a deal about national interest. The anti-imperialist (or the third-worldist) lives in a space outside history—or the nation. Even Nelson Mandela—yes, the Mandela of every third-worldist—has not subordinated his national interest to the rhetoric of struggle and liberation. But there are quite a few Indians who continue to live in the fairytale world of imperialist evil and third-world idealism. That is what happens when fossilised minds confront the new world where every war, every bomb, is an assertion of national interest. India has suffered the burden of borrowed jargons for long. When India wakes up, only dead minds protest.'

It is difficult to decide which is more remarkable: the way contempt for the world's poor (and Hiroshima's victims) is combined with communalism and a soft corner for Bill Clinton (along with a special pleading for the US), or the way bombs, wars and conflicts of national interests are projected as signs of a brave new world.

On to *The Pioneer,* for a more cursory review (so as not to cover the same ground all over again). The immediate response of the paper was essentially the same, though expressed in more euphoric terms. The headline of the frontpage editorial of May 12, signed by Editor Chandan Mitra, said it all: 'Explosion of self-esteem'.

On the CTBT, the paper took a less categorical line, in recognition of the problem of reconciling India's signing of the treaty to the country's past position on it in international fora.

The editorial page has, since the tests, played host to a variety of views on the issue, but the balance of opinion expressed has without doubt been in favour of the bomb. And, the expression hardly suffered from any excessive restraint. Below are just a couple of the more quotable verbal missiles aimed at the anti-nuclear camp in these columns.

From an article headlined, 'Full steam ahead, damn the torpedoes' by M.N. Buch (June 3): 'Unfortunately, we have a number of anti-national do-gooders who have decried the fact that India is now in a position to defend itself. Their constant refrain is that instead of building bombs we should build schools. I was recently in Lucknow where I had the opportunity of observing that icon and messiah of Dalits, Ms Mayawati. Rs 10 crore have been wasted on a granite pillar in Parivartan Chowk. In Ambedkar Nagar, Rs 25 crore have been spent on a VIP guest house, Rs 200 crore on the building of a training centre for scheduled caste candidates for civil services (faculty and educational aids are missing), approximately Rs 250 crore will be spent on a statue of Dr Ambedkar. . . . Neither Kuldip Nayar, nor Praful Bidwai nor Medha Patkar (has) ever questioned the wastage of money. . . The cacophony almost convinces one that these people would be quite happy to see India destroyed in a war by Pakistan. What breed of Indians are these?'

Only someone with no idea at all of the cost of nuclear weaponisation could compare it with the instances of 'wastage' mentioned. It must be added that this section of the elite media did not make any effort either to calculate the cost. The question was ignored as though it were inconsequential.

Popular periodicals in general rely more on reports to make their point. *India Today*, in its special issue of May 25, recorded the moment in rapturous terms:

'For the six men who assembled in the sitting room of the prime minister's official residence at Race Course Road that hot Monday afternoon, it was a tense wait. As three simultaneous nuclear explosions rocked the scorching sands of the Pokhran test range in the Rajasthan desert at 3.45 p.m., the only sound they heard was the purring of an air-conditioner. The Prime Minister's principal secretary Brajesh Mishra lifted the receiver hesitantly to hear an excited voice cry, 'Done!'

'Putting the caller on hold, Mishra re-entered the room. Seeing his expression, Prime Minister Vajpayee, Home Minister L.K. Advani, Defence Minister George Fernandes, Finance Minister Yashwant Sinha and Planning Commission Deputy Chairman Jaswant Singh could barely control their feelings. Advani was seen wiping away his tears. Picking up the receiver, Vajpayee, in an emotion-choked voice, thanked the two scientists who made it happen—Department of Atomic Energy (DAE) chief R. Chidambaram and head of the Defence Research and Development Organisation (DRDO), Abdul Kalam.'

There were no dry eyes among the readers, one is tempted to add.

The June 1 issue (with the cover story on Hawkish India and a tricolour hawk on the cover) dealt with the hard-headed nationalism that Pokhran was supposed to have given notice of.

From the Editor-in-Chief, a regular letter to the readers from Aroon Purie, said: 'Lord Palmerstone, a former British prime minister and a noted nationalist, once said: "A country does not have permanent friends, only permanent interests." It is a philosophy India's BJP-led government would undoubtedly approve of. Last fortnight's nuclear tests may not have won it too many friends abroad. An unruffled government, however, is convinced it is acting in the national interest.'

It added: 'For decades, India's foreign policy was based on conciliation. The nuclear test have radically altered that. With India adopting an aggressive posture. The message is obvious: a nation ignored must now be noticed. . .'

The cover story said: 'The Pokhran tests have radically redefined India's foreign policy. It is now seen as a nation pursuing its interests aggressively, discarding its self-righteous halo.'

A report on the Prime Minister's visit to the Pokharan site declared: 'For once, his eloquence wasn't called for. Braving the desert heat . . . Prime Minister Atal Behari Vajpayee stood at the edge of the crater caused by India's recent nuclear blasts in Pokhran and simply flashed the 'V' sign. That was vocal enough. In the world of diplomacy, Henry Kissinger observes, a loaded gun is more potent than a legal brief. Or, even speech.'

Interesting light was thrown, in the same issue, on how the media was won by (Editor) Prabhu Chawla. In an article headlined 'Vajpayee's blitzkrieg Spin doctors work overtime to give the PM a facelift', in his column Race Course Road. Chawla said: '. . .the sudden avalanche of press briefings and selective leaks last week by mandarins of the Prime Minister's Office (PMO) have jaded even the ever-hungry journalistic palate. Rarely in recent times have scribes covering the PMO and the Ministry of External Affairs been wined and dined in the manner that the movers and shakers of the BJP-led coalition have been doing. The sumptuous meals were accompanied by an overdose of India's nuclear case. . . . The hidden agenda behind this excessive interaction with the fourth estate: to change Atal Behari Vajpayee's image from that of an indecisive prime minister to an assertive chief executive. . . .'

The column talked of a committed PMO and a Clinton-style media management: 'Vajpayee has drafted a highly motivated group to project him and protect the government . . . so you have a Rose Garden-style press meet venue on the lush lawns at 7 Race Course Road, complete with a teak rostrum, behind which the tricolour is artfully draped. For the first time, the prime minister has put together a team which comprises people with ideological commitment to the ruling party. . .'

With good results, concluded the article. 'If excessive media blitz-krieg was aimed at neutralising an orchestrated anti-government senti-ment, the crack PMO team did deliver handsomely. Within a week, most Indian newspapers and fringe armchair intellectuals were bend-ing over backwards in joining the jingoistic chorus.'

And, jingoism finds as odious an illustration as any in (Deputy Editor) Swapan Dasgupta's column 'The Usual Suspects' in the same issue. The article under the headline, 'The Steeling of India Celebrations over, time to win the psychological war' projects the opponents of Pokhran as quislings collaborating with the nation's external enemies.

'. . .For the avant-garde minusculity,' the article said, 'this is the high noon of contrariness. It is an "obscenity", decries academic Shiv Visvanathan on the Internet, "the new Indian self violates . . . my emo-tion of being Indian". The N-tests have "lowered India's global stature and (are) likely to cause the people serious economic hardship", activist Praful Bidwai informs Pakistani readers of *Dawn*. . .'

The Pokhran patriotism could not quietly let such things pass. The article added: '. . .The BJP machinery is formidable, but its leverage over the centres of intellectual power in the country is nominal. The state-funded, left-leaning edifice created by Indira Gandhi in the early 1970s is disoriented, but firmly intact. Now, bereft of Marxist susten-ance, it is shifting its gaze (to the US) . . . the escalating campaign to denigrate India's nuclear achievement is, for example, strongly net-worked to US think-tanks and institutes. The clout of the comprador intelligentsia could have been glossed over if India had no overpowering ambition to be counted on the world stage. Today's agenda calls for the active nurturing of a new intelligentsia committed to the post-nuclear resurgence.'

The column could not have kept silent over the observance of the Hiroshima Day on August 6 with an anti-Pokhran thrust in India. Under the headline, 'Basu's Red Republic: Does India have any juris-diction over West Bengal?' (dealing with different issues altogether), it treated the occasion as one of importance to the Left alone:

'When a US Air Force plane nuked Hiroshima . . . Josef Stalin was both angry and jubilant. Angry because he didn't have the latest weapon of mass destruction and jubilant because the devastation gave him the opportunity to grab some of imperial Japan's territory. This, of course, is history, a history that the lost intelligentsia, now dancing attendance to India's left, is anxious to gloss over. Selective indignation and spurious moralising were, after all, at the heart of last week's Hiroshima Day that so enthralled the editors of *Star News*.'

To sum up. This section of the media sought to sell Pokhran as a package of special appeal to its specific audience. It did so by claiming the tests to be based on a national consensus as well as a break with the past. It did so in the name of Indian science and nationalism of a new, ruthless realpolitik. It did so by presenting Pokhran as a passport to an elevated world status for India. It did so by ignoring the economic implications of nuclear weaponisation almost in their entirety. It sought to damn the anti-Pokhran camp by identifying it with Leftism and 'Third-Worldism' and damning both.

To repeat a point already made, the above is only a broad review based on a roughly representative sample. Readers are most welcome to bring to my notice aspects of the subject that may have been missed here.

Nostrums of Nuclearism

K. VENKATARAMANAN

In May 1982, a US official sent a memorandum for the President's consideration, advocating a 'concerted media blitz' as a response to the anti-nuclear challenge. According to Robert Jay Lifton and Richard Falk, the memorandum analysed the anti-nuclear movement as one consisting of 'such perennial elements as the old-line pacifists, environmentalists, the disaffected left, and various communist elements' but admitted that there was also participation on an increasing scale in the US of the churches, the 'loyal opposition' and, most importantly, 'the unpoliticised public'.[1]

Not only does this episode show how difficult nuclear weapon policy-makers find it to comprehend, not to speak of countenancing, dissent. It also underscores their recognition of the potentially tremendous capacity of the media to influence collective thinking on issues that require a wide debate, if not the scope for it to spread the kind of awareness that it takes to reverse the phenomenon of nuclearism.

Sixteen years later, in May 1998, India and Pakistan joined the grand hypocrisy fostered by the so-called superpowers that the possession of nuclear weapons somehow enhanced a sense of security. Barring a few exceptions, the Indian media's response to this sordid of spectacle of two neighbouring nations, both ruled by insular nationalist absolutists, playing out a politically and psychologically visible arms competition, was barely edifying. Far from exposing the illegitimacy of nuclear weaponisation, the media succumbed to the two regimes' propagandist

concerns, their vague appeal to nationalist sentiments and their successful attempts to engender the self-defeatingly ironic idea that security can be achieved only by militarist postures.

This paper seeks to document the role of popular Tamil magazines in endorsing the nuclearist syndrome, mostly uncritically, but sometimes with the accompaniment of arguments about the risks associated with nuclear weapons and feeble questions about the rationale and timing of the latest blasts and counterblasts in the subcontinent. All the journals chosen for this brief analysis have a reasonably wide circulation, with each having a niche market for itself. While the reader response to these magazines' coverage of the nuclear tests, especially in the immediate aftermath of the Pokhran vs Chagai competition, cannot be accurately assessed, it can be seen that editorial policy won over by the bomb's enchantment was by and large oriented towards furthering the nuclearist cause—by describing the tests as the ultimate achievement in science and technology, besides being a political masterstroke that ought to silence the nation's belligerent adversaries into non-action, at least for the present.

Among the mainstream magazines, it was *Kalki*, a weekly with a reputation for sobriety and restraint since the early 1940s, that unambiguously criticised the nuclear tests from day one, advancing trenchant arguments in support of its stand. *Nakkeeran*, the sensationalist tabloid too analysed the dangers of nuclearisation in an article that also gave a historical account of the development of nuclear science in India since the days of Homi Bhabha and the circumstances of Pokhran I under the supervision of H.D. Sethna.

However, major Tamil dailies led the media support regime for atomic adventurism, with the second largest circulated Tamil newspaper, *Dinamalar*, being the most outstanding example of nuclear idolatry, virtually worshipping the bomb and its makers. To be fair, the newspapers provided quality news coverage to the tests, seeking to explain with not merely news stories, but also articles, graphics and interviews the nature of the bombs, the details of the tests on both sides and the worldwide reaction to the issue. However, *Dinamalar*, which does not carry editorials, resorted to a clever mixture of headlines and display to categorise opposition to the tests as threats instigated by the United States or expressions of frustration and helplessness by countries envious of India, and to play down the economic implications of the Western sanctions.

In a highly rhetorical gesture, the daily carried an appeal on its front page (May 14, 1998) under the heading 'Let us strengthen the Prime Minister's hands,' calling upon its readers to send telegrams to Vajpayee that they whole-heartedly supported the nuclear tests and that they would stand behind him in the national effort to defeat Western sanctions. It also carried a number of interviews with young men and women, and prominently announced that Pokhran II had universal support in the country.

The most popular Tamil daily, *Dina Thanthi*, which has the largest circulation drawn from the lower and middle strata of society, provided in its well-established style, good, non-commentative coverage of the nuclear tests, but indirectly projected the tests as a major achievement, a landmark event in the country's history and essentially something that could form the foundation for national pride. In the only instance of commentative coverage, it published a frontpage cartoon, depicting Uncle Sam as venturing to give some gratuitous advice to Vajpayee even while holding a bomb himself (May 15, 1998). This lone instance sought to reinforce the propaganda that India was going ahead with the tests with great fortitude and in defiance of motivated opposition from the United States. One of its news stories (May 20) was about the mythical existence of a 'nuclear button'. It claimed that the Prime Minister had had a nuclear delivery system installed in his office so that he could launch a nuclear-tipped missile on his whim by the press of the button.

Dinamani, from the Indian Express group of publications, which caters to the elite and educated sections, gleefully supported the tests in its coverage and its editorials, but also published a few articles critical of the tests, and presented varied viewpoints about the hazards of nuclear war, the implications of a nuclear-weaponisation programme on the economy and so on. It commented in a leader on May 13 that the tests were a 'security imperative' as well as a prior requirement in the present geopolitical context for India to make a claim for permanent membership of the UN Security Council. The daily highlighted customary opinion in India about the discriminatory nature of the Nuclear Non-Proliferation Treaty and the Comprehensive Test Ban Treaty and their 'uselessness' in eliminating nuclear armaments. However, it called for a global disarmament effort. In yet another editorial on May 18, it hailed Vajpayee's leadership and said the nation was attaining 'new dimensions' under him.

The very next day, it came out with another editorial that rhapsodised over the operation codenamed 'Shakti', pointing out its 'appropriateness' for the emergence of a resurgent force in India. In the process, it also coopted the pre-nuclear-age Tamil poet Subramania Bharathi's support, quoting an extract from one of his poems to claim that his vision of a 'primal force' to protect the motherland from various evils had at last borne fruit. It betrayed no qualms about misusing a devotional song from one of the country's most catholic poets for endorsing the government's agenda of nuclear militarism.

However, with almost predictable irony, the same daily suddenly voiced concern about a possible arms race in South Asia. The occasion was, as one could expect, provided by the counterblasts of Pakistan on May 28. On May 30, *Dinamani*'s editorial titled 'Test for Peace' referred to the possible collapse of the economy if the two neighbours entered into a mad nuclear armaments race—a point that was equally valid after the Indian nuclear salvo, but which occurred to the Indian media only when Pakistan scored its equalisers. The paper also sought to distinguish the Indian bomb from the Pakistani bomb by saying India's was based on indigenous technology, while the latter was developed by using 'stolen technology'. The daily's attempts to look for means to score moral points over Pakistan was also seen in its comment that Pakistan had at last attained its 'dream of developing an Islamic bomb'.

This (probably) unconscious change in attitude towards the nuclear issue after the Pakistani tests is also perceptible in other publications, notably *Ananda Vikatan*. Its issue dated May 24, 1998, had a cover illustration symbolically saying that the tests were an occasion for great national pride. It showed an Indian commoner sitting atop the Ashok Pillar, the tricolour in hand and a triumphant smile on his face, with a photograph of a mushroom cloud in the background. The Tamil world 'vallarasu' (superpower) was printed on the illustration, with the letter 'va' being stylistically represented in the shape of a bomb, and the symbol of the atomic field sketched within it. Thus, it used multiple symbolism to glorify the tests.

The same issue also carried a cartoon representing the proverbial dove of peace as flexing its 'nuclear muscle'. On the facing page was an editorial titled 'Atom Bomb and Ahimsa'. Opening with the analogy of Buddhist monks in the Shaolin Temple mastering kung-fu, the leader sought to emphasise that a country that had adopted the Dharma Chakra as its symbol was unlikely to use the weapon except in self-defence.

It went on to claim that nobody but demons need to be afraid of the 'chakrayudha' in the hands of Maha Vishnu. It also claimed that the government would surely have considered the consequences of conducting the tests and quotes a Kural that runs: 'Think deeply before acting, but having second thoughts after the action is a matter of shame.'

On the lighter side, the issue carried an imaginary interview with Vajpayee showing him as talking only about the nuclear tests in response to a wide range of questions on contemporaneous crises and controversies, in the process, exposing a 'bomb' mindset. The cover story was a laudatory piece on the nuclear tests, but also raised questions about the timing of the tests and elicited positive replies from the establishment. IGCAR Director Placid Rodriguez and Anna University Vice-Chancellor R.M. Vasagam justified the tests and sought to answer criticism in their brief interviews.

A translation of a Hindi poem by Vajpayee with a pacifist theme was published to portray the Prime Minister as endearingly peace-loving. In an interesting side-bar, a despatch from Rajasthan said the residents of Pokhran and its surrounding villages were deeply gratified by the tests, despite 80 per cent of the huts in some places being damaged beyond repair.

In a question-and-answer column, the weekly's associate editor Madan described the tests as something akin to Vivekananda's majesty, in which saintly patience could co-exist with physical prowess. The next issue of *Ananda Vikatan* (May 31) published half-a-dozen letters praising the editorial and the cover cartoon. There were none voicing any other point of view.

The issue featured an interview with Dr. R. Chidambaram's wife and a small note credited to Dr. K. Venkatasubramanian, former of Vice-Chancellor of Pondicherry University, highlighting the 'Tamil fragrance' on Pokhran's soil—a reference to Chidambaram, Abdul Kalam and Santhanam all being Tamils. Another noteworthy feature of the issue was the publication of cartoons from various magazines, including one titled 'Rogue Elephant' published first in *The Sunday Times*, depicting India as a rogue elephant trampling the world under its feet.

The next issue (June 7) covered Pakistan's 'counterblasts' in terms exactly opposite to the its coverage of India's tests. The editorial, written in the form of a letter to 'Our Friend Pakistan', chastised the country for chronically being envious of India. Patronisingly acknowledging that 'you, too, are a great soldier', the editorial compared Pakistan to Duryodhana (after reminding the country that the character represented envy and ill-will) and concluded by saying: 'Never in history have Duryodhanas ever won.'

The accompanying cartoon depicted Pakistan as a poor family living in a small hut, with a huge bomb jutting out of its roof, and the head of the indigent family wearing a smug smile on his face. It also reproduced a cartoon from its sister publication—*Vikatan Paper*—portraying Pakistan as a drunken lout holding the bomb like a bottle and challenging the world with the words: 'Who said only you can have it, as though we can't?'

By its contemptuous portrayal of Pakistan as an undeserving holder of a nuclear weapon, the magazine presented India's nuclear tests as something inevitable and logical in the face of Pakistan–India hostility, and seemed to enjoy the ill-will between the two countries.

However, in its next issue (June 14), the magazine came out with a cartoon showing Vajpayee and Nawaz Sharif standing face-to-face and both saying, 'I am ready for talks,' while their mouths were sketched in the shape of atom bombs. It appeared to depict the hypocrisy of two nuclearised states talking the language of peace.

The most popular weekly *Kumudam* treated the Pokhran tests in a most perfunctory way initially, and the only serious comment/coverage is found in the issue dated May 28, which featured a discussion between a BJP state office-bearer and a CPI(M) leader, allotting a page each for expressing diametrically opposite views on the nuclear tests. The issue carried an editorial hailing and even worshipping the nuclear scientists and describing the tests as a major step towards national resurgence. It went on to talk about the possible adverse effects of Western sanctions and recalled that India had overcome such crises in 1965–66 and 1972.

However, the leader gave a twist to the whole issue in a concluding paragraph that spoke about the cost of India's decision to conduct the tests. 'The Prime Minister is duty-bound to explain what the dire necessity is now to conduct the test, knowing that India will have to pay heavily for it,' it concluded. An accompanying cartoon depicted the bomb as Vajpayee's weapon to outwit his troublesome alliance partners, while a mock-biodata of the Prime Minister ended with the suggestion that what he required immediately were not bombs, but plans for the nation.

The magazine's highly popular question-and-answer column (June 4, however, imparted its editorial policy an element of ambiguity, as it spoke in unqualified terms of the tests as a positive development, one that would help 'the younger generation keep its head high.' An insightful question by a reader about India going in for the tests within a couple of days of George Fernandes describing China as 'enemy number one' elicited a detailed reply from the editors, but, strangely, the reader's attempt to contextualise the tests was ignored. Instead, the answer offered what it believed was the 'inside story'. It claimed that the decision to conduct the tests had been made even during the 13-day rule of Vajpayee in 1996, and that the government collapsed just a couple of tests before the tests were done. It claimed that Deve Gowda shot down the proposal after he took over. In 1998, it said Vajpayee had a discussion with Dr. R. Chidambaram on March 20 and subsequently a telephone talk with Dr. Abdul Kalam. An invitation to Dr. Kalam to join the Cabinet, it said, was turned down. The two scientists were given the green signal on April 8—before, the magazine helpfully added, 'Amma (AIADMK leader J. Jayalalitha) began giving (the government) headaches.' And they were asked to report from time to time to Brajesh Mishra. None but these four knew about the tests until May 9, the day the ruling coalition's coordination committee met. On that day, George Fernandes was informed, while other important ministers and the three service chiefs got to know about it the next day. The President was informed a mere 24 hours before the actual tests, it said.

It proceeds to give a fanciful account of Kalam informing Brajesh Mishra over the telephone with a single word 'Done', and the Prime Minister thanking 'the two Tamils' for 'fulfilling a cherished dream'. When the news was broken to the other ministers, there was a 'flood of ecstasy' in the room. Advani wept tears of joy. 'Like Ayodhya and uniform civil code, the nuclear bomb was one of the BJP's dreams. The brahmacharis have silently fulfilled this,' the answer concluded.

The very next question was about the difference between Buddha's Smile and Shakti's victory. The answer gave an explanation about the difference between the 1974 explosion (based on nuclear fission) and the 1998 blasts (based on nuclear fusion). It also explained that the thermonuclear device (hydrogen bomb) first required a fission-induced blast to generate the minimum heat required for nuclear fusion to occur, and thereafter, the effect was enhanced 10 times when the hydrogen atoms came together to go off. There was another advantage in the tests, the reply claimed: no further explosions were necessary to enhance India's nuclear capability, as only computer-generated data were henceforth needed. 'So far, this technology was available only to the US and France, and now it is with us,' it said. To another question on the approximate cost of making an atom bomb, the magazine put it at Rs 1 crore.

An interesting question from a reader raised a simple problem: Were the tests an achievement or a misery? The reply listed two achievements. One was that the tests were a triumph of indigenous research as both Dr. Kalam and Dr. Chidambaram were educated in India and had not worked abroad. The second was that it was a 'victory for secularism', as a Hindu and a Muslim who were both educated in Christian institutions (Kalam in St Joseph's College, Tiruchi, and Chidambaram in Madras Christian College) had come together as 'Indians' to successfully conduct the tests! 'If these two achievements are borne in mind by the younger generation, India need not bow its head before anyone.'

However, Pakistan's counterblasts on May 28 brought the magazine back to its earlier sceptical approach to the idea of nuclearising the subcontinent. In a perceptive editorial (June 11), *Kumudam* said: 'The BJP government has staked the future of the younger generation in a major gamble. Where will this lead to?' It roundly denounced the 'arms race' in the region, as evidenced by Pakistan's counter-move which, it said, 'was both expected and feared'. Pointing out that the question of who turned out to be the ultimate winner or loser was irrelevant, as 'there is certainly going to be no end to a war of egos,' it expressed concern over the price that the two countries would have to pay for the nuclear tests. It also raised the economic problems concomitant on increasing spending on armaments acquisition, when there were more crying socio-economic problems that needed attention.

Significantly, the weekly also placed its finger on what it considered the exact nature of the problem. It said India's tests alone were not the immediate provocation for Pakistan to follow suit, but it was the unrestrained rhetoric resorted to by important functionaries of the government, including the Home Minister and Defence Minister, after the Pokhran tests. 'One can understand the extent to which internal pressure must have played a role in the Pakistan government embarking on the nuclear tests, despite being clearly aware that it might have to face economic sanctions, besides international odium, as a result of the tests. Our ministers' statements paved the way for such domestic pressures to build up.'

Weekly *Kumkumam* came out with an analytical article in its May 22, 1998, issue about the nuclear tests, and sought to place the issue in the context of what it called the BJP's ideological commitment to 'Greater India'. Because of this ideology, the BJP was constrained to show that India was a strong nation. It claimed that India's decision to conduct the tests were born out of both domestic compulsions and geopolitical reasons.

Elaborating on the former aspect, the article said Vajpayee wanted to extricate himself from the persistent problems within the coalition and he cleverly exploited the fact that the Indian nuclear programme was fairly advanced by then. Though it was a courageous' decision, Vajpayee had taken it primarily to send a message to the world that he was an assertive leader capable of decisive actions. It was quite possible, it said, that he had given proper consideration to the adverse fallout from the nuclear tests. 'He probably has an action plan to counter the problems arising out of the tests. He has to have it,' it said.

It ended on a sceptical note, claiming that while the 1974 tests had sent a message that India could make peaceful use of nuclear energy, the 1998 test explosions had proclaimed to the world that India could use nuclear power for 'destructive purposes' too.

The article was accompanied by the opinions of a few members of the public, all of whom welcomed and justified the tests. On the very next page, it featured three known public figure and their reactions were on expected lines. S. Gurumurthy and Cho S. Ramaswamy, both RSS sympathisers, spoke of the tests as something that was long overdue and that gave India a distinct identity as a superpower. Both of them linked a nation's standing in the world to the possession of nuclear weapons. Only the mighty were wise, they said. The third opinion was that of Tamil writer Gnani, who criticised India for violating its commitment to confining the use of nuclear energy to peaceful purposes. He also questioned the rationale of embarking on an expensive nuclear programme when basic problems of the people remained unsolved.

In a separate article, the magazine described the adverse fallout from the nuclear tests, reporting that Japan had cancelled a meeting in Tokyo to discuss an aid package to India, including an assistance of Rs 12 crore for the anti-polio programme. It also mentioned the sanctions imposed by the United States and the condemnation of England, Canada and Norway. Only Russia and France appeared sympathetic to the Indian point of view, it said, but added that even Russia had expressed concern over the development.

The issue's gossip column also devoted some space to the nuclear tests, claiming that Vajpayee was following Indira Gandhi's tactic of using issues of national interest to divert people's attention from her political problems. It sought to link the timing of the tests with the meeting of the coordination committee of the ruling coalition held on May 9, 1998.

Its June 5, 1998, issue did not have any direct comment or coverage of the issue, but it gave prominence to the release of a video album titled 'Blast' which celebrates the Pokhran tests. The article briefly describes the nationalist symbolism in the video and quotes its authors to the effect that every Indian should celebrate this great victory. In a related article on the achievements of Anna University's Crystal Growth Centre, the magazine praised its Director, Prof. Ramaswamy as one who had brought international fame to Indian science 'long before the nuclear tests'. The next issue gave a brief biographical note on Kalam and Chidambaram, but the magazine appeared to have ignored the nuclear tests by Pakistan altogether.

Among the mainstream Tamil magazines, weekly *Kalki* stands out, as it unambiguously condemned the nuclear tests and refuted all popular arguments in favour of the measure. In a lengthy and scathing editorial (May 24), it said the Pokhran success represented the Prime Minister's failure. 'It proved neither the BJP's valour nor the country's strength.' Warning that the tests might lead to a dangerous arms race with neighbouring countries, the piece also underscored the fact that the tests had enhanced the possibility of a nuclear war. It was meaningless on New Delhi's part to claim now that the country went in for the tests only to increase the 'feeling of security' among the people.

'India has now lost the moral authority to say with pride that though it had the capability to produce such weapons it had refrained from producing them in the interest of peace and global security.' It also pilloried the claim that making the bomb was a 'great scientific achievement' and wanted the nation's scientists to concentrate on more productive research ventures.

The magazine also touched on the possible radiation hazards as a result of the tests and claimed that residents of Pokhran had been afflicted by radiation in 1974. 'It is a suicidal step to stockpile a weapon that creates alarming consequences even at the time of testing.' Apart creating such dangers for the people, the government has also invited economic sanctions and market instability on itself. It ended with an exhortation to the government to sign the Comprehensive Test Ban Treaty, pointing out that in the changed circumstances, India's traditional argument that it would not sign a discriminatory document that allowed nuclearised nations to retain their nuclear armaments had lost its moral underpinnings. It concluded by observing that the 'outrage' had taken place on Buddha Purnima, a day associated with ahimsa and compassion.

Notes
[1] Robert Jay Lifton and Richard Falk, *Indefensible Weapons: The Political and Psychological Case Against Nuclearism*, (New York: Basic Books Inc., 1982).

The Uncounted Costs

B. BASKAR AND R. SURESH

Sections of India's elite had a hard time dealing with the 1998 nuclear tests. Their economic sensibilities were in conflict with their support for the bomb. This shaped the debate that took place in key sections of the English language Indian press.

The article 'The Meaning of Pokhran II' which appeared in the *Financial Express* a day after India conducted the nuclear tests extended unequivocal support to the tests. In fact the stand taken by its author R. Jagannathan is very similar to that of the front-page editorial in the *Indian Express*.

The article starts out by congratulating the government for having the '. . . guts to do what is right for itself.' It also calls the timing of the tests '. . . noteworthy because over the last few weeks the government has been the target of a sustained pressure campaign by political opposition and a pusillanimous intelligentsia to abandon its nuclear power forever.' Now we all know who these pusillanimous intellectuals are.

Nuclear weapons are also supposed to be cheaper than conventional armoury! The article debunks the economic arguments against the nuclear bomb in an almost offhand manner, by very casually stating that '. . . resources for development cannot be obtained by sacrificing security unless one wants to repeat 1962.' And this in a country where almost 40 per cent of the population still lives under abject poverty. The now familiar language of Cold War politics and deterrence is also used to buttress support for the tests. In fact the language used in this article would have made that high-priest of deterrence Henry Kissinger proud.

Routine comparisons with China are made, about how successful it was in building a nuclear arsenal and how that was used to its economic advantage in the global economic sphere. The comparisons with China make little sense since, even 20 years ago, when China first started cautiously opening up its economy, its economic position was far superior to that of India. The arguments used in this article may sound familiar as they are popular with at least a section of the vocal middle-class. The reason why these tests are hailed as a major scientific achievement is largely due to the gigantic inferiority complex that the English speaking middle-class Indian suffers, not only vis-à-vis its Western counterparts but also its Chinese counterparts. China's experience with nuclear bombs keep cropping up as its experience in playing the zero-sum game of international diplomacy is largely seen as a successful one compared to the 'hypocrisy' of Nehruvian non-alignment.

The article 'A Test of Nerves' that appeared on May 14, after the second round of tests, largely focusses on how India should brace up to the economic consequences of the tests. 'Some international commentators and domestic cry-babies have already warned us that there will be an economic price to pay for the nuclear tests, but this price is worth paying in the short and medium running view of the country's long-term objectives in conducting the tests in the first place.' This statement just about sums up the stand take by its author. A routine references to China is again made '. . . One objective is to force the international community to treat India as a responsible nuclear state, on a par with China.'

On how India should tackle the impact of sanctions, '. . .the answer is boldly and with cunning.' A greater push on the liberalisation front as a bait for foreign investors to nullify the impact of sanctions is suggested. The jury on whether the reforms started in 1991 have made any real impact on poor is still out. But the fact that even with 'impressive' results, liberalisation can leave a sizeable section of the population untouched is something which even the Fund-Bank consensus acknowledges. But, for the author of this article, there is almost a reflexive connection between more reforms and more public welfare. Now comes the 'cunning' part and easily the most dangerous part.

To quote: '. . . there is the option of subtle blackmail: India must tell the world in no uncertain terms that just because it has abstained from exporting nuclear or missile technology in the past, it cannot be assumed that it will continue to be so restrained in future.' Now, if having nuclear weapons was not bad enough, we are also supposed to 'threaten' the West with 'subtle blackmail' of exporting them to other 'rogue nations'.

In an effort to counter the loud chest-thumping and mutual back-slapping between the government and scientists, the article which appeared on May 13, 'Pokhran II: What the recoil could mean' by R. Venkata Subramanian goes about puncturing some the myths paraded by the government as certainties.

It questions the geopolitical assumptions made by the government for conducting the tests. To quote: 'It's unlikely that the explosions will not leave a ripple effect in the geo-political axis around the country, and in the event shift the balance, perhaps forever. For one, Delhi's image as a 'bully' in the region will be reinforced. Did the country need to answer Pakistan's test-firing of Ghauri missile? And if had to, was this the best way of doing it?'

The author alludes to the danger of Pakistan retaliating with a similar test at Chagai Hills, and retaliate it did. But even if it had not retaliated, China would step up its conventional arms exports to Pakistan and Pakistan will surely '. . .stoke insurgency in the much-battered Kashmir valley in the form of 'political and moral support' to separatists'. The author is also convinced that India will not be able to bear the impact of the sanctions as the economy is already in doldrums. The article ends with a quotation from Roman warrior Pyrrhus: 'One more victory like this, and we are undone.'

The response of *The Economic Times* (reports from issues dated May 12 to May 15, 1998) to the Pokhran nuclear blasts by India can be largely divided into two categories: relating to (1) security implications and (2) economic implications.

In contrast to *The Financial Express*, *The Economic Times* has taken a sober view of the nuclear tests. Though its objections did not stem out of any pacifist position and were based mainly on realpolitik considerations such as security and the impact on the economy, it did not indulge in any jingoistic muscle-flexing.

Dealing with security implications, the paper has largely questioned the wisdom of the government in going in for the nuclear tests. It holds that India had an edge over Pakistan in the conventional arms race and the nuclear tests negated whatever strengths India had. However, the reports are ambiguous on whether they support a conventional arms build-up. An article titled 'Economically dangerous delusions of grandeur' by Swaminathan S.A. Aiyar (May 12) says that rhetoric on deterrence is hollow, it only leads to mutually-assured destruction. The BJP is using the 'language of attack, not deterrence'. Nuclear bombs do not offer security, 'they merely ensure self-devastation . . . this ability to raze Pakistani cities five times over does not improve India's position over its ability to raze Lahore alone. In any event, Pakistan can raze any Indian city, so war should be unthinkable.'

Aiyar adds: 'Creating deterrence capacity is cheap and affordable. Fissile nuclear material for possible 80 small bombs has already been created and these can be assembled at short notice. But if we wish to get into a major nuclear war capacity, that is a totally a new ball game, demanding budgets that even superpowers find difficult to manage.' It is clear from the language used by the author that India has to maintain its superiority over Pakistan which he feels was neutralised by the nuclear tests.

The argument used here is not an unequivocal abandonment of nuclear weapons. It almost seems to say that unless you are a superpower economically, you have no business conducting nuclear tests.

This point is reiterated in the editorial 'Strategically irrelevant' (May 15), which talks of how the conventional superiority of India has been neutralised (as Pakistan also has the wherewithal and technology to conduct N-tests, and conduct it did). The claim made by scientists and military men that these tests enhance security is hollow, it says. The editorial adds: 'In conventional war, 40 tanks can win against 30 tanks. But in N-war, 40 bombs cannot beat 30, that merely ensures mutual reduction to radioactive rubble. If Delhi, Mumbai and Jaipur are destroyed, it will be no consolation that Karachi, Lahore and Islamabad will be destroyed five times over.'

The editorial 'How to beat the sanctions' (May 13) says: 'The triple explosions does not, in our view, improve the security of India significantly. The 1974 tests already gave India a credible deterrent and the 1998 blasts do little more to confirm that. Lots of jingoistic Indians are delighted that India has established N-biceps, but actually the news is 24-years-old. What is new is bicep-flexing which will now attract economic penalties.'

It advocates signing the Comprehensive Test Ban Treaty (CTBT) to contain the damage of sanctions, etc. Though the support for signing the CTBT is for containing the damage caused by sanctions, this argument also comes dangerously close to the one advocated by the people in power, for whom signing of the CTBT is conditional on viewing India as a mature nuclear-weapons state.

The editorial of May 14 'Damage control' says: 'In for a penny, in for a pound, in for a few kilotonnes more. Irrespective of the desirability of the three N-tests conducted by India on Monday, having conducted them, it made sense to carry out any further tests needed to complete the series thereafter. . . . By conducting another set of tests, the government has signalled that it refuses to be cowed down by the threat of sanctions by foreign powers.' The editorial says the government has to now focus on minimising damage. And work on ways of lifting sanctions using the divergent global opinions on the US-led sanctions.

In an editorial-page article on May 15, 'Closing an economic option,' Narendar Pani says: 'In a unipolar world with the increasing marginalisation of the NAM movement, India could have stepped under the nuclear umbrella of the US and focussed its energy on the economy. This would have been a sufficient and credible deterrent against Pakistan and China.' The examples of post-war Japan and Germany are quoted. The author is not unduly concerned that this would have only been achieved at a considerable loss of sovereignty on the part of India and that whatever autonomy India had under the 'hypocritical' Nehruvian worldview and NAM would have been eroded significantly.

The stories on the economic implications of Pokhran II make interesting reading. One set of stories reflects the view that the tests have led India to the brink of disaster and that sanctions and withdrawal of loans by multilateral lending agencies will cause huge damage to the economy. It also fears that the reforms process will slow down as a result of this. The other view is that the impact of sanctions will be minimal and India can absorb the shocks. This viewpoint highlights the fact that, given the nature of India's market, it will be very difficult for the Western countries to sustain sanctions as they will be the net losers. Interestingly, all the leading chambers of commerce share this viewpoint.

In his article of May 12 previously referred to, Aiyar also highlights the economic costs that have to be paid by India for conducting the tests. He says that the economic risks are high and that this will have an adverse impact on the already volatile rupee. His views on the tests and the sanctions are as follows: (a) India could have deployed nuclear weapons without testing and suffered no economic sanctions. (b) This would have enabled the BJP to reap domestic political capital without incurring serious foreign costs. (c) Pakistan may not retaliate and leave India isolated in facing the sanctions (Of course, this did not happen). (d) US investments, technology transfers, bank credits from multilateral agencies may get hit. Other foreign investments are under threat, aid from other donors are also under threat.

The article of May 13, 'US may find imposing sanctions difficult' says the same thing. India is too big a market to be ignored by the US. It says India is pinning faith on the US business lobby (which may be the net loser) to reverse sanctions. A report headlined 'WTO meet likely to be rough riding for India' says developed countries will put pressure on India to open up the services sector to foreign investments, scrapping of quantitative restrictions, etc. Under the headline 'Impact of sanctions will be limited, says industry,' another report says that leading chambers of industry and commerce such as the FICCI, ASSOCHAM, and the CII played down the impact of sanctions. Most in fact supported the blasts. They held the view that, since the sanctions would be at the inter-governmental level, private capital flows will not be affected. It will be interesting to know what the 'Bombay lobby', which has been crying foul over the entry of MNCs and demanding a level playing field, had to say on the blasts.

Since there is a broad, favourable consensus on the efficacy of economic reforms among the mainstream papers, the reason why the nuclear tests disturb these people is that it may derail the reforms process. As reforms critically hinge on the inflow of foreign capital, whether in the form of direct investments or the inflow of 'hot money', the tests are seen as a 'deterrent' to further investment flows.

The symbolism of reforms seems to be overwhelmingly in favour of the entry of MNCs in the consumer goods sector and the entry of prominent international brand names—be it Levis jeans, RayBan sunglasses or MacDonald's—has hogged disproportionate newsprint, largely biased towards the 150–200 million-strong middle class aspiring for Western standards of living. The support for weapons of a section of this middle class has its logic, therefore, as a further extension of superpower aspirations.

The Media and Nuclear Nationalism

ZAFFARULLAH KHAN

The Pakistan Federal Union of Journalists (PFUJ) and the Indian Journalists Union (IJU) were the first sister organisations in the new nuke states, India and Pakistan, to issue a joint statement urging both countries, 'not to build up tension in the subcontinent by participating in [a] senseless arms race towards the end of twentieth century when the entire world was moving towards a peace loving society, particularly when both the nations are celebrating the golden jubilee of independence.' Both bodies appealed to the political parties and governments of these countries to desist from building up nuclear weapons and other destructive arms. 'Let both the nations compete with each other in eradicating poverty and illiteracy, and attain self-sufficiency in all major fields and let us not divert our precious resources to destructive purposes,' was their main message.

Contrary to these words of rationality from the sister organisations of working journalists in India and Pakistan, the response of Pakistani print and electronic media to the nuclear tests by and large remained hawkish and it purposefully created a loud din in favour of the test option. The protagonists of non-proliferation were castigated as 'traitors' in the game of patriotism, which was well played through jingoistic rhetoric during the two weeks in between the Indian tests and the Pakistani equalisers.

Unlike the Indians, the price of going nuclear 140 million Pakistanis subsequently had to pay included being deprived of all the 21 fundamental rights guaranteed to them as citizens under the constitution. The suspended rights include freedom of speech, freedom of peaceful assembly and freedom of movement. The country's courts also could not come forward to declare any action of the state void or inconsistent with the law. There were no more safeguards available against arrest and detention, and no right to have a lawyer of choice. This midnight blast by the President was ignored by the majority amid the euphoria of nuclear tests.

Another price; the rich ones lost their foreign exchange accounts. Now the Pakistani rupee is eroding and the economy is sliding, putting question marks over the very existence and viability of the re-awakened state with its nuclear nationalism.

The rationale of the hawkish rhetoric churned out by the state-controlled electronic and private print media in Pakistan could be traced in a couple of inter-linked developments. Soon after the Indian nuclear tests, the Pakistani premier said, we can pay India back in the same coin within 24 hours. Instead of summoning an emergency session of Parliament to devise a consensus-based national response, the Prime Minister preferred to consult the owners and editors of the national press to chart out the country's response. Premier Nawaz Sharif's meeting with the editors/owners who en bloc advocated a matching response, was twice telecast on state-controlled Pakistan Television. (Only a few were silent, and only one, Mujeebur Rehman Shami, advocated prior calculation of the economic pros and cons of going nuclear.) This gesture of the press clearly conveyed that there was no space left in the newspapers for dissenting views on the nuclear issue. Hence, the minor peace lobby tried to make best use of the Internet and E-mail. These two modes of communication experienced pluralistic debate on the issue, a debate that still goes on. The total number of E-mail and Internet users in Pakistan exceeds 60,000.

Coming back to the premier-press meeting, the mainstream press embarked on a well-orchestrated campaign to create jingoistic hysteria and tried to exacerbate traditional tensions between India and Pakistan. Amid such situations, there is a practice in Pakistan that self-appointed custodians of the 'national interest' buy space in newspapers. In the wake of recent nuclear developments, a number of 'ghost writers' monopolised the newspapers' space. The state bore the cost through its numerous 'secret funds'.

The state-controlled electronic media, Pakistan Television (PTV) and Pakistan Broadcasting Corporation (PBC) also contributed its share in cultivating jingoistic chauvinism. A private company that offers the economic news bulletin *Tijarti Khabrain* on PTV aired opinions of a few independent economists and columnists, who appeared to be in support of non-proliferation just a day before the country opted to explode its nuclear devices in Chagai. Since the opinions in the said bulletin were overwhelmingly against mimicking India, the very next day the company was asked to pack up its business. However, things got settled with an unwritten agreement that in future the bomb option will be duly magnified.

Another factor that shaped the press response was the irresponsible attitude and taunting statements of the Indian home minister, which re-enforced pro-bomb thinking as vital for national security and finally played the role of a catalyst in convincing Pakistan to walk on the 'MAD' [mutually assured destruction] path.

The Day After
More shockingly, the news story on Pakistan's state-controlled electronic media on May 28 did not tell the details about the test site, type of tests and other specifications. Rather the entire time was consumed on the Prime Minister's self-congratulatory speech declaring Pakistan a nuclear state. The photograph of the test site was released almost after a week. Another communication gap that confused people was foreign minister Gohar Ayub Khan's claim that Pakistan conducted two more tests on May 30, whereas foreign secretary Shamshad Ahmed maintained that the country had conducted just one test that day.

Later, Prime Minister Sharif and information minister, Syed Mushahid Hussain took two separate groups of journalists to the test site. Only then, it was revealed that the country had conducted its sixth test in the Kharan desert (Balochistan). Significantly, independent journalists and foreign media crews are still not allowed to visit the test site and write about the possible radiation in the vicinity. The state-controlled television did not miss the opportunity to belittle opposition leader Benazir Bhutto on the nuclear issue and mixed up two statements by her to make humiliating news copy.

In the print media, the coverage in the national Urdu press was by and large emotional, instead of being informative. It appeared to be extra-jubilant over Pakistan matching the number of Indian tests.

A glimpse of headlines from the Urdu press: 1. 'Five thappers (slaps—worthy rejoinders) on the face of Vajpayee' (*Daily Khabrain*, Islamabad) 2. 'Allah-u-Akbar, Five tests of Islamic Bomb' (*Daily Ausaf*, Islamabad) 3. 'Al hamdullilah, Islamic bomb tested' (*Daily Nawa-i-Waqt*, Islamabad). 'The print media, seething with rage, had already fought and won many crusades before the nuclear dust raised a tempest,' wrote a columnist because, before the Pakistani tests, the vocabulary used by the Urdu press in its post-Indian test reporting kept up the emotional upsurge and inculcated a single-track thinking that the Indian nuclear tests should be retaliated against with 'our tests' alone. Had it been a cricket match, it would have ended in a draw, but, this was a game frought with danger. At risk are over a billion people living in South Asia with numerous problems like under-development, poverty, illiteracy, etc.

The Hindu religion and Indian mentality were diagnosed in more than one way, to reiterate all stereotypes with which Pakistanis are living since the partition of subcontinent. To be precise, the hangover of the two-nation theory attained a new connotation—'two-nations, with their separate Hindu and Muslim bombs.' The media quite conveniently ignored the odd paradox that both the Hindu and the Muslim bombs in India and Pakistan, respectively had been fathered by Muslim scientists.

At the same time, the print media did not miss the opportunity to sensationalise the tirades by Pakistan's nuclear scientists who were fighting among themselves for 'monopolising credit' of bestowing the capability on the country. However, the government that was propagating an image of national unity in the wake of the nuclear tests had to intervene and ask the scientists to end their war of words.

The national English press remained pluralistic in terms of offering a modest space for dissent. It also lived with the argument that it was a 'now-or-never game' for Pakistan to divorce its policy of nuclear ambiguity. Post-test comments and analyses appearing in the press ignored safety aspects like radiation, etc. Only a few English newspapers raised concerns on issues like an effective, cautious and transparent command and control system.

Journalists as Activists

Right wing journalists sabotaged a press conference by the Pakistan–India People's Forum for Peace and Democracy in Islamabad. They attacked Dr. Eqbal Ahmad and Dr. A.H. Nayyer and abused female peace activists. *Shabab-i-Milli*, the youth wing of *Jama'at-i-Islami*, joined this crusade. Two days later, *Shabab-i-Milli* staged a demonstration in front of the Parliament building and criticised all non-governmental organisations (NGOs) for being anti-nuclear. They dubbed NGOs as the agents of America, 'Yahood' (Jews) and India, 'Hanood' (Hindus). An editor of the Islamabad-based English daily *Pakistan Observer* hosted a reception in honour of *Shabab-i-Milli* to acknowledge its 'national services'. The reception was disturbed by the newspaper's employees who had not been paid their salaries for the last six months.

Cartoons are not a norm in Pakistan's Urdu press but during the period of nuclear hysteria, lines and caricatures were used to translate un-repeatable insults against India and against 'doves' supporting non-proliferation. Most of the English newspapers also came up with similar stuff. However, Zahoor, the cartoonist of the *The Frontier Post*, Peshawar, came up with a series of anti-nuclear cartoons. Bravo, Zahoor!

Regardless of whether or not India and Pakistan will ever be able to live in peace like good neighbours history tells us that on December 14, 1948, through a Delhi agreement, the two states recognised and sought the cooperation of the press, asking it not to indulge in propaganda against one another and refrain from presenting exaggerated versions of news or publishing material likely to exacerbate acrimony. A similar clause also figured in the joint statement issued on the conclusion of foreign secretary-level talks in Islamabad in June 1997. But, in the wake of 'May madness' initiated by India and followed by Pakistan, the press played the role of agent provocateur. Now with the dust of nuclear tests settling and harsh economic sanctions and realities eating up the nuclear euphoria, the press in both countries needs to dispassionately analyse its role and promote a culture of dialogue instead of showing people the path of mutual destruction.

Of Science and Nuclear Weapons

T. JAYARAMAN

The current euphoria about Indian science and technology generated by the recent nuclear tests conducted by the government has little parallel in the history of independent India. All official pronouncements, statements by leading political figures or non-left political parties and media commentaries have invariably begun by hailing the event as a triumph of Indian scientific expertise.

But even as it becomes clear that the new policy has no deep vision underlying it and is no more than a leap in the dark initiated by an act of nuclear adventurism that was Pokhran II, the political stock of Indian science and technology remains high. Despite the sharp internal political divide that has emerged on the nuclear issue, with the opposition parties directly questioning the motivations, timing and wisdom of the BJP government in conducting the tests, the atomic energy and the defence research establishments have not yet been subjected to any searching public or parliamentary criticism.

In fact, it has been an integral part of the BJP-led government's strategy to use the 'scientific' argument, and the general public appreciation of Indian science and its successes to justify its reactionary departure from India's established nuclear policy. Initiating the parliamentary debate on the nuclear issue, Prime Minister Atal Behari Vajpayee claimed that India's newly acquired, 'nuclear weapons state' status was, 'an endowment given to her by scientists and engineers'. In another instance, Parliamentary Affairs Minister Madan Lal Khurana claimed that the tests were a scientific necessity.

These appeals to science as justification for an essentially reactionary political decision have wide currency. The chorus of support for these arguments has served to confuse and blunt criticism from sections of public opinion that would otherwise have reacted more sharply to the overturning of established policy. At least temporarily, the impression of a broad national consensus for the new line, especially among the middle-class and the intelligentsia, has been created.

Science and its political role are very much part of the issue here. The actual content and significance of the claims of high scientific and technological achievement need to be examined with care and placed in the proper perspective. We also need to examine the political role of sections of the scientific establishment, in particular the atomic energy and the defence research sectors, in the run-up to the tests and later.

These questions need to be discussed publicly and not confined to purely professional circles. They cannot be brushed aside by citing the excuse of the inviolability or 'neutrality' of expert scientific opinion, nor can questions of scientific credibility be dismissed by mere statements of patriotic faith in Indian scientists.

In this chapter, we will attempt a preliminary discussion of some aspects of these issues.

The technically noteworthy features of the tests that tested a range of nuclear devices for weapon designs, as claimed by the Department of Atomic Energy (DAE), appear to be two in number. The first, of course, is the explosion of a thermo-nuclear device, also popularly known as the hydrogen bomb. One of the significant features is that India has reportedly developed a significantly cheaper, quicker and more efficient method of producing the hydrogen isotope, tritium, used in the device. The second is the explosion of fission devices that are of low-yield; three such explosions were conducted. These tests, it is contended, will permit the gathering of data that will allow the further testing of fission devices purely by computer simulations, etc., without recourse to actual explosions. Such low-yield devices are also the elements of tactical or battlefield nuclear weapons though this aspect has not been particularly emphasised publicly.

The second feature in particular, relating as it does to methodologies that are known to be in use only in fairly recent times even in countries like the United States and France, appears in particular to have been significant. The suggestion is that India can seek to join the select band of nations that can undertake what is known as sub-critical testing. Apart from these features, reliable reports from various sources indicate that there were other significant technical inputs involved, including high-quality computer programmes and expertise from the fields of high-pressure physics, reactor physics and experimental ballistics.

While the second achievement of undertaking sub-kilotonne explosions has not been seriously challenged (the little data independently available to observers do not contradict this), the first claim, i.e. of the explosion of a thermo-nuclear device, has been more controversial. The claim has been challenged primarily on two counts. One is that there is a discrepancy between the seismographic data of the Indian sensors and foreign sites, with the evidence of the foreign sites suggesting that the explosions were significantly less powerful than that claimed by the DAE. The second according to some expert opinion, is that even the claimed power of the explosions seems to fall outside the class of true thermo-nuclear devices.

The criticism of the DAE on the question of seismic data has come primarily from a nuclear scientist and former Indian Navy captain, Dr. B.K. Subbarao, who has made out a case that the discrepancy between the data recorded by the Indian sensors and the foreign ones is clearly untenable. Why should the interference effect, which the DAE claims caused the data discrepancy in the foreign sensors, not affect Indian sensors?

It is not unknown in science, that under political pressure, experiments can produce results that reflect what is desired, rather than what actually happened or data is produced that does not correspond to what was measured. This may well have happened in the case of the Indian seismic data.

Apart from this discrepancy, there was also a discrepancy between yield estimates from foreign seismic data and Indian official figures. Though the DAE's original interference explanation is rather weak and has rightly been challenged, some foreign experts have now changed their original estimates to those that are reasonably consistent with official Indian ones. One must add here that it is a well-known practice in nuclear weapons technology to set off multiple explosions in order to confuse foreign sensors.

From the seismic data, it is also quite difficult to estimate yields exactly. Several factors such as site preparation, the nature of the soil in the region of the explosions and sub-surface formations can actually affect the final calculation, leading to considerable uncertainties in the final yield figures.

Major suspicions in the foreign media about whether India really has a thermo-nuclear weapon centre essentially around the low explosive power of the devices. In general, the data appear consistent, according to foreign experts (cited in a *New York Times* article by William J. Broad) with a 'boosted' fission device. However, the DAE has chosen aggressively to counter the doubts with an explicit claim that it was indeed a genuine hydrogen bomb, with two explosive stages, a secondary fusion device' with a 'fission trigger'.

It is true that advanced design thermo-nuclear devices of explosive power ranging from a few tens of kilotonnes upwards are known to be present in various nuclear arsenals and have been tested. In general, however, they have been the result of several years of testing and research, involving both a boosted fission stage and a mega-tonne thermo-nuclear stage. In the absence of such stages in the Indian development of a thermo-nuclear device, the DAE claim, suggesting that India went directly to a third-generation thermo-nuclear device appears exaggerated. There have, however, been some specialist opinions that suggest that such a low-yield thermo-nuclear device could well be the correct technological route.

It is obviously important that the question of exactly how far the Indian nuclear establishment is on the road to thermo-nuclear capability is answered. From the viewpoint of scientific credibility and informing the nation of what exactly happened, it is important that this issue be clarified. Conflicting signals emerged from scientific and political establishments after the first few days of the blast. Peculiarly enough, while the DAE has been forceful in claiming a thermo-nuclear explosion, it has not really pressed a claim that it has, in fact, tested an advanced third-generation device. The sole exception to this has been a press interview given by Dr. P. Rodriguez, the director of IGCAR, Kalpakkam, where the explicit claim was made. Dr. Raja Ramanna, an acknowledged spokesman for the nuclear establishment, in a lengthy television interview to Doordarshan on May 27, 1998, did little to clarify this question and simply dismissed criticism. Strangest of all, the Prime Minister's *suo moto* statement of May 27, to Parliament is completely silent on the subject of a thermo-nuclear device having been developed, while acknowledging other scientific advances like the capability of sub-critical testing.

The celebration of Indian science and technology that followed the tests necessitates the placing of these achievements in the limited domain of weapons technology in a broader perspective. Perhaps the first question to consider is, how advanced is this advanced technology that Indian nuclear scientists are supposed to have mastered? In this regard, it is worth noting that the time-lag between the development of these testing methodologies in the US and its adoption by other weapon states has itself been quite short. This suggests that the degree of complexity and sophistication required may not be quite so large as has been made out. To obtain a better idea of the scale of advanced technology involved, we can compare the reported achievements in nuclear testing to the degree of advance Indian nuclear scientists have made with regard to the development of fast-breeder reactors suitable for power generation. The Fast Breeder Test Reactor (FBTR) at Kalpakkam was generating power and was connected to the grid only last year, twelve years after it attained criticality in 1985. Even that stage was several years behind schedule, with a good part of the delay being due to the breakup of the international collaboration with France. A full-scale power-producing fast-breeder reactor is still on the drawing boards. The point really is that weapon technologies in the nuclear field are in several respects simpler than those relating to peaceful uses like power generation, where India's performance though noteworthy in several respects, still leaves tremendous room for improvement.

It is also useful to note that much of nuclear weapons technology is secret in nature and this contributes something extra to the feeling of triumph that accompanies the acquisition and mastery of such technology. This secrecy also contributes to the ease with which the bogey of the competitor having stolen a march on us can be raised, a feature well known throughout the period of the Cold War.

In India, major achievements and milestones in the development of indigenous capabilities in science and technology have always been greeted with justifiable enthusiasm. But in the case at hand, the abandoning of any sense of proportion in the celebration of India's mastery of advanced scientific knowledge points to an entirely different motivation—driven more by ultra-nationalism and jingoism than any nationalist spirit. Indian science is seen as having established India as a nuclear weapon power, making it a 'global player' who cannot be 'ignored' by the other nuclear weapon states.

A second question with regard to these claimed advances in the arena of nuclear weapons testing is what gains have really accrued, or will accrue, in terms of strategic and tactical advantages in relation to the powers and forces that are perceived to threaten India. In this regard, two simple points are clear from the long history of the Cold War. The first is that leads in weapons technologies will always be shortlived. The other side will catch up at some point, taking desperate measures if necesssary. The second is that it is not exactly necessary that the sophistication of the armaments needs to be perfectly matched on both sides. Even with one sophisticated player, the other player needs only a few weapons of just the Hiroshima category with rudimentary delivery systems, in order to significantly raise the dangers of nuclear confrontation. Thus, hailing the 'achievements' of Indian scientists in these tests and claiming that they have delivered 'security' to the people, as scientists like Raja Ramanna are doing, is to take a somewhat short-sighted view.

This point has been brought home sharply in the aftermath of the Pakistani tests that followed close on the heels of Pokhran II. There is little doubt that Indian science and technology go deeper and are more sophisticated and broader in scope than anything that Pakistan can boast of. Nevertheless, Pakistan has clearly demonstrated a nuclear weapons capability. Irrespective of the fact that the level of technical sophistication may not match the Indian tests and irrespective of the fact that Chagai I does not demonstrate an indigenous scientific capability to the same extent as Pokhran II, we now have an incipient open nuclear arms race in the sub-continent. The over-blown estimation of the superiority of Indian science and technology appears to have blinded important sections of the ruling establishment to the extent that post-Pokhran II little thought was given to the possibility and consequences of tests by Pakistan.

The contribution by the atomic energy and defence research establishments to Pokhran II was by no means purely scientific or technical in character. It is becoming increasingly clear now that they have played a pro-active role in the build-up of pressure to conduct the tests and have provided important support to the BJP project of nuclear hawkishness.

The evidence for this was originally indirect, based mainly on the strong political support that was provided by top scientific spokesmen for the nuclear energy establishment to the government's decision to conduct the tests, in language that went well beyond any demands of scientific clarification. But more direct evidence is provided by the May 15, 1998, letter of former prime minister H.D. Deve Gowda in his letter to Vajpayee. Deve Gowda states clearly that the 'scientists had approached two previous governments to continue the tests, once in 1995 and then in 1997.' He adds that like Narasimha Rao before him, 'I was requested to make a decision to conduct fresh nuclear tests. I convinced the scientists that the time was not ripe. . .'

Some DAE scientists, in public comments and in off-the-record statements to journalists, have expressed happiness that this government has given them the chance to demonstrate their capabilities and their competence.

This attitude is an unacceptably naive standpoint on the question of the political role of science and scientists, especially in nuclear weapons technology. Undoubtedly, DAE and DRDO scientists have, in their research programmes, to fulfill the mandate that is given to them by the overall policy orientation. But they cannot claim a right to extend the scientific part of the mandate to the point where it goes against the basic political tenets on which the policy is based.

It is even more serious when a critical section of the scientific leadership goes over to an active advocacy of testing and weaponisation, furthering the creation of a mood that has helped the present government to overturn a peace-oriented nuclear policy.

A striking example of this is provided by the Press Trust of India (PTI) report of an interview given to them by the chairman of the Atomic Energy Commission, Dr. R. Chidambaram, on March 3, 1998, (and published in *The Deccan Herald,* March 4, 1998), when the possibility of a BJP-led government had become clear. While nominally asserting that the final decision was political, Chidambaram argued that tests were a necessity. According to the report, in reply to the question whether the country could go nuclear as outlined in the manifesto of the BJP, Chidambaram 'said that the country was technologically ready and the capability was proved long back'. He added that 'this preparedness itself was a testimony to the deterrent capability possessed by the country.' Further, when asked whether the country

could go ahead only with the help of simulations and by avoiding ·
actual ground experiments he retorted, 'then what was the use of some
countries going for 2000 explosions.' The PTI report adds: 'Speaking
in favour of nuclear explosions to increase the database for the country,
he said computer simulations alone could not stand and huge actual
database was required for simulations.' The report continues: 'There
was huge difference between theoretical studies and practical experiments,' he said, adding, 'if you are weak, people will try to take advantage
of it.'

Clearly, the DAE leadership was all set to bury the earlier Indian
policy line of conditional self-restraint on the nuclear option. It found
in the ascent to power of a government led by the BJP, with its long-
standing dream of nuclear weaponisation, a congenial political climate.

It is important to tackle directly here the argument of 'scientific
necessity' for Pokhran II. The basic rationale for testing with respect to
any technology is, of course, that one must be certain that the projected
designs will work. But this argument cannot be extended indefinitely
to situations where the consequences of testing will have an immense
political or social fallout. The political, social and other aspects must
have over-riding priority here. This argument is by no means new or
unique to the nuclear field. In the field of genetic engineering, for
example, certain classes of cloning experiments involving human
DNA, have been simply disallowed in several countries, irrespective of
any potential scientific value.

Undoubtedly, non-testing may require scientists to take more innovative routes, of a much more theoretical or controlled laboratory
nature, to validate their designs. If such a discipline is imposed by
political requirement or desirability, then science must necessarily
accept this, even if this retards further 'scientific' advance. In any case,
as the experience of Pokhran II has made clear, the necessary steps to
testing could have been undertaken in short order if there was indeed
a genuine need for it. And Chidambaram, while invoking the argument
of necessity, was clearly aware that the existing technological level and
preparedness itself kept India's nuclear option alive and active.

This pro-active stance of a small group of scientists in positions of
administrative importance and political influence on nuclear weapons
testing and their increasingly open advocacy of the weaponisation
option, is a significant departure from the public style of the Indian
scientific establishment that has prevailed so far. The boastfulness of

scientific spokesmen, post-Pokhran II has been notable. Prof. A.P.J. Kalam claimed that the nuclear threat to India had been 'vacated', while Dr. Raja Ramanna claimed that the tests had provided security to India. These claims, as we noted earlier, have proved to be baseless. Chidambaram himself returned to his vision of a strong India in an interview to *Frontline* magazine (June 5,1998). His reply to the question 'Should we have nuclear weapons or keep the option open?', is worth quoting in full: 'No comment. . . . The most important thing is that India must become strong. The greatest advantage of recognised strength is that you don't have to use it . . . everybody knows you are strong. Only when people see you as a weak country, they pressure you. We are a big country. We must learn to behave like a big country of one billion people. We should constantly remind ourselves of our strength.' This is a remarkable statement marked both by hawkishness as well as a dangerously simplistic understanding of politics.

It is probably overstating the case to speak of the militarisation of parts of the scientific establishment. But clearly a section of top scientists, in the process of helping to overturn established nuclear policy and subsequently defending the new line, has not merely provided support to the pursuit of the jingoistic agenda of a particular political formation, they have contributed to dangerous illusions of strength and invincibility on the subject of national defence and security.

The current euphoria over nuclear science and defence research has obviously made most senior scientists wary of speaking out critically. Several others labour under the illusion that there is a purely 'scientific' question of nuclear tests that justifies Pokhran II, and that this should be considered independent of the political background which led to the tests. Fortunately, some voices of dissent have emerged from within the scientific community on the nuclear weapons issue. Though still a minority, these voices, we hope, will eventually help turn science in India more firmly in the direction of peace and development.

One of the most disturbing outcomes for the public perception of science in the current situation is its delivery as a tool into the hands of ultra-nationalistic jingoism. We have come a long way from the original vision of Homi J. Bhabha and others of his era like Vikram Sarabhai, who saw science as an integral tool in the task of development. We have travelled very far from the vision of Pandit Jawaharlal Nehru, who saw in large projects 'the modern temples of independent India' to an insecure nationalism that sees nuclear explosions as the only means to secure 'respect' for India in the community of nations.

Even if the earlier Nehruvian vision of science had its share of naivete in its underplaying the role of socio-political change as an important aspect of development (thus, land reforms were never as important as the Green Revolution), it nevertheless had the not-inconsiderable merit of a humane and peaceful world-view as its fundamental premise. The current scene seems to have room only for an unrelieved hawkishness, cloaked occasionally in the language of strategic analysis, that sees scientific achievement purely in terms of the power advantages that it claims to bring. Characteristic of the current jingoistic euphoria is the impatience with all subtleties in nuclear policy, foreign affairs, or related questions.

But, perhaps the most disgusting and distressing aspect of the nature of current public discourse on the nuclear question is the complete absence of any sense of horror at the induction of such weapons of mass destruction, or even a sense of sober reluctance at the thought of their possible use. Television discussion panel participants, talk show hosts, members of studio audiences, scientists in talk shows of various kinds (with some honourable exceptions) sustain the discussion in the bland language of strategic analysis. 'Nuclear weapons are not weapons of war' intones an analyst on a BBC discussion panel, 'they are political weapons'.

The Prime Minister, speaking to a cheering crowd in front of his residence, assures them that 'we will not hesitate to use nuclear weapons if we need to, in self-defence.' Where exactly will he explode them? Will it be in Punjab, or in Kashmir? If it is exploded on foreign soil, will we remain uncontaminated by the fall-out? Such questions are not asked in the din of celebration and euphoria that follows such triumphalist statements.

If the politics of nuclear weapons is an inexact science, as the history of the last fifty years makes painfully obvious, there is nothing inexact, scientifically speaking, of the horrendous effects of a potential nuclear war. It is the subject of detailed scientific analysis and several years of study whose results are widely available. The analysis has been corroborated by 'experiment', if one may abuse the term to describe the effects of the bombs dropped over Hiroshima and Nagasaki. The bottomline is that there is no scenario in which a nuclear confrontation in the subcontinent will not become one of humankind's worst disasters.

If there is one lesson from the years of tension that was the result of the US-imposed Cold War, it is this: Nuclear weapons do not add to security. Nuclear weapons breed tensions, their induction and further development breed only endless cycles of destructive competition that developing countries in particular can ill afford. And once countries begin to travel down that slippery slope it is not easy to stop.

All through the years of the Cold War, the consistent Indian position on nuclear disarmament remained a beacon of hope to democratic and progressive forces in the Third World and in developed countries. India was often joined in its efforts by the best scientific minds throughout the world, many of whom spent a serious fraction of their time fighting for peace and against nuclear war. From the great Albert Einstein onwards, through the years, in movements like Pugwash and others, scientists consistently fought the idea that nuclear weapons provided security or that nuclear conflicts could be won.

While standing firmly against nationalist chauvinism and jingoism, progressive intellectuals and scientists in India and in South Asia, in general, need to go back to the lessons and inspiration of that experience.

Based on a paper presented at the Delhi Convention Against Nuclear Weapons, held on June 9, 1998.

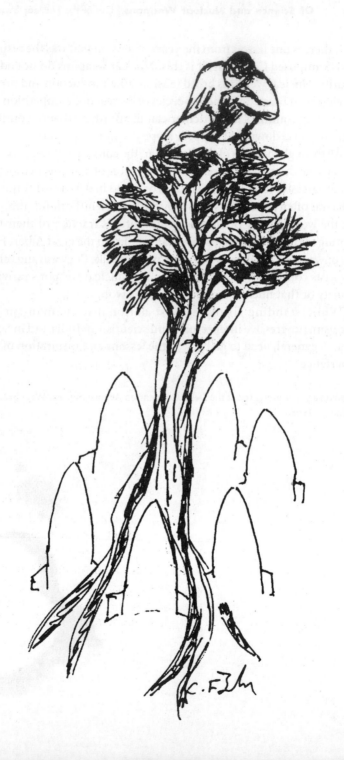

Bombs, Missiles and Pakistani Science

PERVEZ HOODBHOY

Ten days of officially sponsored celebrations, leading up to the nuclear tests of May 28, were scheduled to culminate with the award of prizes and honours by Prime Minister Nawaz Sharif to the leading members of Pakistan's nuclear establishment. In preparation of this grand finale, Pakistan Television continuously exhorted its viewers to celebrate Pakistan's power for wreaking apocalyptic destruction. The Chagai tests, together with the more recent Ghauri-II and Shaheen-I missile launches, have been deemed heroic symbols of high scientific achievement.

Making bombs and missiles has indeed demonstrated a high level of engineering and management skills, and the individuals to be decorated are undoubtedly competent, resourceful and dedicated to the task they were assigned. But these programmes have little to do with cutting-edge science, original scientific research, high technology, or the country's general scientific progress. Testing even a hundred bombs or missiles cannot change this reality by the tiniest bit.

The truth about science in Pakistan flatly contradicts all claims of scientific progress. But it is pointless to answer hyperbole with more hyperbole. Therefore I shall first define suitable criteria for gauging scientific achievement.

One key criterion of progress is to see what new scientific discoveries, analyses, inventions, or processes a country's scientists have produced. Since modern science is about the discovery and invention of new knowledge in highly specific areas, all scientists need to establish their professional credentials by publishing their work in internationally referred journals or filing patents.

Pakistan's international status can be determined from publications of the Institute for Scientific Information that regularly tabulates the scientific output of each country. Professor Atta-ur-Rahman, Pakistan's leading chemist, quotes the following facts published by the Institute. In the period 1990–1994, Pakistani physicists, chemists and mathematicians produced a pitiful 0.11 per cent, 0.13 per cent, and 0.05 per cent, respectively of the world's research publications. Pakistan's total share of world research output in 1994 was just 0.08 per cent.

These painfully small numbers are even more painful if one also looks at the usefulness of these papers as measured by the Institute. The average number of citations per paper was around 0.3, which is barely above zero. In other words, an overwhelming majority of papers by Pakistani scientists had zero impact on their field. Atta-ur-Rahman also points out that between 1947 and 1986 the total number of PhDs produced in the sciences by all Pakistani universities and research institutes was 128. In comparison, India produces over 150 science and engineering PhDs in one single year.

With fewer than 40 active research physicists in the country, about 100 active chemists and far fewer mathematicians, Pakistan is starved of scientists. Even in nuclear physics, contrary to what may be suggested by Pakistan's successful nuclear weapons programme, there are just a handful of nuclear physicists. Ill-informed journalism is responsible for certain popular misconceptions. For example, Dr. A.Q. Khan, the pre-eminent architect of Pakistan's nuclear programme, is often called a nuclear physicist when, in fact, his degrees and professional accomplishments belong to the field of metallurgy, which is an engineering discipline rather than physics. When Dr. Khan visited the physics department of Quaid-e-Azam University about two months ago, he endeared himself even more to his admirers by wistfully saying he wished he could come someday to this university to study physics.

The small size and poor quality of Pakistani science owes squarely to the miserable state of Pakistani universities, which rate among the poorest in the world. There are few qualified and motivated faculty, student quality is low, rote learning is normal, academic fraud is widespread, and student violence common. Pakistan thus does not satisfy the first criterion.

The second criterion for scientific achievement is the degree to which science enters into a nation's economy. Again, the facts are stark. Pakistan's exports are principally textiles, cotton, leather, footballs, fish, fruit, and so on. The value-added component of Pakistani manufacturing somewhat exceeds that of Bangladesh and Sudan, but is far below that of India, Turkey and Indonesia. Apart from relatively minor exports of computer software and light armaments, science and technology are irrelevant in the process of production. Here again, Pakistan fails.

Third, and lastly, a nation's scientific level is estimated by the quality of science taught in its educational institutions and the extent to which scientific thinking is part of the general public consciousness. It is not necessary to say very much in this regard. Even our leaders admit that the country's schools, colleges and universities are in shambles. An internationally administered test in 1983 established that 6th grade Japanese students performed better in physics and mathematics than 11th grade Pakistani students. And with creeping Talibanisation, the dawn of scientific enlightenment among the masses recedes daily. Pakistan fails the third criterion as well.

The arguments given above must have left some readers puzzled, and others angry, but still confident that I am taking them for a ride. Everyone knows that nuclear bombs and long-range missile technologies are extremely complex systems. So, if a country is indeed scientifically impoverished, how can it possibly manufacture them?

A large part of the answer lies in the modular nature of modern technology and the ease with which separate modular units can be transported and then joined together to form highly complex and effective systems. You only need to know how the units are to be assembled, not how they work. Therefore, making bombs and missiles of the type Pakistan and India possess is now the work of engineers and no longer that of scientists. Even here, global technological advancement has created enormous simplifications.

Consider, for example, that 30 years ago an electronic engineer working on a missile guidance system had to spend years learning how to design extremely intricate circuits using transistors and other components. But now he just needs to be able to follow the manufacturer's instructions for programming a tiny microprocessor chip, available from almost any commercial electronics supplier. Today sophisticated motorists and hikers can buy so-called GPS units costing a few hundred dollars to determine their coordinates and similar units can guide a missile launched thousands of miles away to better than fifty metres accuracy.

Modular technology applies also to rocketry, including engine design and aerodynamic construction. Computer-controlled machines have made reverse engineering of mechanical parts easy. No longer is 'rocket science' a correct expression for indicating scientific complexity. Famine-stricken North Korea, with few other achievements, clearly has a very advanced missile programme. In fact, it has been repeatedly accused of transferring this technology to Pakistan, Iran and Iraq. None of these countries has a reputation for scientific and technological excellence, yet all three have intermediate range missiles.

The facts about nuclear weapons are equally stark. Unquestionably the first atomic bomb was a exceedingly brilliant, if terrible, achievement by the world's finest physicists. It required the creation of wholly-new physical concepts, based on a then very newly-acquired understanding of the atomic nucleus. The ensuing technological effort, the Manhattan Project, was quite unparalleled in the history of humanity for its complexity and difficulty.

But here too the passage of five decades has changed everything and the design of atomic weapons, while still non-trivial, is vastly simpler than it was. Basic information is freely available in technical libraries throughout the world and simply surfing the Internet can bring to anyone a staggering amount of detail. Advanced textbooks and monographs contain details that can enable reasonably competent scientists and engineers to come up with 'quick and dirty' designs for nuclear explosives. The physics of nuclear explosions can be readily taught to graduate students.

Implosion calculations are also far simpler now. This owes to the free availability of extremely powerful, but cheap, computers as well as numerical codes that allow one to see how a bomb's characteristics change as one changes sizes and shapes, purity of materials, etc. In contrast, the early bomb calculations had been painfully carried out by hand or by programming huge and primitive vacuum-tube computers. Today's pocket calculator, worth only Rs 500 has more computational power than the room-sized early computers worth millions of dollars.

In a world where science moves at super-high speeds, nuclear weapons and missile development is today a second-rate science. The undeniable fact is that the technology of nuclear bombs belongs to the 1940s, and the furious pace of science makes that ancient history. Nevertheless, the reader may still demand an answer to the question: Exactly how hard is it to make nuclear weapons?

Hard and easy are relative terms. Therefore, to make things more precise, consider the following hypothetical situation. Let us suppose that the developed countries exercise no export controls, or that a given Third World country has a sufficiently clever purchasing network to get around these controls and hence that it can obtain all the non-military technologies it wants. Assume also that it has the cash to pay for such commercially available equipment, electronic systems, machine parts, special steels and materials, and so forth, that are needed in a modern industrial setting. And, finally, suppose that the country either possesses naturally found uranium, or waste material from some reactor. What, then, would be the chances of success?

Botswana, Lesotho and Somalia still couldn't make it, I'm afraid. Nor could Madagascar or the Maldives. Libya or Saudi Arabia would also have great difficulty unless they hired scientists and engineers from abroad. But one can count more than sixty countries currently without nuclear weapons, which could very well have them if the conditions of the above hypothesis were fulfilled—and, of course, if they wanted the weapons.

It is not my purpose to denigrate the considerable achievement of Pakistani and Indian nuclear and missile experts. They have accomplished their goal of being able to reduce each other's countries to radioactive ashes in a matter of minutes. This is no mean feat because even today substantial engineering ingenuity is required to make any textbook method actually work. It takes intelligence to get complex machines to work and reliably convert formulas given in books and documents into bombs and rockets. But this does not amount to scientific genius or to meaningful overall advancement of the nation's technology.

Does it really matter that making bombs and missiles is no longer high-science? The answer is, yes, for three reasons. First, making these weapons no longer impresses the rest of the world. There was indeed a time when being nuclear and missile-armed meant that a country was big and powerful, but today's international pecking order is determined by a nation's economic, not military, strength. India had hoped for a Security Council seat after the May 11 tests but miserably failed.

Second, the highly focused, and hugely expensive, Pakistani and Indian weapons programmes are wasteful because they use scientific principles discovered and developed elsewhere and so cannot produce any important spin-offs. In contrast, the strongly research-oriented military-industrial complex in the US has often produced new spin-off technology with enormous applications, the Internet being one example.

Third, the irrelevance of high-science to bombs and missiles has yet another, and still deeper, implication. Pakistan has established that even a scientifically impoverished country can, with minimal infrastructure, produce bombs that will go off and missiles that will fly. The prescription for success is sufficient money and resources, a few hundred engineers working under the direction of effective and intelligent group leaders, an international buying network and the will to do it all. Therefore one does not need high-class research scientists or world-class universities. A couple of good engineering institutes will suffice, together with a few good schools and colleges. More would be welcome, but an expensive luxury. Hence, Chagai cannot give an impetus for resurrecting an education system that collapsed over a decade ago.

The Pakistani state has declared bombs and missiles as the touchstone of scientific progress and its present elation is understandable. But it has been able to acquire these without having created an educated society, or working science institutions, or even attempting to move towards a society where science can ultimately develop. Historically, every society where science has flourished has necessarily submitted to the power of reason and been radically transformed. When science came to Europe three centuries ago, it swept away the old theocratic medieval order and replaced it with ideas of progress, humanism, and rationalism. Curiously the offspring of science, technology, has been summoned to serve and defend an increasingly Talibanised Pakistan. The country's emerging new medieval theocracy, which now impatiently awaits its turn for power, counts upon having at its disposal the power of fiery jinns to use as it wills.

Nuclear Power and Human Security

ITTY ABRAHAM

At the present moment, there are a number of very real dangers that lie ahead for the people of India and Pakistan. Some have been the stuff of expert commentary, both in the subcontinent and in the west. They include the possibility of war over Kashmir leading to the use of nuclear weapons, the absence of secure command, control, communication and intelligence facilities increasing the danger of weapons being used in error or miscalculation, the small number of weapons on both sides producing a logic of 'use them or lose them', the chance of accidents and mishaps leading to nuclear detonation, the possibility of preemptive strikes, and so on. While not discounting any of these and other prognostications, the greater danger in my view is that we get trapped in a conceptual box bearing the stamp, 'Made in the Cold War'.

As the outlines of an explicitly nuclear South Asia take shape, the only thinking that seems possible comes from the experience of the Cold War. We see this in a number of ways: Recounting the similarities and differences between the Pakistan–India and the USA–USSR relationships as a way of explaining why nuclear conflict is more or less likely in South Asia, borrowing strategies and ideas that are supposed to have reduced tensions between the superpowers, or more insidious, the US offering incentives to India and Pakistan not to go further down the nuclear road that replicate the unequal international structure of that period. But why is mimicking the Cold War experience the correct path to take?

Cold War Realists

Do we really want to end up where the US and Russia are now, with thousands of missiles still pointed at each other, with merely a small number of warheads removed from missiles still in their silos, with nuclear weapon-armed submarines still cruising with arsenals still stacked with nuclear-tipped artillery shells, with new sub-critical and hydrodynamic testing facilities coming into being, with testing ranges still open and ready for use, with thousands of nuclear scientists still employed by weapons labs. How can an end like that seem like a solution? To which problem is it a solution?

The seduction of the Cold War (and its 'end') is what unites the glee of Indian right-wingers who have now found their masculinity and the cold-blooded approval of the votaries of 'political realism', both here and abroad. The conclusions they draw from an uncritical acceptance of a particular understanding of the political history of the last half century can be reduced to these: For the realists, nuclear weapons provide the ultimate security of the state and a stable condition can be achieved between nuclear rivals through the import of the logic of deterrence. For the formerly emasculated, every country desires nuclear weapons because countries with nuclear weapons are the ones that count. India's destiny lies in possessing nuclear weapons because it is a great civilisation. Are these statements as self-evident as they are made out to be?

It is easy to dismiss the presumptions of the raw nationalists of the right. First, it is a logical fallacy to assume that because all the present permanent members of the Security Council have nuclear weapons, possession of nuclear weapons will entitle any country to a permanent seat on the Council. The world now measures international influence in other ways. Second, not every country desires nuclear weapons. Two countries in a somewhat similar position to India and Pakistan— Brazil and Argentina—have recently given up their fairly well-developed nuclear programmes. It is not a coincidence that this was done at the moment when the military regimes that had dominated both countries for much of the post-war period finally returned to their barracks. South Africa's former apartheid regime did the same— renounce nuclear weapons—in its historic transfer of power to the black majority. But, it could be said, perhaps these are special conditions. What about Australia and Sweden, both of which had active nuclear programmes, but gave up the search for weapons in the 1950s?

What about Japan and Germany, both of which have large scientific communities and who sit on large stocks of fissile material—neither show signs of developing weapons programmes. What about the other 40 countries around the world that could do it but have not? There is no truth to the assertion that those that can do it, will, or that international acclaim and respect follows those who are acknowledged nuclear powers.

Remember that during the 1995 Non-Proliferation Treaty negotiations, the nuclear powers were forced by non-nuclear countries to accept the importance of Article VI, the demand that nuclear powers work toward general disarmament as a condition to the treaty's indefinite extension. Recall also the international fury that ensued when France blithely set sail toward the South Pacific to run a series of nuclear tests before signing the Comprehensive Test Ban Treaty—the reaction so shocked the French establishment that they hurriedly cancelled their last few tests, claiming they had all the data they needed.

Nuclear Deterrence?

What about the 'realists' who want to copy the actions and rhetoric of the nuclear powers? The condition that is supposed to have prevented war between the USA and the USSR during the Cold War is based on the horror of the destructive potential of these weapons. Whether for those who believe what happened in Hiroshima and Nagasaki in 1945 was so terrible that it should never happen again, or for the nuclear strategists who believe that no government would be so irrational as to risk the massive destruction of its own people in order to pursue belligerent aims against another country, the present system is built on the premise that nuclear weapons cannot be used. That simple hope is the basis of 'successful' nuclear deterrence between the USA and Russia.

But remember, 'successful' nuclear deterrence does not make conventional warfare less likely. If anything, the historical record shows that the nuclear powers, successfully deterred from dropping missiles on each other, continued to fight each other through a variety of surrogates, in Africa, Latin America and Asia, for nearly half a century. The price for the Cold War was paid with the lives of black, brown and yellow people—not a sign of success if you lived anywhere other than the US or USSR. For India and Pakistan, there's nowhere else to go, or, nuclear weapons on both sides says nothing about the likelihood of peace breaking out. Rather, the presence of nuclear weapons may make policy makers more sanguine about resorting to conventional and unconventional forms of warfare.

The moral sanction of not using nuclear weapons because of their destructive power is soon trumped by the peculiar form of 'rationality' that becomes the norm for strategic discourse once nuclear weapons are in place. As nuclear war fighting plans are drawn up, policy makers are 'rationally' led to make calculations on the basis of the threat potential of relative destruction. Does a destroyed Karachi equate to a destroyed Bombay, or should New Delhi be added in order to make the relative loss to each country the same, they ask each other. Are nine million Indian dead the same as one million Pakistani dead, given the population differentials of each country? That even asking questions like this betray a fundamentally immoral condition is soon forgotten, once the rational game theorists and strategic thinkers start ruling the roost.

What deterrence promises is a condition where an absurdly heightened state of fear is seen to be the only way to maintain the status quo: It normalises pathology. For example, the lesson of the Cuban missile crisis is not how tough US President Kennedy was in making the Soviets back down, or how cleverly Khrushchev saved Cuba from US invasion, rather it is how easily a situation like that emerged and how difficult it was to back away from the crisis.

When the measure of international stability becomes an exchange of threats and counter-threats, we are already in a state of crisis. As we get deeper into the nether world of deterrence thinking, policy makers will agonise over whether the signals of threat escalation are being read clearly by the other side—that uncertainty will lead to greater insecurity on both sides as time goes on. And, when the state of security is reduced to the intangible feeling of how willing someone is to push the nuclear button—the reliability of the threat—sooner or later, the button will be pushed.

Western-style deterrence thinking is a call for extremists on both sides of the border to come to centre stage, because their threats are more credible to the other side. When we accept deterrence as the mechanism to keep war from breaking out, we leave ourselves permanently hostage to the whims and fears of men whose names we don't even know, whose mental state is never quite assured, and whose own sense of masculinity is always in doubt. We will not even be told when the two countries go to the brink of war, because national security concerns are at stake. Deterrence thinking helped perpetuate the Cold War; it legitimised the production of more weapons of ever-increasingly destructiveness. Deterrence knows no way of ending a hostile stand-off, only its management. Deterrence cannot help us move toward a safer and more secure existence and hence, it must be rejected.

In sum, I believe that nuclear weapons and their associated ways of thinking have become internationally sanctioned means for political leaders to avoid dealing with ongoing conflicts, whether real or ima-gined. The immediate task is to prevent nuclear weaponisation and deployment in South Asia. But we can only do that if we know where to look and how to understand what we see.

In this context, it is necessary to remember that for the most part, western strategic thinking followed advances in weapons technology, not the other way around. Contrary to the sanitised versions of US Cold War history that make it appear that a grand strategic plan was set in motion after World War II to contain and defeat the Soviets, in fact, a far more ad hoc system was the norm. Weapon developers and uni-versity scientists, driven by huge budgets and a culture of technological oneupmanship, were principally responsible for the shift from a dete-rrence strategy called 'counter-value', with population centres as prin-cipal targets, to 'counter-force' strategies, a far more dangerous option that could take away an opponent's second strike capability and thus increase the chances of war. By their focus on increasing the power, accuracy and efficiency of first bombs, then missiles and now lasers and other anti-missile devices, scientists forced the strategists to come up with new ways of rationalising their technical accomplishments into a new equilibrium of terror. Once new generations of weapons were built, strategists worked hard to develop new iterations of old theories. It would not be inaccurate to say that the greater foes of arms control between the Soviets and the US were not each other, but their own scientists and weapons developers. Is it any different in India ?

Nuclear Complexes

The problem of nuclear weapons is larger than its purported role in international relations. We need to understand, first, that the nuclear crisis in South Asia is part of a larger global crisis, which is the existence of huge arsenals of nuclear weapons in a number of countries; second, that only domestic pressure will be sufficient to close these nuclear complexes down, international treaties are necessary, but not enough; and third, that those who have the most to fear from these arsenals are the domestic populations of nuclear weapon states.

Let me focus on this last point. Nuclear complexes across the world constitute, apart from their destructive potential, a continuing source of danger to the populations they are meant to serve. We have seen, for the last fifty years and across the world, the cost of nuclear decision-making for popular security and well-being. We have documentary proof that US and Soviet nuclear scientists exposed human subjects and soldiers to nuclear radiation, that unprotected casual labourers were used to clean up radioactive leaks and spills in India, that serious environmental and human disasters were caused by accidents in nuclear power reactors all over the world, and that aboriginal people in Australia and native Americans were pushed off their homelands when uranium was discovered there. At the same time, we hardly know about the means by which highly contaminated nuclear wastes will be stored until safe to dispose of, or the extent of genetic mutation and radiation sickness among populations in the neighbourhood of reactors, mines and testing grounds, or about the huge and scarcely accounted resources that have been spent on these complexes over the last five decades. It must be noted also that when most of these cases were exposed, the first response of those in charge were cover-ups, stonewalling, denials and attempts to intimidate and coerce the victims.

These problems are not the result of the actions of a few misguided individuals. The kind of behaviour that the nuclear complexes of the world induce is built into the constitution of modern, large, capital intensive technological systems. The scale, size and complexity of these systems—from nuclear power stations, large dams, chemical factories and oil super tankers to intercontinental airplanes and their associated sub-complexes of airports, stations, pilots and traffic controllers, etc.—bring with them two things. For all their superb engineering and the material ease they make possible, the size of these complexes also entail a scale of destruction and damage that is beyond most imagination; more important, they carry a built-in danger of breakdown and failure due to their very complexity. Indeed, we have developed entirely new notions of risk and uncertainty, in both actuarial and phenomeno-logical terms, in order to cope with the dangers embedded in these systems.

These systems are, of technical necessity, extremely centralised and hierarchical in organisation, involving small numbers of highly-trained skilled workers and expert managers to run them. Information flows are carefully coordinated and only run along approved circuits. The difficulty of maintaining this rigorous system requires constant policing of the boundaries of the complex. Endless screens are set in place to prevent the intrusion of extraneous factors—whether environmental or infrastructural. However, due to the complexity of these systems, this policing is directed not towards eliminating all potential sources of disaster, but reducing the inherent likelihood of failure to 'acceptable levels'.

The public is rarely or never consulted about the trade-offs embedded in the definition of 'acceptable levels' of risk, about failure rates, or international standards of fault tolerance. Rather, once a system is in place, the public must be kept at bay for their foolish, uninformed concerns constitute a threat to the ongoing efficiency of the system. Over time, and especially as system failures are limited or managed in-house, the distance between those within and those outside the system grows. The privileging of scientific expertise produces a sense of infallibility: this eventually becomes a licence to claim a superior understanding of the common good. Of necessity, restricting information and secrecy becomes the standard operating procedure of these systems.

With a number of the more everyday technological complexes, the public has developed an ad hoc consensus for trusting their functions and accepting their costs. At various moments, especially just following a major disaster—an air crash, tanker spill, or reactor meltdown—the public has been drawn into expert discussions about the conditions under which the functioning of these systems takes places. Even if the public is not polled about its opinions, it is represented in the discussions—as victims of these catastrophes, if nothing else. The interiors of these black boxes become partially visible in a crisis, creating over time a tacit social understanding that helps absorb the fear of their presence. But, with the nuclear power complex that is not possible.

Nuclear power, apart from epitomising all the centralised, hierarchical and concentrated tendencies of large technological systems, is always clouded in the public eye because of its association with national security. From its arrival in the world, nuclear power's first association was with massive destruction, a destruction that soon became identified as the defining feature of national security. Since then, even when associated with peaceful uses, as with producing electricity, nuclear power carries with it the trace of its original sin. We know only too well from the Indian experience, public scrutiny is habitually rejected, ridiculed, or denied through the exaltation of expert knowledge, imposition of definitions of risk and efficiency that favour these systems, or by the invocation of larger social interests. The most opaque and powerful of these larger interests is national security.

What Next?

Where should we go? Even as the BJP government's definition of real and imagined threats to national security is being contested on many fronts, other tasks need to be taken on.

The first step to breaking the chain leading to nuclear disaster lies in far greater domestic oversight of the nuclear and space complexes— India's 'strategic enclave'. The current omnibus legislation that insulates the atomic energy complex from all scrutiny needs to be replaced by more specific, targeted laws that recognise the public's right to know what goes on in their name. Given the Lok Sabha's historic lack of will to take on the task of overseeing, an independent commission staffed by judges, scientists, economists and doctors needs to be set up to conduct a complete social accounting of the Indian strategic enclave. This commission must be given access to all official records and data, and allowed to conduct its own interviews with those within this enclave as well as those affected by it. Apart from informing us what has been done with the enormous funds spent on this sector, public accountability for decisions taken over the last fifty years will finally become possible.

These activities must be carried out in conjunction with citizen's groups from around the world, especially in the declared nuclear weapons states. Names of military scientists and weapon developers from around the world must be made public, so as to increase pressure on them to relinquish these activities and to remind them that they are being constantly monitored. Pressure must be put on national legislatures to ratify signed treaties. A parallel system of verification of weapons states' treaty obligations by domestic groups, with the necessary expertise to carry out scientific studies and publish reports, must be created (countries like China without internationally credible domestic monitors must be pressured to permit teams of international observers from non-nuclear weapons states to verify treaty compliance). This set of linked activities will not be complete until internationalised, but need not wait until the whole system is in place. The people of India can take the lead.

Do Nuclear Weapons Provide Security?

M.V. RAMANA

Having a gun pointed at you is an unnerving experience, even if you yourself are pointing one at the other person. With the recent tests, India and Pakistan are in a similar situation. They are now certainly targets for the nuclear missiles of all the other nuclear weapon states, as well as each other. This may or may not have been true earlier, but one can be sure it is the case now. It is, of course, not just the populace of India and Pakistan who are in the bull's eye. Despite having thousands of missiles, people in the US and Russia have lived in the constant fear that Washington, Moscow, or their own city could be destroyed in a moment. Knowledge that they are being targeted cannot provide security, only insecurity, to the people of the US and Russia, as well as to those India and Pakistan.

From Crisis to Disaster

What then is the security rationale for building nuclear weapons? The usual justification offered is that nuclear weapons are needed to deter the use or threat of use of nuclear weapons by another country. Underlying the concept of deterrence is the idea of mutually assured destruction—that any use of nuclear weapons by two countries possessing large nuclear arsenals would lead to massive destruction in both countries.[1] The idea of deterrence is that faced with this prospect of destruction, no country would initiate war. This notion of nuclear

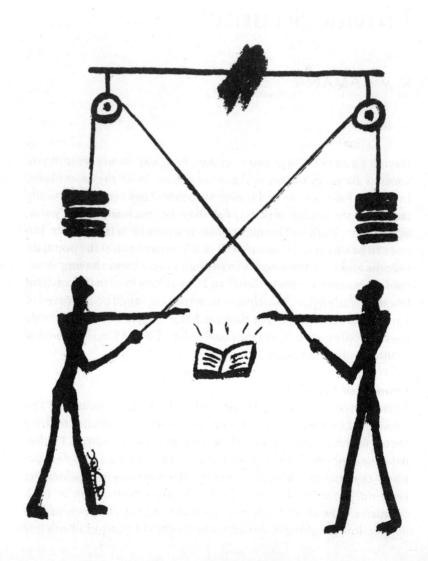

deterrence, by being articulated often enough, seems to have become accepted as true.

Deterrence, however, is not a law of nature like the theory of relativity. Underlying it are various assumptions, any of which may turn out to be false at any given point in time. And, the result of any failure could be catastrophic.

The most basic assumption is that states are unitary, with rational decision-makers trying to maximise their expected utility.[2] In reality, of course, this is far from true. Nevertheless, international relations scholars often assume this because it makes it easier to make predictions. Both the assumptions of unitary actors and rationality become particularly problematic during periods of crisis, especially war. Then, the multiplicity of individuals, institutions and interests that shape decision-making become crucial and could lead to outcomes that would be termed irrational.[3]

Irrational behaviour could also manifest itself at the individual level. An example of this was Richard Nixon who, under the strains of this final days in the presidency, is said to have sobbed, beaten his fists on the floor of his office and to have mused about his ability to release the forces of nuclear disaster. The (then) Defense Secretary Schlesinger took special precautions to prevent any of his orders to nuclear forces from being carried out.[4] Had there been an international crisis during that period, there is no way of knowing how Nixon would have acted. Use of nuclear weapons by Nixon, or by any other leader at any other time, would have meant the death of deterrence—and millions of people.

The counterparts of Nixon in South Asia could be Vajpayee or George Fernandes or Mulayam Singh Yadav or Nawaz Sharif or Gohar Ayub Khan. The question to think about is if anyone would, or should, feel secure with the knowledge that these people have the lives of millions of people in South Asia at their mercy. Nuclear war could result from either a wrong judgement on their part or by genuine mistakes.

Despite these unwarranted assumptions, as the main piece of evidence for trusting their arguments, believers in nuclear deterrence offer us the fact that the US and the Soviet Union did not go to (major) war against each other during the Cold War. Political scientists and historians have long contested the suggested explanation that it was nuclear weapons that kept the peace. Many, even believers in deterrence, point to a whole range of factors that aided stability—the legacy of the Second

World War, bipolarity, economic independence rather than inter-dependence, and so on.[5] It has even been argued that 'while nuclear weapons may have substantially influenced political rhetoric, public discourse and defence budgets and planning, it is not at all clear that they have had a significant impact on the history of world affairs since World War II.'[6] Thus, evidence for deterrence is weak, at best. Further, the absence of war so far does not imply that the same will hold true during other circumstances and for all time.

Over and above these arguments on why deterrence may not be based on well-founded assumptions, it is worth noting here that a growing number of military officials with concrete experience of work-ing with nuclear weapons, have questioned the logic of deterrence. Commander Robert Green, a retired British naval officer, calls nuclear deterrence a 'dangerous illusion'.[7] According to General Lee Butler, who headed the US Strategic Air Command, the world 'survived the Cuban missile crisis no thanks to deterrence, but only by the grace of God.'[8]

Thus, to reiterate, deterrence is based on faulty assumptions and may break down, especially in crisis situations. For example, a single rash act, or even rumours of a planned attack by an adversary, may trigger off nuclear war. If that happens, the massive destructive power available to both sides, intended precisely to strengthen deterrence, will ensure large-scale death and destruction.

For the present, let us grant the votaries of deterrence their security blankets and see what else needs to be in place for nuclear arsenals to even pretend to offer security.

The Sentinels of Doom

Having a large nuclear arsenal alone does not seem to be sufficient for deterrence. The US and Russia live in perpetual fear that the other may launch a first strike and hence have put into place early warning systems. Multiple satellites monitor the whole world looking for signals of missile launches. Once detected, there are early warning radars that take over and follow missile trajectories and pass on the data to proces-sing centres. From thereon, there are communication systems that attempt to ensure that information is conveyed to more senior decision-makers.

These satellites and early warning radar systems give them inform-ation within one-and-a-half minutes of the possible launch of a missile.

The analysis of this data takes about two-and-a-half minutes. During the next few minutes, decision-makers discuss the likelihood of the attack being real. If no other explanations are found for the signals, the President notified and he can call the other side to check if there has been an accidental launch of the missiles. All this is possible because missiles take about 25 minutes to travel from one country to the other. Further, this also allows various fail-safe measures to be built into the system as a hedge against miscalculation. The system, thus, provides for many layers of evaluation of accuracy of signals and decision-making.

Despite the enormous financial and technical resources invested in setting up and running these early warning systems, and trying to make them fool-proof, these systems failed frequently. Information on these failures is largely kept secret. It is known, however, that between 1977 and 1984, the US early warning system showed over 20,000 false alarms of a missile attack. Over 1000 of these were considered serious enough for bombers and missiles to be placed on alert.[9]

There were similar scares on the Russian side as well; a recent example is worth recounting. On January 25, 1995, military technicians at several radar stations across northern Russia thought they had seen a single missile from a US submarine coming towards Russia. This information was passed on through the chains of command to President Yeltsin who activated the 'nuclear briefcase', thus putting Russian forces on high alert. Subsequently, after about eight minutes, senior military officers determined that the rocket was headed far out to sea. The rocket turned out to be an American scientific probe to study the Northern lights.[10]

In the case of South Asia, even if such systems could be set up at enormous financial costs that we can scarcely afford, they would just not suffice. Both India and Pakistan are adjoining nations with a long border. Missile and airplane flight times are very short. A Prithvi missile will take between three and five minutes to reach almost anywhere in Pakistan. A Ghauri missile will take about five minutes to reach Delhi. Where then is the time for analysis of signals from satellites and radars, or to discuss the threat? How can leaders on both sides talk and check if the launch was accidental or intentional?

Because of this short warning time, both nations are likely to adopt a policy of launching their missiles as soon as there is a likelihood of the adversary launching an attack, or risk the prospect of losing their missiles on the ground. In light of the multiple possibilities for false alarms, this policy will almost ensure that nuclear weapons are used, sooner or later. If missiles like Prithvi and Ghauri are loaded with nuclear warheads and deployed on hair-trigger alert, the people of India and Pakistan are doomed to living in constant insecurity.

Remembering Dr. Strangelove

Even if one were to believe in deterrence, nuclear weapons pose conflicting demands. On the one hand, they have to be dispersed and in the hands of the military so that they can be used as soon as there is warning of an attack by the adversary. On the other, the decision to use these weapons is so momentous that one would like only the highest levels be able to order their use, that too after due deliberation. A third dimension is added by the widespread, large-scale effects of nuclear war—these could disrupt communication systems that allow leaders or commanders to communicate with field personnel.

Command and control systems are systems put in place to minimise the chances of inadvertent or unauthorised use of nuclear weapons. This is an arrangement of facilities, personnel, procedures and means of information acquisition, processing and dissemination used by a commander in planning, directing and controlling military operations.[11]

Most discussions of command and control emphasise the technical measures, implying in the process that if the technology is available, then one can feel secure. However, even the most sophisticated technical devices can be rendered worthless if improperly implemented.[12] For instance, one popular device to block unauthorised detonations is called permissive action links (PALs). It is possible to imagine a PAL-code arrangement in which, due to concern about the possible breakdown of communication with the field commander, higher authorities allow local access of the code. In such a case, regardless of how sophisticated the PAL hardware may be, unauthorised launch is possible. Even the most advanced command and control systems are not foolproof.

One only has to see Hollywood movies, starting with the classic *Dr. Strangelove*, to visualise possible scenarios under which unauthorised attacks could take place. Here, as in other realms, truth can indeed be stranger than fiction. Given the novelty of the situation, despite assurances by the Prime Ministers of India and Pakistan, it is highly unlikely that any foolproof command and control system will have been worked out. Indeed, Prime Minister Vajpayee has even said that India does not intend to 'replicate the kind of command and control structures' possessed by other nuclear weapon states.[13]

Thus, at the current moment, once weapons are assembled and handed over to the military, there is always a constant fear that some official, for whatever reasons, may decide to launch an attack against the 'enemy'. The way to avoid such issues is simply not to assemble nuclear weapons. Even some advocates of nuclear deterrence in India, recommend keeping nuclear weapons dismantled and their components stored separately.[14]

Nuclear Weapons Accidents

Setting up these early warning systems and command and control mechanisms do not preclude the possibilities of accidents involving nuclear weapons. Despite safety and security measures, such accidents continue to occur around the world. Between 1950 and 1990, the United States alone had over 175 accidents involving either nuclear weapons or vehicles that are suspected to have been carrying nuclear weapons.[15]

The greatest danger, which has fortunately never happened, would come from the accidental full-scale detonation of a nuclear weapon. There have been numerous accidents in which the chemical explosive surrounding the radioactive core of a nuclear weapon has exploded. For example, on 17 January, 1966, a B–52 bomber and a KC–135 refueling tanker collided in mid-air near Palomares, Spain. The B–52 crashed and four hydrogen bombs (15–25 megatonnes) were separated from the plane. The chemical explosives in two of the bombs exploded leading to release of radioactive material in the middle of a populated area. A similar accident near any of the densely populated South Asian cities could make Bhopal pale in comparison.[16]

A Mini Chernobyl?

If the number of accidents involving nuclear weapons seems high, the number of accidents (or incidents, as they are referred to by officials) in nuclear reactors would be even more. Many, of course, are in reactors used primarily to produce energy. Most of them do not lead to any large-scale consequences. The main people at risk are the workers in these facilities. But, as the Chernobyl accident showed, when there is a major accident in nuclear reactors, then huge regions are at risk. For example, even in Connecticut, USA, there was a 26 per cent increase in thyroid cancers due to radiation from Chernobyl.[17] While the Chernobyl reactor was primarily intended for the production of nuclear energy, even accidents at reactors that produce plutonium for nuclear weapons, which are typically smaller and somewhat different in the details of construction and operation, would lead to qualitatively similar consequences.

Even under normal conditions, the facilities involved in manufacturing nuclear weapons, which include uranium mines, fuel element manufacturing plants, nuclear reactors, reprocessing centres and spent fuel storage sites,[18] cause radiation-related diseases to people living in their vicinity.[19] Further, nuclear weapons, as we have seen recently, have to be tested. It has been estimated that nuclear testing the world over would lead to over 430,000 cancer fatalities.[20] So far, these victims of nuclear weapons manufacturing and testing have been the main casualties since Hiroshima and Nagasaki. Except under the narrowest definitions of security, the nuclear weapons complex will certainly count as a source of insecurity, especially to communities living near any such facility.

Non-Nuclear Threats
Nuclear weapons also pose non-nuclear threats. For nearly the whole period of the 'long peace', the US and the Soviet Union were engaged in a series of proxy wars of which Korea, Vietnam and Afghanistan are just the most prominent examples. Nuclear weapons, by seemingly protecting their homelands, allowed these wars to be fought.[21] It is no wonder then that violence and militarism in Kashmir intensified around the period when Pakistan started claiming and feeling confident about its nuclear capability in the late 1980s.

Despite claims that the establishment of nuclear capability in South Asia would freeze the Kashmir conflict, recent acts of terrorism in the Valley have demonstrated that nuclear tests have not changed the situation. The security of the people of Kashmir, as well as of those living in other arenas of covert warfare between India and Pakistan, is certainly not enhanced by the bomb-making capabilities of the two countries. Further, there is also the risk that even a small battle can escalate into nuclear war.

Conclusion

In summing up, we see that nuclear weapons lead to different kinds of insecurity. Some like those from proxy wars or from accidents in facilities involved in producing nuclear weapon components do not even involve nuclear weapons in any way. But the great danger comes from the possibility of a nuclear explosion, by mistake or otherwise. It is worth emphasising what this could lead to. If a small nuclear weapon with the same yield (15 kilotonnes) as the one that was dropped on Hiroshima more than 50 years ago was exploded over Mumbai (Bombay) or Karachi, the number of immediate deaths could be as high as half a million.[22] This does not include the deaths that would arise from cancers and other diseases that result from the long-term effects of radiation. Further, in the event of such an attack, it is not just those who are in Mumbai or Karachi at the time of the explosion who will be affected. Radioactive fallout could spread across large regions due to wind and radiation levels will remain high for a long period of time. Thus, the range of the destruction extends across space and time. India and Pakistan now have to come to terms with Robert Jay Lifton's statement: 'The central existential fact of the nuclear age is vulnerability.'[23]

The way out of this predicament is to work for the abolition of nuclear weapons—both locally and globally.

Notes and References

[1] Mutually Assured Destruction, like much of the language that is used in discussing nuclear weapons, camouflages what is being talked about. Even official policy makers occasionally admit this. For example, Fred C. Ikle, who went on to be the US Undersecretary of Defense during the Reagan administration, says, 'Assured destruction fails to indicate what is to be destroyed; but then 'assured genocide' would reveal the truth too starkly . . . keeping ready arsenals for instant and unrestrained slaughter of men, women and children is likely to impose a wrenching perspective on the officialdom of both nations.' See, Fred C. Ikle, 'Can Nuclear Deterrence Last Out the Century', *Foreign Affairs* 51, 1973.

[2] Honore M. Catudal, *Nuclear Deterrence: Does it Deter?* (London: Mansell Publishing, 1985, p. 56).

[3] Patrick M. Morgan, *Deterrence: A Conceptual Analysis*, (Beverly Hills: Sage, 1977, pp. 101–02).

[4] Bruce Russett, *The Prisoners of Insecurity: Nuclear Deterrence, The Arms Race, and Arms Control* (San Francisco: W.H. Freeman and Company, 1983, p. 121).

[5] John Lewis Gaddis, 'The Long Peace: Elements of Stability in the Postwar International System', *International Security*, Spring 1986, Vol. 10, No. 4.

[6] John Muller, 'The Essential Irrelevance of Nuclear Weapons: Stability in the Postwar World', *International Security*, Fall 1988, Vol. 13, No. 2.

[7] Commander Robert Green, 'Why Nuclear Deterrence is a Dangerous Illusion', *Agni: Studies in International Strategic Issues,* January–May 1998, Vol. 2, No. 3.

[8] General George Lee Butler, 'Time to End the Age of Nukes', *Bulletin of the Atomic Scientists,* March/April 1997, pp. 33–36.

[9] H. L. Abrams, 'Strategic Defense and Inadvertent Nuclear War', in *Inadvertent Nuclear War: The Implications of the Changing Global Order,* edited by H. Wiberg. I.D. Petersen, and P. Smoker (Oxford: Pergamon Press, 1993, pp. 39–55).

[10] Bruce G. Blair, Harold A. Feiveson and Frank von Hippel, 'Taking Nuclear Weapons off Hair-Trigger Alert', *Scientific American,* November 1997.

[11] Paul Bracken, *The Command and Control of Nuclear Forces* (New Haven: Yale University Press, 1983, p. 3).

[12] Peter D. Feaver, 'Command and Control in Emerging Nuclear Nations', *International Security,* Winter 1992/93, Vol. 17, No. 3.

[13] Kenneth J. Cooper, 'Leader says India has a "Credible" Deterrent', *Washington Post,* June 17, 1998.

[14] General K. Sundarji, 'Imperatives of Indian Minimum Deterrence', *Agni: Studies in International Strategic Issues,* May 1996, Vol. 2, No. 1.

[15] Shaun Gregory, *The Hidden Costs of Deterrence: Nuclear Weapons Accidents* (London: Brassey's, 1990).

[16] It has been estimated that dispersal of kilogram quantities of plutonium (used in nuclear weapons) could cause a few thousand deaths due to cancer. See Steve Fetter and Frank von Hippel, 'The Hazard from Plutonium Dispersal by Nuclear-warhead Accidents', *Science and Global Security,* 1990, No. 2, pp. 21–42.

[17] Permanent People's Tribunal, *Chernobyl: Environmental, Health and Human Rights Implications* (Geneva: International Peace Bureau, 1996, p. 133).

[18] One of the largest nuclear disasters prior to the Chernobyl accident was the explosion of a storage tank containing high-level nuclear waste at the Chelyabinsk–65 nuclear weapons complex. The story of this disaster and the efforts to suppress knowledge of this may be found in Z.A. Medvedev, *Nuclear Disaster in the Urals* (New York: Vintage Books, 1980).

[19] *Nuclear Wastelands: A Global Guide to Nuclear Weapons Production and its Health and Environmental Effects,* edited by Arjun Makhijani, Howard Hu, and Katherine Yih, a Special Commission of International Physicians for the Prevention of Nuclear War and The Institute for Energy and Environmental Research (Cambridge, USA: The MIT Press, 1995).

[20] International Physicians for the Prevention of Nuclear War and Institute of Energy and Environmental Research, *Radioactive Heaven and Earth* (London: Zed Books, 1991).

[21] See, for example, Gar Alperovitz and Kai Bird, 'The Centrality of the Bomb', *Foreign Policy,* Spring 1994, pp. 3–20.

[22] M.V. Ramana, 'Bombing Bombay? Effects of Nuclear Weapons and a Case Study of a Hypothetical Explosion' (Cambridge, MA: International Physicians for the Prevention of Nuclear War Report, 1999).

[23] Robert Jay Lifton and Richard Falk, *Indefensible Weapons: The Political and Psychological Case Against Nuclearism* (USA: Basic Books, 1982).

India's Draft Nuclear Doctrine: A Critique

ACHIN VANAIK

The Draft Nuclear Doctrine (DND), formulated by the National Security Advisory Board (NSAB) and released in August 1999, marks a further hardening of India's nuclear posture since Pokhran-II. Sixteen months after New Delhi first began talking about constructing a 'minimum nuclear deterrent', the DND is pushing India towards an open-ended, potentially huge, triadic (land, air and sea-based) nuclear force of enormous lethality. The DND's publication marks a triumph of the maximalist or extreme standpoint and expresses the dominance of the classical Cold War mindset within the country's nuclear lobby. It will, if implemented, ignite a nuclear arms race in Asia as well as grievously damage the prospects of global disarmament. The DND is yet to be adopted by the National Security Council or the Union Cabinet, but it is clearly driven by the government's need to legitimise the systematic development and deployment of a nuclear weapons system.

Political Expediency in the Timing of the DND Release
The curious timing of the DND's release must be noted. It is hard to believe that its publication, over a year after the actual testing of Indian nuclear weapons, was so pressing an issue as to be completely unrelated to the elections at hand (September-October 1999), to the effectively caretaker status of the government at the time, or to the partisan desire to make political electoral capital out of nuclear jingoism. No such desire to inform the public in advance was evident at the time of the

WIND

MAY the great breathe PURiFication upon you

MAY the WATERS rain immortality upon you

MAY the SUN warm your BODY with blessing

MAY DEATH show YOU mercy!

Do not Perish!

actual tests in May 1998. The only people in the know appear to have been the BJP's ideological mentors in the RSS, since even the coalition partners in government were caught unawares. Indeed, the Indian people were told nothing at first, except a bare statement of technical facts. It was only after writing (in a letter dated May 11, 1998) to the US President giving reasons for the tests that the Vajpayee government felt it necessary to explain its rationale to the people of India. Clearly, the sudden discovery of the virtues of transparent public debate on the part of the BJP-led government hides ulterior motives.

Cosmetic Exercise in Nuclear Legitimisation
Apart from topical electoral concerns, a major ulterior motive is the attempted legitimisation of India's nuclear weapons through the DND. One component of this attempt is the desire to divert public concern and discussion away from the issue of the rights and wrongs of 'going nuclear', that is actually manufacturing and deploying such weapons. It is incredible that the first-ever national nuclear doctrine draft does not even attempt to discuss the relative merits and demerits of a non-nuclear weaponised stance in any depth. Instead, it assumes that India has to have nuclear weapons and proceeds to lay out the kind of weapons systems it feels are required. This omission makes the DND part of the ongoing cosmetic cover-up to treat the Indian nuclear arsenal as a legitimate fait accompli. By focusing public awareness mainly on the 'issue' of what kind of weapons system India should have, the DND deliberately tries to make it more difficult for people to think of reversing India's nuclear weapon-related direction at a time when this is very feasible, as well as desirable and necessary. A second dimension of this attempt to achieve legitimisation is international. The political climate worldwide about nuclear weapons has changed during the decades-long gap in nuclear proliferation prior to May 1998. International opinion against nuclear weapons is now far stronger and more widespread than in the 1960s, leaving India (and Pakistan) in considerable diplomatic-political isolation on the issue. In this context, releasing the DND in the name of 'democratic debate' and offering to discuss the DND with other nuclear weapons powers is a way of working around international pressure to further develop and eventually deploy nuclear weapons under the guise of a 'responsible', 'open-minded' and 'consultative' process. This symbolic value of the DND has nothing to do with its actual contents, which are far more

adventurist than would have been expected from government spokes-people making so-called reasonable calls for 'minimum nuclear deterrence'.

The DND's Fatal Flaw

India's DND is open to two major levels of criticism. The first and most important level is the fundamental flaw embodied in all nuclear doctrines. This has to do with the inescapable and irreconcilable dilemma of deterrence. At the second level lies a more detailed criticism of specific proposals made in the DND. The first flaw is addressed here, while the actual provisions of the Indian DND are addressed later.

Deterrence is an attempt to achieve security by threatening someone else's security. It is an attempt to avoid war by preparing to fight a war. It seeks security for one country by generating fear and hostility in the other. Not surprisingly, deterrence frequently breaks down and there are actual wars. In the non-nuclear case, life carries on despite conventional wars even for the loser. However, in the case of nuclear deterrence, this cannot be, since there is no way of maintaining civil society for the losers (and even for the winners) after a nuclear exchange. Therefore, unlike for non-nuclear deterrence, the only purpose of preparing for a nuclear war is to avoid it. If nuclear deterrence breaks down (and it is illogical and irrational to believe that it cannot break down, especially since non-nuclear deterrence clearly can, and does), all security collapses, as does most life.

Why can nuclear deterrence break down? It can because it is based on a limited, frequently uninformed, erroneous, and changing perception of how opponents will think about and respond to the threat of nuclear war. In fact, mutually hostile countries would always be tempted to strike first, regardless of commitments given, because it is easy to believe that to do so confers 'great advantage' over a hostile opponent. In the nuclear deterrence framework, the initiator can hope to knock out most of the nuclear might of its opponent especially if it also tries to 'decapitate' the political leadership of the 'enemy'. The country that strikes second is no longer acting to enhance its security, so nuclear retaliation is an act of revenge, not of security.

Pursuing security through nuclear deterrence is therefore always a dangerous gamble where the consequences of failure are horrendous and unthinkable—there is no second chance after a breakdown of nuclear deterrence. Relying on nuclear weapons for security creates two major insecurities the regular and continuous insecurity of an escalating arms race between rivals as each tries to prevent the other side from getting an 'advantage', and the ever-present fear that the worst,—'a breakdown of deterrence'—might happen sooner or later.

To sum up, nuclear deterrence, the most 'reasonable' foundation of all nuclear doctrines aiming at security, is nothing but the irrational hope that a terrible fear of the consequences of nuclear war will continuously promote wise decisions by fallible human beings, operating under intense pressure in changing circumstances they can never fully control. All nuclear doctrines are thus basically nothing, but hope masquerading as operative strategies. The Indian DND is no exception.

Specific Features of the Indian DND

As noted earlier, the DND is an attempt to serve as a framework for the limited debate about what kind of nuclear weapons India is to have. The DND is thus a statement of intent and will be treated as such for the moment, although the issue of the lack of India's capacity to build what the DND claims is necessary is itself a major point of concern.

Paragraph 2.1 says that building a deterrent force is 'consistent with the UN Charter, which sanctions the right of self-defence'. This extension of the cover of the UN charter to nuclear weapons is illegitimate and hypocritical. This is especially so, given the ruling of the International Court of Justice (ICJ) that rejected any such right in regard to nuclear weapons, except in the case of the most 'extreme circumstance of self-defence' on which it has given no ruling at all. Nuclear weapons are instruments of revenge or offence, not defence. In fact, in 1995, the Indian government had submitted its own memorandum to the ICJ insisting that the use of nuclear weapons, the threat of their use (deterrence), their development and deployment, and even preparations to build such weapons were immoral, illegal and unacceptable 'in all circumstances'!

Summary of the Major Points Made in the DND

The DND is made up of eight sections, each with their subparagraphs. The sections are (1) Preamble, (2) Objectives, (3) Nuclear Forces, (4) Credibility and Survivability, (5) Command and Control, (6) Security and Safety, (7) Research and Development, and (8) Disarmament and Arms Control. The major points made are:

- India's DND is based on the principle of pursuing security through reliance on the presumed efficacy of nuclear deterrence. The DND, however, admits that such deterrence can fail, in which case India promises adequate punitive retaliation.
- India's nuclear arsenal must be such that it will always provide maximum credibility, effectiveness and survivability. Therefore, the size of the arsenal cannot be fixed but its nature must be dynamic and flexible enough to respond to changes in the security environment (such as changes in the weapons postures of perceived rivals), to changing security needs (as defined by state elites), and to technology advances.
- India's nuclear might must deter any state with nuclear weapons. India will pursue triadic deployment and have multiple redundant systems, that is, more than just a 'bare minimum'.
- India will not strike first but will carry out the promptest possible retaliation, which will also be punitive, meaning massive enough to be unacceptably damaging to the opponent.
- The nuclear arsenal will be tightly controlled by the political centre, namely the Prime Minister, but will also be of a highly mobile and dispersed nature.
- The safety and security of the weapons system is of paramount importance, and all precautions will be taken to ensure against sabotage, theft and unauthorised or inadvertent use of nuclear weapons (the DND says nothing on how this is to be achieved or ensured).
- India will not accept any restriction whatsoever on its research and development capabilities or activities in regard to nuclear weapons and related areas.
- India promises 'no-first-use (NFU)' against nuclear weapons states and 'no-use' against non-nuclear weapons states, except where the latter are aligned to nuclear weapons states.
- India will pursue arms control measures and believes in the goal of complete, global disarmament, which it will also pursue.

Punitive Retaliation and Potential Targets

Paragraphs 2.3 and 2.4 of the DND admit that deterrence can fail but say that in that case there will be 'punitive retaliation'. Punitive retaliation comes when 'nuclear security' has failed. But the DND fails to acknowledge the basic insoluble dilemma of nuclear deterrence. Of course, the DND also does not admit that such retaliation, even if possible, is simply a senseless and suicidal act of revenge since it will lead to continuing nuclear exchanges. Given this context of punitive retaliation, the DND is covering up the fact that once deterrence fails there is permanent collapse of security.

Paragraph 2.4 says 'Indian nuclear weapons are to deter use and threat of use of nuclear weapons by any State or entity against India.' Paragraph 4.1 says 'Any adversary must know that India can and will retaliate to inflict destruction that the aggressor will find unacceptable.' These stances are so open-ended that they can assert a need for nuclear deterrence against almost anybody, including major nuclear weapons states such as the US as well as entities such as NATO. This would require a huge weapons system for 'credible' second-strike capacity. These stances effectively commit India to an arms race with the major nuclear weapons states—an economically, politically and socially suicidal policy.

In paragraph 2.5, the DND says there will be no use of nuclear weapons against non-nuclear states if they 'are not aligned with nuclear weapons powers'. So Japan, for example, may not get an assurance of non-use, only of no-first-use (NFU). This ambiguity not only dilutes India's earlier NFU commitment but is more objectionable than, say, China's NFU commitment, which specifically excludes use against any non-nuclear state regardless of whether or not it is allied to a nuclear state. This paragraph also flatly contradicts paragraph 8.3 in the same document which says, 'Having provided unqualified (our emphasis) negative security assurances, India shall work for internationally binding unconditional (our emphasis) negative security assurances by nuclear weapons states to non-nuclear weapons states.'

Paragraph 5.2 talks of 'sequential plans', 'flexibility and responsiveness', an 'integrated operational plan' and 'a targeting policy'. These make sense only in relation to identified, actual opponents. This flatly contradicts the government claim that India's weapons are 'not country-specific'. Such a posture in practice will clearly vitiate India's immediate security environment further rather than improving it.

The Notion of 'Minimum' Deterrence

Paragraph 3.1 talks of triadic deployment and 'sea-based assets', 'multiple redundant systems, mobility, dispersion and deception'. Paragraph 2.2 talks of developing a capability of 'maximum (our emphasis) credibility, survivability, effectiveness'. What all this means is simple. In defining its 'minimum deterrent', the DND is so ambitious and open-ended that it makes a mockery of any even remotely reasonable notion of 'minimum'. Britain has moved towards a single system of deployment; France is moving towards it and NATO in practice no longer has triadic deployment (it has some airborne and submarine deployment). In this background, India's idea of triadic deployment as a 'minimum deterrent' appears especially bizarre.

The DND also talks of 'sea-based' rather than strictly submarine-based nuclear weapons, which leaves open the option of tactical nuclear missiles on surface vessels. 'Tactical' nuclear weapons are not, incidentally, explicitly repudiated anywhere in the DND. Since such weapons are irrelevant even to the notion of nuclear deterrence, there is ground for legitimate concern that the DND has a hidden agenda extending beyond even 'minimum nuclear deterrence' to nuclear weapon-based attempts at hegemony.

Paragraph 3.2 commits India to shift from 'peacetime deployment to fully employable forces in the shortest possible time.' When this is linked with the requirement for 'mobility, dispersion and deception', and with paragraph 5.5 which talks of executing 'operations in an NBC environment' ('NBC' refers to 'nuclear, biological and chemical' weapons) what emerges is a rationalisation of two actions.

Firstly, it implies possible delegation of authority to use nuclear weapons, which contradicts talk of centralising such a decision at one point (the Prime Minister). Certainly, all nuclear weapons systems and nuclear deterrence ideologies suffer from this inescapable and unresolvable contradiction, and it would have been astounding if the Indian DND, with its far-beyond 'minimum' stances, were to be any exception. If there is a 'decapitating first strike' which is even partially successful, who will decide on the launch of the remainder of the weapons, and how will this decision be taken if delegation has not been allowed for? Against this, delegation of any sort weakens central control and is more provocative and dangerous.

Secondly, the DND demands the quickest possible retaliation, which has to mean launch-on-warning of an enemy attack, or launch-under-attack, or immediate launch-after-attack. In all these modes, there is a requirement for a nuclear weapons system at a high-level of operational alert and readiness, with regular training exercises for maintenance. All of these 'aggression-as-a-routine' postures are bound to be deeply expensive, provocative and destabilising—none of them good indicators of enhanced security.

Furthermore, paragraphs 7.1 and 7.2 insist on continuous and unrestrained research and development in nuclear weapons. Once again, this indicates the shifting base of the DND's notion of 'minimum deterrence', and demonstrates that the DND is tacitly accepting the inevitability of an arms race, committing India to enthusiastic participation in that doomed exercise.

Costs Implicit in the DND

How much is the nuclear arsenal envisaged by the DND likely to cost? This is hard to answer, in part because the DND excludes nothing in principle. Triadic deployment in operational readiness is explicitly envisioned. Tactical weapons are not excluded, neither is a 'credible' second-strike capacity against large nuclear weapons states such as the US, nor a ballistic missile defence system, nor continuous research into ever more advanced nuclear weapons, nor 'space-based assets' for early warning and damage monitoring. In fact, nothing in the DND suggests any bar to spending on the scale of the nuclear weapons programme of, say, the US. In such a situation cost estimates can only be highly speculative, uncertain and subject to constant escalation. Even an adequate breakdown of the costs of the different components of the weapons system cannot be made.

Further, the DND recognises that there is no such thing as a 'stable minimum posture' in terms of defined quantities, estimates of which would be needed if costs are even to be guessed at. The DND also talks of flexibility and responsiveness to changing force structures of other nuclear powers and to technology advances, compounding the open-ended nature of expenditure.

However, the 'base' that the DND aims for is already so advanced (triadic rather than single-system deployment) as to impose an enormous burden. In addition, it is reasonable to assume that there will be difficulties because of supply obstacles, external restrictions, construction failures and over-runs, and costs will skyrocket. This is when only the initial development and manufacturing costs are considered. There are constantly recurring (annual) costs for maintenance and replacement-improvement, which can be anything between 30 per cent to 50 per cent of the total costs incurred in institutionalising a nuclear weapons system. Producing nuclear bombs takes usually around 10 per cent of the total cost. Command, control, communications, intelligence mechanisms account for about a third, and over 50 per cent goes towards the delivery systems. And finally, all these costs are in addition to rather than substituting for conventional defence costs (a point made depressingly clear by the Kargil confrontation in mid-1999), which themselves are likely to rise as the security environment degrades further in mutual suspicion and provocation.

Although no definitive numbers can be guessed at, what range of spending is likely to be necessary? One way is to ask the NSAB panel that produced the DND. While the DND itself is silent on the issue of costs, a member of this panel has said that costs for the proposed 'minimum deterrent' can be anything from Rs. 70,000 crore to Rs. 700,000 crore, or $15 to 150 billion. A second method is extrapolation. Earlier estimates of a 'small' 100-warhead arsenal are of the order of Rs. 40,000 to 50,000 crore. The arsenal envisaged by the DND, which could well have 400 plus weapons, is likely to cost several-fold more. A third way is to look at what other countries have spent. Its nuclear deterrent has cost the US over $5.5 trillion (5,500 billion). The Chinese 'minimum' has so far cost well over $100 billion or Rs. 450,000 crore. Even if the unrealistic assumption is made that a 'modest' Indian deterrent is going to be somewhat less expensive than the Chinese arsenal, the figure of Rs. 70,000 crore is a hopeless underestimate.

What Does the DND Represent?
Clearly, this is not a doctrine that is any less awful than others around the world. The DND is adventurist, aggressive and destabilising like others of its kind. It makes a mockery even of the so-called 'reasonable' notion that India should have a small 'minimum' deterrent, that there will be no competitive arms race with rivals and that the construction of a 'minimum' will be cheap. If implemented, the DND can only push India further into the nuclear abyss. The DND thus reinforces the view that the Indian government's decision to 'go nuclear' was not determined by any changes in threat perceptions, nor by any degradation of national security, but instead by the obsession with nuclear weapons as 'status symbol' and 'power currency', which needs an open-ended and highly ambitious arsenal, regardless of the cost to the nation. The DND is entirely in keeping with the self-righteous and grandiose

'nationalism' of the BJP-led government and of its ideological mentors, which makes the people subservient to the 'state'.

India can either relentlessly pursue a global nuclear disarmament programme or recklessly join the nuclear arms race. It cannot move in these diametrically opposite directions at the same time. The claim of the DND that it intends to pursue both these goals simultaneously is a blatant contradiction and its proposed espousal aims to mislead not only the people of India but of the entire world.

Returning to Our Own Agenda: Why India Should Sign the CTBT?

ACHIN VANAIK AND PRAFUL BIDWAI

What is at Stake?

At the time of writing, it remains uncertain whether or not India will sign the CTBT. A significant section of those who have supported India going openly nuclear are now prepared to go along with the CTBT in return for a behind-the-scenes deal involving the effective lifting of sanctions and greater freedom for India to import dual-use technologies relevant for the continuation and upgradation of its nuclear and missile development programmes. After all, accepting the CTBT does not prevent India from going ahead with its current plans to weaponise and deploy a nuclear delivery system, or to set up the associated command, control, communications and intelligence networks. For this section of Indian pro-nuclearists, acceptance of the CTBT is the minimum price the Indian government will have to pay if it wants to end its current international political isolation and make some mark as a supposedly responsible *de facto* nuclear weapon's power by involving itself in ongoing international arms restraint activities. However, this does not mean that India will eventually or soon enough sign the CTBT.

Opposition to the CTBT remains significant. It exists inside the government and bureaucracy, inside the Sangh combine and certainly amidst the opposition parties of which the CPI and CPM are the most vocal. The Congress, in its latest official statements, has also indicated that it will consider the CTBT only if there is some adequate pay-off, not only in terms of dual-use technologies and the lifting of sanctions but also in some form of explicit recognition by the existing five nuclear weapons powers of India's newly acquired status.

This may just be a way of the Congress trying to distinguish itself from the BJP and seeking to embarrass the ruling party while actually it is itself willing eventually to go along with the CTBT. Nonetheless, the Congress' formal stand is of some importance because a Congress-led coalition of parties, supported from the outside by the mainstream Left, might soon replace the current BJP-led coalition government. Since such a government would be crucially dependent on the Left for its survival, then given the intransigent opposition of the Left to the CTBT, it will make it that much more difficult for India to sign the treaty, no matter what the dominant view is inside the Congress. As it is, there exists a strong section amongst the nuclear hawks who believe that India should retain the option to test and even carry out more tests if that is what is required to develop a 'sophisticated' nuclear weapons system of 'sufficient' credibility, especially vis-à-vis China. India's ability to carry out sub-critical testing is suspect. Some believe (no matter what the Indian scientific establishment may say) that sub-criticals and computer simulation do not adequately substitute for explosive testing when it comes to making significant qualitative advances in nuclear weapons' designing and engineering.

The time period in which a decision has to be made is short. If India does not sign the CTBT, then the centre of gravity of the whole nuclear discourse in the country will again shift (as it did during the 1995–96 debate on the CTBT) to the right, making it more likely that India goes ahead not just in accelerating the process of weaponisation and deployment but even towards further testing. If the logic of earlier refusing to sign the CTBT was then to move towards testing (what was the point of not signing the CTBT and condemning it as an American-led trap but then acting as if India was still in the trap by refusing to test?), then the logic of once again defying the CTBT regime is to go further ahead to carry out more tests in the name of enhancing one's weapons capability and sophistication levels, all in the name of protecting 'national security'. If India does test again in the future, then it is almost certain that the CTBT regime will unravel completely and that some (e.g. China, US, Russia) if not all, the existing nuclear weapons states will resume explosive testing. The impact of such a development on the momentum towards greater nuclear restraint, reduction and disarmament will be nothing short of disastrous. As it is, US Senate ratification of the CTBT is unlikely to take place unless India accedes to the Treaty; and if the US does not ratify it, then China and Russia most likely will not. If support for the CTBT has now come from a section of nuclear hawks, there has also been steady, consistent support from a small minority of anti-nuclearists who have always argued that the CTBT is a worthy restraint measure that should be welcomed by all those opposed to regional and global nuclearisation.

Some of those who are opposed to any further testing by India may now come around to this view. However, the mainstream Left, which also wants such a permanent end to testing believes that, as a matter of principle, continued opposition to the CTBT is essential. If, for the sake of argument, we temporarily accept this claim, then the Left must put forward a viable and superior alternative to the CTBT and outline how this can be feasibly achieved. This it has not done. In reality, the choice is: either the CTBT or nothing! Certainly, any other arrangement, even if possible, would be qualitatively inferior. Consider the following. The current government has suggested that it is prepared to give its prevailing moratorium on further testing a *de jure* status.

This is not the same as a permanent ban on further testing. It is difficult to believe that any future government, barring one led by the Left (which is not a realistic short- or medium-term possibility), would enact legislation to ensure such a permanent ban. Even, if we assume, once again for the sake of argument, that this is a possibility, can we honestly believe that this will come about soon enough to halt the rightward shift of the general terms of the nuclear discourse that will be promoted by rejection of the CTBT? Assuming that such a self-denying ban through an Act of Parliament is achievable soon enough, can we expect such a ban to include sub-criticals and computer simulation? If it does not, will the Left oppose such a national ban on the grounds of its fraudulence, since this is one of its central criticisms of the CTBT itself? It would appear strange indeed, if the Left did not insist that any such Indian law or resolution of Parliament should include such a denial. Does it believe such a comprehensive test ban is achievable nationally? This is not all. What about a genuine national monitoring system which will be fully transparent and accountable to the Indian public so as to ensure that there is no cheating? Sub-kilotonne tests, for example, are not easily detectable by outside monitoring. Can we seriously believe that such a fully transparent and publicly accountable national monitoring system will ever be set up by any government, barring that of the Left, given the character not only of other parties but of the Indian scientific and technical nuclear establishment itself? Or are we to assume that it is not necessary to set up such a national monitoring system? Furthermore, assuming the virtually impossible, i.e. that such a national monitoring system is set up, in what way would it be superior to the international monitoring system of the CTBT regime? Why should we prefer a purely national monitoring system, howsoever transparent, to one which is international in character and, therefore, gives reassurance to the peoples and governments of other countries that there is no cheating by any of the nuclear weapons states? Why shouldn't Pakistan have transparent access to information concerning possible Indian cheating and vice versa?

Some Indian critics of the CTBT have made superficial and misleading comments about the supposed dangers of intrusive procedures of onsite inspections by the CTBT regime (which criticisms of which will be dealt with later). But they have never pointed out what is the obvious truth about the treaty. The CTBT is the first ever nuclear arms-related treaty to be genuinely multilaterally negotiated! It is also the first-ever treaty in nuclear-related fields, if and when, it enters into force, which will set up a genuinely international monitoring system (not a US-dominated one) that limits national sovereignty on the question of testing, thereby establishing a crucial and vital precedent for the development of genuine international mechanisms of control and authority of the kind that will have to eventually emerge if we are to have a truly global structure for ensuring universal and total nuclear disarmament. Before coming to the provisions of the treaty itself and to a rebuttal of the main lines of criticism of it, let us take a look at the early history of the Indian CTBT debate.

The Early History of the Indian CTBT Debate

Before early 1994, no one in India—neither pro-nuclear hawks nor any leftists—opposed a CTBT. Indeed, it was repeatedly asserted, both officially and by those outside the government, that the CTBT precisely exemplified the kind of universal and non-discriminatory restraint and pro-disarmament measure that should be supported in contrast to selective or 'discriminatory' or regional disarmament measures, like the call for a South Asian nuclear weapons-free zone (NWFZ), which had to be rejected. The first stirrings of unease about the CTBT begin in early 1994 and then opposition to it grew, especially through-out 1995–96, reaching a domestic crescendo by mid-1996 when the Government of India formally announced its decision not to accede to the CTBT. Why this change from a position held for decades by everyone in India–hawks, ambiguists, doves and leftists-of support for the CTBT? In fact, it was Nehru who in 1954 became the first world statesman to propose such a comprehensive test ban!

Two kinds of arguments were proffered to explain and justify this volte face by the new-found opponents of the CTBT, which included Leftists. First, it was claimed that India was not opposed in principle to a CTBT and thus there was no shift from prior positions. It was opposed to this particular CTBT i.e. to its particular failings and deficiencies. However, this argument could not but sound extremely hollow when coming from the Indian government and its hardline supporters since the Congress Party, it is now revealed, was seriously considering carry-ing out a test in December 1995 (military logistics began in March 1995), when the serious nitty-gritty of negotiations on the CTBT had not begun and its likely shape was, therefore, unknown. The absolutely central issue of the very scope of the treaty only began to take shape in December 1995. Subsequently, all opponents of the CTBT focused on specific criticisms of the supposed failings of this treaty as justification for an Indian rejection.

The difference between Leftist opponents and others was that among the ranks of the former could be found a number of people who rejected it solely on the grounds of such putatively inherent failings and did not use 'national security' arguments to justify their opposition. These specific criticisms will be taken up later. The second line of argument for rejecting the CTBT revolved around the claim that the general political context had changed and therefore what was deemed appro-priate and necessary earlier had now to be discarded. Here, there were two favourite candidates for substantiating this changed context claim. Both were liberally used in the Indian debate, separately and in conjunc-tion. The end of the Cold War, it seemed, had now so dramatically changed the overall context, i.e. the US had come into unipolar global dominance, that the issue of a CTBT had to be reassessed anew. But the Cold War began unravelling from the mid-1980s and the Gulf War (the peak of US post-Cold War euphoria) was over in 1991. And yet no Indian talked of reassessing the CTBT till years later, in 1994–95. Did they only then recognise that the end of the Cold War had 'changed the context'? For other critics, the decisive moment when the 'political context changed' was in April 1995 when the NPT was indefinitely and permanently extended.

This was supposed to signal a new phase in the US-led nuclear imperium in which the CTBT issue had now to be placed. But since the outcome of these NPT negotiations was not evident till the very end and attacks on the CTBT had started a year earlier, this too is not a particularly convincing claim. There is a larger issue about the relationship of the NPT to the CTBT and the question of whether the CTBT is part of the discriminatory non-proliferation regime sought to be institutionalised and consolidated by the nuclear weapons states. This will also be taken up later. But the key point here is that the claims about how a changed context now rendered older, more favourable perspectives about the CTBT redundant, were really little more than exercises in self-delusion or deceit. The principal reason why criticisms of the CTBT only surfaced sometime in 1994 and not earlier is strikingly obvious. Negotiations on the treaty only began in early 1994 and it was only in September 1994 that some kind of a working draft or 'rolling text', as it was called, was established.

As long as the CTBT issue was something distant, abstract and not likely to be realised imminently, India could try and occupy the high moral ground by claiming to be for the CTBT as distinct from other supposedly non-universal and selective measures. The moment, however, that it became something eminently and imminently realisable, then the implications of the CTBT on India's position of ambiguity became a matter of urgent and unavoidable consideration in which simply continuing with a long-practised form of moral posturing would no longer do. India's position of ambiguity, which enjoyed support from all the political parties—with only the BJP insisting for decades that the country should openly nuclearise—was always combined with the commitment to continuously and regularly upgrade this option technologically. It was this capacity to upgrade the Indian option that was now threatened by the possible emergence of a CTBT. This focused Indian minds, as never before, on the question of whether or not to test, whether or not to accept the CTBT, whether or not to maintain the posture of ambiguity or to go openly nuclear.

The overall result was that the CTBT debate became the most intense public debate ever since 1947 on any nuclear weapons-related issue.

It was no surprise, moreover, when not only the general anti-CTBT lobby but the government itself finally broke with longstanding official policy and cited 'national security' reasons as well as explicit criticisms of the CTBT draft for its rejection of the treaty. This marked the first time since Independence that the Indian government had officially endorsed nuclear deterrence and linked it to national security perspectives. Before then, it had always held nuclear deterrence to be 'morally abhorrent' and a delusory and unacceptable foundation for the pursuit of nuclear security for any country including India. The anti-CTBT lobby, with only the partial exception of some Leftists, therefore, justified their opposition to the treaty, both on the grounds of its weakening Indian national security and on various other grounds of its deficiency as a nuclear restraint and pro-disarmament measure. This way, not only could India adopt the position that it was simply safeguarding its national interests and security, but that it was also placing itself in the forefront of a morally legitimate crusade to promote genuine nuclear restraint and disarmament by exposing the supposedly fraudulent character of the CTBT itself.

What resulted, of course, was one of the most shameful, deceitful, ignorant (and in some cases downright dishonest) public debate on any issue in the last 50 years in India. As bad, if not worse than, the actual fact of India's rejection of a worthy treaty (which could also have been made better) was the terrible distortion of the very terms of the discourse on the CTBT issue. The effect was to shift the centre of gravity of all discourse on the nuclear issue well to the right, paving the way for the BJP–RSS to hijack the nuclear agenda and to eventually do what they did in May 1998. The general elite 'common sense' that emerged from this deeply distorted debate was that the CTBT was not only against Indian interests, not only thoroughly deficient in itself, but also a US-led 'trap' aimed particularly at containing nuclear threshold countries like India, Pakistan and Israel, especially India, which unlike the other two, is no US ally. A powerful political logic had thus been created to move inexorably towards testing and, as importantly, to secure widespread support for doing so. What after all, was the point of formally rejecting the CTBT but then in practice not testing and thus acting as if one was prepared to remain forever in this supposed US-led trap?

The Finalised CTBT

The final treaty was not passed as it should have been by the Conference on Disarmament (CD) because of an Indian veto, ostensibly made because of India's desire to change Article XIV of the treaty on 'Entry Into Force', but actually made to weaken the CD since India was fully aware that its veto would not change the Article in question. It was passed by an overwhelming majority in the U.N. General Assembly. The Treaty comprises a preamble, seventeen articles, two annexes and a protocol. As would be expected from a multilaterally negotiated treaty, the final agreed text represented a compromise in which no country got everything it wanted and all major players had to make concessions of one sort or the other to arrive at a final consensus document.

The real character of the final treaty, then, is at variance from the view adopted by Indian critics that it was essentially an artefact of the nuclear weapon states (led by the US) to perpetuate their 'nuclear hegemony'. Precisely because this was not the case, the preamble of the finalised treaty has had to be misinterpreted and misrepresented by the US executive so as to make it more amenable to manipulation in line with its possible future and contemporary interests. In this preamble the key statements are the following: (a) the 'objective' of the Treaty is 'to contribute effectively to the prevention of the proliferation of nuclear weapons in all its aspects, to the process of nuclear disarmament, and therefore to the enhancement of international peace and security,'; (b) 'that the cessation of all nuclear weapon test explosions and all other nuclear explosions, by constraining the development and qualitative improvement of nuclear weapons and ending the development of advanced new types of nuclear weapons, constitutes an effective measure of nuclear disarmament and non-proliferation in all its aspects.' The US President in his message to the Senate of September 23, 1997, presented an interpretation which tried to obliterate the distinction in the Preamble between 'development and qualitative improvement of nuclear weapons' and 'development of advanced new types' in order to obscure the fact that the CTBT recognises that the treaty will 'end (emphasis added) the development of advanced new types of nuclear weapons' and thus reduce it to what the current US executive would like the treaty to be but is not—namely, that the CTBT merely constrains such activities. In short, for US hawks to get their way, they have to try and undermine the CTBT's provisions in

letter and/or spirit; they cannot scrupulously obey a treaty supposedly fashioned to promote their interests. Incidentally, even these
hawks acknowledge that the CTBT 'constrains' the US's qualitative
weapons advancement. Regarding the seventeen articles, the most
important that need to be briefly outlined and explained are articles I,
II, IV, VII, VIII, IX and XIV.

Article I refers to the scope or basic obligations of all signatory
members. Each such signatory must abjure 'any nuclear weapon test
explosion or any other nuclear explosion' no matter how small in
yield on its territory and prevent any such occurrence under its jurisdic-
tion. Nor can any state party cause, encourage or participate in any
way in such test or other nuclear explosion. This is what is meant by
the famous 'zero yield' formulation that was, after much wrangling,
put forward during the negotiations in August 1995 and became the
basis of the, till then elusive, agreement on scope by the five major
nuclear weapons powers, each at a different level of nuclear weapons'
technological and scientific capability and potential.

Article II gives the character, functions and distribution of powers
and responsibilities of the different tiers of the organisation of the
CTBT or CTBTO. The three levels of the organisation are the Conference
of States Parties, the Executive Council (EC) and the Technical
Secretariat which includes the International Data Centre. While the
CTBTO will co-operate with other international organisations such as
the International Atomic Energy Agency (IAEA) it is an independent
body. The supreme decision-making body is the Conference of States
Parties in which each member has one vote only. This conference
meets (once the treaty comes into force) regularly (annually if accepted)
besides any special sittings that may be requested by the Executive
Council, the conference, or any state party if supported by a majority
of members. On 'matters of substance' decisions 'shall be taken as far
as possible by consensus'. If this is not possible, than it has to be by
two-thirds majority of members present (a majority constituting a
quorum). The single-most important official position is that of the
Director-General of the International Secretariat. This will be decided
by the conference with each term lasting four years and renewable for
one more term only. Between the Conferences of States Parties, the
decision-making within the parameters set by the treaty will be by the
Executive Council consisting of 51 members to which each member
has the right to serve on in due course and by rotation taking into

account geographically distributed quotas. There are no permanent members of the Executive Council and all members are treated as equal and eligible, regardless of their weapons status. The EC membership will be selected by the conference with reference to stipulated geographical and technical criteria laid down in the treaty and the EC is accountable to the conference. The EC is charged with seeing to the 'effective implementation of, and compliance with, this treaty' and with supervising the activities of the Technical Secretariat as well as with organising the regular and other meetings of the conference. The Technical Secretariat is responsible for carrying out the practical verification of compliance, i.e. to ensure that there is no cheating by any member signatory regarding a nuclear explosion, test or otherwise. The Technical Secretariat supervises and co-ordinates the International Monitoring System (IMS), comprising variant forms of monitoring stations and activities as well as operating the International Data Centre and to process, analyse, evaluate all relevant data.

Article IV deals with the character of the proposed verification regime which has (a) an International Monitoring System; (b) provisions for consultation with and clarification from requested and requesting states parties; (c) onsite inspections (OSI); (d) confidence-building measures. All monitoring facilities of the IMS shall be owned and operated by the states hosting them or otherwise responsible for them as per the protocol of the treaty. But they will be placed under the authority of the Technical Secretariat and their functioning cannot be impeded by national governments. All data, raw and processed is available to all states parties. No state party is 'precluded from using information obtained by national technical means of verification' (e.g. satellites) to judge whether a demand, for example, for onsite inspection of a particular country should be made. But this information must be obtained 'in a manner consistent with generally recognised principles of international law, including that of respect for the sovereignty of States.' This is generally interpreted to mean that information from illegal spying activities is not allowed. The crucial issue, of course, is the impartiality and rigour of the procedures for sanctioning and then carrying out on-site inspections. Any state party has the right to request (from the director-general and the EC) an onsite inspection of another member country's facilities only for determining whether Article I has been violated. But even so, the requesting country must obey established procedural norms regarding the provision of adequate information about the environment of the event triggering the request, the estimated time of the triggering event and it must provide all data on which the request is based. Before the question of whether or not to sanction such a request arises, there is a stipulated procedure concerning the communication of the request to the said country as well as to all other states parties, the awaiting of the said country's clarifications and communication of that to the requesting country. If the requesting country is still not satisfied and insists on an on-site inspection, then this will be undertaken only if 30 or more out of the 51 members of the EC agree. It can take up to eight days for this procedure of initial request–clarification–sanction of OSI to be completed. If an OSI is sanctioned, this must be carried out according to strictly laid down procedures in the treaty. There can be no simultaneous OSIs on a given territory. The inspected state party has the 'right to take measures it deems necessary to protect national security interests and to prevent disclosure of confidential information not related to the purpose of inspection.' Representatives of the inspected state party will be present throughout the inspection and the inspection team will wherever possible 'begin with the least intrusive procedures and then proceed to more intrusive procedures only as it deems necessary to collect sufficient information to clarify the concern about possible non-compliance with this treaty.' The final report of the inspection team will be transmitted to the requesting state party, the inspected state party, the EC and to all other state parties. The EC will then decide whether there has been non-compliance and whether, even if there is deemed to be compliance, the request for OSI was an abusive request or not. In the case of an abusive request, the EC can require the state party concerned to defray the costs of the preparations of the Technical Secretariat. It can go further and suspend the requesting state party's right to request future OSIs for a period of time determined by the EC. It can further suspend the right of the requesting state party to serve on the EC for a period of time.

Regarding the issue of non-compliance with Article I deemed to have been shown by an OSI, it is the conference that will decide what to do taking into consideration the EC recommendations. The rights and privileges of a state party can be restricted or suspended by the decision of the conference. The conference can recommend collective measures to the states parties against the non-complying country but these have to be 'in conformity with international law'.

Article VII concerns amendments to the treaty. This can only be done by an amendment conference. Such a can be called if a majority of states parties want it. But no substantive amendment to the treaty can be carried out unless there is a positive majority vote with 'no State Party casting a negative vote'. That is to say, each state party has veto power. Everybody doesn't have to say yes, a majority will do. But nobody should say no, not even one country!

According to Article VIII there will be (unless a majority decides otherwise) a review conference ten years after the treaty comes into force. This review will take into account any new scientific and techno-logical developments relevant to the treaty. Every ten years, there can be a review conference or even at lesser intervals if so decided by the Conference of States Parties.

Article IX concerns duration of, and withdrawal from, the treaty. The treaty is of unlimited duration. As is standard in treaties whose signatories are sovereign national states, each state party has the right to invoke jeopardisation of its 'supreme interests' in order to withdraw from the treaty.

Article XIV deals with entry into force. Here the key point is that the treaty can only enter into force if it is signed and ratified by 44 countries listed in Annexe 2 of the treaty which are deemed by the IAEA as having nuclear power or research reactors. Specifically, the CTBT cannot enter into force unless two countries, India and Pakistan, which have so far refused to accede to the treaty, sign and ratify it. This is clearly unfair to the two countries concerned and seeks to coerce India and Pakistan into going along with a Treaty they have rejected, as is their sovereign right to do so. But far worse than this unfairness to India and Pakistan—an earlier hold-out, Israel, has now signed the CTBT—is the unfairness of this provision to the Treaty itself. Its coming into force should not have been made contingent on the accession to it of countries that did not wish to accede to it. It should have been allowed to come into force excluding India and Pakistan leaving it to them to decide whether or not they wish to reconsider their decision at some later date. The sooner a CTBT comes into force covering most of the world, the better. Regarding the powers of the review conference that took place in September 1999, three years after the CTBT was passed in the UN, these were strictly defined. Only ratified member-signatories have voting power with non-ratifying, but signing mem-bers, enjoying observer status. These conferences cannot impose sanctions on countries that are not so far signatories to the CTBT like India and Pakistan. They can only consider what measures 'may be undertaken to accelerate the ratification process in order to facilitate the early entry into force of this treaty.' However, such measures have to be decided by 'consensus' and in a manner 'consistent with international law'. International law, and the Vienna Convention on the Law of Treaties, does not allow for any treaty to endorse collective punishment of any sort on a country or countries that refuse to be a party or parties to the treaty in question!

Indian Criticisms of the CTBT

There have been five main lines of criticism of the CTBT in the Indian debate. (i) The CTBT was not linked to a time-bound schedule for global nuclear disarmament if it is to be acceptable. (ii) The CTBT is discriminatory in character. (iii) The CTBT is decisively flawed and rendered effectively worthless, at least for the US and perhaps France and possibly for Britain, China and Russia. This is because the CTBT, in its present form, allows sub-critical testing, does not prevent advances in computer simulation techniques which will set up a 'virtual testing regime' or 'informational test ground', and allows research and development of direct fusion weapons to continue through such institutions as the planned National Ignition Facility in the US and the Laser Megajoule facility in France. (iv) The CTBT is another building block, after the NPT, in the perpetuation and strengthening of 'nuclear hegemony' practised by the nuclear haves against the nuclear have-nots, led above all by the US. (v) Specific criticisms of some provisions of the CTBT, most notably Article XIV on 'Entry Into Force'; the supposed pressure likely to be imposed on India by the 1999 review conference; and the 'intrusive' dangers of the verification procedures embodied in the treaty. Each of these criticisms will be taken up in turn and refuted.

1. Take the first line of criticism. Time and again, countries opposed to positive nuclear restraint or reduction measures have used a standard argumentative technique. Commitment to a grand goal, e.g. global nuclear disarmament, with which every sane person can agree, is cited precisely in order to block the process of incremental steps by which we can move towards that goal. India was doing exactly this with its demand for a time-bound schedule. A few of us at the time pointed out that this demand from the Indian government was little more than

a stalling tactic to justify its opposition to the CTBT for other 'national security' reasons. The fact that after the tests the Indian government has dropped this demand in regard to the CTBT and the fissiles materials cut-off treaty or FMCT (supported in this dropping by most of those who earlier insisted on this linkage) shows how cynical the bulk of the former anti-CTBT lobby was. But, of course, some who accepted this linkage argument were sincere and continue to adhere to this position. India has a past record as a country more committed than most to the cause of nuclear disarmament. This, and the fact that for so long it did not go openly nuclear despite having proven its nuclear weapons capability, had given it a certain moral capital which inclined a large number of non-nuclear weapons states to give it the benefit of the doubt as to its motives in proposing this linkage.

But the important point is that the other non-nuclear weapons states did not join India in making or endorsing this explicit linkage between a time-bound schedule for global disarmament and the CTBT. They did not do so because they valued the CTBT in itself sufficiently so as not to try to make the best the enemy of the good and thus jeopardise the very possibility of a CTBT coming into existence. In a sense, there were three basic positions during the CTBT negotiations that can be elaborated in the form of an analogy. If the relationship between a measure like the CTBT and global nuclear disarmament is visualised as a descending staircase at the bottom of which is the common goal of complete disarmament, with the CTBT representing the first step down towards this goal, then the position of the nuclear weapons states, especially of the US, could be characterised as follows: they are prepared in their words to go this first step down, but are not prepared to be pressured any further. They will decide whether, when, or how they will take further steps down this staircase.

The second position was that of the overwhelming majority of non-nuclear weapons states barring India. The value of the CTBT in their eyes lies not simply in its specific merit but also as a measure promoting the momentum towards further disarmament. In short, they wanted the nuclear weapons states to give a more serious commitment to moving further down this staircase and not just stopping after the CTBT. The third position was India's. Not only did India not regard the CTBT as a step downwards (at least for the US and possibly France), but it would not itself take this one step unless the nuclear weapons states gave a categorical commitment not only to move all the steps down towards total global disarmament but provide a definite time schedule for doing this! India cannot, of course, give a time-bound schedule for solving the Kashmir problem or its own problems of poverty, communalism or literacy but it demanded on so difficult an issue as getting global nuclear disarmament, that the nuclear weapon states provide just such a timetable right away!

The absurdity of this position was reinforced by the fact that the Indian government was effectively putting the cart before the horse. Before one can sensibly talk of securing a time-bound schedule for global disarmament one first has to secure and institutionalise a genuine, multilateral body that has a mandate accepted by both nuclear and non-nuclear weapons states to negotiate such universal disarmament. Getting such a body into existence or effectively preparing the ground for this is going to take many years of arduous diplomacy and struggle, given the current reluctance of the nuclear weapons states to countenance such a body. One does not jeopardise the efforts to secure such a crucial breakthrough by insisting that the very birth of such a body be made contingent on the nuclear weapons states now agreeing to accept a time-bound schedule for total disarmament. In fact, the two most important efforts to secure such a body are the pursuit of the formation of an ad hoc committee on global nuclear disarmament in the CD, and the setting up of a nuclear weapons (abolition) convention or NWC. Both efforts need to be pursued simultaneously and continuously. The first was exactly what the large majority of the non-nuclear weapons states in the CTBT negotiations were pursuing, hoping that they could get a commitment from the nuclear weapons states on agreeing to such a body at least with a discussion mandate, if not a negotiating one, to begin with. Such a commitment could have been embodied in the preamble of the CTBT. Had India been serious about helping to institutionalise such a body, then it could have employed powerful leverage to get this as the price of its acceptance of the CTBT.

This emerged as a real opportunity in the crucial weeks before India's June 1996 rejection of the CTBT. However, opposing the CTBT because it would affect its (wrongly) perceived national security interests, India was never interested in seriously negotiating to bring about a stronger or better CTBT even more in line with the aspirations and hopes of the majority of the non-nuclear weapons states and other anti-nuclearists worldwide. Regarding the NWC, India pays lip service to it. But insisting that the NWC's very inception be made dependent on the nuclear weapons states accepting a time-bound schedule within it for disarmament is nothing but obviously ill-motivated, shallow and hypocritical moral posturing out of synchronisation even with those non-nuclear weapons states most committed to rapid global disarmament that make no such demand. This is an outrageous and ridiculous 'big bang' conception of how global nuclear disarmament must take place. The Indian government has now dropped this demand but this isn't from any sophisticated or deep-seated new found commitment to disarmament. Rather, it now wants to pose as a 'responsible and moderate' nuclear weapons power.

2. The second criticism was about the supposedly discriminatory character of the CTBT. It is one thing to consider a treaty flawed. On this there can then be a debate on how significant are the flaws and whether the treaty is thereby rendered worthless for one or more of its signatories. It is another thing altogether to make the more morally charged accusation that a treaty is discriminatory. Who after all wants to be on the side of discrimination? Such a criticism has a much more general appeal to a public otherwise unfamiliar with the technical dimensions of nuclear arms development, which is necessary to assess how technically flawed the CTBT is. To call something discriminatory is therefore a politically damaging accusation. Which is why the sheer irresponsibility of the charge is so great. The claim that the CTBT is discriminatory betokens precisely that imprecision of language and thought that can often bedevil a proper assessment of an issue. The CTBT imposes the same obligations on all member signatories. In this respect, it is fundamentally and decisively different from the NPT, which has discrimination legally enshrined within it by having differential obligations for different classes of members to the treaty. In the NPT, the two different classes of members are the nuclear and the non-nuclear weapons states, and the treaty refers to them as such, and also spells out a range of different obligations and privileges for each. In the CTBT, the very language shows the absence of any such enshrined discrimination. The only term used for all members are 'states parties' or 'states members'. There are no separate obligations nor separated classes of members.

It can, of course, be argued or claimed by critics of the CTBT that behind the formal or legal 'impartiality' and 'non-discrimination' of the treaty in question there exists a prior context or situation on the ground of discrimination between the nuclear haves and have-nots that the CTBT does not address adequately. But this is fundamentally and conceptually different from a claim that the CTBT itself is inherently, or by its nature, discriminatory. It is, in fact, an implicit claim that the real problem with the CTBT is not that it is discriminatory but the very opposite! It does not do what its critics think it should do—discriminate positively, or in favour of the nuclear have-nots, so as to help rectify the real situation of discrimination that exists regardless of, and prior to, the CTBT! Perhaps the appropriate analogy here is the famous comment of Anatole France that the law in its impartial majesty equally penalises the rich and the poor for sleeping under a public bridge! The point being that the rich do not have to so sleep and therefore the effects of this law are so uneven as to cause no problems for the rich but many for the poor. Is the CTBT, then, something like this, having strong and genuine restraining effects on the non-nuclear weapon states, on nuclear threshold countries like Israel and India and Pakistan (before their tests), on possibly some of the nuclear weapons states but not on others most notably the US? In fact, this too, is a misleading analogy. The CTBT powerfully restrains all the nuclear weapons states including France and the US.

3. This brings us to the third line of criticism about the supposedly fatal technical loopholes that exist in the treaty because it allows sub-criticals, computer simulation and R&D on direct fusion or fourth-generation nuclear weapons. This is related to, but distinct from, the previous line of criticism. Does the pursuit of such activities violate the letter of the CTBT? It does not. But it certainly violates the general spirit informing the treaty, which intends to move away from efforts to qualitatively enhance nuclear weapons development. Of course, no treaty can effectively monitor and thereby curb computer simulation. Does the existence of these possibilities for carrying out sub-criticals, computer simulation and direct fusion R&D weaken the CTBT to the point of making its restraining effect on all nuclear weapon states including the US, effectively nugatory or inconsequential or of little consequence? Here, the answer is a categorical and emphatic no! The CTBT remains a powerful and worthwhile restraint measure. The refutation of the claim that these activities constitute fatal loopholes in the CTBT relies on both arguments and evidence of a technical nature as well as on evidence of a non-technical and political nature, which can plausibly convince non-specialists about the efficacy of the treaty.

We will take the more technical arguments first. Sub-criticals, computer simulation and direct fusion weapons R&D must each be dealt with separately because of their quite different purposes and aims. Sub-critical experiments (SCEs) are those that do not lead to a nuclear chain reaction but remain below that critical point. Their nuclear yield is therefore zero. These experiments are designed to study the dynamic properties of ageing nuclear materials. They can incorporate what is called hydrodynamic testing, which helps in the study of the other non-nuclear components in a weapons assembly. But neither hydrodynamic tests nor other kinds of SCEs are of much use in weapons designing beyond first-generation weapons, knowledge regarding which is already widely available in public literature. The real danger represented by SCEs is that they can 'creep up' to the level of hydronuclear testing (HNEs), which is of significant help in the designing of very small yield weapons. HNEs, because they achieve slight supercriticality, are banned by the CTBT. Preferably, there should be no SCEs. But if they are carried out, the central problem with them is that their conduct should be sufficiently transparent so that there is public assurance that they have not been allowed to 'creep up' to the level of HNEs. But SCEs in themselves are not a serious problem, let alone a fatal loophole in the CTBT with regard to qualitative nuclear weapons advancement.[1]

What about computer simulation and the possibility of establishing an 'informational test site' or 'virtual testing' that would effectively do away with the need for explosive testing? Here, the crucial issue is whether or not computer simulation alone can lead to the emergence of a new generation of sufficiently accurate weapons codes, which are crucial to developing a new generation of nuclear weapons or making significant qualitative advances in weapons designing even within the existing generation of weapons? What are weapons codes? Think of weapons codes as something like a shelf or even shelves of a very large number of books that provide or attempt to provide a deep and integrated knowledge of an extremely complex and vast array of issues. Nuclear weapons codes establish linkages between the empirical evidence gained from previous explosive tests and laboratory work, the existing (though incomplete) state of knowledge about the basic physical processes involved in a nuclear explosion and the specific design parameters of the device under consideration. They are, in fact, the principal tool of nuclear weapons designers. The US, not surprisingly, is the country that has invested the most in the effort so far to develop an 'informational test site' through its Accelerated Strategic Computing Initiative (ASCI) being carried out in collaboration with five major US universities. What has now been realised from ongoing efforts is that though computer simulation most certainly helps in the development of such weapons codes it nonetheless suffers from insuperable problems. The issue is not whether a new weapon will work or not but whether it will work in the way its designers want it to work, i.e. whether it will properly fulfil the function for which it has been designed?

Such is the limitation of existing knowledge about what takes place in advanced nuclear weapons explosions (especially regarding what are called the 'secondaries') and the complexity of the way various processes are connected, that codes generated by computer simulation alone are simply inadequate. These connections are so complex and their basis still so incomprehensible that if weapons codes are made or adjusted to be more accurate in one direction, then for reasons unknown, they become more inaccurate in other directions. The significance of these 'fudge factors', as they are called, has been repeatedly affirmed by the comparison of results achieved by computer simulation alone when compared to known parameters of devices already established through previous explosive testing. The effort to establish 'virtual testing' is thus deeply ironic. It has led to the greater recognition of the importance of ultimately resorting to actual proof-testing or explosive testing in order to finally design advanced or new generation weapons.[2]

Far from substituting for explosive testing, such simulation efforts create pressure for eventually resiling from the CTBT if the US is going to make serious qualitative advances in nuclear weapons development and weaponisation. Thus, what the existence of facilities for carrying out SCEs, direct fusion weapons R&D and ASCI do is to keep the necessary software (the small pool of highly specialised scientists) and much of the hardware in operation so that if in the future the US decides to break out of the CTBT it can move towards the development and deployment of a new range of weapons in the shortest possible time. What all this indicates is not the irrelevance of the CTBT but, in fact, the vital importance of securing it and keeping it in place permanently. Finally, there is the issue of fourth-generation or direct fusion weapons, such as laser beam weapons, etc.

The CTBT and the banning of explosive testing does not theoretically present an obstacle to the development of such weapons. So the

CTBT does not render their development impossible. But to claim that the CTBT is rendered worthless on this count is absurd. The leap from third-generation to fourth-generation weapons is far greater than from first-generation to third-generation weapons. In fact, nobody can say with any confidence that such a leap will ever be made. The physics is simply unknown. The National Ignition Facility seeking to develop the key technology of inertial confinement fusion (and France's Laser Megajoule) are deeply speculative ventures to produce 'pie-in-the-sky wonder weapons', whose chances of success are regarded as small. The overwhelming majority of knowledgeable nuclear physicists give these facilities less than a 10 percent chance of success. The very small minority who are most committed to these projects are themselves not prepared to give it more than a fifty-fifty chance of success.[3]

With a CTBT in place, today's US can do, and not do, the following: it cannot go ahead to develop any third generation nuclear weapons such as particle beam weapons, enhanced or reduced radiation weapons or battlefield micro-nukes, electromagnetic pulse bombs, etc. It cannot certify any nuclear weapon. Within the range of second-generation weapons, which is where the US is currently situated (but ahead of any other country in this range) it can, even with the CTBT in place, develop weapons that represent new applications of existing or known designs such as 'deep penetration earth bombs', etc.

In respect of newer weapons (but not new-generation weapons), the closer their designs are to known designs, the easier they are to make even if the CTBT prevents certification of all weapons. But the further away the new designs are from existing designs, then the more difficult they become to make, and indeed after a shortly arrived point of distance from existing knowledge, they are effectively not possible to design with the necessary confidence that they will work as they are supposed to. But it is not necessary to be a nuclear physics expert in order to realise that the CTBT is a genuine and powerful restraint measure on all the nuclear weapon states. The non-technical evidence is there for all to see, except for those most determined not to see it. In all the nuclear weapon states, there exist powerful lobbies primarily centred around sections of the weapons laboratories, defence forces and ardent arms-racers (usually positioned on the hard right of the political spectrum) that have strongly opposed the CTBT precisely because they have understood full well its powerful restraining effect. In the US, they have gathered around a section of the Republican right with the result that Senate ratification of the CTBT remains deeply uncertain. How is it that the more rightwing, gung-ho section of the US establishment is so reluctant to support the CTBT if it is a measure which is meant to serve US imperialist interests and is not a serious restraint on that country's qualitative weapons advancement?

The effective answer to Indian critics of the CTBT, notably the Left is, and has to be, the absurd argument that the Democrats and supporters of the CTBT in the US are the more intelligent and sophisticated imperialists, but these rightwing Republicans and others are the more stupid imperialists who don't properly understand how US imperialist interests should be best pursued. Such critics of the CTBT have hardly been swayed, dismayed or even shaken out of their complacency by the fact that virtually the whole of the international anti-nuclear movement and the overwhelming bulk of the international left have, with varying degrees of enthusiasm, supported the CTBT! The overwhelming majority of international anti-nuclear groups and activists, most of whom have a more consistent record than the Indian Left in their opposition to all nuclear weapons-related activity (whether by capitalist or communist countries) and which include top world-class nuclear physicists, including former nuclear weapons designers have also supported the CTBT with varying degrees of enthusiasm. The Indian Left should realise that the division between pro- and anti-CTBTers in the US does not correspond to the absurd and artificial division between smart and naive imperialists postulated by them. Rather, it reflects the obvious fact that after the end of the Cold War there is a division between arms-racers in the US on one hand and arms reducers/arms moderators on the other. There is no significant or powerful section of arms-eliminators amongst the US nuclear elite, although the number of voices demanding complete arms-elimination is growing.[4]

But after the end of the Cold War, the category of those who no longer see the purpose of continuing with the quantitative and qualitative advancement of nuclear weapons by the US or any other country has grown stronger. Most of them want an end to this race and considerable reductions in nuclear weapons even though they do not countenance complete elimination on the part of the US and are far from becoming opponents of US political imperialism. There is further non-technical evidence. The idea that other nuclear weapons states like Russia and China would ever have agreed to a CTBT that was fatally flawed is absurd. In fact, the CTBT only became a possibility when the 'zero yield' formulation was agreed upon by the US on August 11, 1995. Before that, the US had been pressing for a very small loophole allowing explosive testing up to 2 kg. yield.

The position of the Russia and China, was that if a loophole of any sort was to be allowed then it had to be big enough so that they themselves, at a lower level of weapons technology than the US, would nonetheless be able to benefit. Thus, the Russians demanded a loophole of ten tonnes while the Chinese wanted allowance of up to several hundred tonnes. It should be self-evident to Indian critics of the CTBT that the nuclear and scientific establishments of Russia and China (which can safely be assumed to be far more advanced than that of India) went on board after the zero-yield proposal because they recognised that while anything else would have constituted a debilitating flaw in the CTBT from which the US alone would significantly benefit, a treaty allowing SCEs, computer simulation and direct fusion R&D was not similarly flawed. Unfortunately, as in the case of the Republican right opposing the CTBT in the US, the fact of Russian and Chinese acceptance of this treaty despite these presumed flaws has only led to tortuous Indian efforts at rationalisation.

Among the more ridiculous of such attempts are claims that the US so badly wanted a CTBT that they were prepared to share knowledge and equipment i.e. give away their technological edge in these areas with Russia and China. Thus, whereas once it was argued the US so badly wanted this 'flawed' treaty because they alone could monopolise the benefits of its failings; later it was argued (often by the same critics) that the US so badly wanted the treaty that they were willing to give up their monopoly of benefit from its supposed flaws! Other equally desperate and far-fetched explanations claimed that the Chinese were primarily bent on sustaining the imbalance in their nuclear relationship with India. So long as this was on the cards, the Chinese were not too bothered about allowing the qualitative nuclear technological imbalance between itself and the US to grow, calculating that they had enough of a minimum deterrent against it.[5]

Some such critics also claim that the Russian and Chinese insistence that the CTBT only enter into force if India, Pakistan and Israel join it constituted a second line of defence against the treaty ever coming into existence and thus preventing the US from monopolising the benefit of its 'biased' operation. This is, of course, an extraordinary argument. For its logic, strictly speaking, must lead to the conclusion that should Indian and Pakistani accession to the CTBT become likely in the future (and thus its entry into force) then the Russians and/or the Chinese will resile from the treaty! In fact, Russian, Chinese and British insistence on Indian, Pakistani and Israeli accession to the treaty before it could come into force simply and obviously reflected their concern that the 'sacrifice' imposed by the CTBT upon them was not being shared by the nuclear capable threshold states staying out of the treaty, and that given the strength of the anti-CTBT lobbies within their own countries, this was a way of stalling the treaty's operation though certainly not of guaranteeing that it would never come into operation.

For such a period then, the CTBT would constitute a moral-legal norm of restraint and behaviour on its signatories but not a punitive one. The behaviour of the other NWSs, notably Russia and China, indicates by all reasonable and balanced inference, that the CTBT was perceived by them as a genuine restraining measure on all countries, including the US. The whole controversy over the 'Entry Into Force' clause (Article XIV) thoroughly undermines the argument that the CTBT was primarily (or even secondarily) a US-led 'trap' aimed at containing the threshold nuclear powers and especially India that, unlike Pakistan and Israel, is not deemed a formal or strategic ally by any section of the US foreign policy establishment. Indian critics who have claimed as much have never bothered (understandably, since it so seriously weakens their case) to either state or emphasise the following facts. India formally announced its refusal to sign the CTBT in June 1996. A month earlier, in May when it became increasingly clear that India was going to reject the Treaty, the US was the first and only nuclear weapons states to publicly appeal to India that it would accept India's rejection but that it should not block the passage of the Treaty in the CD.[6]

Moreover, the US did not attempt to coerce India by insisting on its signature as a precondition for the treaty to enter into force. It initially opposed the stands of Russia, China and UK in this regard and even sought to get these countries to withdraw this demand in the interests of enabling the treaty to go through. Strange behaviour indeed for a country supposedly aiming to 'trap' India through the CTBT! While the US could have handled the UK, the Russians and Chinese were adamant, the former as much as, if not more so, than the latter. The US then accepted the Russian and Chinese condition because it was important to get these two countries on board the treaty and because even if this condition was withdrawn, India would still have nothing to do with the CTBT. Incidentally, Russia, China and UK insisted on this clause only after India made its rejection to the Treaty clear in late June 1996.

4. The fourth line of criticism is that the NPT is the central pillar of the non-proliferation regime sought to be sustained by the nuclear weapons states (led by the US) and that the CTBT is another building block in the effort to perpetuate and strengthen this regime. The first part of this claim is fundamentally correct but the second part is not, being based on a gross misrepresentation. Before investigating the true nature of the relationship between the CTBT and the NPT, it is necessary to say something about the NPT, in particular about the utterly unbalanced and inaccurate manner in which it has been criticised in India. In the mid-1960s, India played a major role in pushing for the NPT and in seeking to draft it. The final draft represented the consensus view of the US/UK and USSR (China and France only joined the NPT in the early nineties) brought about by their own separate discussions and as such had formulations that were not as satisfactory to a number of non-nuclear weapons states of the time, including India. However, the standard criticism that the NPT was inherently discriminatory was not—to begin with, nor at the time of signing—the real problem for the non-nuclear weapons states including India.

It became convenient for Indian critics subsequently to make this discriminatory character the centrepiece of its case against the NPT but this represents a misleading simplification. At the time of drawing up the proposed NPT, there were only two choices. Either the treaty should be completely non-discriminatory with equal obligations for all member signatories—in which case the nuclear weapons states would never accept it and would have to be excluded from the treaty. Or, in order to get the nuclear weapons states in, the proposed treaty would have to have two classes of member-signatories with the principle of differential obligations enshrined within it. This was because, at least for some period, the nuclear weapons states would not renounce their possession of nuclear weapons while this would be the condition demanded of all other signatories. Sensibly enough at the time, most non-nuclear weapons states felt there would be no purpose in having a treaty which excluded the nuclear weapons states. A basic bargain was thus established when the treaty was finalised in 1968 and came into force in 1970. In return for the non-nuclear weapons states accepting the enshrinement of the principle of discriminatory obligations in the treaty, the nuclear weapons states would commit themselves to move eventually towards complete nuclear disarmament.

It is this bargain that is embodied in Article VI of the NPT. The failure of the NPT since its inception—and the main reason why it has become over the years the central pillar of the non-proliferation regime (and thus deserves criticism and condemnation)—is not so much its inherently discriminatory character but the fact that the nuclear weapons states failed to live up to their end of the bargain by their perfidious disregard for the letter and spirit of Article VI in the NPT. Whatever disarmament has since taken place (after the end of the Cold War) is certainly not because of the NPT but despite it. The subtle but important difference between highlighting the central weakness of the NPT as lying in the perfidious behaviour of the nuclear weapons states and not in its discriminatory provisions becomes acutely relevant when it comes to assessing why India did not sign the NPT. This was not primarily because it was discriminatory and India was initiating some sort of moral-political crusade against the 'pernicious' NPT. While the principle of discrimination between nuclear haves and have-nots was accepted within the Treaty this did not mean that there had to be as much of an imbalance as there was in regard to other differential obligations between the nuclear and non-nuclear weapons states in regard to technology transfers, IAEA safeguards, etc. But this too was not sufficient explanation for the Indian refusal.

Like a number of potential nuclear powers close to the threshold of achieving weapons capabilities, e.g. Brazil and Argentina, India, too, did not want to foreclose this option at the time. Already after the death of Nehru, there had been a subtle shift in official thinking from a posture of 'no bombs ever' to one of 'no bombs now' as well as the emergence of a new kind of official discourse in which it was now being simplistically claimed by New Delhi that continuing vertical proliferation would be the direct cause of further horizontal proliferation instead of acknowledging that the latter had an independent dynamics as well. The NPT banned even peaceful nuclear explosions, which is how the Indian government described its 1974 Pokhran test.

All this weighed heavily in shaping the Indian decision. But the decisive factor in leading to the Indian rejection of the NPT was almost certainly the Chinese refusal at the time to sign the NPT even as a nuclear weapons state. Nonetheless, any balanced assessment of the NPT (rarely present in the Indian debate and certainly never during the hysteria of the anti-CTBT 1994 to 1996 period) would have to point out that it was also initially directed against Japan, Germany and Italy, the losers in World War II, each with the capability to produce nuclear weapons. This was something to be supported, not opposed. Later, it became a way for the nuclear weapons states to maintain non-proliferation amongst the non-nuclear weapon states and to rationalise in the longer term (after its unwarranted and condemnable permanent extension in April 1995) their own possession of nuclear weapons.

However, it is also necessary to note that the NPT still contains the only international legal commitment that has ever been made by the five major nuclear weapons states to carry out complete nuclear disarmament. Many anti-nuclear activists, not surprisingly feel, that this does provide an important point of legal-moral international leverage, which in the absence of anything else, can still be of some use in the struggle for global disarmament. They are thus not prepared to go so far as to call for the treaty's dismantlement or to declare its complete irrelevance or to condemn it totally. This is not a view of the NPT shared by the authors of this article, who reject it on much more comprehensive grounds than most Left critics in India.[7]

But this position, when coming from anti-nuclearists, should not be seen as simply dishonourable or 'supporting nuclear imperialism' or other such over-simplifications forwarded by Indian critics with a much less balanced or sophisticated understanding of the NPT and the historico-political context surrounding it. Let us come now to the question of the real nature of the relationship between the NPT and the CTBT. So strongly committed are non-nuclear weapons states to the idea of the CTBT that even during the effort to draft the NPT, countries like Mexico, Burma and Ethiopia wanted a CTBT to be reached in conjunction with the NPT. In fact, for the non-nuclear weapons states that were considering signing the NPT, a CTBT was seen as the single most important expression of the commitment of nuclear weapons states to pursue disarmament as embodied in the terms (Article VI) of the treaty. The three nuclear weapons states preparing to be a party to the NPT—USSR, US and UK—adamantly opposed this. Subsequently, at every five year review conference of the NPT, 1975, 1980, 1985, 1990, the issue of the CTBT was repeatedly raised by non-nuclear weapons states and consistently opposed by the nuclear weapons states.

In fact, in the view of many countries the NPT would itself only survive in the longer run if there were effective international safeguards and a CTBT.

Thus there has always been a historical connection between the CTBT and the NPT but of a kind very different from that which has been made out by Indian opponents of the CTBT. When in 1995 the issue of the NPT's extension came up it was inevitable that the issue of the CTBT would surface. The nuclear weapons states only succeeded in getting what they wanted—the permanent and indefinite extension of the NPT—by resorting to very considerable behind-the-scenes arm-twisting of many non-nuclear weapons states. This permanent extension was extremely unfortunate because it eliminated that degree of leverage the non-nuclear weapons states would have continued to possess if they agreed only to the NPT's short-term and conditional extension before reviewing it again in the future. Although the nuclear weapons states got what they wanted, they had to pay a price. That price was an explicit and time-bound commitment for the first time ever to completing a CTBT. In the 1995 review conference, new 'Principles and Objectives' were established whereby a CTBT had to be completed before the end of 1996. Far from the CTBT being another building block after the NPT in the nuclear weapons states supposedly calculated attempt to promote their 'nuclear hegemony', it was a concession forced upon them by the non-nuclear weapons states that the nuclear weapons states had to make because otherwise the NPT's permanent extension and its authority would have been gravely undermined.[8] As it is, a number of non-nuclear weapons states had become deeply critical and frustrated by the nuclear weapons states' behaviour inside and outside the NPT, with some like Mexico even threatening to withdraw from the NPT. The Indian government had no reason to explain to its public what actually went on in the 1995 review conference attended by numerous anti-nuclear groups, NGOs and individuals so that the pattern and manner of negotiations were public knowledge. But the refusal of the Indian Left to even look seriously at what actually happened in those negotiations, let alone at the general history of the relationship between the NPT and the CTBT, is deeply disturbing.

5. The fifth line of criticism centres around certain claims regarding the iniquity of Article XIV on 'Entry Into Force' in the CTBT; on the supposedly pressing danger to India of the 1999 review conference, thereby justifying the timing of the Indian nuclear tests; and on the

putative dangers of excessive 'intrusiveness' embodied in the CTBT's verification regime. The first two points have already been covered in this text. Regarding the third, the basic parameters have also been laid out in the discussion on Articles II and IV in the CTBT. The Chemical Weapons Convention (CWC) served as an important precedent for the CTBT in respect of how the principle of balancing between concerns of 'national sovereignty' and 'effectiveness' of international monitoring could be handled. India endorsed the CWC procedure without serious reservations. It only needs to be added here that the two most secretive nuclear regimes are those of Israel and China. There were hard negotiations before the specific provisions concerning verification procedures and authorisation of OSIs were arrived at. The result was a compromise consensus but one which was acceptable to Israel and China which have both signed the CTBT precisely because the final outcome was deemed reasonable by them. On this terrain too, the Indian objections have been couched in vague terms carefully avoiding specifying what provisions are unacceptable and why, let alone why Indian concerns about the dangers of intrusive spying are sharper than Israel's and China's or why these countries are prepared to be 'taken in' by a supposedly flawed verification regime. Is it not obvious that once again, India is resorting to self-serving deception in order to justify its opposition to the CTBT?

Conclusion

For those Indians seriously committed to promoting global nuclear restraint and disarmament, who also oppose Indian nuclearisation, testing and weaponisation, the struggle must obviously take place at home, as well as against external culprits. Signing the CTBT will not stop India's weaponisation programme. Had India signed the CTBT in 1996, we would have been spared the tragedy of May 11 and 13 and then Pakistan's tests on May 28 and 30th. India signing it now (followed or, very likely, preceded by Pakistan) cannot now have anywhere near the same significance. Nonetheless, this paper has tried to show why the CTBT is still relevant and why Indian accession to it is still important. The case made by Indian critics of it is not simply inadequate but utterly barren, mistaken and politically dangerous. Tragically, the Indian left, today one of the crucial and most-valued political forces in the struggle to prevent future Indian weaponisation, has also been a victim of, if not a party to, this misrepresentation of the CTBT. There may be a more foundational reason for this that has to do with the deeper limitations of the Left's thinking on the nuclear question in particular and on international politics in general; a failure that is also connected to the distinctive peculiarities and traditions of Indian Marxism. That is a larger and separate issue that need not be gone into here. But even these legacies do not necessarily prevent a proper and just assessment of the value and worth, and the true strengths and limitations of the CTBT. Whether the Left is willing or able to carry out such a reassessment involving the categorical revision of its stand hitherto on this issue is a crucial question. On it may rest a great deal. But it is still not too late for such a rethink. And one can only hope that it will take place.

Notes

[1] An Indian staple is that sub-criticals and computer simulation constitute fatal flaws. The leftwing Indian fortnightly magazine, *Frontline*, has long been carrying on a campaign against the CTBT based on precisely the kind of arguments that have been criticised here as distorted. However, it has, to its credit opposed the recent tests. In its July 17 issue, it carried a rare, technical article titled 'Matters of Authority' of genuine authority and worth about these tests which also accurately portrayed the essential character of SCEs, reinforcing the argument presented here. The spelling and language of the text suggested a US provenance and it is possible that the article was lifted off the Internet. The name of the author was not provided but responsibility assigned to a 'special correspondent' which was itself highly unusual. Certainly, before this article, *Frontline* had not carried anything of comparable technical authority on CTBT-related matters by any Indian writer. From time to time, Indian critics have cited in a very selective fashion the technical criticisms of sub-criticals and computer simulation by Western experts known for their general anti-nuclear stance, such as C.E. Paine, Ted Taylor and Frank N. von Hippel (a particular favourite) but without ever pointing out that these experts have, with various reservations, supported the CTBT, indeed have been advocates of it as well as of rapid nuclear disarmament. Such activities in the US also come under the umbrella of the government-sponsored 'science-based stockpile stewardship and management programme' (SBSS&MP), which too has been severely and correctly criticised as intending more than it formally says, i.e. to help in weapons designing and not just to check the 'safety and reliability' of the existing aging stockpile. The authoritative and regular reports of the Natural Resources Defense Council (NRDC)—a Washington based NGO—have been of particular importance in this regard. What has not been pointed out is that the SBSS&MP has been attacked by the NRDC not just for promoting efforts at weapons designing despite the CTBT, but also for being financially wasteful and promising more than it can deliver. For an authoritative account of the post-CTBT sub-criticals carried out by the US in 1997 emphasising

the importance of ensuring transparency, see Suzanne L. Jones and Frank N. von Hippel, 'Transparency Measures for Subcritical Experiments under the CTBT' in *Science & Global Security*, Vol. 6, 1997, pp. 291–310.

[2] See in particular, the 'Nuclear Weapons Databook' series brought out by the NRDC, especially Explosive Alliances: Nuclear Weapons Simulation Research at American Universities by M.G. McKinzie, T.B. Cochran, C.E. Paine; Washington, January 1998; and End Run: The U.S. Government's Plan for Designing Nuclear Weapons and Simulating Nuclear Explosions under the CTBT by C.E. Paine and M.G. McKinzie, Washington, April 1998.

[3] The SBSS&MP justifies the development of facilities such as the Dual Axis Radiographic Hydrodynamic Test Facility (DARHT) at Los Alamos and the National Ignition Facility (NIF) at Lawrence Livermore. The key area of dispute is over the possible relationship of NIF and Inertial Confinement Fusion (ICF) technique to the development of fourth-generation fusion weapons. The theory behind ICF is that giant lasers yet to be built at NIF will produce concentrated pulses of ultraviolet light to explode a tiny gold capsule called a hohlraum, itself comprising a pellet of deuterium and tritium. Just before the hohlraum explodes, it is supposed to émit a powerful beam of X-rays that will compress and heat the pellet to more than a 100 million degrees Celsius causing deuterium and tritium to fuse as in a nuclear bomb but on a very much smaller scale. The chances of this ever working are, as pointed out, very dim. But the NIF is obviously one of those 'big science toys' that keeps weapons labs and their scientists and administrators active and happy. Promising these facilities was one way of overriding, and buying off much of the opposition from these quarters to the CTBT and getting them to reluctantly accept the latter. See J. Bairstow, 'Switch Off the National Ignition Facility' in *Laser Focus World*, Sept. 1997.

[4] The Nuclear Posture Review brought out by the US government in September 1994, and the Presidential Decision Directive-61 (which was the outcome of a seven-year review process and officially declared in November 1997) are key documents in this regard. Their purposes are to rationalise officially the retention of nuclear weapons for the future but in recognition of the changed post-Cold War context in which a new nuclear strategic doctrine would have to be established. New enemies have to be found, hence 'rogue states'; and a much smaller number of nuclear weapons are being asked to fulfil newer, yet to be fully worked out, strategic tasks. PDD–61 is the first such directive related to nuclear weapons after Reagan's last directive in 1981 and reverses that earlier commitment to fighting 'winnable' nuclear wars. The US has now accepted that such weapons are for deterrence only. The point is not that the US will not continue to elaborate nuclear strategic perspectives (the 'pursuit of nuclear imperialism') but that these changes of perspective have been very substantially pushed upon it by the post-Cold War reality of a new momentum towards disarmament and restraint which the US finds difficult or undesirable to buck completely but can try to dilute or outflank as best as it can. The relationship of these particular planning perspectives to restraint measures like the CTBT must be clearly understood. They are not efforts at reorganising strategic nuclear perspectives through the CTBT but despite or apart from the CTBT.

[5] This extraordinary claim, along with a series of tendentious, politically mistaken and technically ill-informed attacks on the CTBT, is to be found in S. Varadarajan, 'Testing the World Order' in *Seminar*, No. 468, August 1998. The Chinese have always been concerned about their imbalance with the US. Their strike force— of an estimated mere 13 to 18 long range land-based ballistic missiles capable of hitting the US mainland—has always been vulnerable theoretically to a US first strike, located as it is in only two northeastern bases. So much for their possessing at the moment an 'adequate' or 'credible' second strike capacity against the US. The Chinese are currently particularly disturbed by possible developments in regard to the US's Theatre High Altitude Area Defence (THAAD) preparations which in conjunction with rightwing efforts to undermine the 1972 ABM Treaty might eventually lead to that 'pale' or 'soft' version of a 'Star Wars' system of defensive missile interceptors, etc. that in its stronger version was once so seriously pressed for by President Reagan. Should this happen and such a ballistic missile defence system be established, then even if the currently feeble Chinese capacity to hit the US in a second strike was somewhat strengthened, it could well be rendered worthless.

[6] India did not have to block the passage of the CTBT in the CD after rejecting it. It claimed it had to do so after the emergence of the new 'Entry Into Force' clause so as to put pressure on changing it. But New Delhi was fully aware that blocking the Treaty's passage in the CD would have no effect in this regard. It did so for two reasons—as a symbolic gesture of defiance; but more importantly, to deliberately weaken the stature of the CD in keeping with an evolving diplomacy. To be sure, if the 'Entry Into Force' clause had not been changed in the way it was, the CTBT text would probably not have been blocked by India in the CD. But this still does not excuse what India did. India even went to the shameful extent of vetoing the passage of an otherwise consensus factual report of the CD on its activities over the previous two and a half years. This report would merely have concluded that there was a consensus that there was no consensus! But the report's acceptance and formal passage would have salvaged some credibility for the CD by recognising and acknowledging its efforts and workings despite its failure to reach the desired final consensus.

[7] The NPT has a built-in contradiction. To soften the stick of renunciation of nuclear weapons by non-nuclear weapons states, it offers the carrot of technical support on the civilian side of nuclear energy production—thus helping to provide the wherewithal for building nuclear bombs. This contradiction has been taken advantage of by, at least, Iraq and North Korea. Moreover, the very fact that the NPT promotes the civilian nuclear energy programme can be condemned by those who believe that as an energy and power source this too is unacceptable for the innumerable problems, dilemmas, inefficiencies and dangers it poses. The Indian Left does not oppose the production of nuclear energy for civilian purposes. It should take a second, critical look at the issue. The NPT is also a weaker disarmament measure than NWFZs because unlike the latter it allows nuclear weapons states to station nuclear weapons on the territory of non-nuclear weapons states.

[8] Throughout the 1995–1996 debate on the CTBT it was rare indeed to find an Indian critic of the Treaty who was even prepared to acknowledge that the CTBT was a concession forced upon the nuclear weapons states to secure the NPT's permanent extension, let alone that without this concession the NPT regime could have unravelled. More recently, this has been more widely acknowledged but in such a manner as to try and rob the point of its legitimate impact. Some such critics (belonging to the left) insisted wrongly for so long that the CTBT was effectively a building block after the NPT in the general architecture of the non-proliferation regime through which 'nuclear hegemony' was to be strengthened. In order to somehow preserve the basic thrust of this charge, they now have to carry out a desperate intellectual-political contortion by simultaneously acknowledging that the CTBT was indeed a concession (purely token according to them, but still a concession) to ensure the consolidation, even the continued survival of the NPT, and yet insisting that the CTBT is an integral part of the architecture of 'nuclear imperialism' centred on the NPT. As if the difference between a Treaty which is sought after by the nuclear weapons states (most notably the US) because it will enhance the NPT regime and one which is finally conceded in order to preserve this regime, is not a fundamental one, providing two distinctive judgements on the character of that Treaty itself. See S. Muralidharan, 'Unequal Bargain' in *Frontline*, July 3, 1998; and S.M. Menon, 'The Nuclear Imperium and its Vassal Kings' in *Economic and Political Weekly*, August 1–7, 1998.

Turning Pakistan Away from the Nuclear Abyss

PERVEZ HOODBHOY AND ZIA MIAN

Caught between the desire to match India's nuclear tests and the fear of devastating sanctions, Pakistan vacillated for two weeks before testing its own. Subsequently, Prime Minister Nawaz Sharif went on television and declared 'This auspicious day is an historic event for us.' Anticipating the price the country would have to pay, he urged 'sacrifices' and stated 'if the need arises be ready to go hungry.' But amid the public celebrations most people in Pakistan preferred to hear only his opening words.

Now, with sanctions imposed by its international creditors, and private capital scared away, the spectre of Pakistan's economic collapse looms large. The currency has fallen sharply and may well go into free fall, driving up inflation and increasing the difficulty of finding resources to pay the debt. Foreign debt is around $30 billion. This may seem small, but not for Pakistan. Debt servicing was set at 45 per cent of government expenditure at the time of the June budget, before the collapse of the currency. Debt repayments amount to more than $350 million per month and, with less than $1 billion dollars of reserves left, default lies in the cards.

As the economy falters, institutions of society, weak even before the testing, could soon collapse. Should there be a breakdown of governance, Nawaz Sharif, as well as the current chief of the army, a moderate, may be replaced by hard-liners from Islamist groups. Within the army, fire-breathers such as retired General Hamid Gul, the former

head of Pakistan's Inter-Service Intelligence Agency, stand to gain. These groups are the ones who rejoiced most loudly at Pakistan's tests. They are pathologically anti-Indian, and determined to settle scores once and for all with India. What this means in the nuclear age is terrifying.

The internal situation is so grim that in the months ahead it may become too difficult for any stable government to manage. When Muslim-hating Indian BJP hardliners incited and enticed Pakistan into testing (the first time a state has tried to compel an adversary to test nuclear weapons!), they may have hoped for a repeat of Cold War history. The BJP would like to see Pakistan exhausted and broken by an arms race and, quite possibly, might get their wish. But unlike the steel cage of the Soviet state, which ensured that some crucial structures of governance survived even as everything else collapsed, Pakistan's state is already fractured by multiple violent ethnic and religious conflicts. Disintegration into molecular civil war with fiefdoms and warlords is a terrible possibility. Should this occur, India will have created a South Asian nuclear Somalia for a neighbour.

To be sure, while recent events have greatly accelerated it, the dire situation that Pakistan finds itself in pre-dates its debut into the nuclear world. Today, the Pakistan state is not able to provide even the basics of a viable education system, health care, housing, or jobs to its people. This is because, for almost all its fifty years of independence, the limitless avarice of Pakistan's tax-dodging elite has allied with a desperate sense of insecurity about India to ensure that the military got the lion's share of what few public resources were available. This fundamentally untenable situation was sustained largely by military and economic aid, especially from the US in exchange for Pakistan's loyalty in the Cold War. But the collapse of the Soviet Union meant the end of Pakistan's free ride, and sanctions because of its nuclear weapons programme. Left to its own resources and never having been able to create institutions to manage them efficiently, Pakistan plunged deeper and deeper into debt. Debt servicing replaced military spending as the largest item in government spending and 1990 was the last year military spending equalled development spending.

In the last few years, the need to address this economic and social crisis had slowly dawned on some in government and the military. There were the beginnings of a quiet revolution; military spending unobtrusively started to decline in real terms and as a fraction of government spending. Astonishingly, just weeks before the Indian tests, General Jehangir Karamat, the head of Pakistan's army, publicly identified the state of the economy and internal problems as a more serious threat to the future of Pakistan than India. All this changed after India's tests on May 11. The stock of the hardliners has risen, India is now back as enemy number one, and the 14 per cent increase in India's military budget has led Pakistan to increase its military spending by 8 per cent. This was only for openers. India's Defence Minister has promised further large increases in military spending.

Pakistan's disintegration will have calamitous consequences for South Asia and must be averted. But, the situation may be too far gone for Pakistan's leaders to handle it alone. Therefore the international community must act as a community to help out. The first thing it must do is ensure the situation is not made worse. Sanctions applied for punitive ends, and which take no account of political constraints and possibilities, are part of the problem. The longer they are applied the quicker will Pakistan's structures of economy and society collapse. Secondly, the international community should realise the potential of Kashmir as a flash-point for a nuclear conflagration. Today Pakistan's leaders privately admit they can't win Kashmir but, in the same breath, stress that they cannot be seen to give up on the issue. They are now prisoners of their success in manufacturing public consent to a particular solution to Kashmir. They desperately need a fig-leaf. What can this cover be? An excellent beginning could be to make use of the UN military observers who have been in Kashmir for almost 50 years. They could be increased in numbers and authorised to separate the two armies and keep them out of each others artillery range, and prevent illegal movement across the border.

However, this is only a stop-gap measure. The international community must try harder to break the impasse between India and Pakistan on Kashmir. At present, the two states cannot even agree on what are the terms for talking about Kashmir. Pakistan believes the basis for any discussion must be the 1948 and 1949 UN resolutions on Kashmir, agreed to by India, which envisaged the United Nations Commission for India and Pakistan supervising a settlement in Kashmir 'in accordance with the will of the people', which was to be determined through a 'plebiscite'. India argues the 1972 Simla Agreement has to be basis for talks; signed after the 1971 India–Pakistan war, it makes no mention of the UN, instead it commits the two states to settle their disputes 'through bilateral negotiations or by any other peaceful means mutually agreed upon between them.' An international contact group, consisting say of judges from the international court of justice, may be able to help the two countries work through these competing claims of the legal basis for proceeding on Kashmir.

Given their vulnerability, Pakistan's leaders also cannot afford to be seen as caving in to pressure on arms control measures such as the Test Ban, no-first-use of nuclear weapons and a ban on fissile material production. Pakistan's statements about undertaking a strategic review and possibly de-linking their policy from India's positions on these treaties can be positively interpreted as signs of a willingness to move forward. But the international community should be not blinded by its wish to see progress in this direction. It must resist efforts to push things along by offering conventional weapons and dual-use technology to Pakistan or India. Such deals amount to helping South Asia jump out of the nuclear frying pan into a conventional fire. This fire has burned both countries three times already.

What Pakistan needs is the time and resources to dig itself out of the hole it is in. The back-breaking sanctions presently imposed by the international community must be lifted. Instead, it must be given help to create and manage the urgently needed social infrastructure of schools and hospitals, and to put its economic house in order. Social peace, something Pakistan has rarely enjoyed, can create the basis for peace with India. Nothing else may.

A version of this article first appeared in *the Bulletin of Atomic Scientists*, September–October 1998.

Education for Peace

LALITA RAMDAS

I speak here not as an expert, an economist, a scientist, a military person or a journalist, nor as a politician. I speak primarily as a citizen and a woman, one who is not a member of any political formation, but who has clear and strong political views which I hold dear as a part of my democratic rights and duties.

Backdrop

On the night of the Pokhran blasts—May 11 1998—certain things changed within me for all time. I sat up all night hitting at my computer keys, to churn out a piece entitled '*Has the Buddha Smiled?*', and was startled by the intensity of my own feelings. I kept asking myself why this action had stirred me to the depths as nothing else had for the past many years? The answers came slowly but they came surely. And it is this that I would like to share, hoping that it will provide some food for thought, and provocation for action.

My overwhelming emotions on that night were anger, sadness, fear; and what I can only describe as an all-consuming determination to fight a leadership that could take such cynical and dangerous decisions in order to hold on to power. Until the night of May 11, I too was half willing, like several others, tired and weary of the corruption, the infighting and inability to govern, displayed by the many alliances of political parties, to 'give the BJP a chance'! May 11 marked a turning point—what a grotesque travesty of Buddha's philosophy. Since that night, I have spent most of my waking hours engaged in one way or other with this question of dealing with a nuclear India, a nuclear Pakistan, the related issues of nuclear apartheid and the hypocrisy of the 'nuclear have' nations, and the role of citizens in this context.

Before dilating on the question, it might not be out of place to spend a few minutes on what I do. My field has been education—formal, non-formal, informal—with a special emphasis on issues of access, equity and social justice for large sections of those deprived and marginalised because of gender, class, race, religion and ethnicity. My experience over three decades has spanned urban and rural areas, national, regional and international forums, and has moved between the micro level and actual delivery systems, to policy and advocacy issues at the macro level.

Over the years, it has become an article of faith that education in its broadest definition offers us the only real possibility of building a true democracy and of creating the kind of awareness that can lead to social and political transformation. Our failure as a nation and people to have made the right investments in ensuring universal access and quality education for our people has cost us dearly in many ways—most starkly in the kind of leadership that we continue to elect and trust. Why am I against the bomb and the decision to go nuclear? My own strong reaction to the nuclear tests are based on certain fundamental premises.

1. Conviction

The most compelling one comes from a long-standing conviction that nuclear weapons are evil, inhuman and should be destroyed and banned. A visit to Hiroshima in 1995 served only to reinforce this stance. India was among those nations that introduced and piloted the bill before the International Court of Justice, The Hague, to declare the use, or even the threat of the use of a nuclear weapon as unlawful, illegal on the basis of the existing canon of humanitarian law.

It is incomprehensible that a government that does not even have a clear majority in Parliament could choose to exercise the nuclear option in such total disregard of the country's own established and documented positions on this question. But it is even more incomprehensible that so many of us, the so-called educated, so completely misread the intentions of this, and previous governments, and did nothing over the years to spread a better and wider awareness of the horrors of what this phrase 'keeping the nuclear option open' actually means.

2. Contradictions

Our existing notions with regard to nuclear power and the whole notion of Atoms for Peace are fraught with contradictions and nuances that need far more in-depth analysis. A recent film made [clandestinely] by Yorkshire Television exposes the stark reality of the horrendous situation caused be the laxness of safety regulations in our nuclear power plants—from Tarapore to Kalpakkam—and the suffering of countless villagers and residents in the vicinity. The tragedy is that most victims of our callousness (not peculiar to just the nuclear industry by the way), are poor, voiceless and certainly not organised enough to do what the residents of one group of locals did in the USA, near the Fernald Plant—a nuclear bomb processing facility. They fought a five-year legal battle claiming that the plant had 'dumped 400 thousand pounds of uranium into the air and 150 thousand pounds into the local Miami river and nearby streams' causing radioactive pollution and widespread health disorders in the community. The US Department of Energy was ordered by a federal Judge, to pay US$ 73 million in damages to the community (Isa Daudpota in *Viewpoint*, Nov. 16, 1989).

Not many of us know that in India (possibly in Pakistan too) there exists a special set of laws governing everything to do with atomic energy, the department, its institutions and decisions, which are exempt from discussion and questioning—even in Parliament.

3. The Nature of the State

The next equally strong ground for opposition to the decision to test at Pokhran is related to the sheer hypocrisy, inconsistency and dishonesty with which our leadership has behaved on this issue. After two months of travel and intensive reading and conversations, I am clearer than ever that the demands of political expediency, a long-standing ideological compulsion, and not 'national security', influenced the decision to test. This, in turn, has clearly exacerbated the 'security' environment in our region and turned back the clock of the tentative peace-building exercise with Pakistan. One has only to listen carefully to the way the hawks in both our countries are talking today, to understand that weaponisation and a new arms race has to follow, unless there is a very powerful movement and expression of popular opposition

This display of wanton jingoism and cynical disregard of all ethics, morality or humanity by those in power throws up some fundamental questions with regard to the nature of the state, the role of citizens in a democracy and the right to information and debate about the underlying assumptions of India's role in the world, her priorities and responsibilities to her people. In any other functioning democracy, such a gross transgression of time honoured and accepted norms and codes on the decision to exercise the 'nuclear option' by the government of the day without even the pretence of a debate, would have resulted in a widespread protest, questioning and opposition. Alas, in this country, it led to the opposite—a thoughtless and mindless expression of euphoria and popular support by the public, and a complete confusion in the ranks of the existing political opposition.

4. Defining Nationalism and Patriotism

Sadly, the debate about the bomb has got hopelessly entangled with the question of demonstrating one's loyalty to the country. I believe we must challenge this at every quarter. While a BJP government might have added an extra edge to this, to my mind this is an underlying thread that has been running through our political system about which, for the most part, we do not talk. Recently in Toronto, I was accosted by the representative of the Vishva Hindu Parishad and harangued for my opposition to the decision to go nuclear, which he equated to my being anti-national. The same gentleman, when I suggested that Canadian-Indians might chose to demonstrate their concern for India as they celebrated the end of the Golden Jubilee year by making a commitment to ensure that every child in India was in school within the next decade, said that it was for different groups to decide what they saw as priorities. With a few notable exceptions, most of the Indo-Canadian business community really did not want to hear of the anti-nuclear voices being raised back home.

To the best of my belief, I am as much a patriot as the next man or woman, and this has nothing to do with my religion, community, or having been a service daughter and a service wife. I totally reject any suggestion that those of us who have spoken up against the bomb are in some way less nationalistic than those who mindlessly support the bomb. Perhaps some of you have heard or read a wonderful presentation made by Professor Amulya Reddy in which he speaks of 'poverty being the defining characteristic of India', and the need to use the Gandhi Talisman of recalling the face of the poorest man before deciding on whether a decision of yours will truly help him or her. So says Dr. Reddy, 'Poverty reduction should be the touchstone of our reaction to the nuclear tests.' And as to the question: what is patriotism? 'It is repaying the people the debts one owes them.' Patriotism consists of 'wiping every tear from every face'. So, those who stress that making bombs increases tears are patriotic; those who divert attention from the central reality of India—its poverty—are anti-national.

5. Nuclearisation, Defence and the Right to Information
For more than half of my life, I have 'bought into' the web of myths and beliefs surrounding all matters connected with the Armed Forces, the government of the day and their inviolability and immunity from any form of questioning. It goes without saying that the 'Sacred Cow' of defence secrets formed a major part of one's socialisation—and this applied to everything from something as innocuous as taking photographs at our [sadly ancient] airports, to getting accurate infor-mation about the way the defence budgets are actually designed to conceal more than they reveal!

About two decades ago, when I first began questioning and challenging that nebulous thing called the 'system' and the 'establishment', it was focussed entirely on one person who symbolised that power and authority. And I am referring to none other than my partner and husband of 37 years, the newly-turned anti-nuclear activist (some choose to use the term 'peacenik' in a somewhat derisive sense), the former Chief of the Navy [of India]. It is a tribute to his innate openness and integrity that our marriage, and our family, survived, even thrived, on the furious debates and arguments about education versus defence, bread versus guns, feminism versus military machismo, and most critically, the true meaning of nationalism and patriotism that raged in our home.

6. Bringing Women Centrestage in the Peace Movement
A linked issue about which I have been thinking a great deal—and which is again directly linked to the nature of our education and social systems—is questioning the relative (deafening) silence of women

and the women's groups on this issue, on the one hand, or the mindless expression of self-righteous support, on the other. Here again, I believe it is because of two typical kinds of confusion which must be addressed. For most of us women and wives brought up in typical middle class homes, especially in the post-Independence government service milieu, there was absolutely no way that we dared to doubt or question the 'sacred patriotic and nationalistic' motivations of all those who wore uniform or worked for the government. This was forbidden territory filled with a carefully cultivated mystique.

Even for those of us who came from a history of academia or activism, when Indo-Pakistan or Indo-Chinese issues came up for debate, the most militant among us would opt for a 'nationalist' line. This was marked during each one of our conflicts with Pakistan, and was particularly evident in the pre-conference meetings before Beijing.

The bulk of the poor, on whom the burden of violence is greatest, are hardly encouraged to make these linkages, but fed with propagandist messages of nationalism and patriotism against which it is hard to put up a fight. In her recent article in *Manushi* [an Indian feminist magazine], provocatively titled 'War-gasm', Madhu Kishwar has addressed some of these dilemmas and contradictions. And I argue here that this issue in particular needs to be explored if we are able at all to mobilise women to raise their voices against nuclear weapons in particular, and militarisation in general.

The impact of nuclearisation, as indeed of all forms of militarisation, is hardest on women, and in an increasingly hierarchical and patriarchal set-up, women will be ever more marginalised. We have only to look at the recent debacle in the Indian Parliament on the Women's Representation Bill.

7. Defining a Vision for India, and for South Asia

The reason I have chosen to elaborate on some of these concerns is in order to make an important point, namely, that there is need for each one of us to re-examine our own positions on several questions relating to the issue of how we understand development and the future of the people of India and her neighbours—the people with whom geography and history has determined that we relate, live and work together. For too long, we have allowed ourselves to be led by the nose to follow a pre-set agenda on who decides and what constitutes national priorities —which, in turn, leads to a kind of collective paralysis when called upon to take positions and clearly articulate a point of view on questions ranging from the nuclear issue to reservations or making elementary education a fundamental right. Preceding the issue of whether we want to see India as a nuclear power is a set of other basic questions regarding the kind of India we want to build.

What is our vision for the next century and what really constitutes national security? Is it more important that we gate-crash into the nuclear club and desperately seek a place in the Security Council, or that we target taking India to the top 50 in the UNDP Human Development Index from our present position of 138 out of 175?

Critically, in the present context, what can and should be the role for science and technology, our huge resource bank of scientists, and our institutions of higher learning which have, tragically, remained elitist, even militarist and removed from the needs of that 80 percent of people in this country who continue to struggle against the elements, and for whom applied science and technology could transform their present realities?

I was amused to read recently that one of our most respected nuclear scientists spoke of how 'peaceful nuclear explosions' can be used to divert river beds and for oil exploration. True? False? How do we deal with radiation? Will the experts tell us, please? But, even if true, did we really have to wait to test in the name of security in order to explore these possibilities? The K.L. Rao and Dastur plan on linking India's rivers has been gathering dust in governmental archives. Surely scientists and planners could have got together three decades ago to see how our already existing nuclear capability could be harnessed for national development.

Instead, millions of our people continue to suffer year after year from the ravages of floods or drought, which no scientific policy has seriously sought to solve. None of the esteemed gentlemen (and a few women too), who are writing reams about how 'we can now talk to the US (Mr. Talbott—a third rung official) as equals, and that we are now willy-nilly members of the charmed Nuclear Club (that we have abhorred), and how we can now look people in the eye', have touched upon what, to my mind, constitutes one of the major features of the nuclear option, namely, the environmental cost and the deadly kiss of radiation. The secrecy and inefficiency surrounding many of our own nuclear energy establishments in this region has been kept under wraps by scientist, bureaucrats and politicians alike.

Our current pseudo-nucleonic discourse conveniently chooses to ignore the fact that eminent scientists from Einstein to Rotblat, and political and military leaders like General Eisenhower, Admiral Leahy and General Lee Butler also turned their backs on this lethal and immoral source of potential destruction for reasons they have eloquently articulated. But in an area of such widespread lack of information, it is easy to manipulate and use facts and statistics selectively.

8. India and our Neighbours—Big Brother Syndrome

Bully or friend? India's decision to test in May shattered the carefully built up strategy to work for peace in the region. I find it hard to forgive this piece of chauvinism and, yes, 'anti-national' behaviour. The post-Pokhran months have been full of all manner of academic, strategic, political and other discourse carried by the mainstream (particularly English speaking) media with regard to 'geo-political compulsions in our region'. Many of us have reached a point of total saturation. In such situations, I often find myself turning to my conversations with cab drivers in many parts of the world as a source of infinite wisdom and down to earth commonsense.

One of the clearest expositions on the entire question of Pakistan-India relations (and for that matter relations with any of our neighbours) came from a Pakistani cab driver in Copenhagen. When a South Asian encounters South Asians abroad, there are some interes-ting, unspoken dynamics that take place in the first few minutes! I have now learned to use to maximum benefit the fact that I have a Pakistani son-in-law and how he and my daughter are forced to live in the US so that I rarely get to see my little grand-daughter. This disarms the most hostile of them! Amin Bhai was clear that there was racism, arrogance and hypocrisy among the developed nations, especially the Nuclear Big Five that must be challenged. But he also pointed a finger at India who, as the bigger brother, should play a much more responsible role. '*Behanji*', he said, 'suppose in a family, the big brother who is 6 feet tall and physically more powerful, is always beating and pushing and bullying a weaker '*chhota bhai*' (younger brother), will not the younger brother start hating the big brother? We have always looked up to our big brother for a different kind of role. Why should India be frightened of Pakistan? Do you seriously think that Pakistan can walk in and capture India? Why can we not trade together, come together and only then we can teach these 'b......s (i.e. the west, the whites) a lesson. *Magar jab thak hum aapas mein ladte rahenge, hamaara ihi nuksaan hogaa, aur yeh log aur bhi bandook aur bum bechenge!* (Till such time as we keep fighting among ourselves, it is only we who will suffer, and they will continue to sell us guns and bombs. . . .)'

9. Building Democracy—the Role of Education, Information, Analysis

Clearly these and many more questions must become the subject of a really widespread debate at the level of *panchayats* and *mahila mandals* and village education *samitis*. Until such time as this can happen, successive governments—the powerful politico-administrative, military, and largely elitist nexus—will continue to interpret national goals, national security, and nationalism itself according to their world view, their inherited and inflated ambitions to put India on some world map where power and position are determined by very different and questionable criteria.

As an education and development activist, I cannot but conclude by touching on my favourite subject, namely, that of setting out our priorities and understanding better the link between national security and education and development. Many years ago, in my capacity as head of the Women's Welfare Association of the Navy, I invited a senior expert from one of our premier institutions of defence and strategic analysis, to give us a talk on national security and development. I still recall his clear and powerful statement which essentially said that the ultimate yardstick of national security can only be an internal situation where there is food in every stomach, where every child is in school, where there is indeed health and employment and shelter and drinking water for every Indian. Where did those words of wisdom go? How did we lose our way in the jungle of nuclear muscle flexing and nationalistic jingoism of the narrowest and most sectarian kind?

10. An Agenda for the Future—the Way Ahead

Ironically, the one good thing the tests have done is to bring some of these issues and debates to the surface. The months since Pokhran II have been very revealing in terms of attitudes and perceptions of different people in different places. This might provide some insights into what needs to be done in the coming times. There is really no one formula, except a fundamental commitment in your hearts to waging peace, a determination to bring a better quality of life to our people, and extension to all those with whom our lives are inextricably tangled.

We are a society and a region beset by every possible kind of complexity and diversity. A beginning can only be made by recognising and saluting this richness which provides us with our real characteristics and strength. This is the kind of philosophy of inclusion and plurality that must infuse the very fabric of our society and its institutions, especially educational. (And I am not speaking here only of the exclusive private/public schools but also of the mainstream education system where the bulk of our children are). I could provide a long list of actions possible and actions already underway for those who are interested.

It has been heartwarming to see the kind of communication and exchanges over the Internet, by literally thousands of students, activists, trade unionists, journalists, writers and academics, especially Indians and Pakistanis, all determined that this madness must stop. The challenge is to transform this into a much more broad-based, democratic, educational movement of the people, beyond just the English speaking elite. Provide us resources—human and material—who will translate and adapt till they drop! Then only can we bombard the vernacular press, educational institutions and mass- and community-based organisations with the information and knowledge they too deserve access to. In our villages, frankly most people do not understand the difference between an Anu-bam (atom bomb) and any other kind of bomb. And yet, because of a forced insularity, their vote goes by default to whoever offers some kind of hope. At the same time perhaps, this is the moment to build some kind of truly grassroots-based alternative political front, which people might be inspired to see as a real, viable alternative. In the ultimate analysis, change will have to be fought on the political battlefield and there can and should be no place in this land of the Buddha, for any political philosophy or formation which is exclusivist, fascist and fundamentalist in its outlook. Living as we do in village India—Alibad, Maharashtra—without the familiar organisational structures of the NGO and other groups that were my support group in Delhi or Mumbai—we are now devising completely unorthodox methodologies for opening up the subject, drawing links between local issues and nuclear weapons of destruction. We have located sympathetic individuals even in this stronghold of fundamentalist politics who have translated articles, done interviews, are willing to give publicity to Hiroshima Day and the peace initiatives all over, especially in India and Pakistan. I carry leaflets and white ribbons to the local bank, the fax and xerox shops, the village and taluka and district meetings of school teachers, principals of colleges, the village *sarpanches* and *sabhapathis* (headmen and women) and grab a few moments to explain, to distribute and to mobilise.

People in villages are also essentially tradition bound and god-fearing. A recent article pointed out that the face of Brahmanical Hinduism was essentially militant, with most of our Gods carrying some form of 'asthra' (or weapon). As we went over the pantheon, we realised that Saraswati, Lakshmi, Krishna and Ganesha were among the few who carried instruments of music, and were dedicated to both fun and learning! It is time to discuss how we can and must re-appropriate these cultural spaces for a progressive, democratic and peace agenda. So we are trying to make a beginning by re-orienting the upcoming single-most popular festival of this region, dedicated to Ganesha, the Lord of wisdom, of knowledge and auspicious beginnings, and propagating a message of peace and learning, of tolerance and harmony, of *shanti* and *vidya*. The struggle is long, the issues are deep-rooted in our histories and our sociologies, as much as in our economics and politics.

I have just picked up the newspaper with a headline 'India, Pakistan fail to make headway at SAARC.' The ultimate way ahead will be to strengthen the voices of the millions of our people through a patient process of education to really stake their claim in the decisions that affect our common futures.

And finally, a lament by a Japanese girl who died in Hiroshima, which my children and hundreds of their friends who studied at Springdales school, Delhi, sang together with other songs against apartheid, against war, against violence and for peace over a decade ago:

I'm only seven , although I died, in Hiroshima, long ago
I'm seven now, as I was then
When children die, they do not grow
     My hair was scorched by burning flames
My eyes grew dim, my eyes grew blind
Death came and turned my bones to dust
     And that was scattered by the wind

I need no fruit, I need no rice,
I need no sweets, not even bread
I ask for nothing for myself
For I am Dead, For I am Dead
 All that I ask is that for Peace, You Fight Today.
 You Fight Today, so that the children of this world,
 May live and grow and laugh and play

Based on a presentation made at the Anti-Nuclear Convention in Chennai, July 26, 1998.

STATEMENTS

Indian Scientists Speak Out Against the Indian Nuclear Tests

In the last few days, India has conducted five nuclear tests, including the explosion of a thermonuclear device. The tests, which are claimed to have become necessary due to strategic compulsions affecting our national security, have also been claimed to be a major scientific and technological achievement.

We, scientists in various disciplines, while expressing our deep dismay and unhappiness at this action of the Indian government, wish to point out the following:

The magnitude of the achievement in conducting these nuclear tests should not be blown out of proportion. The technology involved is for the most part decades old, and the aura of achievement stems mainly from the secrecy that surrounds its acquisition and mastery. It must also be seen in relation to far greater technological challenges like the designing, erecting and successful running of safe nuclear power plants. This is something we have been doing for a long time now and we are justifiably proud of it.

These tests are bound to vitiate the atmosphere in the South Asian region, triggering a nuclear weapons race in the region, exacerbating the tensions that already exist and making even more difficult the achievement of peaceful co-existence and co-operation amongst the peoples and the nations of this region. The Government of India has adopted the same cynical language as the nuclear weapon powers by claiming that these tests will contribute to disarmament.

These nuclear tests have undone the consistent position that has been taken over the years on nuclear disarmament. While making it clear that we had the relevant technological capability, India had nevertheless not taken the step towards weaponisation in order not to initiate a nuclear arms race in the sub-continent. At the same time, we had taken a firm stand against signing both the Nuclear Non-Proliferation Treaty (NPT) as well as the Comprehensive Test Ban Treaty (CTBT) because of their discriminatory nature. Strangely enough it is now argued by sections in the government as well as the media, that we should accept and sign the CTBT!!

The country has been committed to an expensive weapons programme without a national debate. We do not see what immediate threats to national security 'forced' this move, particularly when people's needs in terms of education, health, infrastructure and industrial development are urgent. The present government had promised on assuming office that a debate on national security issues would take place, but has in fact initiated a sharp policy turn with wide-ranging implications without the slightest debate.

We wish to recall here, emphatically, the horror that is nuclear war. We stand firmly with the long tradition of eminent scientists who have consistently argued against the induction of nuclear weapons. The horrors of nuclear war cannot be forgotten, whatever pride we feel in achievements, or whatever tactical calculations we make. After all, we still hear of the strategic 'compulsions' that led to the bombing of Hiroshima, and many of us were disgusted by the way the American media turned the 1991 Gulf War into a show of technological supremacy. Moreover, can we feel happy and secure in a world in which every country feels proud of its nuclear weapons capability and is convinced of the deterrence tactic?

May 18, 1998

Signed by:
T.R. Govindarajan, Kamal Lodaya, Krishna Maddaly, Kapil Paranjape, Venkatesh Raman, R. Ramanujam, Sudeshna Sinha, R. Shankar, T. Jayaraman, V.S. Sunder, G. Rajasekaran, Madan Rao, G. Baskaran, Tapobrata Sarkar, Arundhati Dasgupta, Suneeta Vardarajan, Saurya Das, Subrata Bal, Sarasij R.C., I. Suresh, Radhika Vathsan, G.V. Ravindra, R. Srinivasan, Sreedhar Dutta, K. Srinivas, M.V.N. Murthy, Mitaxi Mehta, Abhijit Kar Gupta, Anup Mishra, Meena Mahajan (*The Institute of Mathematical Sciences, Chennai*)

D. Indumathi, Pramathanath Sastry,Ashoke Sen, Joydeep Majumdar, Sujan Sengupta, D. Shubashree, Anirban Kundu, Amber Habib, (*Mehta Research Institute of Mathematics and Mathematical Physics, Allahabad*)

Jaikumar Radhakrishnan, Sumit R. Das, Satya N. Majumdar, Swagato Banerjee, Pranab Sen, Abhisek Dhar, Keshav Dasgupta, Dibyendu Das, Satyaki Bhattacharya, Amit Ghosal, Pratik Majumdar, Shouvik Datta, K. Sheshadri, Saumen Datta, Prasenjit Sen (*Tata Institute of Fundamental Research, Mumbai*)

Alok Kumar, Somendra M. Bhattacharjee, Ajit M. Srivastava, Shikha Varma, Supratim Sengupta, Bikash C. Gupta, Subir Mukhopadhyay (*Institute of Physics, Bhubaneshwar*)

Alladi Sitaram, V. Pati, G. Misra, N.S.N. Sastry, S. Thangavelu, C. Varughese, S. Ramasubramanian (*Indian Statistical Institute, Bangalore*)

Dipan Bhattacharya, Maitreyee Saha (Sarkar), Jyotsna Chatterje, Asimananda Goswami, Binay Dasmahapatra, Sudeb Bhattacharya, Manoranjan Sarkar, Amitava De, Kamales Bhaumik, Swapan Sen, Pravat Kumar Gupta, Kallol Bhattacharya, Netai Bhattacharya, Manoranjan Bhattacharya, Sanjukta Ganguly, Barnana Pal, Chandidas Mukherjee, Atri Mukharjee, Raj Kumar Moitra, Kajal Ghosh Roy, Bijay Bal, Mohan Lal Chatterjee, Harashit Majumdar, Padmanava Basu, Subinit Roy, Polash Bannerjee, Asit kumar De, Triptesh De, Gautam Ghosh, Debajyoti Bhaumik, Samir Mallick, Polash Baran Pal, Brhmananda Dasgupta, Anjali Mukherjee, Debasis Mitra, Kaushik Chatterjee, Ushashi Dutta-Pramanik, Pradipta Das, K. Chabita (Saha), Tamal Sengupta, Kasturi Mukhopadhyaya, Rupali Gangopadhyaya, Dilip Kumar Debnath, Brahmananda Chakraborty, Jhimli Dasgupta, Sumana Roychoudhury, Biswanath Chattopadhyaya, Sandip Sarkar, Somapriya Basu-Roy, Indrani Roy, Indrajit Mitra, Debrupa Chakraborty, Abhee K. DuttaMajumdar, Surasri Chaudhuri, Subhasis Basak, Krishnendu Mukherjee, Rajen Kundu, Somdatta Bhattacharya, Asmita Mukherjee, Sebanti Bagchi, Bhaswati Pandit, Sheuli Chaudhuri, Jaya Pal,Debashish Mukherjee, Mita Sen, Poonam Agarwal, Shankhashubhra Nag, Amit Dutta (*Saha Institute of Nuclear Physics, Calcuttai*)

Parongama Sen (*Surendranath College, Calcutta*)

K.V. Subrahmanyam (*SPIC Mathematical Institute, Chennai*)

Enakshi Bhattacharya, Hema Murthy, Suresh Govindarajan (*Indian Institute of Technology, Chennai*)

Ashutosh Sharma, Gauri Pradhan, Manojit Roy (*University of Pune*)

Tapas Kumar Das, Indranil Chattopadhyay, Subhradip Ghosh (*S.N. Bose National Centre for Basic Sciences, Calcutta*)

D.P. Sengupta, Arnab Rai Choudhuri, Priti Shankar, Ahmed Sayeed, Kiran Kolwankar, Sumit Basu, Nandini Gupta (*Indian Institute of Science, Bangalore*)

Diptiman Sen, B. Ananthanarayan (*Centre for Theoretical Studies, Bangalore*)

Sabyasachi Chatterjee, Parthasarathi Joarder, S. Mohin, Sonjoy Majumder, Projval Sastri, Angom Dilip, Joydeep Bagchi, V. Krishnakumar (*Indian Institute of Astrophysics, Bangalore*)

Prabir Purkayastha (*IEEE Computer Society, Delhi Chapter*)

D. Raghunandan (*Centre for Technology & Development, Delhi*)

Amit Sengupta (*Delhi Science Forum, Delhi*)

Mohan Rao (*Community Health and Social Medicine, Jawaharlal Nehru University, Delhi*)

Kamal Mitra Chenoy, Sankalpa Ghosh, Shailesh K Shukla, Debasish Bose (*JNU, Delhi*)

Dhruva Raina, Dinesh Abrol, Usha Menon, Irfan Habib (*National Institute for Science Technology and Development Studies, Delhi*)

Tabish Qureshi (*Indira Gandhi Centre for Atomic Research, Kalpakkam*)

Partha Bhattacharya, Dipankar Sarkar (*Indian Institute of Technology, Kharagpur*)

Anurag Mehra, Rowena Robinson, Bharat Seth (*Indian Institute of Technology, Mumbai*)

Subhasis Banerjee (*Indian Institute of Technology, Delhi*)

Gautam Sengupta (*Indian Institute of Technology, Kanpur*)

Arvind (*Guru Nanak Dev University, Amritsar*)

Avijit Chatterjee, Santosh P Koruthu, S. Jawahar (*Aeronautical Development Agency, Bangalore*)

A.P. Balachandran (*Syracuse University, USA*)

Rukmini Dey (*SUNY at Stony Brook, USA*)

K. Varghese John, K.S. Narain, Amol S Dighe, S. Raghavan (*International Centre for Theoretical Physics, Trieste, Italy*)

Muktish Acharyya, R.S. Chakrawarthy (*Cologne University, Germany*)

B. Biswal (*University of Stuttgart, Germany*)

Haranath Ghosh (*Univ. Federal Fluminense, Brazil*)

Ansuman Lahiri (*Karolinska Institute, Sweden*)

Biologists in India
for Nuclear Disarmament

In the wake of the nuclear weapon tests in South Asia in May 1998, it has become imperative to remind ourselves and each other of the unique evil that nuclear weapons represent. They are not simply another way of waging war, but weapons non-selective by their very nature, since every nuclear explosion releases radioactive fallout. This radioactive dust is spread by wind and rain, contaminates water and air, is taken by plants and enters the food chain right at the bottom, and persists for thousands of years. It will leave effects transcending generations; not only innocent people but their unborn children will be deeply damaged, as will be the world around them, by even a 'small' nuclear weapon. There will be horrific degradation of the environment, with devastating effects on human communities. Hiroshima, Nagasaki, Chernobyl and the many nuclear test sites around the wrold, old and new, are 'living' evidence of this. Nuclear weapons are, therefore, quintessential terrorist instruments inappropriate for democratic societies anywhere. It is a matter of common sense that making nuclear weapons and deploying them steadily increases the chance that they will be used, by 'mistake', 'inadvertently', 'just to be on the safe side.' In addition to the geographical realities of South Asia, the heightened tensions, confrontational attitudes and worsened neighbourly relationships enhance these risks, negating any claims of enhanced national security. In fact, South Asia now has all the ingredients for a regional nuclear arms race that would exponentially increase these risks and prove socio-economically ruinous. It is essential to condemn the hypocrisy of the nuclear weapons states in maintaining huge nuclear arsenals while making pious pronouncements and imposing sanctions under a discriminatory and unethical global nuclear regime. This can only be done by returning to ethical and consistent positions on global nuclear disarmament through renouncing nuclear weapons manufacture and deployment, not by joining the nuclear weapons states in their insanity.

It is a sorry comment on the scientific establishments of South Asia that the copying of fifty-year-old technology available in the public domain for decades, needs to be propped up as a major claim to fame for sub-continental science. The point and purpose of innovative science is to comprehend our world and hopefully, ourselves, and that of innovative technology is to use the comprehension (and perhaps wisdom) gained to improve the quality of life of all human beings, everywhere. Nuclear weapons do not fit this bill. Ever since Hiroshima and Nagasaki, the bulk of the scientific community the world over has consistently argued that it is irrational to be steadily increasing the chances of use of weapons that simply cannot be used, and has been in sustained and vehement opposition to nuclear weaponry. There is every pressing reason for the scientists and technologists of India to join their voices to those of their global communities and urge their fellow-citizens to reject the acquisition of nuclear weapons; not because somebody compels us, but because reason impels us.

June 1998

Signed by:
Satyajit Rath, Sandip K. Basu, Vineeta Bal, Chandrima Shaha, R.P. Roy, Ayub Qadri, Pramod Upadhyay, R.A. Vishwakarma, Rahul Pal, Seyed E. Hasnain, Anna George (*National Institute of Immunology, New Delhi*)

K. Srinath Reddy, Anoop Saraya, Sarman Singh, Anjan Dhar, Dinesh Kumar, Yogesh Jain, M.R. Bhagat, K.K. Ray, S. Bhan, A.B. Dey, A. Sood, D. Prabhakar, P. Chopra, M. Vijayaraghavan, Ruma Ray, Subrata Sinha, O.P. Kharbanda, Ritu Duggal, N.K. Arora, S.K. Acharya, Arvind Kumar, S. Guleria, T.K. Chatterji, M. Ramam, J.K. Grover, V.P. Choudhry, V. Bhatnagar, C.S. Panday, N.G. Desai, M. Mehta, R.S. Tyagi, Raka Jain, G.P. Bandhopadhyay, S.S. Chauhan, Rajeev Jain, Kaushal K. Verma, H. Krishna Prasad (*All India Institute of Medical Sciences, New Delhi*)

Shahid Jameel, Chetan Chitnis (*International Centre for Genetic Engineering and Biotechnology, New Delhi*)

Anil K. Tyagi (*Delhi University, South Campus*)

Alok Bhattacharya, Mohan Rao, Santosh K. Kar, Sudha Bhattacharya, Ritu Priya (*Jawaharlal Nehru University, New Delhi*)

D. Sengupta, A.B. Banerje, H. Bhattacharya, Chittaranjan Bhattacharya, D.J. Chatto-padhyay (*Calcutta University, Calcutta*)

Gautam Basu, Anuradha Lohia (*Bose Institute, Calcutta*)

Susanta Roychoudhury, Anjana Mazumder, Chitra Dutta, Salil C. Datta, Rukhsana Chowdhury, Hemanta K. Majumder, Santu Bandyopadhyay, Tushar Chakraborty, Tuli Biswas, Pratap K. Das, Partha Chattopadhyay, B. Aihari, P.K. Dutta, S.B. Mandal, Anup Bhattacharya, B.C. Pal, T. Mukherjee, A.N. Bhaduri, C.N. Mandal, A.K. Ghosh, S. Sengupta, Sumantra Das, Madhusudan Das Keya Chaudhuri, Debashish Bhatta-charya, Syamal Roy (*Indian Institute of Chemical Biology, Calcutta*)

F.U. Ahmed (*Government Medical College, Dibrugarh*)

Amit Mishra, Satyavan Singh, A.K. Dwivedi, Prem Prakash, S.K. Bhatnagar, S. Bhatta-charya, L. Srivastava, Anuradha Dube, Vinod Bhakuni, Raja Roy, Sudhir Sinha, R.P. Satpathy, W. Haq, Uma Roy, Safia Nasim, Bamani Sur, Vinod Bihari, G.K. Jain, Srikanta K. Rath, P.S.R. Murthy, M.M. Singh, D.C. Kaushal, R. Raghubir, P.Y. Guru, D.S. Upadhyay, Ram Pratap, O.P. Asthana, Saman Habib, Mehrotra N.N. (*Central Drug Research Institute, Lucknow*)

Ashis K. Das (*Birla Institute of Technology and Science, Pilani*)

V. Rodrigues, K.S. Krishnan, Rohit Mittal, Zita Lobo, B.J. Rao, Shobhona Sharma, M.M. Johri, Gotam K. Jarori, Krishanu Ray (*Tata Institute of Fundamental Research, Mumbai*)

Rita Mulherkar, C.N. Shenoy, Archana Wagle, Rajiv Sarin (*Cancer Research Institute, Tata Memorial Centre, Mumbai*)

B. Ravindran (*Regional Medical Research Centre, Bhubaneswar*)

A.P. Dash (*Institute of Life Sciences, Bhubaneswar*)

Dipankar Chatterji, Usha K. Srinivas, Ravi Sirdeshmukh (*Centre for Cellular and Molecular Biology, Hyderabad*)

Satyajit Mayor, Obaid Siddiqi, M. Vijayraghavan, M.M. Panickar, Jayant Udagaonkar, Manjari Mazumdar (*National Centre for Biological Sciences, Bangalore*)

Madan Rao (*Raman Research Institute, Bangalore*)

Rohini Balakrishnan (*Indian Institute of Science, Bangalore*)

[*Though signatories are identified by their institutional affiliations, their signatures reflect their individual concern as global citizens rather than institutional views.*]

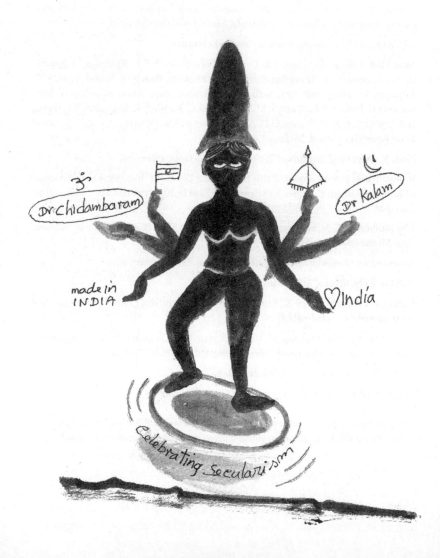

Protest Against
Nuclear Bomb Tests
Scientific Workers' Forum, West Bengal

This is to express our dismay, shock and anguish at the recent nuclear bomb tests by the Government of India. The use of N-bombs in Hiroshima and Nagasaki is a shame for humanity. But the run for aquiring such weapons of mass destruction is still on. Present day nuclear weapons are much more destructive in nature in terms of short and long term effects. It is distressing that India has become a party to trigger arms race involving such weapons in this part of the continent. There are a million issues which need urgent attention and yet our government is diverting the country's efforts and scarce resources to a non-issue. It is a well accepted fact in knowledgable circles today that nuclear weapons are not at all effective as deterrent. Before being happy about the achievements of our nuclear tests we should pause to think about our limited achievements in several domestic matters of grave importance. We continue to be in the list of one of the least developed countries. We have one of the lowest per capita incomes. Half of our population is illiterate. Our education system is in a complete mess. There doesn't exist such a thing as health care. Even hospitals in urban areas lack basic facilities and in rural areas they are abominable. Millions are forced to live in slums in subhuman conditions. We are a country where child labour and female infanticide still continue to exist and over 1.5 million children die annually due to diarrhoea. The list is unending. We believe that there are better ways of building the county's defence. The best way would be to develop better relations with our neighbours. We should not start with the assumption that peace with our neighbours is impossible. We believe that this act of our government will add to the tension already prevailing in this region and will give rise to a nuclear and conventional arms race. The latter will only benefit the arms selling countries. The best defence of any country is freedom from hunger, disease, illiteracy and harmony with its neighbours. The government has adopted the same cynical language as the nuclear weapons powers by claiming that these tests will contribute to disarmament. While making it clear that we had the relevant technological capability, India had nevertheless not taken the step towards weaponisation in order not to initiate a nuclear arms race in the sub-continent. At the same time, we had taken a firm stand against signing both the Nuclear Non-Proliferation Treaty (NPT) as well as the Comprehensive Test Ban Treaty (CTBT) because they contained discriminatory clauses. Strangely enough it is now argued by sections in the government as well as the media, that we should accept and sign the CTBT!! We should guard against being swayed by chauvinistic feelings. Unbridled chauvinism has led to catastrophies in the past. We urge all people believing in peace and true progress to take a strong stand against such acts of our government.

This statement was modelled on the declaration signed by scientists of the Tata Institute of Fundamental Research, Mumbai, the Institute of Mathematical Sciences, Chennai, and some other institutes.

May 18, 1998

Stop This 'Scientific' Jingoism

An Appeal by Journalists Against
Nuclear Weapons (JANW)

The Journalists Against Nuclear Weapons (JANW) draws the urgent attention of the public in general, and specially the scientific community, to disturbing attempts at identifying Indian science with militarism. These attempts need to be countered and curbed before it is too late. The country has been witness in recent days through our mass media, to the unedifying spectacle of a nuclear militarism being peddled in the name of an allegedly patriotic science. The nuclear tests themselves have, right from May 11, 1998, continued to be described and defended, above all, as a proud scientific achievement. Any opposition to the nuclear tests and what they signify has thus been projected as an affront to Indian science and scientists. That was bad enough. Worse by far is what has followed.

Those at the helm of the science establishment, associated and identified with Pokhran II, have been lionised in well-publicised fora. And they have been feted as patriots par excellence. These scientists have seized the occasion to make observations of a partisan character and even statements approximating to policy pronouncements.

One of them, Dr. A.P.J. Abdul Kalam, has been quoted as contemptuously directing the opponents of the tests and the nuclear weaponisation programme to go stage their protests and demonstrations in Washington and Moscow—as though those against India's bomb were not opposed to nuclear weaponisation elsewhere and everywhere. Like other organisations that demand dismantling of all nuclear arsenals

and universal nuclear disarmaments, the JANW cannot but repudiate the presumption. In the latest example, another of these scientists, Dr. K. Santhanam of the DRDO, is reported to have declared that India can make the neutron bomb and added: 'We have no plans as of now to do so, but should anyone ask us (the scientific community) to do so, we will do it.'

The implications of leaving national security issues to be pronounced upon by such a section of scientists are evident. Even more dangerous, however, is the trend towards identifying science, and Indian science itself, with jingoism.

Some sections of the scientific community have, fortunately, come out against the tests and the nuclear weaponisation drive and exposed the hollow claims behind it. The JANW assures these sections of full support in efforts to prevent Indian science from being misused to further a militarist agenda.

September 15, 1998

Protest Rally at Hutatma Chowk

Anubam Virodhi Andolan, Mumbai

In response to the 10 nuclear explosions that have rocked the sub-continent in the last month, the Anubam Virodhi Andolan (Movement against Nuclear Weapons) held a protest rally at Hutatma Chowk in Mumbai starting at 3.30 pm on June 10th, 1998. AVA believes that the atomic explosions and the rhetoric and jingoism that has accompanied them in India as well as Pakistan are an inmitigated disaster and a looming threat to humanity in general and our region in particular. They are indefensible morally, militarily, economically and psychologically. Morally because we have no right to threaten the lives of millions of human beings alive today and the many millions who will never be born for thousands of years after a nuclear war. Militarily because neither India nor Pakistan have become more secure because of these tests. Both countries are vulnerable to the pressure of their fanatics. Apart from this even a minor accident can start a nuclear war between India and Pakistan as both lack the sophisticated fail-safe mechanisms that America and Russia possessed despite which accidental nuclear war was barely averted on numerous occasions. Economically, because our two nations are poverty striken and a nuclear arms race is a criminal waste of national resources. Psychologically, because the explosions and subsequent jubilation in both countries over the acquisition of weapons of mass destruction can only be regarded as brain damage. The Anubam Virodhi Andolan while condemning India and Pakistan is not unaware that the USA, Russia, the UK, France and China as well as other soon to be nuclear states are equally to blame for not having the courage and wisdom to give up the nuclear path.

The AVA is a coalition of individuals and groups in Mumbai including Ekta, National Alliance of People's Movements, Sarvodaya Mandal, the Republican Party of India, Nirbhay Bano Andolan, Nivara Hakk Suraksha Samiti, The Humanist Movement, Lok Shahi Hakk Sanghatana, Indian People's Media Collective and others.

June 10, 1998

Sabarmati Declaration
Anu Virodhi Shanti Samiti

A meeting of eminent thinkers, Gandhian activists, scientists and concerned citizens met at Sabarmati Gandhi Ashram in Ahmedabad to discuss growing weaponisation in general and the implications and fallout of the Pokhran nuclear tests in particular.

After considering diverse views, discussing various aspects of the Pokhran II and the country's nuclear policy, the gathering came up with the following declaration:

Nuclear explosions conducted by India at Pokhran on 11th and 13th May 1998 were without the democratic consent of the people of India. We believe that, under the pretext of 'secrecy for security reasons', people's right to information has been totally neglected.

We believe that this myopic and thoughtless move in the name of 'national security' is anti-people, because, as everyone knows, in a nuclear war there are no winners, but destruction results in both camps.

Pokhran II has adversely affected our country politically, diplomatically, economically, socially and ecologically. Our relations with our neighbors have deteriorated. Internationally, now, we no longer have the same locus standi on global disarmament. Apart from the dwindling flow of development funds from the west, Pokhran II has affected and will continue to adversely affect our internal economy. The fallout from Pokhran II will have radioactive nuclear waste in our air, soil and ground water. The effects of radioactive waste are too well known to require any specific explanation. Whereas we have inherited rich cultural heritage from our ancestors, we will leave behind dangerous nuclear waste for our future generations!

On the much-discussed theory of deterrence, we conclude that deterrence is an irrational and strategically unsound proposition. Deterrence will lead to arms race and will tax internal economics of both the rival countries.

We believe that the money being used for weaponisation in general and nuclear arms in particular should be channelised to fulfill the basic needs of the country's millions who do not have access to appropriate and adequate drinking water, primary education, basic health services and benefits of welfare schemes. We believe that to divert funds from such uses to building up nuclear armament is immoral, unethical and suicidal.

We also believe that changing our earlier nuclear policy without a national consensus and without explaining its rationale was a treachery of the people of India.

We propose the following action agenda to address some of the issues and to create a massive public opinion against nuclear armament and in the interest of World Peace.

Widespread public awareness campaigns should be undertaken using tools like posters, street theater (special programmes should be planned between 6th and 9th of August)

Bold initiatives should be taken by peace lovers to pressurise the Indian government for an arms-free India. Signature campaigns may be used as a tool.

As a people inheriting the legacies of Gandhi, Buddha and Ashoka, India should take a lead in not only building international opinion on de-weaponisation but also should endeavour to form a league of nations against nuclear weapons and to pressurise the international 'haves' to defuse their nuclear arms.

Peace groups should support the bill in favour of people's right to information so that in future such major policy shifts and also defence expenditures are not kept secret from the people of this country.

The Anu Virodhi Shanti Samiti (Peace Committee Against The Atom) is based in Ahmedabad, Gujarat.

July 18–19, 1998

Join the Struggle
Indian Writers and Poets

On the 6th of August, 1945, the first atom bomb was dropped on the city of Hiroshima. A similar bomb was dropped three days later on Nagasaki. Over 200,000 people died in the immediate aftermath; thousands continue to die every year from the after-effects of the bomb. The message of the hibakusha—the survivors of the bomb—is the best argument for global disarmament.

In May this year, the BJP-led Indian government conducted nuclear tests in Pokhran. The Pakistani tests in Chagai followed two weeks later. Together these tests have catapulted South Asia into a dangerous new chapter of its history. It is ironic that in this, the 50th year of our independence—when we have barely begun to understand the tragedy of partition—these new horrors have been unleashed on either side of the border. Already these tests and the accompanying jingoist rhetoric have undermined popular initiatives to forge peace and friendship among the people of the region. And in the future, these weapons could mean worse, not just a partition, but death and destruction on both sides, on a scale difficult to imagine.

Both India and Pakistan now have the capability to perpetrate the horrors of Hiroshima and Nagasaki on each other, not once but many times over. The people of India and Pakistan must stop this madness which threatens us with mutual annihilation.

This is why August 6th, Hiroshima day is such an important reminder to us this year. This is why we call upon all Indians, all those who love their country, all those who love life, to join in the struggle against nuclear weapons and for global nuclear disarmament. We must show the rulers of this country that we want to stop their weapon-isation program and its deployment. We must demand that the discriminatory and hypocritical global nuclear regime be dismantled. To this end, India must return to the global nuclear disarmament agenda and stop any further moves to induct and deploy nuclear weapons. Pakistan too must reciprocate with matching measures.

August 6, 1998

Signed by:
Amrita Pritam, Arundhati Roy, Bhisham Sahni, Githa Hariharan, J.P. Das, Khushwant Singh, Krishna Baldev Vaid, Krishna Sobti, Mrinal Pande, Mukul Kesavan, Nirmal Verma, Rajendra Yadav

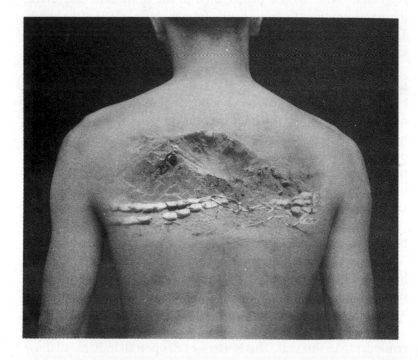

Return to the Disarmament Agenda
Indian Journalists

On the 6th of August, 1945, the first atom bomb was dropped on the city of Hiroshima followed by a similar bomb three days later on the city of Nagasaki. Over 200,000 people died in its immediate aftermath and thousands continued to die every year from the after effects of the bomb. The message of the Hibakusha—the survivors of the bomb—has been a powerful force for global disarmament.

With the May 11th and 13th nuclear weapons tests by the Indian government, followed by the Pakistani tests two weeks later, our region has now entered a dangerous phase. The tests and the provocative rhetoric by BJP leaders that succeeded them have only heightened tensions in the region, worsened relations with our neighbours and undermined popular initiatives aimed at forging peace among the people of the region.

India and Pakistan now have the capability to perpetrate the horrors of Hiroshima and Nagasaki on each other, not once but many times. Hence, the need to remember August 6th, Hiroshima day, is particularly important this year. The people of India and Pakistan must stop this madness which threatens us with mutual annihilation.

Concerned citizens of the Capital, cutting across political divides, have taken the initiative to mobilise public opinion on the issue. It is intended to convey to the government that the average Indian does not want nuclear weapons and demands a halt to the program of nuclear weaponisation and deployment. also seeks to drive home the point that India, which was aways for disarmament and against the discriminatory global nuclear regime, cannot now make efforts to become a party to the same exclusivist club. The attempt by the present government to join the nuclear club must be condemned as it is against all that this country has stood for.

The hypocritical concern of the nuclear weapons powers about proliferation of these weapons of mass destruction cannot be countered by its home grown version. In order to resume India's due role, India must return to the global nuclear disarmament agenda and stop any further measures towards induction and deployment of nuclear weapons. Pakistan too must reciprocate with matching measures.

June 1998

Signed by:
A. Raghavan, Achin Vanaik, Ajaz Ashraf, Ajith Pillai, Ajoy Bose, Amitabha Roy Chowdhury, Anita Anand, Bishaka De Sarkar, E.P. Unny, Faraz Ahmed, G. Chandrashekhar, Javed Faridi, Jawid Laiq, John Cherian, John Dayal, K.K. Pande, Kuldip Nayar, Madhu Kishwar, Pamela Philipose, Paranjoy Guha Thakurta, Pradeep Magazine, Ram Sharan Joshi, Ravindra Prasad Rabbi, Ruchira Gupta, S.K. Pande, Seema Mustafa, Shankar Raghuraman, Siddharth Varadarajan, Sujata Madhok, Sukumar Muralidharan, Suresh Bafna, Sumir Lal, Vishnu Nagar, Yogesh Vajpeyi

A Call for Peace
Indian Medical Professionals

On this day, some fifty years ago, the first nuclear weapon was used. The whole city of Hiroshima was erased from the face of this earth. About one lakh human beings, including women and children who had nothing to do with war or politics became corpses in the wink of an eye. Many of those who survived died agonising deaths due to burns and cancers. We, the members of the medical profession spend our whole lifetime fighting illnesses and trying to save individual lives. We know that nuclear weapons are like no other weapons; medicine is helpless before its horrifying consequences. Therefore, we are deeply saddened that the governments of India and Pakistan have field tested nuclear weapons which are far more destructive than the one dropped on Hiroshima. We hold that nuclear weapons cannot solve any of the problems of the people of this subcontinent. On the one hand, they can start a very costly and senseless arms race which would impoverish the region, and lead to an enormous increase of poverty-related diseases. There is nothing that can be achieved by mere possession of nuclear weapons. They cannot guarantee a victory in tactical warfare. Vietnam proved that beyond any doubt. They cannot guarantee the stability of a country. The disintegration of the former USSR proves that. On the other hand, there is nothing that cannot be solved by dialogue held with mutual respect. The people of India and Pakistan share similar problems. Any problems between us should be settled by dialogue—after all what could not be settled by two wars cannot be settled by a third one—even if it is a nuclear one. Perhaps the only certainty of a nuclear war is mutually assured destruction. We, the members of the medical profession, on this day remembered the world over as Hiroshima day, appeal to the governments of India and Pakistan to abandon the nuclear option altogether and return to the negotiating table. This we do in the name of the innocent victims of Hiroshima and Nagasaki.

The following Call for World Peace was released by 350 medical professionals on August 6, 1998, Hiroshima Day, at a public function at Stella Maris College, Madras by Dr A.S. Thambiah, FRCP, a well-known dermatologist and the recipient of the B.C. Roy Award. Some of the prominent signatories were Dr B. Ramamurti (FRCS, neurosurgeon, Voluntary Health Service, Madras), Dr A.S. Thambiah (FRCP, Emeritus Professor, Madras Medical College, Madras), Dr C.N. Devanayakam, FRCP, Supertindent, Hospital for Thoracic Diseases, Tambaram, Madras, Dr Sunil Pandya (neurosurgeon, Jaslok Hospital, Bombay, and editor of Journal of Medical Ethics), and, Dr N.H. Antia, FRCS, former Member of Planning Commission, Government of India.

August 6, 1998

Opposing Nuclear Weapons
Solidarity for Peace

Leading academics, intellectuals, human rights activists, journalists and writers from Andhra Pradesh have condemned the recently conducted nuclear tests describing them as 'anti-people' and indicative of the fascist designs of the Bharatiya Janata Party-led government.

Presiding over an anti-nuclear weapons conference, organised here last night by the Solidarity for Peace, a forum of students of the Hyderabad Central University, Prof. G. Haragopal, vice-president of the Andhra Pradesh Civil Liberties Committee (APCLC) and head of the human rights department of the university, said going nuclear would only lead the country to greater centralisation of power in the hands of poli-ticians, technocrats, bureaucrats and security forces and pauperise, subjugate and render helpless the common people.

He pointed out that history had ample examples of how potential dictators like Adolf Hitler and Benito Mussolini built up a fear psychosis among their people to justify greater militarisation of their countries before embarking upon an all out repressive pogrom. Questioning the motive of the Vajpayee government in conducting the nuclear tests under strict secrecy, Prof. Haragopal said there should have been a full-fledged debate in the country on the pros and cons of the tests before taking the nuclear plunge.

APCLC president M.T. Khan, speaking on the social, political and cultural fall-out of the nuclear tests, quoted Prime Minister Atal Behari Vajpayee's statement that 'we would sacrifice every thing for the country's security.' 'What it means is that the BJP would sacrifice human rights and dub any people's movement, dissent and struggles for life as anti-national,' he added. Mr. Khan said the jingoism of the BJP leaders suited the politicians of Pakistan equally as the cry of patriotism would help them repress any form of dissent.

Prof. Rama Melkote of Osmania University questioned the propriety of the state assuming monopoly over violence and weapons and pointed out that internal security of the state was as important as external security. She said nuclear weapons cannot ensure the security of the country, pointing out the case of the former Soviet Union, which despite having a large stock of nuclear weapons, collapsed under its own weight. She said the welfare of the people and integrating them were a far greater guarantee for the security of a country.

Leading environmentalist Purushottam Reddy wanted a total ban on nuclear establishments in the country and appealed to all the peace loving people to unitedly work for a nuclear free world. Prof. S.G. Kulkarni condemned the militarisation of science and technology and stressed the need for advancement in science and technology for solving the problems of the people. He alleged that the ruling party leaders and technocrats were hand in glove in nuclearising the country which would only promote a dictatorial government which took shelter behind secrecy.

Prof. Probal Dasgupta said there was nothing to gloat about the nuclear tests as our scientists had only duplicated the technology available elsewhere. It would be something worth taking pride in if only our scientists came up with innovative techniques to better the lives of the people.

Journalist Venugopal alleged that the nuclear tests were just a ploy to silence the opponents of the BJP and create a sense of euphoria among the people. He recalled how the then Prime Minister Indira Gandhi went for a nuclear test in 1974 when she was facing the move-ment for total revolution headed by Jayaprakash Narayan. APCLC gen-eral secretary K. Balagopal called upon all the concerned citizens to launch a campaign to concientise mass opinion against nuclearisation.

Hyderabad, May 22, 1998

Call For Urgent And Universal Disarmament
Catholic Bishops Conference of India

The Standing Committee (Governing Body) of the Catholic Bishops' Conference of India, meeting at a time when the entire world and in particular the people of Asia are discussing the eleven nuclear tests conducted by India and Pakistan in May 1998, makes a fervent plea for urgent and universal disarmament.

Now that the nuclear weapons race on the sub-continent of South Asia is a reality, the most urgent need is to restore mutual confidence between the countries of the region, specially between India and Pakistan, to reopen channels of communication, and to defuse the atmosphere of tension and confrontation. With the presence in our sub-continent weapons of mass destruction and the fear that long range missiles may be capped by nuclear weapons, the most urgent and pressing need is to de-escalate the tension through diplomatic and political discussions in an atmosphere of mutual understanding and respect for life and for the common historical and cultural heritage of the two nations and their people.

The Catholic Bishops' Conference knows that peace is inseparable from security. The people of India, the Catholic community, and the Bishops extend their full support to all peace and disarmament initiatives with their prayers.

The CBCI is firmly of the mind that the resources of India and all countries of the sub-continent must be dedicated singularly to the welfare of the people of the region. Resources needed for combating poverty for waging war on hunger and disease, and for empowering the people through education, shelter and a respect for their human rights, should not, and must not, be diverted in a race involving hostility, war and destruction.

The CBCI calls for universal disarmament through democratic international negotiations. A special responsibility in this regard rests on those nations which have huge stockpiles of nuclear weapons.

The stand of the Catholic church has been consistent on this issue from the very beginning of the nuclear era. The Holy Father, Pope John Paul II said in his speech to the diplomatic corps on January 13, 1996 '... in the sphere of nuclear weapons, the banning of tests and of the further development of these weapons, disarmament and non proliferation, are closely linked and must be achieved as quickly as possible under effective international controls. There are the stages towards a general and complete disarmament which the international community as a whole should reach without delay.'

The CBCI in April 1982 noted that 'In a nuclear age there is no alternative to world disarmament.' Disarmament is the only realistic form of national defence. It was Mahatma Gandhi's conviction that 'the world is sick unto death of blood spilling and looks for a way out.' War is our common enemy and all that can be done must be done against it and its root cause - the demonic evil of hatred, fear, selfishness, greed and lust. 'They shall beat their swords into ploughshares and their spears into pruning hooks; one nation shall not raise the sword against another nor shall they train for war again.' (Is. 2/4)

Nuclear energy is one of the momentous discoveries of our times. It has been always our conviction that nuclear energy must be used only in the service of people's development and peace, that nuclear research and technology must have the single objective of fighting disease and improving the quality of life. The poverty and underdevelopment in the Indian subcontinent makes it particularly imperative that the region's scientific and other resources and energies are focussed sharply on ameliorating the lot of the people.

The CBCI reaffirms its commitment to peace and calls on all to strengthen the ambience of non-violence and security, so that our people can achieve their potential in a lasting and abiding peace, without fear and without the shadow of a nuclear threat.

June 11, 1998

India Should Not Induct Nuclear Weapons

The Polit Bureau of the Communist Party of India (Marxist)

It is a matter of great indignation that the Prime Minister, keeping the people and the political parties in the dark regarding the reasons leading to the reversal of India's long established nuclear policy, has chosen to write about the same to the US President even before the second round of tests on May 13th.

There had never been any doubt regarding the capacities of the Indian scientists in developing our indigenous capabilities in the field of nuclear technology. In fact, these tests would not have been possible but for the continuous work during the last 24 years since the first nuclear test.

While recognising India's capacities and our internal strength in this field, successive governments had chosen not to make nuclear weapons but to keep the nuclear option open, without jeopardising our national security, as a commitment to India's long cherished goal for achieving universal nuclear disarmament. The BJP, which all along adopted a strident jingoistic position, advocated inducting nuclear weapons. The BJP-led government, however, assured that such a step would be taken after a comprehensive review of our security concerns. It has now gone back on its own assurance that it made to the Indian people by this unilateral reversal. And this has been done by a government which has a precarious majority and yet to prove its stability.

The earlier policy, which stood India in good stead in the past, has now been reversed. The BJP led government has to answer to the Indian people as to what dramatic changes have occurred in our threat perception during the few weeks after it assumed office. It is clear that the BJP is pursuing a domestic political agenda of whipping up jingoism. This is more than clear by its call for celebrations and the simultaneous publication (on May 11) of the RSS mouthpiece, Organiser, exhorting India to become a nuclear weapon State.

Such a policy, apart from undermining the long stand independent foreign policy of India, severely jeopardises the ongoing initiatives taken by India towards improving relations with our neighbours. It negates the advances made during the period of the United Front government. At one stroke the BJP-led government has harmed the atmosphere of good relations being built. The strident anti-China campaign reverses the important initiatives for reduction in arms build up and the confidence building measures that the two countries have arrived at after a decade of diplomatic efforts. The consequences of nuclear arms race in the sub-continent will have a disastrous effect on the Indian economy and the livelihood of millions of working Indians.

While mounting an aggressive anti-China campaign in his letter to the US President, the Prime Minister has deliberately ignored the longstanding threat perception of India concerning the US nuclear military base in Diego Garcia. This Indian Ocean island base has been used by the USA in the Gulf war and its weapons have a range that covers India. Such deliberate silence about imperialist military manoeuvres and support to anti-Indian extremist activities reflect the pro-imperialist shift in Indian policy. Increased tensions in South Asia will enable USA to actively intervene in the region.

The Polit Bureau of the CPI(M) strongly protests against the sanctions being imposed on India by the western powers. The nuclear weapon states and others who have all along supported an unequal and discriminatory nuclear order in the world have no right, moral or otherwise, to impose sanctions on India. All sections of the people will unitedly reject any intimidatory tactics directed against India.

The PB of the CPI(M) warns the BJP led government that the people of the country will not tolerate further attacks on their livelihood through further 'liberalisation' and opening up of the economy to foreign capital in the name of combating the sanctions. Already the government has announced the decision to offer counter guarantees, like in the case of Enron, to three multinational companies for power projects. Accelerating this disastrous course will not combat the effect of sanctions but on the contrary, will make India more vulnerable to imperialist economic pressures jeopardising the country's economic sovereignty and simultaneously, imposing greater burdens on the working people. The arms race, at the same time, will both divert scarce resources away from compelling economic needs and divert people's attention away from pressing problems.

Using the sanctions, greater pressures will be mounted on India by imperialism to sign the unequal and discriminatory treaties like the NPT and the CTBT. The BJP led government will not be allowed to capitulate on India's long standing consensual decision of not signing these treaties.

The Polit Bureau of the CPI(M) demands that the BJP led government openly declare that it shall not induct nuclear weapons and build a nuclear arsenal triggering a nuclear arms race in the subcontinent. This is not in the interests of the country and the people. Further, the government should categorically assure the Indian people that it shall not submit to imperialist pressures to be party to unequal and discriminatory international treaties.

The Polit Bureau of the CPI(M) calls upon all peace loving patriots to rally together in carrying forward India's long cherished desire to rid this planet of all nuclear weapons and force the government to adopt positions which will help preserve peace and security in the region and strengthening good-neighbourly relations.

Delhi, May 29, 1998

A Cloudy Future
Delhi School Children

As school students, we are deeply shocked at the nuclear tests conducted by both India and Pakistan, and by the nuclearisation of the subcontinent. We believe there was no strategic justification behind them and that the exercise is a waste of money in two desperately underdeveloped countries, where nearly half the population does not have access to adequate food, clothing or shelter. We are extremely ashamed that the current arms race should have been initiated by India.

We know of the devastation caused in Hiroshima and Nagasaki by bombs far weaker than any produced today. There are immense radioactive dangers in the development of nuclear technology. It is also illogical to believe that peace can flourish in an atmosphere of constantly accelerating mutual hostility and nuclear proliferation.

Most of all, we are disgusted by the jingoism displayed by the government after the Pokhran tests. These tests are being seen as a measure of national pride. To us, nuclearisation is a matter of shame. As future citizens of this country, we would like to know what legacy we are being left with. We would like to know whether we are to enter the twenty-first century in an atmosphere of peace and amity, or an atmosphere where the possession of weapons of mass murder is a matter of pride. We are unconvinced by the government's protestations of peace, since BJP culture has always been antithetical to democracy, secularism and amity. But as the citizens of tomorrow, we do have a right to know exactly how far the government has plunged us in darkness, and whether we are condemned to a future in the shadow of the mushroom cloud.

Aditya Sarkar (Class XII, Springdales School), Nayantara Sood (Class XII, Air Force School), Meenakshi R Madhavan (Class XI, DPS, RK Puram), Megha Anwar (Class XI, Sardar Patel Vidyalaya) and others, New Delhi.

The Times of India, June 22, 1998

'Candle Light Vigil' Held at Wagha Border

Extending the hand of friendship in a goodwill gesture, hundreds of Indians comprising human rights activists, intellectuals, journalists, artists and prominent citizens held a 'candle light vigil' close to the Indo-Pakistan border here last night on the eve of the 51st Independence Day celebrations.

The participants led by noted journalist and MP Kuldip Nayyar called upon India and Pakistan to break the artificial barriers and open up trade.

The candle light vigil sponsored by the Indo-Pakistan friendship forum for the third consecutive year, however, received no response from the Pakistan side where except for personnel of the Pakistan rangers no civilian was present.

Contrary to the earlier occasions the function this time was held outside the road barrier complex and continued till the early hours of Saturday.

Others who participated in the function included noted film director Gulzar and cinestar turned MP, Raj Babbar.

The Border Security Forces guarding the fence did not allow the crowd to enter the road barrier complex but permitted about fifty people to go upto the zero line holding lighted candles carrying a message for the Pakistani people that despite tension there still existed a ray of hope to bring the two nations closer.

They shouted slogans like Hind-Pak dosti zindabad, Hindu-Muslim bhai bhai, janta ki dosti zindabad. (Long live Pakistan-India friendship, Hindus and Muslims are brothers, long live the friendship of the people).

The road barrier complex on both sides of the border was decorated with flags, coloured lights and banners to mark the Independence Day anniversary.

The participants adopted a number of resolutions on the occasion which condemned the role of political leaders of both the countries for ignoring the interests of the common man.

The resolutions called for halting tension between the two neighbouring countries and called upon leaders to solve the bilateral disputes including the Kashmir issue through peaceful talks.

It sought furthering of bilateral economic relations, opening of the Wagha barrier for free trade besides asking for reduction of the visa restrictions.

Wagha, August 15, 1998

Protest Against
Pokhran II Again
Movement Against Nuclear Weapons

It is two years since Pokhran II, and it is time for the people to protest again. To reiterate with renewed vigour their opposition to all that those deafening blasts of May 1998 in the Rajasthan desert meant.

In this period, all the claims made by the authors and apologists of Pokhran II have been proved absurd, utterly false. Simultaneously, the fears voiced by peace-loving people, by diverse sections of democratic opinion, have been fully vindicated.

As loud as the blasts was the boast of advocates of the Indian bomb that the nation's security had been now assured. They claimed that Pokhran II was a promise of enduring peace in the subcontinent. After Pakistan replied with the resounding tests in the Chagai Hills, they prophesied regional peace with even greater certainty. India and Pakistan, these pundits swore, would never again go to war, not even a conventional war, against each other. The Bharatiya Janata Party government and the tests, they certified, had made no break with the country's proud and traditional policy of commitment to the cause of world peace and nuclear disarmament.

Came Kargil, and the claims lay shattered amid the heaps of Indian and Pakistani corpses on the Himalayan heights. The bus ride to Lahore before the war had proved no journey to India-Pakistan amity. Worse, the conventional conflict brought the prospect of nuclear disaster more perilously close to the subcontinent than ever before. From Pakistan emanated the threat to 'use any weapon' and an organ of the Rashtriya

Swayamsewak Sangh, regarded by many as the real power behind the New Delhi regime, editorially exclaimed: 'Why did we make the nuclear bomb? To keep on the shelf?'

The end of the conflict in Kargil spelt no end to the process of nuclear madness and militarism that had been set in motion. Even before the Defence Minister asked the country to be prepared for 'a hundred Kargils', the government had come out with a Draft Nuclear Docrtrine. The rulers, who had staged Pokhran II without asking the people, were on their own prescribing an absurd and obnoxious programme to make India a nuclear superpower.

The diabolical doctrine, combined with the unabashed ambition to make India a member of the 'nuclear club', left little doubt that a go-by had been given to the nation's anti-nuclear-weapons crusade and commitments. The land of Buddha and Gandhi lost its powerful voice for peace, and none was more gleeful than the powers presiding over the largest of nuclear arsenals. Predictions about the impact of the tests on India-Pakistan relations proved depressingly true. And so did fears about the fallout inside India. Pokhran II proved a prelude to a major offensive of communalism on the country's minorities.

Concern about the economic cost of Pokhran II has also proved entirely warranted. The nuclear weaponisation programme envisaged under the new-found doctrine was estimated to cost about Rs. 45,000 crores over a decade. In the very first year, however, the (increase in the) defence expenditure has been of the dimension of Rs. 13,000 crores. The latest Union Budget provides for an unprecedented increase of 28 per cent in such expenditure. The same budget snatches away paltry concessions for the poor under the public distribution scheme with a proud show of sternness.

The carcasses of animals strewn around the site of the tests in drought-stricken Rajasthan are a terrible illustration of the truth about the much-acclaimed 'achievement' of 1998. Pokhran II stands proved once again as a vicious mockery of the poverty of the vast masses of our people.

Our Demands
Roll back the process set in motion by Pokhran II and reverse the course of nuclear weaponisation.

Abandon the option of further nuclear weapon testing under an Act of Parliament.

- No nuclear weapon tests—explosive or subcritical
- No production of weapo-grade fissile material
- Protect minorities from Pokhran II fallout.
- Spend on national development, not nuclear madness.
- Promote India-Pakistan amity and regional peace for real security.
- Return to the international camp and campaign for peace and universal nuclear disarmament.

Organisations represented in the Movement Against Nuclear Weapons: *Journalists Against Nuclear Weapons, Indian Scientists Against Nuclear Weapons-Chennai Chapter, Tamil Nadu Science Forum, Campaign Committee Against Nuclear Weapons, All-India Peace and Solidarity Organisation, All-India Trade Union Congress, Centre of Indian Trade Unions, All-India Coordination Committee of Trade Unions, All-India Insurance Employees' Association, Bank Employees Federation of India, All-India Bank Employees' Association, All-India Catholic University Federation, Don Bosco Institute of Communication Arts, Physicians for Peace, National Alliance of People's Movements, National Federation of Indian Women, All-India Democratic Women's Association, All-India Progressive Women's Association, Tamil Nadu Women's Forum, Forum for Women's Rights and Development (Mottukkal), Tamil Nadu Muslims Munnetra Kazhagam, All-India Students Association, Students' Federation of India, All-India Students' Federation, Democratic Youth Federation of India, All India Youth Federation, Revolutionary Youth Association, Tamil Nadu Progressive Writers' Association, Tamil Nadu Government Employees' Association, Tamil Nadu Government Employees' Union, People's Union for Civil Liberties, Legal Education Aid Society.*

May 2000

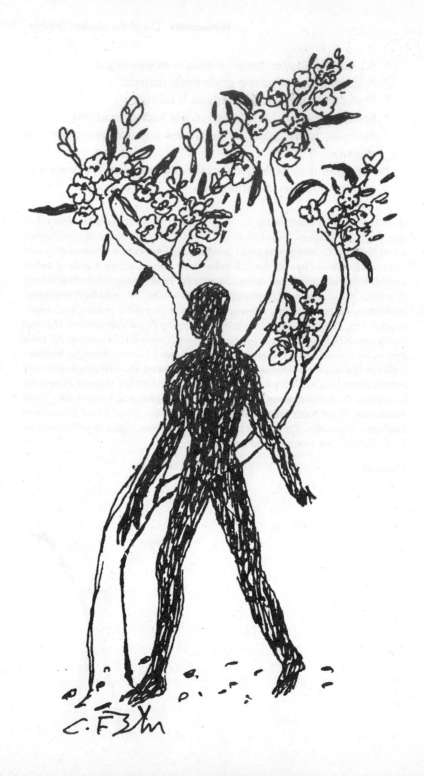

National Convention for Nuclear Disarmament and Peace

As the culmination of two and a half years of grassroots campaigns and mobilisation throughout India in protest against the Pokhran-II nuclear weapon tests by India, and consequent to the Pakistani tests soon after, a National Convention for Nuclear Disarmament and Peace was held in Delhi on November 11-13, 2000. The climax of the 3-day Convention was the launching of a National Coalition for Nuclear Disarmament and Peace committed to seek and campaign for the complete elimination of nuclear weapons worldwide. The Convention was sponsored by 115 organisations and was attended by over 600 delegates from India and abroad, including 50 peace activists from Pakistan. All regions of India were represented. Delegates included grassroots activists, eminent scholars and intellectuals, scientists and doctors, trade unionists and kisan sabha (farmers' association) activists, writers and artistes. Besides the delegation from Pakistan, there were over 30 delegates from Australia, Bangladesh, Britain, Japan, Malaysia, the Netherlands, New Zealand, Sri Lanka, and USA. Among the major international peace organisations that were represented were the Japan Council Against A & H Bombs (Gensuikyo); Japan Congress Against A & H Bombs (Gensuiken); Campaign for Nuclear Disarmament (CND, Britain); Abolition 2000 (USA); Women's International League for Peace and Freedom, New Zealand; and the Pakistan Peace Coalition.

The newly established Coalition for Nuclear Disarmament and Peace gives to India's hitherto heterogeneous peace movement an all-India organisational platform for the first time. This is expected to raise the profile of the nuclear disarmament campaign and give a big boost to its ability to exert pressure on national strategic thinking. The Convention elected a 38-member National Co-ordination Committee. The Convention adopted an Interim Charter for Nuclear Disarmament and Peace calling for a rollback of India and Pakistan's nuclear weapons programmes, cessation of all weapons testing and acquisition of fissile materials, and concrete steps towards global nuclear disarmament. It also adopted an Action Plan for the next one year. A Resolution calling for a concerted campaign against the USA's planned National Missile Defence and Theatre Missile Defence systems which most delegates, including the international activists, proclaimed to be the major future threat to world peace, was unanimously adopted. The Action Plan, the list of sponsoring organisations, the list of National Coalition members and the Charter are presented below.

Action Plan

The Coalition for Nuclear Disarmament and Peace has undertaken to implement over the coming year ending 31 December 2001, the following programme:

1. Establish a central 'clearing house' of information to help indivi-duals and groups wanting to get necessary materials (videos, printed matter, experts, etc.) to generate popular awareness about nuclear weapons and lack of safety and transparency in the nuclear power sector.
2. Co-ordinate ongoing efforts towards regional and then national conventions of anti-nuclear weapon activists. Such regional meetings in the North, South, East, West and Central India to be convened over the next 6 months. There will be separate national conventions for trade unions, scientists, doctors, journalists, artists, lawyers, musicians etc.
3. Press for the institutionalisation of 'Nuclear Disarmament and Peace Week' from August 4-11 every year in as many schools and colleges as possible.
4. To actively engage in dialogue with all political parties and mass organisations as well as with professional associations of all kinds, including industry, religious bodies' etc.
5. Support organisations in Jharkhand fighting the cause of victims of nuclear radiation in whatever way possible to highlight their

plight including official dialogues with the new State government of Jharkhand.

6. Support the efforts of concerned people in Rajasthan regarding secretive government nuclear-related activity including possible dumping of radioactive wastes in their areas.

7. Help to set-up within one year a national federation of radiation victims.

8. Liase with the Pakistan Peace Coalition (PPC) to bring out within a few months a report on joint Indo-Pakistan civil society initiatives that should be carried out to highlight the dangers posed by the nuclearisation of South Asia.

9. Work with the PPC to identify 10 schools and 10 colleges in India and Pakistan respectively, which will be termed as 'sister schools' and 'sister colleges'.

10. Work fraternally with all other genuine nuclear disarmament groups and individuals globally as well as establish links of mutual support with the Indian and South Asian Diaspora in Europe, North America and elsewhere.

Organisations sponsoring the national convention for nuclear disarmament and peace include:

- Akhil Bharat Rachnatmak Samaj
- All India Bank Employees Association (AIBEA)
- All India Central Council of Trade Unions (AICCTU)
- All India Democratic Women's Association (AIDWA)
- All India Federation of Trade Unions (AIFTU)
- All India Insurance Employees Association (AIIEA)
- All India Peace and Solidarity Organisation (AIPSO)
- All India People's Resistance Forum (AIPRF)
- All India People's Science Network (AIPSN)
- All India Progressive Women's Association (AIPWA)
- All India Students Association (AISA)
- All India Students Federation (AISF)
- All India Trade Union Congress (AITUC)
- All India Youth Federation (AIYF)
- Anti-nuclear Movement, Nagpur
- Anumukti, Vedchhi (Gujarat)
- Association of Peoples of Asia (India)
- Bangalore Platform Against Nuclear Weaponisation, Bangalore

[AIBEA (Canara Bank); Alternate Lawyers Forum; BEL Employees Union; Centre for Education and Documentation; Citizens Against Nuclear Energy; Documentation & Dissemination Centre for Disarmament Information; Federation of Voluntary Organisations for Rural Development; Gandhi Peace Centre; General Insurance Employees Union; Indian Scientists Against Nuclear Weapons; International Energy Initiative; Karnataka State Peace and Solidarity Organisation; Manasa; New Entity for Social Action; Peoples Union for Civil Liberties; Pipal Tree; Samvada; Science for Society; Anglo-Indian Guild; Visthar; Bharat Gyan Vigyan Samiti]

* Bank Employees Federation of India (BEFI)
* Campaign Against Nuclear Weapons, Calcutta
* Centre of Indian Trade Unions (CITU)
* Centre for Social Work and Research (CSWR), Tripura
* *Champa*: The Amiya & B.C. Rao Foundation
* Chhattisgarh Anu Mukti Manch, Chattisgarh
* Christian Peace Conference (India)
* Delhi Forum, Delhi
* Delhi Science Forum, Delhi
* Democratic Teachers' Front, Delhi
* Democratic Youth Federation of India (DYFI)
* Dhyan Society, Delhi
* Ekta, Mumbai
* Eklavya, Madhya Pradesh
* Federation of Medical & Sales Representatives Association of India (FMRAI)
* Focus on Global South (India)
* Forum for Science and Development, Karnataka
* Forum of Scientists, Engineers and Technologists, West Bengal
* Gandhi Peace Foundation, Delhi
* Gene Campaign, Delhi
* Greenpeace-India
* Harijan Sevak Sangh
* Haryana Gyan Vigyan Samiti, Haryana
* Himachal Vigyan Manch, Himachal Pradesh
* Human Rights Forum, Hyderabad
* Indian Association of Lawyers
* India Peace Centre, Nagpur

* Indian Radical Humanist Association
* Indian Scientists Against Nuclear Weapons, Chennai
* Indian Federation of Trade Unions (IFTU)
* Indian National Social Action Forum (INSAF)
* Indian Institute for Peace, Disarmament and Environmental Protection, Nagpur
* Indian Social Institute, Delhi
* Jana Natya Manch, Delhi
* Jan Vigyan Vedica, Andhra Pradesh
* Jharkhandi's Organisation Against Radiation, Jadugoda
* Journalists Against Nuclear Weapons, Chennai
* Kerala Shastra Sahitya Parishad (KSSP), Kerala
* Lok Abhiyan, Lucknow
* Lok Sahet Manch, Punjab
* Lok Vigyan Sanghatna, Mumbai
* Lokayan, Delhi
* Madhya Pradesh Vigyan Sabha (MPVS), Madhya Pradesh
* Movement in India for Nuclear Disarmament (MIND), Delhi
* Movement in India for Nuclear Disarmament (MIND), Mumbai
* National Alliance of Peoples' Movements (NAPM)
* National Confederation of Officers Associations of Central Public Sector Undertakings (NCOA)
* National Council of Churches in India (NCCI), Nagpur
* National Federation of Indian Women (NFIW)
* Nishant Natya Manch, Delhi
* Pakistan-India Peoples' Forum for Peace and Democracy (PIPFPD)
* Paschimbanga Vigyan Manch (PBVM), West Bengal
* PEACE, Delhi
* People's Rights Organisation (PRO), Delhi
* People's Union for Civil Liberties (PUCL), Delhi
* People's Union for Civil Liberties (PUCL), Jaipur
* People's Union for Democratic Rights (PUDR), Delhi
* Physicians for Peace, Chennai
* Pondicherry Science Forum, Pondicherry
* Public Interest Research Group, Delhi
* Revolutionary Youth Association (RYA)
* Saheli, Delhi
* SAHMAT, Delhi

- South Asian Network for Alternate Media (SANAM)
- Srujanika, Orissa
- Student Christian Movement, Trivandrum
- Students Federation of India (SFI)
- Tamil Nadu Science Forum (TNSF), Tamil Nadu
- Vikas Adhayan Kendra, Mumbai
- Wan Kamgar Sanghathna, Nagpur
- Women's Association for Peace in South Asia (India)
- Women's Centre, Mumbai
- World Environment Protection and Peace Organisation (WEPPO)
- Workers Solidarity, Delhi
- World Conference on Religion and Peace (India)
- Youth for Nuclear Disarmament (YND), Delhi
- Youth for Unity and Voluntary Action (YUVA)

Coalition for Nuclear Disarmament and Peace
National Co-ordination Committee

1. Achin Vanaik - Delhi
2. Amarjeet Kaur - Delhi
3. Anil Choudhury - Delhi
4. Chenna Basavaiah - Andhra Pradesh
5. Christopher Fonseca - Goa
6. Gautam Sen - West Bengal
7. George Mathew - Delhi
8. George Thomas - Tamil Nadu
9. Gurdiyal Singh Sheetal - Punjab
10. Ilina Sen - Chattisgarh
11. Jaya Velankar - Maharashtra
12. N.D. Jayaprakash - Delhi
13. T. Jayaraman - Tamil Nadu
14. Kamal Mitra Chenoy - Delhi
15. Kavita Srivastava - Rajasthan
16. Lalita Ramdas - Maharashtra
17. Mazab Hussain - Andhra Pradesh
18. Minar Pimple - Maharashtra
19. Nirmala Deshpande - Delhi
20. Paras Ram Rana - Rajasthan
21. Perin Romesh Chandra - Delhi

22. Prakash Meghe - Maharashtra
23. Prabir Purkayasta - Delhi
24. Praful Bidwai - Delhi
25. P. Rajendran - Tamil Nadu
26. N. Ram –Tamil Nadu
27. Ramachandra Guha - Karnataka
28. Admiral L. Ramdas - Maharashtra
29. Sandeep Pandey - Uttar Pradesh
30. Sanjay Biswas - Karnataka
31. R. Shankar - Tamil Nadu
32. Shubha Chacko - Karnataka
33. Smitu Kothari - Delhi
34. Surendra Gadekar - Gujarat
34. J. Sri Raman - Tamil Nadu
35. Vineeta Bal - Delhi
36. Vishwambar Pati - Karnataka
37. Vivek Monteiro - Maharashtra

Coalition for Nuclear Disarmamment and Peace (CNDP) Charter

I. Preamble

India's self-declared entry into the 'nuclear weapons club' in May 1998, when it conducted five nuclear tests in Pokhran, Rajasthan is ethically reprehensible as well as socially, politically, and economically ruinous. India and Pakistan have now joined the original five members of the Nuclear weapons club and Israel who, unmoved by the horrifying experience of Hiroshima and Nagasaki in 1945, have amassed nuclear weapons. Such a legitimisation of nuclear weapons deserves unequivocal condemnation. The Coalition for Nuclear Disarmament and Peace (CNDP) was constituted in November 2000 in response to nuclear weaponisation in India and Pakistan against a background of the global amassing of nuclear weapons.

II. Why We Must Oppose Nuclear Weapons

(a) The Moral Dimension: Nuclear weapons are means of mass destruction regardless of who wields them. They are weapons of genocide. They can impose horrendous suffering on victims across generations. They can destroy the ecosystem. The damage they do is lasting and incurable. The sheer scale and character of the devastation they can cause makes them a profound and distinctive evil. For this and other reasons, the possession, use, or threat of use of nuclear weapons is absolutely immoral.

(b) Nuclear Weapons and International Law: India's nuclear weaponisation, like the possession of nuclear weapons by other nuclear weapons states, flies in the face of the Government of India's written submission to the International Court of Justice (ICJ) in 1995. The Memorial submitted to the ICJ stated that the use, threat of use, or possession of, and even preparation for making, nuclear weapons is immoral, illegal, and unacceptable under 'any circumstances' and also that 'nuclear deterrence has been considered abhorrent to human sentiment since it implies that a state if required to defend its own existence will act with pitiless disregard for the consequences to its own and its adversary's people.' India's nuclear weaponisation, like the possession of nuclear weapons by other nuclear weapons states, also flies in the face of the July 1996 Advisory Opinion of the ICJ which holds that 'the threat or use of nuclear weapons would generally be contrary to the rules of international law applicable in armed conflict, and in particular the principles and rules of humanitarian law.'

(c) Betraying the Past: Until 1998, the official position of the Government of India consistently saw nuclear weapons as evil, and India was a participant in initiatives to restrain, reduce, and eliminate them. This position in favour of nuclear disarmament was abandoned in 1998, without any tenable explanation for Pokhran II and nuclear weaponisation in its aftermath. India and Pakistan have thus joined the ranks of Nuclear Weapons States, which pursue discriminatory and peace-threatening agendas.

(d) The Nuclear Weapons Danger: Nuclear weapons do not provide 'national security' but increase insecurity and paranoia. Time and again since the Nuclear Age began in 1945, the world has come to the brink of a nuclear exchange by design, miscalculation, or accident. If the world continues to have nuclear weapons, it is very likely that they will be used sometime, someplace. In this respect, the India-Pakistan nuclear face-off is an obvious danger, even if not the only one. The myth that nuclear weapons provide security was disproved by the 1999 Kargil conflict. Nuclear weapons and the arms race generate mutual suspicion and fear all round.

(e) The Myth of Deterrence: Nuclear deterrence is a pernicious and discredited doctrine that seeks to legitimise the possession of nuclear weapons. Reliance on such a doctrine serves only to heighten the danger of war and a nuclear exchange. The so-called 'minimum credible nuclear deterrent' announced by the Indian government is no exception. It is a fraud on the people. Since a 'minimum credible nuclear deterrent' is not a fixed position but moves ever upward depending on the changing technologies and preparations of nuclear rivals, such a policy will inevitably lead to further expansion of nuclear weaponisation.

(f) A Diversion from Real Needs: Nuclear arming is not only dangerous but also economically wasteful. It is estimated that building a 'minimum credible nuclear deterrent' for India over the next decade can cost upwards of Rs. 70,000 crore. Alternative use of such resources will eliminate illiteracy, dramatically improve health care, and provide a basic social security net for all Indians. The economic cost of a spiraling arms race will be ruinous and the marginalised will be pushed further to the periphery.

(g) Undermining Democracy: A nuclear weapons regime creates unacceptable levels of secrecy and non-accountability, thus subverting democratic institutions and values. When this regime is linked to, and reinforced by, communal, chauvinist, and militarist ideologies, as is the case in India and Pakistan, the situation becomes qualitatively worse. The very process of nuclear weapons production, particularly when undertaken in secrecy, can destroy soil, water, and lives. The focus on such secretive and destructive technologies damages the project of connecting science and technology to real social needs. The meshing of civilian and military activities in the nuclear field undermines the possibility of ensuring any serious public accountability in the area of nuclear safety. The absence of a nuclear safety authority that is independent of the Department of Atomic Energy is violative of Article 8-2 of the 1994 international Convention on Nuclear Safety to which India is a party. To make matters worse, in April 2000, the Bhabha Atomic Research Centre (BARC) complex, which is the main nuclear weapons-related work centre but which also includes spent-fuel reprocessing plants, the entire Health Physics monitoring and control, and all radioactive waste processing and management, was taken out of the purview of the Atomic Energy Regulatory Board (AERB) by an Order of the Chairman of the

Atomic Energy Commission. The Order stated that 'the regulatory and safety functions at BARC and its facilities hitherto exercised by the AERB will henceforth be exercised through an Internal Safety Committee structure to be constituted by the Director of BARC for the purpose.' To protect the health and safety of workers and local residents and to prevent degradation of the local environment, there must be proper and full transparency with public accountability regarding all nuclear activities of the government and its agencies. Appropriate legislative changes and measures needed to ensure public accountability of the nuclear programme in India must be worked upon.

(h) A Race against Time: Early nuclear disarmament is essential as a crucial link in the struggle for an egalitarian, socially just society and world. Thus the struggle for nuclear disarmament must connect with global, regional, national, and local concerns, particularly in the context of internecine conflicts driven by imperialist, fundamentalist and militarist ideologies in the world today. The struggle must be comprehended by the people of India and all countries to be a race against time. We owe the children of tomorrow a nuclear weapons-free world.

III. Building the Movement

(a) A Unified Focus: An anti-nuclear weapons focus brings together groups that share this basic platform but may have differences of perception on related and important issues, such as how best to handle the tensions between arms control/abolition, between nuclear weapons/energy, and between nuclear disarmament/ general disarmament and peace. These differences of perception can neither be hidden nor ignored but must be creatively explored and integrated into building a united movement AGAINST nuclear weapons which is also simultaneously linked to the various movements FOR social justice and development. Such a nuclear disarmament movement must encourage maximum freedom of discussion and spaces for multiple forms of co-operation among like-minded groups and individuals. The movement must continuously deepen and strengthen overall unity on an agreed minimum programme and platform.

(b) Unity and Diversity: The movement must steadily evolve consensus positions on the core issue of opposition to nuclear weapons and the related matters of nuclear safety, transparency, and public accountability. Beyond this, the movement must forge links with the broader struggles of the people on issues of social justice, development, and security.

(c) A Broad Front: The national coalition will consist not only of organisations, groups, and individuals that work primarily on nuclear disarmament, peace, and related issues (such as nuclear fuel cycle-related issues). It will also include others who work in broader areas but have nuclear disarmament and peace as a part of their agenda. These sensibilities and perspectives need to be respected, learnt from, and integrated creatively, as do the perspectives and strengths of anti-nuclear weapon movements world-wide.

(d) Maintaining Dialogue: It is essential for the movement actively to engage in dialogue at all levels with political parties, and particularly with those parties and sections within political parties opposing India's nuclear weaponisation. The movement must also engage in dialogue with mass organisations, professional and industry associations and groups, religious bodies, and individuals. This dialogue must focus on the need for nuclear disarmament at the national, regional, and global levels and for stopping all nuclear tests and weaponisation. An ongoing and deepening dialogue with the general public is vital to building public opinion in favour of nuclear disarmament and peace.

(e) A Global Perspective: It is necessary constantly to keep in mind the global dimension of an Indian/South Asian struggle against nuclear weapons. Therefore, connections with movements around the world are essential, as is the recognition and integration of all genuine trends towards nuclear disarmament. The culpability of the Nuclear Weapons States, especially but not solely of the United States, must be recognised and every effort must be made to push these states towards rapid and total global disarmament. The 1996 Advisory Opinion of the International Court of Justice unanimously recognises that Nuclear Weapons States are obliged to negotiate complete nuclear disarmament and, specifically, that 'the legal import of that obligation goes beyond that of a mere obligation of conduct; the obligation involved here is an obligation to achieve a precise result—nuclear disarmament in all its aspects—by adopting a particular course of conduct, namely, the pursuit of negotiations on the matter in good faith.' Further, accomplishing the aims and objectives for which the United Nations was founded, is an imperative.

(f) Stocktaking and Coordination: The Coalition for Nuclear Disarmament and Peace must take careful stock of the various resources and capacities collectively available in avenues such as advocacy, school and college programmes, cultural and educational activities, creating pressure through public agitation and mobilisation, interaction with the media, and so on. Such stocktaking will enable groups to plan and carry out sustained coordinated activities at local, regional, national and global levels.

IV. The Common Agenda
A. For India

In order to halt and roll back India's nuclear weapons-related preparations and activity, we demand that the following measures be implemented immediately:

1. No assembly, induction, or deployment of nuclear weapons.
2. No acquisition, development, or testing of nuclear weapons-specific delivery systems.
3. A halt to advanced research into nuclear weapons.
4. No explosive testing, sub-critical testing, or production or acquisition of fissile materials and tritium for nuclear weapons purposes.
5. Complete transparency and independent monitoring of governmental activity in this field and full public accountability on nuclear development and energy matters.
6. Proper compensation and reparation to all victims and their families for damage done to their health and local environmental conditions by activities related to all aspects of the nuclear fuel cycle (from uranium mining to reactor production to waste disposal). Priority must be given to remedial measures for all environmental damage.
7. We demand that India go back to being among the pacesetters in all matters relating to global nuclear disarmament and the abolition of nuclear weapons.

B. For Other Nuclear Weapons, and Nuclear Weapons-Capable, States

1. We demand similar immediate measures to halt and roll back nuclear weapons-related preparations and activities from Pakistan.

2. Given the tensions and potential for war in West Asia, we demand the complete dismantling of Israel's nuclear weapons regime.

3. The five Nuclear Weapons States—the United States, the Russian Federation, the United Kingdom, France, and China—must immediately de-alert their nuclear weapons systems, make a pledge of No First Use (China alone, among the five, has made such a pledge), and stop all research into advanced nuclear weapons. We oppose all efforts to construct an anti-ballistic missile system or missile shield.

4. We demand the rapid, systematic, and continuous reduction by the Nuclear Weapons States of their nuclear weapons down to zero level through unilateral, bilateral, and multilateral agreements and commitments.

5. We want a nuclear weapons-free world and we support all genuine efforts in pursuit of this goal. In this effort, we commit ourselves to the global movement for nuclear disarmament and abolition of nuclear weapons and will strive to strengthen international solidarity in this endeavour.

Against Nuclear Tests and Weapons

Retired Pakistani, Indian and Bangladeshi Armed Forces Personnel

The following Joint Statement Against Nuclear Tests and Weapons signed by sixty three retired Pakistani, Indian and Bangladeshi Armed Forces Personnel is hereby submitted:

> To the Secretary General of the United Nations
> To the Prime Minister of Pakistan
> To the Prime Minister of India
> To the President of the United States of America
> To the President of France
> To the Prime Minister of U.K.
> To the President of China
> To the President of the Russian Federation

Recent developments in South Asia in the field of nuclear weapons and the means of their delivery are a serious threat to the well being of this region. The fact that India and Pakistan have fought wars in the recent past and do not as yet enjoy the best of relations, makes this development all the more ominous. The signatories of this statement are not theoreticians or arm-chair idealists; we have spent many long years in the profession of arms and have served our countries both in peacetime and in war. By virtue of our experience and the positions we have held, we have a fair understanding of the destructive parameters of conventional and nuclear weapons. We are of the considered view that nuclear weapons should be banished from the South Asian region, and indeed from the entire globe. We urge India and Pakistan to take the lead by doing away with nuclear weapons in a manifest and verifiable manner, and to confine nuclear research and development strictly to peaceful and beneficient spheres.

We are convinced that the best way of resolving disputes is through peaceful means and not through war—least of all by the threat or use of nuclear weapons. India and Pakistan need to address their real problems of poverty and backwardness, not waste our scarce resources on acquiring means of greater and greater destruction.

Signed by:

India: Admiral L. Ramdas (Ex-Chief of the Indian Navy), Brigadier John Anthony, Brigadier Madhav Prasad, Commodore Norman Warner, Major Vijai Uppal, Lt Col G.J. Eduljee, Air Commodore A.K. Banerjee, Air Commodore A.K. Venkateshwaran, Commodore K.K. Garg, Lt. Gen Gurbir Mansingh

Pakistan: Air Marshal M. Asghar Khan (*Ex-C-in-C Pakistan Air Force*), Air Marshal Zafar A. Chaudhry, Air Vice Marshal Saeedullah Khan, Air Vice Marshal M. Ikramullah, Air Vice Marshal M.Y. Khan, Air Vice Marshal C.R. Nawaz, Air Commodore S.T.E. Piracha, Air Commodore Rafi Qadar, Air Commodore Ejaz Azam Khan, Air Commodore Qamarud Din, Air Commodore Habibur Rahman, Air Commodore G. Mujtaba Qureshi, Air Commodore A. Aziz, Air Commodore Wahid A. Butt, Wing Commander N.A. Siddiqui, Wing Commander M. Yunus, Wing Commander Shajar Hussain, Flight Lieutenant M.A. Mannan, Group Captain N.A. Sheikh, Group Captain Amir Shah, Group Captain M. Amin, Group Captain G.M. Siddiqi, Group Captain Khalid Jalil, Group Captain Sirajud Din Ahmed, Major Saeed A. Malik, Dr Capt. Tariq Rahman, Brigadier Rao Abid Hamid, Major Ishtiaq Asi, Wing Commander Aameen Taqi, Brig Izzat M. Shah, Sqn Ldr Ihsan Qadir, Lt Col Abdur Rehman Lodhi, Maj Amjad Iqbal, Maj Ishtiaq Asif, Lt. Col. Nadeem Rashid Khan, Brig Shahid Aziz, Brig Bashir Ahmad, Capt Omar Asghar Khan, Lt. Col. Ahsan Zaman, Lt. Col. Azhar Irshad, Brig Jahangir Malik, Lt. Col. S. Imtiaz H. Bokhari, Maj. Gen. Syed Mustafa Anwar Husain, Brig Humayun Malik, Brig A. Wahab, Maj. Naim Ahmad, Brig SE Jivanandham, Brig Luqman Mahmood, Lt. Gen Sardar F.S. Lodi, Lt. Col. Ernest Shams, Lt. Col. Aijazulhaq Effendi, Brig Mir Abad Hussain, ex Ambassador

Bangladesh: Major General M A Mohaiemen

October 1, 1998

Against the 'Limited Wars' Doctrine

MIND and Pakistan Peace Coalition

The recent announcement by Indian Defence Minister George Fernandes unveiling a 'limited wars' doctrine is alarming evidence of the dangerous path along which those who govern India are moving towards. Recent news from Pakistan also suggests a tussle among the ruling generals with significant voices among them pushing for a 'tougher' stand vis a vis India. This coupled with the continuing voices of nuclear threat mongering and blackmail on both sides of the border (especially exchanged during the Kargil conflict), pushes the subcontinent into one of its gravest crises ever.

Several citizens forums have called for the cessation of the present climate of jingoism and chauvinism, and stressed the need for sobriety and peace. The visits last week of several senior retired Army officials from Pakistan and their recognition and commitment (reciprocated by their counterparts in India) to taking bold steps to foster peace in the region are an indication of the possibilities that still exist to urgently initiate a process of mutual restraint and dialogue.

We urge the peoples and governments of both countries to urgently forge a bold plan of action to reverse the present process of sliding into a political deadlock that may justify continuing 'limited wars' at the expense of greater amity and security for the peoples of South Asia.

Signed by:
Pakistan: M.B. Naqvi, Anis Haroon, Karamat Ali, Abdul Khaliq Junejo, Brig. (*retd.*) Abid Hameed Rao, Tahir Mohammed Khan, Sheema Kirmani, B.M. Kutty, A.H. Nayyar, Nusrat Jamil, Beena Sarwar, Jennifer Bennet, I.A. Rehman, Dr Quereshi

India: Sumit Sarkar, Imtiaz Ahmad, Smitu Kothari, Kumkum Sangari, Praful Bidwai, Achin Vanaik, Seema Mustafa, Prabhat Patnaik, Tanika Sarkar, Kamal Mitra Chenoy, Utsa Patnaik, Nirmala Deshpande, Anuradha Chenoy

January 29, 1999

Joint Statement Issued Simultaneously in Karachi and Delhi by Prominent Pakistani and Indian Citizens

'We, the members of Association of People's of Asia, India and Pakistan chapters, and concerned citizens make an earnest appeal to the governments of India and Pakistan to exercise restraint, stop hostilities on the Kashmir front and save our valuable resources for the betterment of the people, specially the poor and the needy of both countries. Both the countries cannot afford such adventures. We also appeal to the people of both the countries to build up a strong peace initiative to bring moral pressure on their respective governments.

Human life on both sides is precious, any killing is a loss to both our countries. Let us follow the path of sanity and develop good neighbourly relations in order to solve our problems.

Pakistan: Dr Zaki Hasan, Dr Mubarak Ali, Mr Shakil Ahmed Baloch, Mr Tahir Muhammad Khan, Mr M.B. Naqvi, Dr Aly Ercelawn, Mr B.M. Kutty, Mr Abdul Khaliq Junejo, Mr Karamat Ali, Mr Rochi Ram Advocate, Maulana Obaidullah Bhutto, Mr Akhtar Hussain Advocate, Mr Ghulam Kibria, Ms Anis Haroon, Ms Iqbal Sultana, Mr Farid Awan, Mr Usman Baloch, Miss Farhat Parveen, Mr Sharafat Ali, Mr Mujahid Barelvi, Mr Baseer Naveed, Dr M.A. Mehboob, Dr A. Aziz, Mr Naseer Rizvi, Ms Sarah Siddiqui

India: Mr Kuldip Nayar, MP, Ms Shabana Azmi, MP, Ms Nirmala Deshpande, MP, Dr Kartar Singh Duggal, MP, Mr Jayant Kumar Malhotra, MP, Ms Sonal Mansingh, Ms Syeda Hameed, Mr Kedar Nath Singh, Prof. Namwar Singh, Mr Sumit Chakravarti, Mr Vedpratap Vaidik, Prof. M.H. Qureshi, Dr N. Radhakrishnan, Father Bento Rodrigues, Rev. Valson Thampu, Dr Gangaprasad Vimal, Prof. Akhtarul Wase, Prof. Imtiyaz Ahmed, Dr Asghar Ali Engineer, Mr Mrinal Sen, MP.

June 1, 1999

Pakistan Peace Coalition Conference

The first conference of the Pakistan Peace Coalition brought together activists from all over the country on a common platform of resisting the nuclearisation of Pakistan, of South Asia, and the world. Until last May, our work for peace, human rights and social justice assumed continuity of both society and state. Nuclear weapons threaten this continuity as nothing else has ever done.

The struggle for peace is a struggle over values. We believe that nothing justifies nuclear weapons, under any circumstances. Nuclear weapons offer no solution to the fundamental political problems of a state, they exacerbate them. We reject these weapons and their attendant nuclear nationalism that is based on hatred and fear, and reinforces existing systems of patriarchy, class exploitation, ethnic and religious differences. The most hurt vulnerable groups are women and children and the marginal and dispossessed.

Welcoming the recent initiatives towards peace by the prime ministers of India and Pakistan, this Conference calls upon them to go beyond the symbolism and goodwill generated by the Lahore Declaration and take concrete steps towards peace and de-escalation of tension in the region. These include the signing of a no-war, no-aggression pact and a commitment not to be the first to use nuclear weapons.

Both governments must commit themselves to total disarmament and to interim, unilateral, bilateral and global steps and treaties that restrict or prohibit the design, development, manufacture, from the region, which should be declared nuclear-free, prohibiting the storage or passage of nuclear materials and weapons on land, sea or air.

Meanwhile, the areas of tension must be dealt with on an urgent basis. There must be an end to the confrontation in Siachin, and Pakistan and India should forthwith implement the accord they reached ten years ago. The conflict over Kashmir is not merely a territorial issue but involves the lives and rights of the Kashmiri people. We demand the withdrawal of troops as well as an end to foreign sponsored militancy in the region.

Kashmir should not be allowed to hold back Pakistan-India cooperation in all possible fields, especially trade and culture. This cooperation can only be possible if the people of both countries are allowed to emerge from the paranoia that has marked the Pakistan-India relationship. This requires free movement of citizens between the two countries, and a sharing of media and culture, including an exchange of newspapers and periodicals.

This Conference calls for wider public participation in setting national priorities, especially on defense expenditure, which should be reduced forthwith. It urges transparency and political accountability, especially of nuclear-related military expenditure.

This Conference denounces the rise in intolerant fundamentalist ideologies and violence, whether sectarian or communal. This, coupled with the trend of settling disputes and differences with guns has negatively impacted vulnerable groups, particularly women, who become the targets of a male dominated culture that seeks to restrict their freedom.

The mass media, education system and the practices of everyday life all contribute to internalisation of an intolerant and violent mindset. These need to be liberated from this mindset in order to create a space for the culture of peace and pluralism to flourish and empower the marginal and dispossessed in our society.

In our struggle, we are joined by fellow activists from South Asia and around the world. We salute this struggle, and re-commit ourselves here today to this resistance in all its forms.

Resolution: Commission on Security
The Pakistan Peace Coalition Conference resolves to set up a Commission on security, comprising Air Marshal (Retd.) Zafar A. Choudhry

(convenor), Dr. Mubashir Hasan, Dr. Pervez Hoodbhoy, Mr. Shahid Kardar and Brig (Retd.) A.R. Siddiqui and Mr. M.B. Naqvi, with the following terms of reference.

(a) To examine the implications of nuclearisation and suggest confidence building, arms control and disarmament steps necessary to protect the people of Pakistan and the sub-continent against the danger of a nuclear war;
(b) To determine the parameters of legitimate security arrangements for Pakistan;
(c) To prepare an alternative defence policy and affordable defence budget

The commission may co-opt new members as and when required and call upon experts, specialists, and activists for the realisation of its objectives.

Resolution on Minorities

Convinced that the treatment of minorities in South Asian states contributes to confrontation and conflict both within their societies and between states, the Pakistan Peace Coalition Conference resolves to sponsor a meeting of eminent personalities from the South Asian region to decide on the modalities of setting up a high-level South Asia Peoples' Commission on Minorities and determine its terms of reference and procedures. The Conference nominates Ms. Asma Jahangir as the convenor of the eminent persons' group and requests her to report to the Coalition no later than June 15, 1999.

The protection of the people around Chagai

The conference calls upon the government to undertake a comprehensive public study involving independent scientists of the effects of the nuclear tests in Chagai on local communities and the environment and take all possible measures to protect them from the hazards they may have been exposed to.

Issued by the coordinating committee of the Pakistan Peace Coalition.

February 28, 1999

Condemning the Nuclear Arms Race
Joint Action Committee for Rights, Lahore

A resolution passed at a meeting convened by the Joint Action Committee for Peoples Rights strongly condemned nuclear arms and the nuclear race, and the emergency in Pakistan. It also demanded that the issue of Kashmir be decided on an urgent basis. The meeting was attended by over 200 people from different walks of life, individuals as well as representatives of trade unions, human rights and womens' rights organisations, teachers, economists, lawyers. A four-point resolution unanimously passed at the meeting expressed fears about the danger of a nuclear war in the region, given that the BJP government is a fanatical government, and Pakistan's own affairs are controlled by elements who also have fanatical leanings.

Regarding Kashmir it said: As human rights and social organisations, we believe that the issue of Kashmir needs to be decided immediately, and not on religious but on democratic lines. Pakistan's policy on Kashmir should be apparent and transparent. We have not been sincere to the cause. Our politicians have been taking lakhs of rupees to lobby for Kashmir in international circles, without knowing anything about the issue. It is our policies which have led to the installation of the BJP government, the resolution regretted.

Secondly, condemning the emergency, the resolution noted that in reality, Pakistan had no external compulsions for conducting the nuclear tests. Rather there were internal compulsions which were used to hide the government's own weaknesses. 'We have been asked to make sacrifices, and we are willing to do so, but for peace, for democracy, for education, for development and not for presidential ordinances bulldozed through a Punjab-centred assembly.' The meeting condemned the isolation of the smaller provinces, particularly expressing solidarity with the people of Balochistan and condemning the action on their land, without their permission.

Thirdly, it condemned the role of the official and state-controlled media, particularly radio and television for projecting a one-sided view of the situation. This is the same Pakistan Television which turned a blind eye to the happenings of 1970 and presented lies to the people, agreed the participants, objecting to the projection of Pakistan's nuclear bombs as Islamic or Muslim.

Fourthly, they stated that the issue of religious intolerance and protection of religious minorities must come on the agenda of talks within and by both India and Pakistan for a long term solution, and that both countries must undertake to protect their religious minorities. There is a need to end the impression that being nuclear is grand. What is grand is when there is democracy and when people are not hungry. We cannot compare Pakistan and India with other nuclear countries, said the resolution.

Participants pointed out that the defence expenditure must be debated, as the current nuclear programme is likely to make life even more difficult for ordinary people.

They expressed concern about the lack of awareness regarding the horrors of a nuclear war and the long term environmental impacts even of nuclear tests. They slammed the concept that responsible states can possess the bomb and 'irresponsible states' should not posses it, pointing out that it was a so called responsible state, the USA, which has been the only country to actually drop a nuclear bomb.

Prominent among those who addressed the meeting included Dr Mubashir Hasan (PPP-SB and former finance minister), Khaled Ahmed (editor *Aj-Kal*), Prof. Mehdi Hasan (academic), Asma Jahangir, Hina Jillani (Human Rights Commission of Pakistan and AGHS Legal Aid Cell), trade unionists Farooq Tariq (Labour Party) and Altaf Baloch, Naseem Shamim (Pakistan National Party—Bizenjo Group), social scientist Dr Rubina Saigol, and Neelam Hussain (Simorgh and Women's Action Forum), among others.

Lahore, June 11, 1998

Against the Nuclearisation of South Asia

Action Committee Against Arms Race

This document is the end-product of the discussions, which took place in a series of meetings, held in Karachi and attended by representatives of several political parties and labour, social and women's organisations.

The original text of the document reflected the reaction of the participants against the five underground nuclear tests conducted by India and the possibility of Pakistan replicating them.

A Committee was formed in that first meeting to chalk out a programme to mobilise public opinion against the nuclearisation of the subcontinent. It was named 'the Action Committee Against Arms Race (ACAAR)', considering that all kinds of arms race, be it conventional or nuclear, are immoral as they not only rob the people of their right to health, education, housing, employment and other basic needs, but put their and their progenies' existence as human beings, in peril.

Since then, Pakistan has conducted six tests in Chagai, confirming our worst fears that a nuclear race in South Asia would soon be on, with all its horrendous consequences. Along with the nuclear tests came the imposition of Emergency and suspension of the fundamental rights of the people of Pakistan. The Committee took stock of the new situation and introduced relevant amendments in the original document, giving space to the series of new developments leading towards a South Asian nuclear race between two under-developed countries whose people are these days fighting street battles for drinking water and electricity, leave alone schools, hospitals, roads, housing and jobs.

The Document

The recent series of 5 nuclear tests by India and 6 by Pakistan (a body blow to the ongoing efforts to improve Pak–India relations), the ongoing escalation of missile race by both the countries, and the general militarisation of the region are matters of grave concern, not only for the people of the two countries but for the whole of South Asia. Although all this is being done in the name of national security, these actions serve only to heighten tensions and hostilities in the region, further aggravating insecurities for each country. It is tragic that precious resources that should be used for the welfare and betterment of the people are instead being squandered on weapons of mass destruction of unimaginable proportions.

The nuclear tests carried out by the BJP-led government in India had exposed the true designs of that fascist, religious fundamentalist party of the upper castes. The BJP which had polled hardly 30 per cent of the votes cast in the recent Indian general elections had no mandate from the people of India to indulge in such a criminal exercise which has taken the India–Pakistan cold war and arms race to a new stage of nuclearisation of the subcontinent with all its alarming consequences. Similarly, in the 1997 elections the people of Pakistan had not given the Pakistan Muslim League or Nawaz Sharif any mandate to conduct nuclear tests or make nuclear weapons.

While the BJP and its allies were rejoicing amidst the euphoria generated by India's nuclear tests, their counterparts in Pakistan like Jamaat-i-Islami and its fellow-travelers were clamouring for giving a befitting reply to India by conducting Pakistan's own nuclear tests. It was pathetic to see the Pakistan People's Party and its leader Benazir Bhutto trying to outdo the religious, sectarian and jingoist elements in this campaign in support of the nuclear bomb. And, it is disgusting now, after Pakistan has carried out six tests, to hear the same person warning everyone of the dangerous implications of the Pakistani nuclear tests for national security.

In their blind pursuit of paranoid nationalism, the vainglorious elements in both countries remain blissfully unaware of the mass destruction potential of nuclear weapons. They do not understand that nuclear weapons are evil, mass annihilators of human life and are morally indefensible, which no country should possess and that it is the moral responsibility of the citizens of every country to try and prevent their country from ever possessing these terrible weapons.

Even some of the leading military generals in the West who had their fingers on the nuclear buttons have publicly come out to say no to nuclear weapons. How can countries like India and Pakistan which cannot even bear the burden of buying, leave alone manufacturing conventional weapons, except at the expense of the basic needs of their peoples, bear the astronomical cost of testing and manufacturing nuclear weapons? And, has anyone among the protagonists of the nuclear bomb ever thought of not only the massive destruction and devastation in terms of human lives that a nuclear bomb of any denomination will bring upon the targeted territory and far beyond but also its devastating consequences upon generations upon generations of human beings, animals and plants for decades to come? We do not wish to quote figures because they are too frightening to look at. The worst victims of this war-mongering, arrogant and competitive nationalism (fraudulently rationalised in the name of 'security') are ordinary people. The social and economic costs of development, forgone thanks to military posturing, have already proved onerous. For all the official bluster about pursuing 'national greatness', India and Pakistan both feature, by all accepted indices, at the bottom of the human development ladder.

As for Pakistan (which is also applicable to India) an economically stable Pakistan with strong democratic institutions and without nuclear bombs will be many times more secure than an economically shattered Pakistan with a few nuclear weapons in its arsenal but with a population robbed of their basic human right to a decent existence. This is a lesson one should have learnt from the fate of the mighty Soviet Union which collapsed and disappeared, not because it had no nuclear weapons and delivery systems but in spite of having so many of them. Soviet economy fell victim to the armaments race, the nuclear race and crashed under its weight, and with it went down the Soviet State.

The already entrenched international Nuclear Club has already demonstrated its inability to stop any country from going nuclear. If the countries of this exclusive club are sincere about every country signing what they call the Comprehensive Test Ban Treaty (CTBT) and Non-Proliferation Treaty (NPT), they should set an example by starting to dismantle their own nuclear arsenals first.

The United Nations should make nuclear non-proliferation an integral part of its programme rather than an exclusive club dictating terms to other countries.

In the face of the ongoing jingoistic rhetoric of the nuclear lobbies of the two countries, followed by the suspension of people's fundamental rights under a state of emergency in Pakistan, there is an urgent need to take a bold initiative towards developing a people's peace movement in the subcontinent, and also globally, that aims at people-to-people reconciliation and maximal economic, political and social progress for all the peoples of South Asia through close regional cooperation. To promote peace and peaceability is the most urgent task of all the people of goodwill and liberal outlook. It is high time the peoples of South Asia took a bold initiative and forced their governments to publicly announce the renunciation of nuclear tests and production of nuclear weapons and missiles.

It is heartening to see peace-loving forces in India too protesting everywhere against the Indian nuclear tests and condemning the BJP government. We appeal to all such organisations and individuals in Pakistan who are striving from different platforms for peace in the subcontinent, to link up with the ACAAR so that a grand national peace movement may emerge as part of a larger South Asian and international movement for peace and democracy at this hour of grave peril to our very existence.

Yusuf Mustikhan (*ACAAR*); Usman Baluch (*PNP*); Comrade Maqbool (*CMKP*); Sheikh Saleem (*LPP*); A. Hai (*HRCP*); Issa Khan (CMKP); Z.A. Beedri (*PILER*); Khawaja Najeebuddin (*Anjuman Taraqqipasand Musannifeen*); Mohd. Sabir (*CMKP*); Haji Iqbal Baluch (*PNP*); Sabaun Bangash (*CMKP*); A. Sami Soomro (*PNP*); Shuja Baluch; Fasih Salar (*AJP*); A.R. Arif (*CMKP*); Muslim Shamim (*Progressive Writers Association*); Jawed Shakoor (*Railway Mehnatkash Union*); Sharafat Ali (*Social Democratic Movement*); Mohammad Hashim (*Khoso Jeaye Sindh Mahaz*); Muhammad Yusuf Khan (*Niazi Saraiki National Party*); Yusuf Mustikhan (*PNP*); Namat Khan (*Tehreeki Istiqlal*); Sheen Farrukh (*Forum for Peace & Development*); Tauqeer Chughtai ('*Jafakash'-Idara-e-Aman-o-Insaf*); M.B.Naqvi (*Social Democratic Movement*); Farhat Parveen (*PILER*); A.Khalique Junejo (*Jeaye Sindh Mahaz*); Nuzhat Shirin; Azra Babar (*Baan Beli*); Sheema Kermani (*Tehrik-e-Niswan*); Dr. S.T.Sohail; Jamaluddin Naqvi (*Forum for Social Studies*); Naheed Afzal Khan (*Tehreeki Istiqlal*); Husain Askari (*The News*); M.Ahmed Drra (*Tehreeki Istiqlal*); Baseer Naweed (*Social Democratic Movement*); Karamat Ali (*Pakistan Workers Confederation*); Shahid Fayyaz (*Social Democratic Movement*); Moazzam Ali (*HRCP*); A. Ali Memon; Musadiq Sanwal; Khurram Mustikhan; A.Samad Panjguri (*PNP*); M. Farooque Baloch (*PML*); Javed Baloch (*BNM*); Mohammed Ali (*NSC*); Mir Hammal Khan (*PNP Sindh*); B.M.Kutty (*PNP-PNC*); Aly Ercelawn (*Creed*); Aziz Fatima; Zulfiqar Ali (*PILER*); Qamar ul Hasan (*PILER*); Khalid Ahmad (*Tehrik-e-Niswan*); Seemin Bashir; Nuzhat Kidvai; Nasir Baluch *(LPP)*; Farooq Rehman (*Catholic Social Services*); Augustine Massey (*Catholic*

Social Services); Sabeen Mahmud; Zaheer A. Kidvai (*Hamdard Institute of Information Technology*); Dr. Asad Sayeed (*PILER*).

PNP: Pakistan National Party
CMKP: Communist Mazdoor Kisan Party
HRCP: Human Rights Commission of Pakistan
PILER: Pakistan Institute of Labour Education and Research
LPP: Labour Party of Pakistan
PML: Pakistan Muslim League
AJP: Awami Jamhoori Party
PNC: Pakistan National Conference
BNM: Balochistan National Movement

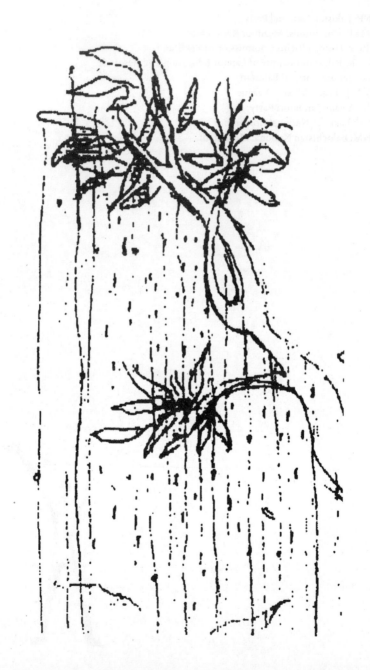

Condemning Nuclear Tests and Weapons

Pakistanis Across the World

To:
Mr. Muhammad Nawaz Sharif
Prime Minister of Pakistan and
Mr. Atal Behari Vajpayee
Prime Minister of India

Dear Prime Ministers,
On behalf of more than 200 Pakistanis—scientists, academics, educationists, architects, doctors, editors, engineers, journalists, jurists, lawyers, publishers, teachers, writers, poets, artists, filmmakers, cultural workers, human rights activists, women rights activists, anti-child labour and anti-bonded labour activists, development and environment experts, human resource developers, economists, political workers, students and others—we would like to send this petition to you against nuclear tests and weapons.

The May 28 and 30, 1998 detonations of nuclear devices by Pakistan and similar tests conducted by India a few days earlier on 11 and 13 May pose an incalculable danger and threat to peace and stability in the region. Thus far only the ability to detonate a nuclear device has been demonstrated by both sides. Whether effective delivery systems have also been developed, remains unclear. If at all these blasts prove anything, it is the horrendous realisation that the chauvinistic and jingoistic lobbies in the two countries now have at their disposal the means to inflict irreversible and irreparable destruction and suffering upon the peoples of the Subcontinent. The worst imaginable scenario could be that the whole region slips into oblivion in the event of a war involving nuclear weapons, leaving behind enough radioactivity and other lethal agents to menace the health and safety of regions far beyond and for a long time to come. There is, of course, the argument that the possession of nuclear weapons enhances security and thereby contributes to peace, simply because if both sides possess them then neither can use them with impunity. This is apparently a strong cold-blooded, rational, argument. However, in the Pakistan-India context it can be shown that such an argument is a bad one. Here are some points to consider:

1. Nuclear weapons may be an effective deterrent against total war, but are useless as a means of preventing small-scale terrorist activities of the intelligence services of hostile countries. It is widely believed that at least since the beginning of the 1980s both sides have been involved in dastardly acts of terrorism against innocent men, women and children. Bombs have been planted in market-places, buses, offices, trains, railway stations and other such places where people congregate in large numbers. As a result, many people have been maimed, killed or simply traumatised. Against this ongoing undeclared war nuclear weapons are no deterrent. In fact one can suspect that they will only embolden the secret services to intensify their nefarious activities and indulge their sadistic impulses with relish in the vain belief that a large-scale war is now impossible.

2. Low-intensity battles have been going on for years between Pakistani and Indian troops along the cease-fire line in Kashmir. Casualties, including deaths, have occurred on both sides. Nuclear weapons are of no use in deterring such blood-spilling. On the other hand, the assumption that a full-scale war is now impossible may perversely encourage local commanders to accelerate their war games.

3. Nuclear weapons are a deterrent only if the belligerents are in possession of superior technology to monitor the situation and ensure that accidental outbreak of war can be prevented. However, no foolproof technology exists anywhere. As recently as 1995 a stray Norwegian rocket seemingly threatening to enter Russian airspace led the Russian armed forces to alert President Yeltsin. They subsequently determined that the missile was not headed for

Russia and called off the alert. As we know, neither Pakistan nor India can claim access to sophisticated technology at present. This greatly increases the chances of an accidental use of nuclear weapons. In the final analysis, nuclear weapons can never guarantee real and lasting peace.

We, Pakistanis (included are persons of Pakistani origin and expatriates), therefore exhort the two governments to seek other ways and means of promoting peace and security. They must focus on the ethical and material well-being of their peoples. It is especially shameful that while the vast majority of the people in these two countries have to wage a daily struggle for survival their governments waste scarce resources on building weapon arsenals. The ancient Indian tradition of ahimsa is part of the common heritage of all the peoples of this region. Many Sufi ideas are also supportive of peace, tolerance and respect for life. The ultra-nationalist and militarist postures of the present regimes, however, negate these humane values. This must change. Relations between Pakistan and India and their peoples should be based on goodwill and a commitment to resolve all controversial issues through discussion and mutual accommodation.

We do not, therefore, find the present policies of the governments of Pakistan and India on defence and security, especially the acquisition of nuclear weapon capabilities, justifiable on any grounds. We also find that the present arrangement that the USA, Russia, France, Britain and China can continue to possess nuclear weapons, arbitrary and flawed. We urge, therefore, the two governments to work towards a global regime dedicated to bringing about the total destruction of all nuclear weapons within a specified period of time, without linking it to their own right to nuclearise. As an immediate step, both countries should declare that they will not embark upon a programme of building nuclear weapon systems.

Signed by:
Dr. Fatima Husain (*London*); Ijaz Syed (*San Jose, CA, USA*); Sain Sucha (*Sollentuna, Sweden*); Riaz Ahmed Cheema (*Stockholm, Sweden*); Prof. Hassan Gardezi (*Canada*); Ayyub Malik (*London*); Amena H. Saiyid (*Missouri, USA*); Nusrat Malik (*New York*); Waseem Hussain (*Zurich*); Dr. Yunas Samad (*Bradford, UK*); Dr. Faheem Hussain (*Trieste, Italy*); Mohammed Yusuf Rahat (*Virginia, USA*); Zulekha Yusuf (*Virginia, USA*); Farina Sial (*New York*); Dr. Ahmed Shibli (*Surrey, UK*); Tazeen Ali (*Sydney, Australia*); Mahir Ali (*Sydney, Australia*); Mujahid Tirmizey (*London*); Saeed Minhas

(*Pakistan*); Rafi Khawaja (*California, USA*); Dr. Bilal Hashmi (*USA*); Tazeen Bari (*Pakistan*); Sehba Sarwar (*USA*); Dr. Zarina Salamat (*Pakistan*); Dr. Khushi M. Khan (*Oldenburg, Germany*); Dr. Saghir A. Shaikh (*Sacramento, CA, USA*); Mustafa Hussain (*Lund, Sweden*); Dr. A.H. Nayyar, (*Islamabad*); Irfan Malik (*Austin, Texas, USA*); Irfan Malik (*Arlington, MA, USA*); Bakhsh Lyallpuri (*London*); Furrukh Khan (*Kent, UK*); Razia Malik (*Chicago*); Dr. Fayyaz A. Malik (Prattville, Alabama, *USA*); Dr. Sohail Inayatullah (*Brisbane, Australia*); Aisha Gazdar, Nosheen Imran, Sohail Akbar Warraich, Bushra Rehmat, Nighat Hafeez, Fazila Gulrez, Fauzia Rauf, Insha Hamdani, Amtul Naheed, Naveeda Hashmi, Shabana Naz, Naureen Tawakkal, Naila, Ambar Naveed, Muhammad Anwar, Muhammad Alamgir, Khawar Mumtaz, Farida Shaheed, Abbas Rashid, Kamil Khan Mumtaz, Tasnim Beg (all of *Shirkat Gah, Lahore*); Zubair Faisal Abbasi (*Lahore*); Rafiq Khan (*Stockholm, Sweden*); Ilyas Khan (*Stockholm, Sweden*); Faiza Inayat (*Islamabad*); Dr. Zahid Shariff (*Olympia, Washington, USA*); Amar Mahboob (*New Jersey, USA*); Prof. Ziauddin Sardar (*London*); Dr. Iftikhar Malik (*Bath, UK*); Nighat Malik (*Oxford, UK*); Farooq Malik (*Brighton, UK*); Sidra Malik (*Oxford, UK*); Abdul Majid (*Lahore* and *Stockholm*); Mirza Tassaduq Baig (Vaxjo, *Sweden*); Zahoor Malik (*Chicago*); Nadeem J.Z. Hussain (*Ann Arbor, MI, USA*); Zafar A. Malik (*Hounslow, Middx, UK*); Sameena Z. Malik (*Middx, UK*); Saad A. Malik (*London*); Saeed Anjum (*Oslo, Norway*); Ahmed Afzal, (*Rawalpindi*); Tanveer A. Janjua (*Sacramento, CA, USA*); Hafsa Rai (*Cairo, Egypt*); Prof. Pervez Hoodbhoy (*Pakistan*); Dr. Amjad Ali (*Durham, NC, USA*); Dr. Arif Azad (*London, UK*); Prof. Riffat Hassan (*Louisville, Kentucky, USA*); Mishka Zaman (*Islamabad*); Masood Munawer Bhatti (*Drammen, Norway*); Khalid Salimi (*Oslo*); Azad Kausary (*Lahore*); Harris Khalique (*Karachi*); Ahmed Faqih (*Sollentuna, Sweden*); Surraya Faqih (*Sollentuna*); Sunil Faqih (*Stockholm*); Adeel Faqih (*Sollentuna*); Sonia Faqih-Zadef (*London*); Sheeba Z. Malik, Madiha Z. Malik, Khawar Z. Malik (all of *Chicago*); Amanullah J. Kariapper (*Lahore*); Fatma Shah, Abbas Hasan, Amenah Hasan (all of *Islamabad*); Foqia Sadiq Khan, Dr. Jennifer Bennett, Sajid Kazmi, Dr. Kaiser Bengali, Zubair Murshid, Dr. Shahrukh Rafi Khan, Atif Rizwan, Masood Hussain Qureshi, Arshad Khurshid, Dr. Shahid Zia, Iqbal Haider Butt, Saba Khattak (all of *SDPI, Islamabad*); Faisal A. Gilani (*Rawalpindi*); Dr. Arshad Waheed (*Islamabad*), Imran Baig (*Solna, Sweden*); Uzma Jalal Haque (*Baltimore, USA*); Mustafa Kamal Ahmed (*Cambridge, MA, USA*); Dr. Ghazala Anwar (*Philadelphia, USA*); Mohammed Naim Ullah (*London*); Mohammad Shamoon Chaudry (*New York*); Hasan Rizvi (*Islamabad*); Isa Daudpota (*Islamabad*); Safiya Aftab (*Islamabad*); Prof. Asghar Qadir (*Islamabad*); Mehreen Hosain (*Islamabad*); I.A. Rehman (*Lahore*); Aziz A. Siddiqui (*Lahore*); Hussain Naqi (*Lahore*); Mehboob Khan (*Lahore*); Ashar Rahman (*Lahore*); Tahira Mazhar Ali Khan (*Lahore*); Athar Rahman (*Multan*); Zaman Khan (*Lahore*); Saeed Ahmad Khan (*Multan*); Safdar Hasan Siddiqui (*Lahore*); Rao Abid Hamid (*Lahore*); Rashed Rahman (*Multan*); Sahr Ataullah (*Lahore*); Ayesha Vawda (*Washington, DC*); Dr. Mohammad Tanveer (*Lahore*); Aziz Mazhar, Rashed Rahman (*Lahore*); Jalees I. Hazir, Muhammad Akram Dail, Vajdaan Tanveer, Fozia Tanveer, Farah Zia, Hussain Sajjad, Noman Yawar, Saleem Akhtar (all Pakistani journalists); Sarmad Manzoor, Amna Rizwan Ali (*Islamabad*); Shahbano Aliani (*New York*); Najeeba Khan; Mona Ahmad Ali (*New York*); Maqbool Aliani (*Virginia, USA*); Dr. Altaf Memon (*College Park, MD, USA*); Ayesha Muzaffar (*Islamabad*); Saleem H. Ali (*Boston*); Nadeem

Omar Tarar (*Lahore*); Asif M. Mohammad (*California*); Saad Muftı (*Virginia, USA*); Rahil Ahmad (*Sollentuna*); Jan Mohammed Baloch, Humair Baloch, Mahroze Baloch, Fiza Baloch (all of *Los Angeles*); Saira Latif, Aisha Masood Rashid, Khurrum S. Bhutta, Saara Salim, Majid Munir, Ameel Zia Khan (all of *Lahore University of Management Sciences*); Zahra Shamji (*Ljunby, Sweden*); Hameed Ahmed Sheikh (*Islamabad*); Faisal Kheiri (*Lahore*); Kiran Khan (*Dubai*); Azfar Najmi (*San Diego, CA, USA*); Amer Iqbal (*Cambridge, USA*); Babar Mumtaz (*London*); Zia Akhter Abbas, Irfan Ahmad Khan, Shamsa H. Khalique, Zafar Ahmed, Dr. Shershah Syed, Tariq Khalique, Dr. Rana Tauqir Ahmed (*Karachi*); Bilal Ahmad (*Lahore*); Amjid Bhatti (*Islamabad*); Adil Manzoor (*Canada*); Zahra Hassan (*Lahore*); Dr. Hameed Toor (*Islamabad*); Naseer Ahmad (*Malaysia*); Ibrar Hamayun (*Islamabad*); Prof. Tariq Rehman (*Islamabad*); Saeed Ur Rehman (*Australia*); Dr. Durre S. Ahmed (*Lahore*); Iqbal Jatoi (*Islamabad*); Khalid Hussain (*Lahore*); Mahmood U. Hassan (*Cambridge, UK*); Irfan Mufti (*Lahore*); Tanvir Ahmad (*Lahore*); Khalid Umar (*Lahore*); Syed Sirajus Salekin (*Sollentuna, Sweden*); Ali Amjad (*Ohio, Delaware, USA*).

The statement was prepared by Dr. Ishtiaq Ahmed, Associate Professor (Reader), Department of Political Science, Stockholm University, 106 91 Stockholm, Sweden. *The signatories have signed in their individual capacity.*

August 11, 1998

A Call for Revival of the Lahore Process

Leaders of public opinion from South Asian countries today called upon India and Pakistan 'to take urgent and decisive measures to defuse the tensions' between the two countries 'before it is too late'.

In an urgent appeal made public by the former Indian Prime Minister, Mr. I.K. Gujral, participants at the Neelan Tiruchelvam Commemoration Programme here, urged the leaders of the two countries 'to revive the Lahore process so that both India and Pakistan, along with other South Asian neighbours march together building a vibrant and prosperous South Asian community.'

The appeal, signed by leading intellectuals from India, Pakistan, Sri Lanka and Bangladesh, termed the Lahore Summit as one which demonstrated the 'political commitment' of the Prime Ministers of the two countries 'to transcend the burden of their tensions—ridden relations of the past 50 years.'

The 'historic development' had 'heartened' the people of both countries as well as all South Asian countries, who 'perceived that a new dawn of hope and harmony will usher in the era of prosperity and well-being.' However, 'within less than a year the vision for a better and peaceful future has become a distant dream,' the statement said, expressing concern that 'peace is one again in peril in the sub-continent, raising grave apprehensions of the imminent danger of outbreak of armed conflict between India and Pakistan. Such a path will result in unimaginable human and material destruction not only in the two neighbouring countries but also in the entire region.'

As South Asia was 'already marginalised in the world community, an armed conflict will only retard, if not reverse, even the faint hopes of the South Asian people, who constitute one-fifth of the total world population, to respond to the challenges of the emerging interdependent and globalised world community.'

The 'time has come for South Asia to make a critical choice between war and peace, destruction and development, poverty and prosperity,' the appeal said, calling upon the 'public and the media to play a positive role in moulding a climate of peace.'

In addition to Mr Gujral, the appeal was signed by:
Justice P.N. Bhagwati, Ms. Devaki Jain, Mr Bishnu Mohapatro, Mr A.G. Noorani, Mr Ashis Nandy and Ms Veena Das (*all from India*), Ms Asma Jehangir, Ms Farida Shaheed, Mr I.A. Rehman and Mr Niaz Naik (*all from Pakistan*), Mr Kamal Hossein and Mr Imitiaz Ahmed (*Bangladesh*), Ms Radhika Coomaraswamy, Mr Gnananath Obeyesekere, Mr Stanley Thambiah, Ms Kumari Jayawardene, Mr Jayadeva Uyangoda, Mr P. Saravanamuttu, Mr Shibley Aziz and Ms Deepika Udagama (*Sri Lanka*)

Colombo, February 1, 2000

South Asians Against Nuclear Arms

South Asian Forum for Human Rights

To,
The Heads of State
South Asian Association for Regional Cooperation (SAARC)

We, the peoples of South Asia are dismayed and alarmed at the Indian and Pakistan nuclear tests of May 1998. The decision of the two traditional rivals, India and Pakistan, to build and deploy nuclear weapons has put at risk the survival of not only the peoples of India and Pakistan, but also the peoples of all the countries of South Asia. We believe that nuclearisation of the subcontinent is a betrayal of the sacred trust of the peoples reposed in their governments. There can be no justification either for the initial nuclear test by India or the retaliatory tests by Pakistan. No amount of provocation or perceived threat legitimises the development, testing, proliferation or use of nuclear weapons. Nuclear weapons are immoral weapons of mass destruction. It is a crime against humanity even to consider the use of nuclear weapons as an option.

The theory of deterrence based on the logic of Mutually Assured Destruction (MAD) has been shown to be highly unstable and accident-prone. During the cold war years, the world was brought to the brink of an 'accidental' nuclear holocaust on nearly 800 occasions. In the case of India and Pakistan, the nuclear balance will be fraught with even greater risk, as the travel time for a nuclear tipped missile is less than three minutes as against about 40 minutes in the erstwhile US-Soviet nuclear face off. Moreover, the history of animosity between India and Pakistan give us little reason for comfort. The two countries have fought three wars during the last fifty years. Two of these wars were over the possession of the territory of the former princely state of Jammu and Kashmir. Even today, they are engaged in a low intensity war over Kashmir.

Since the nuclear tests, there has been an alarming rise in jingoism and sabre rattling on both sides. It threatens to push back India-Pakistan relations to the dark days of mistrust and mutual hostility. During the last few years the common peoples of India and Pakistan had been encouraged by non-governmental initiatives which had taken the courageous step to go against official hostility and advocate peaceful solution of all conflicts through dialogue. The people of India and Pakistan dared to look forward to peaceful relations. But the nuclear tests have resulted in a major setback to the official dialogue, which was resumed after a gap of four years in 1997. It has also meant a major setback to building of bridges through people to people contacts.

The animosity between Pakistan and India has been the main cause of tension in South Asia. It is their rivalry that created hurdles in the path of the growth of economic, cultural, scientific and technological co-operation in the South Asian region. The internal tensions generated by their rivalry and its corollary—the militarisation of polities of Pakistan-India, has had a spill over effect on the region. The Indo-Pak arms race has not only affected the economy of both the countries, it has held back the development and growth of the entire region.

The nuclear arms race will bring even greater misery to the common peoples of the region. The hungry, shelterless, illiterate, sick, jobless, poverty stricken and the disempowered teeming millions, who are the silent suffering majority in South Asia, can not and do not perceive the acquisition of nuclear power as the means towards security, self respect, status and power—economic and political.

We, the concerned peoples of South Asia, call upon the heads of governments meeting in Colombo, to demonstrate the necessary states-manship to assure the future of a fifth of humanity, now threatened with nuclear annihilation.

We urge the SAARC summit in Colombo to put moral pressure on India and Pakistan to immediately sign a bilateral treaty of peace enshrining the principles of non aggression: no first use of nuclear weapons and abjuring the use of force in settling bilateral difference.

We ask the SAARC summit to persuade India and Pakistan to seriously set about resolving the Kashmir dispute in consultation with the entire population in Jammu and Kashmir.

We urge the SAARC summit to exhort India and Pakistan to resume bilateral co-operation in trade and investment, technological and cultural exchanges and tourism. The growth of regional co-operation demands a conflict free South Asia. Normalisation of India and Pakistan relations is essential if the very first objective of the SAARC chapter is to be achieved—'the welfare of the peoples of South Asia and to improve their quality of life'.

July 29, 1998

Marching for Peace in Nepal

Physicians for Social Responsibility, Nepal (PSRN) an affiliate of IPPNW, organised a peace march on August 8, 1998. More than 200 physicians, health professionals, nurses, medical students, journalists and intellectuals from different professions participated. The procession was led by three big posters showing the devastation caused by the explosions in Hiroshima and Nagasaki. Monk , Bhikshu Ashwaghosh, was just behind the posters. He was followed by physicians, medical students, nurses, representatives from *Martin Chautari* and *Mulyankan* journal. They wore black dresses as a sign of protest to the nuclear testing and wore a bow on their heart to express their solidarity with the people of the sub continent.

In the afternoon, a discussion was organised at the Tribhuvan University Teaching Hosptial. Posters of the devastation in Hiroshima and Nagashaki were displayed . There was a big impressive banner with portraits of Buddha for world peace and Einstein pleading atoms are not for destruction. A skull between missiles in cross was shown over the beautiful globe. The slogan read in Nepali:

Dharti Mata Chahinccha Samhar Haina,
Shakti Jeevanko Lagi Ho Mrityuko Lagi Haina

(Mother Earth Needs Care Not Destruction, Energy is Life Not for Death).

The speakers were:
Dr Mathura P Shrestha (*founding president of PSRN and former Minister of Health*), Daman Nath Dhungana (*Former Speaker of Parliament*), Padma Ratna Tuladhar (*renowned human right activist and politician*), Dr Tulsi Pathak (*Chemist*), Suman Ratna Tuladhar and Dr Ashokanand Mishra (*President of PSRN*).

[After the discussion, there was the film show of *A Mother's Prayer*, and a documentary on the Hiroshima and Nagashaki explosions.]

August 8, 1998

Call for a Nuclear-Free South Asia

Sri Lankan Forum for Nuclear Disarmament

The Sri Lanka Forum for Nuclear Disarmament views with grave concern the failure of India and Pakistan to defuse mutual nuclear tensions fully six months after their governments carried out nuclear test explosions and exposed the region to new and serious levels of militarism, environmental destruction, political and economic instability and nuclear holocaust. The Forum is also concerned about proposed new installations of nuclear reactors such as the one of Chernobyl vintage in Kundakulum, Tamil Nadu, which poses an immediate and serious security and environmental threat to Sri Lanka.

On World Armistice Day (November 11th) which commemorates the veterans of war, the Forum calls for the dismantling of the tools of war. It is a timely occasion to remind ourselves of the urgent need for universal nuclear disarmament and global peace, and the special responsibility that devolves in this regard on the five recognised nuclear weapons-states as well as India and Pakistan. The imperative to keep South Asia a nuclear weapons-free zone has never been more pressing.

The Forum strongly deplores the governments of India and Pakistan for embarking on their nuclear misadventure and destabilising security in the region and the Asian continent as a whole. It will spell a runaway arms race, and enormous increases in already high military spending—to the detriment of development and programmes to alleviate the poverty and deprivation in which large numbers of their citizens live. It will detract from the priorities of healthcare, education, food security, and housing to which their peoples have an inalienable right.

The Forum calls upon the governments of India and Pakistan to heed their own people—and those of the rest of South Asia—who object to nuclearisation as an affront to humanity. We call for disarmament and an immediate freeze on all nuclear weapons and missile-related developments in the region.

November 11, 1998

Call for a United Movement Against Nuclearisation
South Asia Solidarity Group

A meeting organised by the South Asia Solidarity Group and entitled 'India and Pakistan, Imperialism and the Bomb' at the House of Commons on the evening of 22nd June, was attended by more than a hundred people and was addressed by Tony Benn M.P., Amrit Wilson from South Asia Solidarity Group and Amjad Ayub from the Labour Party of Pakistan (ML).

Tony Benn condemned all nuclear weapons whether in the West or India or Pakistan. He highlighted the hypocrisy of sanctions which would hurt only the people and not governments. He pointed out that reasons for opposing nuclear weapons in South Asia applied equally well to Britain, where defence budgets had for too long taken up money which should have been spent on health and education. He called for a revival of a genuine internationalism as opposed to the 'globalisation' of exploitation by multinational capital, and for a linking of world-wide anti-nuclear movements.

Amrit Wilson argued that India's current BJP-led government and the BJP itself were using the nuclear tests to pose as nationalist and anti-imperialist but were in fact fascistic and anti-people. She highlighted their history and their current policies which were communalist and deeply anti-Muslim, anti-lower caste, anti-women and anti-workers. She pointed out that since sanctions have been imposed, the government has signed nearly 150 deals with foreign companies, many of them US oil companies, under conditions which were extremely disadvantageous to India. She called on South Asians in Britain to expose the nature of the BJP and its sister organisation the Vishwa Hindu Parishad (VHP) which is receiving funds from many Local Authorities in Britain, via its branches in the community.

Amjad Ayub spoke about the role of the military in Pakistan which had always been a dominating force in politics even in periods of civilian rule. He described the role of the US which had used Pakistan as a base for its military strategy of dominating the region. This had also had a devastating effect on the poorer youth of Pakistan who were being indoctrinated and inducted via 'madrassas' into government-sponsored 'militant' groups.

The meeting received messages of support from the Concerned Citizens for Democracy in Kashmir, Delhi, the Communist Party of India (Marxist-Leninist), the Anti-Fascist Democratic Committee, Dhaka, the JKLF, the Anti-Nuclear Coalition, Bangalore, and others.

Many of those attending the meeting signed a statement condemning the sanctions as well as the tests in India in Pakistan. This statement had earlier been signed by eleven Labour MPs and a large number of South Asian academics in Britain and elsewhere in Europe.

South Asia Solidarity Group, UK.

June 22, 1998

Raise Your Voice Against the Nuclear Tests in India and Pakistan

South Asians Abroad

An urgent appeal by South Asians in North America and their friends from all over the world
On May 11 and 13, 1998, the less-than-two-month old Vajpayee government of India carried out five nuclear tests in Rajasthan, an incident that jolted the subcontinent and shocked the world. In retaliation, the Nawaz Sharif government of Pakistan on May 28 and 30 tested its own nuclear devices in Baluchistan. Since the blasts took place in India, inflammatory statements and intemperate language have replaced normal political dialogue in South Asia. The voice of those who oppose nuclear weapons in India, politicians as well as common people, has been disregarded in the heady rejoicing about the recently acquired capacity to kill innocent people indiscriminately. In Pakistan, a symmetrical and unreal fervour for nuclear weapons has taken hold of the people and government, beginning with the testing of the intermediate range missile.

In USA and Europe, pro-BJP and pro-RSS groups have been campaigning in support of their parties' action, and are now asking NRIs to flow money into India to bail the coalition government out of its self-inflicted fiscal troubles created due to economic sanctions placed on India by USA, Japan, and quite a few other countries. Similarly, the Pakistani government is soliciting massive contributions from its own citizens living abroad. We say to you: help needy people,

help people who are suffering, but do not pay for war-mongering and arms build-up.

India and Pakistan have fought three wars and have remained hostile to each other since 1947. The intolerance exhibited by the present governments has severed the lines of communication that had recently opened up between the two countries. The implications of the BJP government's radical departure from India's traditional foreign policy for peace in South Asia (a policy that has been based on Panchsheel and compassion) and the ensuing threat of a nuclear arms race in the region are something that should trouble all peace-loving people of the world. Other than the danger of possible radioactive fallouts from such tests, we are deeply concerned that the poor citizens of India and Pakistan will have to bear the brunt of the massive expenses to build nuclear weapons, because such expenses that India and Pakistan can hardly afford are now going to be heaped by these governments on poor people, thereby putting their already difficult lives in serious jeopardy.

We want global peace and disarmament, and not escalation of wars. We strongly deplore the nuclear weapons and missiles programmes in India and Pakistan. The peace-loving people of South Asia must not be provoked by these irresponsible acts. The two countries should enter into negotiations to eliminate the immediate danger of a nuclear conflict, and then to de-escalate gradually in mutually verifiable steps.

Our People Need Peace and Progress, Not Belligerence and Bombs

Signed by:
Partha Banerjee (*NY*); Anurag Acharya (*CA*); Sameer Akbar (*UK*); V. Krishna Ananth (*Chennai*); Solomon Antony (*MI*); Farhat and Ezra Azhar; Nikhil Aziz (*CO*); Sruti Bala (*Germany*); Priyadarshi Banerjee (*MA*); Pratyush Bharati (*NY*); Rajani Bhatia (*Committee on Women, Population and the Environment, MD*); Sadhu Binning (*Canada*); Anita Bohm-Hassani (*TX*); A.J.C. Bose (*Netherlands*); Heena Brahmbhatt (*CERAS, Centre d'études et de ressources sur l'Asie du Sud, Montreal, Canada*); Archishman Chakraborty (*PA*); Sharmila Chakravarty (*MD*); Laxmi Challa; Shankar Chatterjee (*CA*); Amrita Chhachhi; Mona Chopra (*NY*); Geeta Citygirl (*NY*); K. Joseph Cleetus (*WV*); Aniruddha Das (*NY*); Ashesh Das (*PA*); Moni Day (*MD*); Nikhil Desai (*VA*); Sunil Deshmukh (*CT*); Prachi Deshpande (*MA*); Damini Dey (*Canada*); Joyoni Dey, (*MD*); Rukmini Dey (*NY*); Saroj Dhital, (*Nepal*); Shelley Feldman (*NY*); Friendship Action Culture & Empowerment of South Asian Americans (*Houston, TX*); Hassan Gardezi (*Canada*); Shalini Gera (*CA*); Tapasi Ghosh (*PR*); Vinay Gidwani (*Canada*); Mandeep S. Gill (*CA*); Sherna B. Gluck (*CA*); Rajesh Gopakumar (*MA*); Manisha Gupte; Shubhra Gururani (*Canada*); Houston Endorser, F.A.C.E., (*TX*); Shishir K.

Jha (*NY*); Partha Joarder (*Bangalore*); Harsh Kapoor (*France*); Kalpana Kaul (*Calcutta*); Kaleem Kawaja (*MD*); Mary Keller (*Scotland*); Smitu Kothari (*Delhi*); Karl-Heinz Krämer (*Germany*), Nidadavolu Krishnaji (*India*); Sunil Kumar (*Germany*); Amar Mahboob (*NY*); Biju Mathew (*NY*); Sunil Mathrani (*France*); Rinita Mazumdar (*NM*); Ernestine McHugh (*MN*); Shiraz Minwalla (*NJ*); Raza Mir (*MA*); Mizuno Mitsuaki (*Japan*); Anuradha Mittal (*GA*); Sujata Moorti; Saikat Mukherjee (*CA*); Somnath Mukherjee (*CA*); Meera Nanda (*NY*); Shalini Nataraj; Murli Natrajan; Judith Norsigian (*MA*); Prema Oza (*Canada*); Mukund Padmanabhan (*Chennai*); Ravi Palat (*New Zealand*); Tasneem Paliwala (*TX*); Krupa Parikh (*TX*); Shaista Parveen (*TX*); Laurie L. Patton (*GA*); Ram Puniyani (*Bombay*); Usman Qazi (*TX*); S. Ravi Rajan (*CA*); M.V. Ramana (*MA*); Sri Renganathan; Anupama Rao (*IN*); Kunjan Raval (*OR*); Sugandhi Ravindranathan (*Bangalore*); D.J. Ravindran and T.K. Sundari Ravindran (*India*); Indira P. Ravindran (*MD*); Raka Ray (*CA*); C. Rammanohar Reddy (*Chennai*); Hannah Reich (*Germany*); Mousumi Roychowdhury (*TX*); Eugene Ruyle (*CA*); Nandan, Prema, Aleyamma, Nalini, Sandhya, and Prasannan, Sakhi (*Trivandrum*); Chris Salter (*PR*); S. Sankarapandi (*MD*); Ratnabali Sengupta, Forum for Secular India (*MD*); Srinivas Seshadri (*Canada*); Mehar Shah; Sunil Shah (*TX*); Saghir A. Shaikh; Prithvi R. Sharma; Ratnesh K. Sharma (*CO*); Lhakpa Sherpani (*Germany*); Mathura P. Shrestha (*Nepal*); Sandhya Shukla (*CA*); Dina Mahnaz Siddiqi (*PA*); Mohan Sikka (*PA*); Harpreet Singh (*NY*); Jyoti Singh (*OR*), Vandana Singh (*OR*); Aparna Sivasankaran (*MA*); R. Sivasankaran (*MA*); S. Sivasegaram (*Sri Lanka*); Harald O. Skar (*Norway*); G. Srinivasan (*Canada*); Prasad Subramanian (*VA*); Abha Sur (*MA*); Raja Harish Swamy (*MI*); Ijaz Syed (*CA*); Parshu Ram Tamang, Nepal Federation of Nationalities (NEFEN), Nepal Tamang Ghedung (NTG) and Milijuli (*Nepal*); Narayani Tiwari (*Australia*); Rita Tsering (*Germany*); S.P. Udayakumar (*MN*); Phiroze Vasunia (*CA*); Senthilvel Vellaichamy (*MI*); Jyotika Virdi (*MD*); Prema Viswanathan (*Singapore*); Saeeda Wali-Mohammed; Maya Yajnik (*MA*).

Advertisement in India Abroad *and* India West, *June 19, 1998*

Petition Against the Nuclearisation of South Asia

We, the undersigned, express our deep regret at the recent series of nuclear tests by India, the ongoing escalation of missile tests by both Pakistan and India, and the general militarisation of the region. Although the two governments have sought to justify the nuclear arms build up in their respective countries in the name of national security, their actions serve only to heighten tensions and increase hostilities in the region. It is tragic that valuable resources that should be used for the betterment of the people are instead being squandered on weapons of mass destruction. The nuclear and missile tests undermine the ongoing efforts to forge common bonds of friendship between the two countries by those Indians and Pakistanis who have been able to transcend narrow nationalist propaganda. The jingoistic rhetoric of our leaders notwithstanding, we are determined work together toward peace and harmony in the region.

Signed by:
M.V. Ramana (*M.I.T., Cambridge, MA*); Salahuddin (*Boston University*); Pervez (*Boston University*); Zarrar Sainet (*New York*); Azhar Salahuddin (*Boston University*); J.J. Suh (*M.I.T*); Sayan Mukherjee (*M.I.T.*); Anant Sahai (*M.I.T.*); Siva Dirisala (*M.I.T.*); Arvind Mallik (*M.I.T.*); Asad Naqvi (*M.I.T.*); Abira Ashfaq (*Northeastern Law School*); Amita Vasudeva (*Boston*); Joydeep (*Harvard University*); Amer Iqbal (*M.I.T.*); Salal Hussain (*M.I.T.*); Farhan (*M.I.T.*); Bill Bhutta (*M.I.T.*), Jalal Khan (*M.I.T.*); Atif Mian (*M.I.T.*); Atif Zaheer (*Harvard University*); Asma Shaukat (*Aga Khan University*); Anjum Saleemi (*M.I.T.*); Geetha; Aparna Sindhoor, Alliance for a

Secular and Democratic South Asia; Asha George (*Harvard School of Public Health*); Pervez Hoodbhoy (*University of Maryland*); Siddhartha Balachander (*M.I.T.*); Mriganka Sur (*M.I.T.*); Raju Sivashankaran, Alliance for a Secular and Democratic South Asia; Jayanta Dey (*UMASS., Amherst*); Abha Sur (*Harvard University*); Kashif Riaz (*M.I.T.*); Nassem Haq (Cincinnati, Ohio); Faraz Hoodbhoy (*Rensselaer Polytechnic Institute*); Sabrina Hasham; Salima Jinna (*McGill University*); George Varghese, (*Center for Theoretical Physics, M.I.T.*); Bilal Musharraf; Steven Barner; Khizar Ahmad Khan (*Teradyne Inc.*); Faisal Hassan (*M.I.T.*); Abhay Wadhwa; Roohi Abdullah (*M.I.T.*); Ali Mir (*Purdue University, Indiana*); Nayela Khan (*M.I.T.*); Nida R, Farid (*M.I.T.*); Navaneetha Rao (*Harvard University*); David Reiner (*M.I.T.*); Kishore Dasari; Syed A. Maroof; Shomik Mehudirattan; Arvind Rajagopal (*Purdue University*), Anupama Rao (*West Lafayette, Indiana*); Partha Banerjee; Arnab Acharya (*Harvard University*); Dharni Vasudevan (*Duke University*); Madhu Rao (*Duke University*); Shome N. Mukherjee; Demetris Vryonides (*Harvard University*); Amitava Kumar (*University of Florida*); Cyrus Umrigar (*Cornell University*); Sujata Moorti (*Old Dominion University*); Jyotsna Vaid; Shalini Natraj (*Sommerville, MA*); Prasad Venugopal (*U Mass, Amherst*); Sekhar Ramakrishnan (*Columbia University*); Kirankumar Vissa; Ashish Gupta, Buffalo; Mahua Sarkar (*Johns Hopkins University*); Nikhil Aziz (*University of Denver*); Raza Mir, (*U Mass, Amherst*); Anjali Ram (*Clark University*); Kavita Philip (*Georgia Institute of Technology*); Hari Subramanian; Vandana Singh (*Portland*); Ishrat Chaudhuri, M.A., (*Boston*); Padma Latha Channavajhala (*Boston University*); Tito Basu (*U Mass, Boston*); Priya Shamsunder (*Chicago*); Janak Ramakrishnan (*Harvard University*); Sunil Mushran; Anu Saxena; Balakrishnan Rajagopal; Anugraha Palan; Sara Abraham (*New York*); Nalini Visvanathan (*Brattleboro, VT*); Amrita Basu (*Amherst College, MA*); Raj Hasmukh Barot (*Brooklyn Law School*); Balmurli Natrajan; Preeti Kachroo; Aniruddha Das (*SAMAR Editorial Collective, NY*); Sreenivas Paruchuri, U. Paderborn, (*Germany*); Mona Chopra (*New York*); B. Skanthakumar (*Law Department, SOAS, London*); Manabi Majumdar (*Harvard University*); Siddhartha Chatterjee (*Syracuse*); Nalini Ganapati; Jael Silliman (*University of Iowa*); Subramanian Shankar (*Rutgers University*); Alnoor Dhanani (*Harvard University*); Noor Kassamalu; Subir Sinha (*University of Vermont*); Rashmi Varma (*University of Vermont*); Laxmi Rao (*M.I.T.*); Mohan Rao (*Umass, Amherst*); Param Roychoudhury (Cambridge, MA); James Gathii (*Harvard Law School*); Rina Das; Sanjay Asthana; Gonzaga de Gama; Omar Khalidi (*M.I.T.*); Monami Maulik (*Brooklyn, New York*); Radhika Lal (*UNDP, New York*); Badri Raghavan; Amitabha Bagchi (*Baltimore*); Rasheed Khan; Amitabh Chaudhary; Freyan Panthaki; Amrish Kacker; S. Charusheela (*Franklin & Marshall College, PA*); Gunja Sengupta; Nidhi Srinivas (*McGill University, Montreal*); Shelley Feldman (*Cornell University, NY*); Kunal Parker (*Cleveland Marshall College of Law, Ohio*); Baman Das, (*MA*); A.H. Jaffor Ullah; Brij Masand (*Wayland, MA*); Priya Nanda; Nadine Ezard (*School of Public Health, Harvard University*); Sinead Jones (*School of Public Health, Harvard University*); Vijay Prasad, (*Trinity College, CT.*); Indira Ravindran; Swati Shah, (*New York*); Rahul De; Sharmila Chakrabarty; Jayati Lal (*New York University, NY*); Shahbano Aliani (*Center for Economic & Social Justice, NY*); Satya P. Mohanty (*Cornell University*); Ganesh Venimadhavan (*UMass, Amherst*); Radhika Nagpal (*M.I.T.*); Bindu T. Desai (*Chicago*); Shariq Ahmed Tariq; Mangai Gopalan; Bharat Kona; Sagguirty (*Sunnyvale, CA*); Surendra Gadekar (*Sampoorna Kranti Vidyalaya*);

Sanghamitra Desai (*Sampoona Kranti Vidyalaya*); Iftekar Rahman, Isabelle Valois (*South Asia Partnership Canada, Ontario*); Akm. Mahfuzur Rahman; Basav Sen (*Alliance for a Secular and Democratic South Asia*); Satyajit Arvind Vaidya (*UMASS, Amherst*); Harsh Kapur (*South Asia Citizens Web*); Nalini Lamba Nieves (*Wisconsin*); Faisal Hossain (*National University of Singapore*); Godhuli Bose (*Berkeley, CA*); Akeel Bilgrami (*Columbia University*); Modhumita Roy (*Tufts University, MA*); Michael Sprinker, (*SUNY, Stonybrook, NY*); Prasad Rampalli, Intel (*Folsom, CA*); Mridula Udayagiri (*University of California at Davis*); Vasuki Nesiah (*Harvard Law School*); Manishita Dass (*Stanford University*); Mila Mitra; Rummana Alam; G. Asha; Radhika Balasubrahmanyam; Mina Reddy (*Cambridge*); Ram Rammohan; Phiroze Vasunia (*University of Southern California*); Sangeeta Kamat (*Brooklyn College, NY*); Biju Mathew (*Rider University, NJ*); Anibel Comelo (*UCLA, California*); Richa Nagar; David Faust; Medha Faust-Nagar; Faisal Khan (*U.K.*); Meena Tewari, Bhuvnesh Jain (*M.I.T.*),; Sivaram Pillarisetti (*Columbia University*); Martin B. Kalinowski (*IANUS, Germany*); Faheem Hussain (*Abdus Salam International Center for Theoretical Physics*); Sheheryar Salim (*Boston*); Kajoli Banerjee Krishnan (*Bangalore*); Venkat Srinivasan (*Canton, MA*); Pradeep Sopory (*University of Wisconsin at Madison*); David Ludden, (*U. Penn.*); Rizwan M. Tufali (*U. Chicago*); S. Viswanathan (*U. Penn*); Anurag Garg (*UCLA*); Geraldine Forbes (*SUNY, Oswego*); Sidnay L. Greenblatt (*Syracuse University*); Manjari Mehta (*M.I.T.*); Faris Ahmed (*Ottawa, Canada*); Srikanth Sastry (*Gaithersburg, MD*); Anupama Rao (*U. Michigan*); Adil Hussain (*Middlebury College, Vermont*); Ananda Chanda (*Johns Hopkins University*); Yumna Siddiqi (*U. North Carolina, Greensboro*); Smitu Kothari (*Delhi*); Amber Habib (*Mehta Research Institute, Allahabad*); Rishikesha T. Krishnan (*Indian Institute of Management, Bangalore*); Rowena Robinson (*Mumbai*); John Broomfield (*Havelock, New Zealand*); Jo Imlay (*Havelock, New Zealand*); Kamel; Sanjay and Rizwana Talreja (*Mount Holyoke College, MA*); Ansar Fayyazuddin (*Harvard University*); Jatin Hansoty; S. Sabahat Quadii (*Karachi*); Irfan Zaman;John McNamara; Jason Keith Fernandes (*National Law School, Indiana University*); Abha Verma (*MHMR, Texas*); Mofeez Murtaza; Muhammad Raja; Iftekar Zaman (*Colombo, Sri Lanka*); Ali Diwan; Aiko Joshi (*Georgia State University*); Srikanth Nagaraja; Omayr Aziz Saiyid (*Claremont, CA*); Sankaran Krishna (*U. of Hawaii at Monoa*); Lipi Ghosh (*Calcutta*); Vaqar Ahmed (*Westmont, Canada*); Munawar Karim (*St. John Fisher College, Rochester, NY*); Sajjad Mahmood (*Albany*); Shraddha V. Chigateri; Damini Dey; Mire Dey; Jishnu Dey; Ch'ng Kim See (*Singapore*); Vinod Mubayi (*New York*); Mathew John (*National Law School, Bangalore*); Abhijit Banerjee (*M.I.T.*); Nithya Sriram (*India*); Inayatullah (*Islamabad*); Jehan Ara (*Karachi*); Ameena Saiyid (*Oxford University Press, Pakistan*); Asim Hussain; Shahid Mahmud; William J. Willis (*Columbia University, NY*).

May 13, 1998

Demanding Global Disarmament
South Asian Magazine for Action and Reflection

We are outraged by the BJP-led government's decision to conduct underground nuclear tests which have ended the hope for peace in our region. As we gather in protest on the soil of the nation which has chiefly been responsible for obstructing the possibility of worldwide nuclear disarmament, we also wish to condemn the US and the other nuclear weapons states for their sanctimonious responses to outcomes that they have helped to create.

The rickety coalition government currently ruling India was moved by the basest of motives: short term political gain internally, and the wish to strut around self-importantly on the international stage. Their jingoism has uprooted the lines of communication that had only recently opened up between India and Pakistan, and severely damaged India's relationship with China. It has placed in peril the lives of millions of Indians who have never supported an aggressive nuclear policy as well as the lives of millions of inhabitants of neighbouring nations whose real economic and social needs will be sidelined as the nations of the region race to enhance their capacity to kill. In the 50th anniversary year of his assassination, we mourn the obliteration of the Gandhian tradition in India through this violent nuclear gesture. The BJP-led government brandishes its close affinity with the paranoid, hate-filled world view of Gandhi's assassins as it moves to stamp out all that remains of Gandhi's vision of peace and non-violence. Those of us who are Indian citizens feel disgraced by the belligerent actions of our government, and by its portrayal of these nuclear tests as 'anti-imperialist' just as it prepares to barter away the interests of the Indian masses to foreign capital when it signs the World Trade Order.

We are appalled by the hypocritical posturing of the nuclear nations, particularly the US imposed sanctions on India, when these nations have blocked every international move towards a nuclear-free world by their insistence on retaining their own nuclear arsenals. While we may debate the question of whether or not discriminatory treaties like the CTBT are indeed a step in the direction of ultimate global disarmament, we agree that lasting peace is possible only when the nuclear powers agree to disarm. Otherwise, the Indian government's actions will be matched in time by other aspirants to the membership of the nuclear nations club. We categorically oppose the US decision to impose sanctions on India, which will crush the most vulnerable sections of Indian society, the sections most likely to have opposed the decision to go nuclear. As the citizenry of the world today, we demand a just, good faith process towards global disarmament which applies equally to all nations.

SAMAR, USA.

May 19, 1998

Condemning the Indian and Pakistani Government

Des Pardesh, Toronto

We condemn the tests, and we condemn all steps towards weaponi-sation, deployment and a nuclear arms race in South Asia. No govern-ment has the 'right' to test, deploy or use nuclear weapons. No govern-ment has the 'right' to squander precious resources on evil weapons of mass destruction. No government has the 'right' to place tens and hundreds of millions of people under the constant threat of nuclear annihilation. Nuclear weapons increase insecurity; they do not increase security. Des Pardesh also condemns the Canadian government for it's role in the proliferation of nuclear technologies around the world that contribute towards the nuclear weaponisation of the planet. Des Pardesh represents a broad cross-section of people of South Asian origin and others interested in peace, democracy, secularism and social justice on the sub-continent. We are Hindus, Muslims, Sikhs, Christ-ians, Zoroastrians, Jews, Buddhists, agnostics, atheists, of mixed back-ground, women and men, immigrants and children of immigrants from all the countries of South Asia. We stand in defiance of the Indian and Pakistani governments' decision to nuclearise the subcontinent. The two governments claim to have the unanimous support of their respective communities overseas. They do not.

We say, 'Stop the madness!.' We pledge our support to all initiatives inside South Asia aimed at halting the nuclearisation of the sub-continent and at settling conflicts through non-violent and political means. We pledge our support to all initiatives outside South Asia aimed at accelerating worldwide nuclear disarmament.

We call upon the government of Canada to put pressure on all countries to sign the Comprehensive Test Ban Treaty (CTBT) and to desist from its hypocritical policy of selling nuclear technologies that contribute to nuclear weaponisation.

Background

Relations between India and Pakistan had shown signs of improvement before the tests. Relations between India and China had significantly improved since the late 1980s. This fragile progress towards reducing tensions within South Asia and between South Asia and its neighbours has been dealt a major blow by these irresponsible tests and the belligerent declarations that preceded and followed them.

The countries of South Asia have experienced an increase of communal tension and political and economic instability in recent years. The nuclear tests have added fuel to the fire. There is a real danger that matters will escalate out of control, into an increase in violence against minority communities, and even into outright conventional or nuclear war between India and Pakistan. Since the late 1980s there has been slow-but-real progress towards global nuclear disarmament. Yet the nuclear weapons states still have enough bombs to destroy the planet several times over. The USA, for its part, has largely disappointed all those who had hoped for a 'peace dividend' in the post-Cold War world. Its total military spending remains at Cold War levels, it is higher than the military spending of all the other main powers put together. The USA has used the end of the Cold War to perpetuate and extend its domination of the planet in defense of a profoundly unjust economic and political world order.

The hypocrisy and misdeeds of the USA and other world powers, however, in no way justify the recent misdeeds of the Indian and Pakistani governments. India and Pakistan's nuclear bombs in no way challenge the unjust US-led world order. On the contrary, the Indian and Pakistani foreign policy elite see 'the bomb' as a 'short cut' towards carving out a privileged place within this unjust world order. In addition to being cynical, irresponsible and perilous, the decision to nuclearise could well turn out to be a landmark foreign policy fiasco that further isolates South Asia in a world only too ready to do just that. The May nuclear tests have delivered a major blow to the fragile process of global nuclear disarmament. It is now that much more difficult for those outside South Asia to argue for global nuclear disarmament. South Asia has alienated a large number of those peace-loving people in the world that looked to it for leadership. The world needs a universal movement of citizens for nuclear disarmament. Des Pardesh pledges to work with Canadians involved in building such a movement, and to strengthen links with the emerging anti-nuclear movement in South Asia.

Des Pardesh is a group of South Asians based in Toronto, Canada.

August 6, 1998

POEMS

POEMS

Goodbye Gandhi

NARAYAN DESAI

Fifty years ago we took leave of Gandhi
For he was a symbol of the moral power of this nation.
Seeing us at fault He would cry 'Halt'
While returning a debt, he would calculate not what use
    the neighbour would make of it.
Being freed of debts he would try to be righteous
When we opposed the NPT
Our theme was righteousness
With what face were you asking others to desist
While armed with bundles upon bundles of bombs.
The first principle of morality is to wash one's face before
    holding a mirror to others.
When we turned away from CTBT
There were still some shreds of virtue left
What is the point of merely banning testing
While doing nothing about stockpiling and refining newer weapons.
Fifty Years! Today we present you Operation Shakti
Having bid a final goodbye to Neeti
What strength is there where there is no life
What Shakti is there where there is no Neeti

Translated by Surendra Gadekar

I Will See if You
Like It or Not

AMITAVA KUMAR

For Safdar Hashmi
[*This poem mimics Allen Ginsberg's America. 'America when will you
send your eggs to India? I'm sick of your insane demands.'*]

India I have given you all and now
I'm a memory.
I'm a name for a playwright killed and a movement born
    on January 1, 1989.
I can't stand my own countrymen's minds.
India when will we end the daily war?
Go fuck yourself with your nuclear bomb.
India, I'm not Sanjay Gandhi
I don't give a damn about making Marutis.
I will write poems about tyrants spilling blood in the streets.
India when will you be a playground for your children?
When will you celebrate Holi with red flags?
When will you remind the world of the dead in Bhopal?
When will you be worthy of a single landless peasant in Bihar?
India why are the songs of Bhikhari Thakur about lean days?
India when will you stop sending your engineers to America?
I'm sick of the world's insane demands.
When can I appear on Doordarshan and shatter H.K.L. Bhagat's
    dark glasses with my smile?

India after all it is you and I who are perfect not the next world.
Your ministers are too much for me.
You made me want to be poor.
There must be some other way to settle this argument.
Gaddar is in a prison even at home it's sinister.
Are you being sinister or is this a practical joke of the
  Home Ministry?
I'm trying to come to the point.
I refuse to give up my obsession.
India stop pushing I know what I'm doing.
India the gulmohar is blooming.
I haven't read the newspaper for months, everyday somebody
  is accused of wild corruption.
India I feel sentimental about Telengana.
India I became a communist when I was a kid
I'm not sorry.
I sing songs at town squares every chance I get.
I sit in tea-shops for days on end and talk to strangers
  about bringing change.
When I go to a basti we raise the cry 'Halla Bol...'
My mind is clear that they are going to make trouble.
You should join me in reading Marx and Premchand.
The priests say the old order was perfectly alright.
I will not repeat the old half-truths and outright falsehoods.
I have revolutionary dreams and songs about a new world.
India I still haven't told you what you did to Manto when
  he did not leave for Pakistan in '47.
I'm addressing you.
Are you going to let your emotional life be run by television?
I'm obsessed by television.
I watch it every day.
Its eye watches me every evening as I step inside my home.
I watch it with friends in a room in A.K. Gopalan Bhavan.
It's always telling us about the greatness of this country.
Cricketers are great. Movie stars are great.
Everybody's great but us. It occurs to me that I am India.
I could not be talking to myself when I say this.
Alisha sings she is 'Made in India.'
What happened to Mukesh singing 'Mera joota hai Japani,

Yeh patloon Inglistani, Sir pe laal topi Rusi, phir bhi dil hai
    Hindustani?'
I'd better consider my national resources.
My national resources consist of ten glasses of tea,
our nukkad-natak,
The fire in the stomach of my unemployed friends,
The exhaustion on the faces of those productively employed,
    who after work,
put in four or more hours in rehearsals and street-performances.
I say nothing about the factories closed-down the busted trade
    unions the millions who wake under the dying suns of
    flourescent pavement lights.
I have abolished bonded labour in Delhi, dowry deaths is
    the next to go.
My ambition is to have Bertolt Brecht elected the head of
    each gram-panchayat
Despite the fact that he does not belong to any caste.
India how can I write an epic poem in your television soap opera?
I will continue like J.R.D. Tata
My plays are as patriotic as his factories
More so they're also for the working class.
India I will perform a street-play Rs. 50 apiece Rs. 400, 550
    down on your Apna Utsav festivals.
India put behind bars Bal Thackeray.
India save the Naxalites.
India Avtar Singh Pash must not die again.
India I am Shah Bano.
India when I was young my parents had organised mehfils
    in a small garden with communist artists like
    Bhisham Sahni and Habib Tanvir
They had performed with the Indian Peoples Theatre Association
and we started with Machine because in a factory goons fired on
    striking workers who had wanted a tea-shop
And a cycle-stand Comrade Mohan Lal was reminded of
    the martyr Bhagat Singh
And Bhishamji said that a new link had at last been added to
    the freedom struggle
The rhythm of people's heartbeats had found expression once again.
India you don't really want to go to war.

India it's them bad Pakistanis.
Them Pakistanis them Pakistanis and them Chinese.
And them Pakistanis.
The Pakistan wants to make eunuchs of us all.
The Pakistan's terrorist.
She wants to take all our cricketers hostage.
Her wants to destroy our temples.
Her needs a Quran-quoting Times of India.
Her wants our HMT watch factories in Karachi.
Him military government running our corner bania-stores.
That not godly.
Chi! Him convert our untouchables.
Him need the support of all Indian Muslims.
Ha! Her make us all victims of missile attacks.
Help.
India this is quite serious.
India this is the message being repeated by our rulers.
India is this right?
We better get down to the job.
It's true I don't want to train in shakhas of right-wing
    vigilantes or join mobs intent on demolishing mosques,
I'm a Muslim and unwelcome anyway.
India I'm putting my unyielding shoulder to the wheel.

Dear Civilised People

SAHIR LUDHYANIWI

Be this blood ours or theirs
Humanity is bloodied
Be this war in East or West
A peaceful earth is bloodied
Whether the bombs fall on homes or borders
The spirit of construction is wounded
Whether it is our fields that burn or theirs
Life is wracked by starvation
It matters not that tanks advance or retreat
The womb of the earth becomes barren
Be it a celebration of victory or loss' lament
The living must mourn the corpses
That is why, O! civilised people
It is better that war remains postponed
In your homes, and in ours
It is better that lamps continue to flicker

Mankind's Error

KHUSHAL HABIBI

Each morning as I comb my hair
I look into the mirror,
And far beyond my own image
I envision mankind's error.

So as to boost his pride
And further his territorial sphere
It makes weapons of destruction
To kill all living creatures far and near.

In the name of nuclear deterrence
It makes atomic bombs to douse
The world with leathel radiation
Which will blow his own faulty house.

When in the world thousands die
From hunger and disease
The cost of buying lethal weapons
Will forever further increase.

To run the wheel of fortune
Of the dreadful war machines
They are sold to the warlords
Who indulge in fratricidal scenes.

Oh when will this insanity stop
So that death's smell may blow no more
Let there be eternal joy
Without the fighter jet's roar.

Chagai: The White Peak

SHAHEEN RAFI KHAN

I'm withered and deformed—
Mere rubble where once I towered.
My elements are fused;
I exude poison from deep within,
To defile water, air and soil.

Once I was nature's pride,
Rich in her colors did I glow;
My shades of ochre, red and brown
Blazed sharply in the morning sun,
Or blended in the fading light.

Still, silent, serene;
A willing host to flocks,
That grazed upon my craggy slopes;
Or birds that nestled in my folds,
Beneath the eagle's soaring rush
Against a blue and brilliant sky

A tribute to God, to His sublime will;
A stillness where even He could rest,
And rejoice His creation would endure—
A haven in the endless rush of men

Then they came—the faceless ones:
Filled with hatred,
Grim of purpose;
Dark, self-righteous angels
Of a biased God.

Like a relentless flood they bored,
And sowed the seeds of death in me.
Intently they watched, these faceless men
Exulting in the pain they wrought—
In the destructive power unleashed

Now in their soulless, concrete homes
Like jackals they vie for fame—
For a fickle, fleeting thing,
That fades with fleeting time.

With my misshapen form they adorn,
The portals of their sad, grey towns.
Consecrating their fame,
With painted missiles—grim augurs of death,
Exalted with names from a bloody past.

Left to bleed, I mourn the loss,
Of friendly guests;
Of tripping hoofs and rushing wings;
Fleecy enveloping clouds;
Cheerful murmurs in the night;
Glimmering, smoky, orange glows;
Silhouettes of men huddled in camaraderie.

No! men don't come to me now, I go to them,
Infecting them with my poison;
A corrosion spreading sickness and disease:
A barren tribute to martial angst
To all embracing strife,
To everlasting glory and—-oblivion.

'No, O Hunter, No!'

JAY GOSWAMI

According to Indian mythology, the art of poetry was discovered by the sage Valmiki, the composer of the great 'Ramayana'. While taking a morning stroll on the bank of a river, Valmiki saw a pair of water birds mating. Suddenly a hunter's arrow ended the life of the male bird. Valmiki was so deeply anguished by this terrible happening that a few moving words came out of his mouth spontaneously, beginning with Ma Nishada (No, oh, hunter, no). This was the world's first poetry. Valmiki had discovered that words could have a special power when the heart is deeply moved! Goswami's poem is full of evocative images from Indian literature and culture, to make the point that Indian poets through the ages, starting from Valmiki, have always raised their voices against wanton aggressiveness. Some of the most beautiful stanzas of the poem allude to medieval Bengali poetry, which may not be known to readers outside Bengal. Hence, those portions have not been included in the translation.

The silence shatters, a pillar of dust
Pushes against the dome of sky,
Earth's sphere rotates, the fire of hell
Leaps up to devour the sun.

No, not the sun, is it the moon of dark nights?
A black bird flies with the crescent moon in his beak;
A black arrow pierces that moon,

From the bow of the ancient hunter

The ancient hunter whose arrows and spears
Ended the mating of that fated bird couple.
Our first poet's curse still visits on him.
The moon waxes and wanes . . .

Struggles prehistoric—
Struggles to take away the food from the hungry mouth.
A tattered rag to cover a hollow body in winter nights,
The warmth of a morning sunshine on sandy beaches.

The dead and the wounded float in the sea water,
With broken chariots and dead horses.
Two men crawl in the green grass, weapons in hands—
Were they not neighbours once?

I want that land of my neighbour.
I want to rule my neighbour's village.
I want my neighbour king to pay me taxes.
I want my neighbour to fear my weapons.

Will you not mix poison
In my neighbour's wind, sunshine and water?
Intellect and Science crawl like serpents
To dig a hole under the ground.

The fire of hell leaps up in that hole,
A mushroom cloud in the sky, no place to escape.
A burnt house, heaps of bleached bones,
The cracked soil of a barren land.

Many men are dead, many more are born—
With crooked arms, with bodies of monstrous limbs,
Some with no tongues to utter the soul's anguish
Or no leg bones to stand erect.

Poison has entered the seed of man,

Poison has destroyed the fertility of woman and land.
Still we harvest the ripe paddy,
Still we sing the songs of Tulasi and Kabir.

I have seen Tulasi walk by our burnt village,
Kabir sings in the solitary river bank,
The Ramayana lies torn on the dusty road
Where a red-eyed Sadhu roams with a naked sword.

I hear homeless children cry in the footpaths
Through nights of hunger,
I see the owner of a cheap tea-stall
Beat a child labourer.

Let them carry on with their existence.
Even if they starve,
I have got my Weapon
In my mighty hand.

Weapon on the ground, Weapon in the sky,
The horizon is reddened with Weapon's glow,
The red Weapon reflects in the river water
Down which the Grantha Saheb floats . . .

Earth's sphere rotates,
The Jews turn into soil under our feet,
Paddy plants bloom in the killing fields . . .

The sun traverses the sky to rise
In my neighbour's land after mine.
A destitute Muslim offers his daily prayer,
With a white dove flying over his white cap.

A black bird flies with the crescent moon in his beak,
The moonlight shines on weapons of mass murder,
The ancient hunter waits with the raised bow,
The green earth will cease to be when he pushes the button!

Come, O Poet, say once more 'No, O Hunter, No!'

Let the anthills burst apart,
Let the sun and the moon stand on the two sides
And illuminate the paintings of ancient man on cave walls.

Behold the silent night settles on the Ganges,
Behold the solitary boatman rows his boat,
Behold how the whispers of ordinary men
Turn into immortal songs of a nation.

Behold the dust storm has stopped.
The dove of peace has come swimming across the white moonlight
To rest in our yard and pick up grains of wheat.
We work in the fields of wheat and corn.

Behold the silent night settles on the Jamuna,
Behold Krishna and Radha come holding their hands,
Don't you hear Mira singing of love
In the ruined temple?

Is it so easy to kill us all?
We have risen through the cycle of days and nights,
We have traversed the space of the Mahabharata . . .

O Hunter, let your Weapon burn our village
To ashes. I see
An innocent virgin
Rising through those ashes.

The sea waters lie calmly at her feet,
A distant thunder rumbles in clouds over her head.

She takes away the Weapon from your arm,
She throws it in the calm sea waters.

Behold the sun sets in the calm sea waters.

Centuries gyrate—the sun sets . . .

Translated by Arnab Rai Chaudhri

RESOURCES

Selected Bibliography

The scholarly literature on nuclear weapons is enormous. No bibliography can usefully hope to cover more than a small fraction. The list given here reflects works that may be useful as references or starting points for deeper enquiry. The World Wide Web contains many more detailed bibliographies. An introductory list of websites is given separately. We are grateful to Sharon Weiner of Princeton University for her help with the bibliographies.

The Effects of Nuclear Weapons
John Hersey, *Hiroshima* (Vintage Books, 1989).
Samuel Glasstone and Phillip J. Dolan, *The Effects of Nuclear Weapons* (US Government Printing Office, 1977).
Arjun Makhijani, Howard Hu and Katherine Yih, *Nuclear Wastelands: A Global Guide to Nuclear Weapons Production and its Health and Environmental Effects* (MIT Press, 1995).
Carole Gallagher and Keith Schneider, *American Ground Zero: The Secret Nuclear War* (MIT Press, 1993).
Robert Jay Lifton and Richard Falk, *Indefensible Weapons: The Political and Psychological Case Against Nuclearism* (New York: Basic, 1991).
Stephen I. Schwartz, *Atomic Audit: The Costs and Consequences of U.S. Nuclear Weapons Since 1940* (Brookings, 1998).
Kai Bird and Lawrence Lifschultz, *Hiroshima's Shadow: Writings on the Denial of History and the Smithsonian Controversy* (Pamphleteer's Press, 1998).
Paul Boyer, *By the Bomb's Early Light: American Thought and Culture at the Dawn of the Atomic Age* (University of North Carolina, 1994).

Nuclear Weapons Programs

Richard Rhodes, *The Making of the Atomic Bomb* (Touchstone, 1986).

Richard Rhodes, *Dark Sun: The Making of the US Hydrogen Bomb* (Simon & Schuster, 1995).

Thomas B. Cochran, William M. Arkin and Milton M. Hoenig, *US Nuclear Forces and Capabilities—Nuclear Weapons Databook Series Volume I* (Ballinger, 1984).

Thomas B. Cochran, William M. Arkin, Robert S. Norris, and Milton M. Hoenig, *US Nuclear Warhead Production—Nuclear Weapons Databook Series Volume II* (Ballinger, 1987).

Thomas B.Cochran, William M. Arkin, Robert S. Norris, and Milton M. Hoenig, *US Nuclear Warhead Facility Profiles—Nuclear Weapons Databook Series Volume III* (Ballinger, 1987).

Thomas B. Cochran, William M. Arkin, Robert S. Norris and Jeffrey I. Sands, *Soviet Nuclear Weapons—Nuclear Weapons Databook Series Volume IV* (Ballinger, 1989).

Thomas B. Cochran, Robert S. Norris, and Oleg A. Bukharin, *Making the Russian Bomb: From Stalin to Yeltsin* (Westview Press, 1995).

David Holloway, *Stalin and the Bomb* (Yale University Press, 1994).

Robert S. Norris, Andrew Burrows, and Richard Fieldhouse, *British, French and Chinese Nuclear Weapons—Nuclear Weapons Databook Series Volume V* (Westview, 1994).

John Wilson Lewis and Xue Litai, *China Builds the Bomb* (Stanford University Press, 1988).

Avner Cohen, *Israel and the Bomb* (Columbia University Press, 1998).

Seymour Hersh, *The Samson Option: Israel's Nuclear Arsenal and American Foreign Policy* (Random House, 1991).

David Albright, Frans Berkhout and William Walker, *World Inventory of Plutonium and Highly Enriched Uranium* (Oxford University Press, 1996).

Richard Kokoski, *Technology and the Proliferation of Nuclear Weapons* (Oxford University Press, 1995).

Rodney W. Jones and Mark. G. McDonough, *Tracking Nuclear Proliferation: A Guide in Maps and Charts, 1998* (Carnegie Endowment for International Peace, 1998).

Nuclear Weapons in South Asia

George Perkovich, *India's Nuclear Bomb* (University of California Press, 1999).

Praful Bidwai and Achin Vanaik, *South Asia On A Short Fuse: Nuclear Politics And The Future Of Global Disarmament* (Oxford University Press, 2000).

Itty Abraham, *The Making of the Indian Atomic Bomb: Science, Secrecy and the Postcolonial State* (Zed Books, 1998).

David Cortright and Amitabh Mattoo, eds, *India and the Bomb: Public Opinion and Nuclear Options* (University of Notre Dame Press, 1996).

Ashok Kapur, *India's Nuclear Option: Atomic Diplomacy and Decision-making* (Praeger, 1976).

Amitabh Mattoo, ed., *India's Nuclear Deterrent: Pokhran II and Beyond* (Har-Anand, 1999).

Jasjit Singh, ed., *Nuclear India* (Knowledge World, 1998).

Raju Thomas and Amit Gupta, ed., *India's Nuclear Security* (Vistaar Publications, 2000).

Raj Gopal, *Reach for the Stars: The Evolution of India's Rocket Programme* (Viking, 2000).

India and Disarmament: An Anthology of Selected Writings and Speeches (Government of India/Ministry of External Affairs, 1988).

Raj Chengappa, *Weapons of Peace: The Secret Story of India's Quest to be a Nuclear Power* (Harper Collins, 2000).

David Hart, *Nuclear Power in India: A Comparative Analysis* (George Allen and Unwin, 1983).

Ashok Kapur, *Pakistan's Nuclear Development* (Croom Helm, 1987).

Samina Ahmed and David Cortright, *Pakistan and the Bomb: Public Opinion and Nuclear Options* (Notre Dame University Press, 1998).

Zia Mian, *Pakistan's Atomic Bomb and the Search for Security* (Gautam Press, 1995)

Pakistan Peace Coalition, *Pakistan–India Nuclear Peace Reader* (Mashal, 1999).

Nuclear Strategy

Gar Alperovitz, *The Decision to Use the Atomic Bomb and the Architecture of an American Myth* (Knopf, 1995).

Lawrence Freedman, *The Evolution of Nuclear Strategy* (St. Martin's Press, 1989).

Janne E. Nolan, *Guardians of the Arsenal: The Politics of Nuclear Strategy* (Basic Books, 1989).

Peter Pringle and William Arkin, *SIOP: The Secret U.S. Plan for Nuclear War* (Norton, 1983).

Fred Kaplan, *The Wizards of Armageddon* (Simon & Schuster, 1983).

Ernest R. May and Philip D. Zelikow, *Kennedy Tapes: Inside the White House During the Cuban Missile Crisis* (Harvard University Press, 1997).

Bruce Blair, *Strategic Command and Control: Redefining the Nuclear Threat* (Brookings Institution, 1985).

Bruce G. Blair, *Logic of Accidental Nuclear War* (Brookings Institution, 1993).

Kurt Gottfried and Bruce Blair, *Crisis Stability and Nuclear War* (Oxford University Press, 1988).

Paul Bracken, *The Command and Control of Nuclear Forces* (Yale University Press, 1983).

Ashton B. Carter, John D. Steinbruner, and Charles A. Zraket, *Managing Nuclear Operations* (Brookings Institution, 1987).

Desmond Ball and Jeffrey Richelson, eds., *Strategic Nuclear Targeting* (Cornell University Press, 1986).

Scott D. Sagan, *The Limits of Safety* (Princeton University Press, 1993).

Nuclear Energy

Crispin Aubrey, Danielle Grunberg, and Nicholas Hildyard, eds, *Nuclear Power: Shut it Down!. An Information Pack on Nuclear Power and the Alternatives*, Volumes I and 2 (New Malden, Surrey, England: The Ecologist, 1991).

Brian Balogh, *Chain Reaction: Expert debate and public participation in American commercial nuclear power, 1945–1975* (Cambridge: Cambridge University Press, 1991).

Irvin C. Bupp and Jean-Claude Derian, *Light Water: How the Nuclear Dream Dissolved* (New York: Basic Books, 1978).

John Byrne and Steven M. Hoffman, editors, *Governing the Atom: The Politics of Risk* (New Brunswick: Transaction Publishers, 1996).

Steven Mark Cohn, *Too Cheap to Meter: An Economic and Philosophical Analysis of the Nuclear Dream* (Albany: State University of New York Press, 1997).

Daniel Ford, *Meltdown: The Secret Papers of the Atomic Energy Commission* (New York: Touchstone, 1986).

Daniel Ford, *Three Mile Island: Thirty Minutes to Meltdown* (New York: Penguin, 1982).

John G. Fuller, *We Almost Lost Detroit* (New York: Readers' Digest Press, 1975).

Vinod Gaur, ed., *Nuclear Energy and Public Safety* (New Delhi: INTACH, 1996).

Bertrand Goldschmidt, *The Atomic Complex: A Worldwide Political History of Nuclear Energy* (La Grange Park, Illinois: American Nuclear Society, 1982).

James M. Jasper, *Nuclear Politics: Energy and the State in the United States, Sweden, and France* (Princeton, NJ: Princeton University Press, 1990).

Christian Joppke, *Mobilizing Against Nuclear Energy: A Comparison of Germany and the United States* (Berkeley, CA: University of California Press, 1993).

Arjun Makhijani, and Scott Saleska, *The Nuclear Power Deception: U.S. Nuclear Mythology from Electricity 'Too Cheap to Meter' to 'Inherently Safe' Reactors* (New York: Apex, 1999).

David R. Marples, *The Social Impact of the Chernobyl Disaster* (New York: St. Martin's Press, 1988).

Grigori Medvedev, *The Truth About Chernobyl* (New York: Basic Books, 1989).

David P. O'Very, Christopher E. Paine and Dan W. Reicher, eds, *Controlling the Atom in the 21ˢᵗ Century* (Boulder, CO: Westview Press, 1994).

Frank J. Rahn, Achilles G. Adamantiades, John E. Kenton, and Chaim Braun, *A Guide to Nuclear Power Technology: A Resource for Decision Making* (Malabar, Florida: Krieger Publishing Company, 1992).

Piers Paul Read, *Ablaze: The Story of the Heroes and Victims of Chernobyl* (New York: Random House, 1993).

Richard Wolfson, *Nuclear Choices: A Citizen's Guide to Nuclear Technology* (Cambridge, MA: MIT Press, 1995).

Arms Control

Gregg Herken, *The Winning Weapon: The Atomic Bomb in the Cold War, 1945–1950* (Knopf, 1981).

Bruce Russett, *The Prisoners of Insecurity: Nuclear Deterrence, the Arms Race and Arms Control* (Yale University Press, 1983).

Allan S. Krass, *The United States and Arms Control* (Praeger, 1997).

Bruce Larkin, *Nuclear Designs: Great Britain, France and China in the Global Governance of Nuclear Arms* (Transaction, 1966).

Harold A. Feiveson, ed., The Nuclear Turning Point: A Blueprint for Deep Cuts and De-Alerting of Nuclear Weapons (Brookings Institution, 1999).

Frank von Hippel and Roald Z. Sagdeev, eds., Reversing the Arms Race: How to Achieve and Verify Deep Reductions in the Nuclear Arsenals (Gordon and Breach, 1990).

Strobe Talbott, Deadly Gambits: The Reagan Administration and the Stalemate in Nuclear Arms Control (Vintage Books, 1985).

Kosta Tsipis, David Hafemeister, and Penny Janeway, Arms Control Verification: The Technologies that Make it Possible (Pergamon-Brassey's, 1986).

Allan S. Krass, Verification: How Much is Enough? (Lexington Books, 1985).

Peace Movements

Lawrence Wittner, One World or None: A History of the World Nuclear Disarmament Movement Through 1953 (Stanford University Press, 1993).

Lawrence Wittner, Resisting the Bomb: A History of the World Nuclear Disarmament Movement, 1954–1970 (Stanford University Press, 1997).

David Cortright, Peace Works: The Citizen's Role In Ending The Cold War (Westview Press, 1993).

Matthew Evangelista, Unarmed Forces: The Transnational Movement to End the Cold War (Cornell University Press, 1999).

Russel J. Dalton et al., Critical Masses: Citizens, Weapon Production and Environmental Destruction in the United States and Russia (MIT Press, 2000).

Jonathan Schell, The Gift of Time: The Case for Abolishing Nuclear Weapons Now (Metropolitan Books, 1998).

Films

This list has been compiled from various sources. The scale of how many creative film-makers were moved, some of course to sensationalise and treat the nuclear issue as a commodity, is an indication of how deep our collective conscience has been angered by this evil human creation.

Above and Beyond. 1952. Dir: Melvin Frank, Norman Panama
The story of Col. Paul Tibbets, the pilot of the B–29 'Enola Gay', the plane that dropped the atomic bomb on Hiroshima. With the exception of the dropping of the bomb at the end of the film, *Above and Beyond* sets the pattern for later films that deal with SAC's training for war. Also, as in later SAC dramas, war seems secondary to the personal problems of airmen, and the dropping of the atomic bomb seems less a turning point in world history, than an episode in Col. Tibbet's life.

Amerika. 1972–1983. Dir: Al Razutis
This is a feature-length film that tries to serve as an antidote to commercial media myths about Western culture. Reel 1 contains a segment called *Atomic Gardening*. Synopsis is in 'Canyon Cinema, Catalog 6', p. 100.

Andromeda Strain. 1971. Dir: Robert Wise
Based on the novel by Michael Critchton. The *Andromeda Strain* combines nuclear and biological mythology. A town has been wiped out by a virus from outer space, one for which human beings have no natural immunity. Scientists plan to destroy the infected town with a nuclear bomb. Also, they plan to use a nuclear weapon to destroy and decontaminate the research lab in which the Andromeda Strain has broken free. As in the film version of *War of the Worlds*, nuclear weapons fail to provide an effective defense. Scientists realise at the last minute that a nuclear blast will simply cause new mutations in the Andromeda Strain.

Any Given World. 1982. Dir: Eames Demetrios
This is the story of a man on a submarine four years after the end of the world. He has nothing to do all day but watch videocasettes of commercial television over and over. . . . The film includes a 20 minute flashback equating architecture with nuclear war, . . . a concert in a post-nuclear parking lot, and a dance on an unfinished freeway. The plot centres on the use of a nuclear power plant to restrict civil liberties in San Francisco, just before Armageddon.

Atoll K. 1950. Dir: Leo Joannon. Also called *Utopia* and *Robinson Crusoeland*
By 1950, even Laurel and Hardy rely on a nuclear theme in this, their final film together. They inherit an island which contains a uranium deposit.

*The Atomic Cafe.*1982. Dir: Kevin Rafferty
A classic use of documentary footage to capture the 'feel' of the Cold War. Also, the film demonstrates the extent to which nuclear fear and fervour penetrated American culture after World War II.

The Atomic Monster. 1941. Dir: George Waggner
When the movie was re-released in the 1950s, the title was changed from *The Man Made Monster* to *The Atomic Monster*. Lon Chaney, Jr. is immune to the electric chair. Interesting because the title change reflects the waning of electricity as a symbol of modernity after 1945.

The Beginning or the End. 1947. Dir: Norman Taurog
First feature length film about the development of the atomic bomb.

The Bells of Nagasaki. 1950. Dir: Hideo Oba
This seems to be the first Japanese feature film about the atomic bombings. When it was made, the Americans still forbade any overt criticism of the bombing in Japanese films. Instead of showing devastation the film dwells upon the heroism of Dr. Takashi Nagai, upon whose memoirs the film was based. See Tadeo Sato's *Currents in Japanese Cinema*, pp 197–198.

Black Rain. 1990. Japanese
Based on the novel by Ibuse. The film maintains the low-keyed approach of the novel. The title refers to the black rain that fell on a young woman at Hiroshima, and which caused her to fall ill from radiation sickness after the war. The film explores the lingering effects of the war both on victims of the atomic bombings and on those experienced by ordinary soldiers. A classic example of 'post-traumatic-stress.'

Broken Arrow. 1987. Dir: Dina Hect for Channel 4. UK
On January 17, 1966 a US Air Force B–72 crashed into its refuelling aircraft over Spain, rupturing the bomb casings of the four thermo-nuclear bombs on board, scattering plutonium across villages of Palomares and Villaricos. The long term effects are only now begining to emerge—just as the statute of limitations expires.

Children of the Atomic Bomb. 1952. Dir: Kaneto Shindo
A film that caused controversy in Japan because it suggested that something should actually be done for the children of the bombed cities. A reminder to Americans that the survivors of the atomic bombings were often shunned. At the time, the children were often treated as untouchables. Sekigawa's *Hiroshima* was made in the following year to restore the politically correct theme of passive suffering. See *The Japanese Movie*, p. 101.

China Syndrome. 1979. Dir: James Bridges
Reflects an iconographic shift away from the threat of nuclear war to the more immediate danger posed by 'peaceful' uses of nuclear energy.

Crisis in Utopia. 1981. Dir: Ken Ross
Renee Shafransky, writing in *The Villager*, October 29, 1981, described it as an avant-garde version of *War of the Worlds*. See Film-Maker's Cooperative, Catalogue No. 7, pp. 414–415.

Crossroads. 1976. Dir: Bruce Conner
Uses documentary footage from the tests at Bikini Atoll, July 25, 1946. The repetition of the explosion 27 times gradually makes the bomb seem akin to god or nature itself. Canyon Cinema, Catalog 6, p. 54.

The Day After. 1983. Dir: Nicholas Meyer. TV movie
A bland study of the effects of nuclear war. Again, there is a typically American focus upon family crises generated by global thermonuclear war. The best scenes are the shots of American missiles streaming out of their silos: the first warning to citizens that nuclear war has begun.

The Day After Trinity: J. Robert Oppenheimer and the Atomic Bomb. 1981
A documentary about J. Robert Oppenheimer and the atomic bomb.

Day One. 1989. Dir: Joseph Sargent. TV Movie
The story of the making of the atomic bomb, with Brian Dennehy as General Leslie Groves.

The Day the Earth Stood Still. 1951. Dir: Robert Wise
The classic film in which a wise alien warns earthlings to abandon nuclear weapons. Klaatu and his invulnerable robot, Gort, land in Washington. Klaatu is a Christ figure: he warns of the dreadful punishment if the human race fails to heed his message, he is killed by those whom he is sent to save, and he is then resurrected from the dead and returns to the heavens.

Desert Bloom. 1986. Dir: Eugene Corr
A girl grows up in Nevada during the time of the nuclear tests. Another example of the American obsession with how atomic bombs will affect the American nuclear family.

Dr. Strangelove, or How I Learned to Stop Worrying and Love The Bomb 1964. Dir: Stanley Kubrick
The classic satire of nuclear war strategies and of stodgy SAC movies.

Dr. Strangelove is one of the greatest of the mad nuclear scientists of the movies: totally insane, mutilated, and charismatic. Strangelove easily persuades the President and the top brass that the American elite must collect young girls for breeding stock and take refuge from fallout in deep mine shafts; an ironic twist on the convention that 'civilisation' survives underground after nuclear war. By far the funniest movie ever made about the annihilation of the human race in global thermo-nuclear war.

Ek Khoobsurat Jahaz. 1998. Dir: Gauhar Raza, Hindi
One of the first Hindi short films highlighting the history and the effects of nuclear weapons.

Fahrenheit 451. 1966. Dir: Francois Truffaut
Interesting because nuclear war is not included. In Ray Bradbury's original story, two nuclear wars have already occurred when the story begins and a third is pending at the end.

The Final War. 1960. Dir: Shigeaki Hidaka. Japanese
Also known as *World War III Breaks Out.* The world is drawn into a nuclear war after the Americans accidentally detonate an atomic bomb over Korea. Oddly, only Argentina survives.

First Time Here. 1964. Dir: Richard Myers
Uses a model of a city to show the effects of the atomic bomb.

Hellfire: A Journey From Hiroshima. 1986. Dir: John Junkerman, John Downer
A documentary about two painters, Iri and Toshi Maruki, who saw Hiroshima soon after the dropping of the bomb. The Marukis painted 15 murals that reflected their experience.

Hiroshima. 1974.
An episode from the *World at War,* a documentary series for Thames Television, UK.

Hiroshima. 1953. Dir: Hideo Sekigawa
Made in response to Shindo's *Children of Hiroshima.* The latter had not seemed to support the Japanese idea that passive sorrow and

displacement of blame to the Americans was the only honourable course after Hiroshima. Some scenes from Sekigawa's film were reused in Resnais' *Hiroshima, mon amour*, another film that seems to revel in passive suffering. See *The Japanese Movie*, pp. 101–2.

Hiroshima, Mon Amour. 1960. Dir: Alain Resnais. French
A French woman and a Japanese man become lovers. The story suggests a parallel between French 'suffering' brought about by the shame of defeat and collaboration, and Japanese suffering brought about by defeat and the Atomic bomb.

Hiroshima/Nagasaki. 1945
Released 1970, this film was constructed from suppressed footage that had been made in 1945 by Japanese camera persons.

The Hunt for Red October. 1990
Based on Tom Clancy's novel of the same name, the theme is a Russian equivalent of *Dr. Strangelove*, except that the rogue Russian naval officer is not insane like General Jack Ripper. Rather than trying to initiate global thermonuclear war, Sean Connery's character tries to prevent it by defecting to the Americans, along with his missile submarine.

In No Uncertain Terms. 54 mins: Karl Geiringer for Underdog Films, The Netherlands, 1996
Are nuclear weapons legal?—In October of 1995 the World Court of Justice in the Hague heard arguments and received written submissions from 22 countries on whether to make use of nuclear weapons illegal under international law. The film presents an exclusive portrait of the proceedings.

The Journey. 1984–85. Dir: Peter Watkins
This film is probably longer than a real nuclear war: 14.5 hours. It is a multi-part documentary and commentary filmed in various countries. It includes live interviews and documentary footage of nuclear weapons and their effects to give a kind of 'state of the world' message. See *Canyon Cinema*, Catalog 6, pp. 237–240 for descriptions of the many segments of the film.

Kurosawa's Dreams. 1990. Dir: Akira Kurosawa
The theme is the dreadful consequences that follow if man fails to respect the natural order of things. In one segment, the traditional Japanese landscape is filled with mushroom clouds. The clouds do not signify nuclear war, but the destruction wrought by nuclear power-plants.

Last Days of Planet Earth. 1964. Dir: Shiro Moritani. Japanese
Atomic bombs are among the calamities that usher in the last days of planet earth.

Lord of the Flies. 1963. Dir: Peter Brook
British schoolboys are marooned on an island as they flee the nuclear holocaust. There is an American version made in 1990 that omits the reference to nuclear war.

Mad Max. 1979. Dir: George Miller
The outback of post-apocalypse Australia is the setting for this drama. An understaffed police force against gangs of bikers which plunder the wastelands. The director has denied that he thought of the Mad Max films as distinctly post-nuclear in setting, but they are inevitably inter-preted as such by most viewers.

Nuclear Tango. 1992. Dir: Viktor Buturlin for C.I.M.I.R., Russia
A chilling testament to the agony of Russian veterans who participated in the Soviet Union's nuclear tests in the 1950s. The few who survived relate how they were sent in their aircraft to the epicentre of the nuclear explosions to measure radiation, and how they were upheld as heroes but forced to keep silent about events.

Octopussy. 1983. Dir: John Glen
A maverick Russian general plans to set off a nuclear bomb at an American base in England, but he is thwarted by James Bond.

Our Friend the Atom. 1956. Dir: Walt Disney
Disney domesticates the atom. Famous for showing radiation as sparkle dust.

Pattern for Survival. 1950
This is a classic propaganda film: one of the earliest attempts to 'instruct' Americans about how to prepare for nuclear war, mainly by setting up fallout shelters and storing food. The script for this film is reproduced in *Film and Propaganda in America*, vol. 4; edited by Lawrence H. Suid and David Culbert, New York: Greenwood Press, 1991.

The Plutonium Incident. 1980. Dir: Richard Michaels
The story of a woman who protests dangerous incidents in a nuclear power plant.

Radio Bikini. 1988. Dir: Robert Stone
The first part of the film uses documentary footage of the atomic tests at Bikini Atoll, much in the manner of *The Atomic Cafe*. The second half focuses upon the medical plight of a sailor who was exposed to radiation during the tests.

Record of a Living Being. 1955. Dir: Akira Kurosawa. Japanese
A man is obsessed with a fear of nuclear bombs.

Seventh Seal (The). 1956. Dir: Ingmar Bergman
Although Bergman's film is set in the middle ages, it is intended as a filmic premonition of nuclear war. When Bergman was asked if the film was indeed about nuclear war he replied 'That's why I made it.'

Shadow of Terror. 1945. Dir: Lew Landers
Spies attempt to steal the plans for a secret bomb, which is obviously atomic but which is unnamed in the film. The movie was finished before the atomic bombs were dropped on Japan in 1945, and stock footage of nuclear explosions was added later. This is probably the earliest theatrical film featuring the atomic bomb and actual footage of the explosion.

Silkwood. 1983. Dir: Mike Nichols
A docu-drama based on the life of Karen Silkwood who worked in a nuclear factory.

Speak Up, Uncle Sam is Hard of Hearing. 1984. Dir: Karl Cohen
Short films that are intended as anti-nuclear 'public service' messages.

Their intent is to help galvanise viewers and to enlist them in the anti-nuclear movement. Includes a *Newsbreak* that announces the coming of UFOs to warn us about the perils of nuclear armaments.

The State of Things. 1982. Dir: Wim Wenders
A film within a film. In the beginning, a director is making a film about life in the post-nuclear world.

Suicide Mission to Chernobyl. a NOVA documentary
A Nova film crew revisits Chernobyl and the result is the most bizarre and chilling of all nuclear documentaries. The most sobering scenes are those of Russian scientists working with crude tools inside the 'Mausoleum', the primitive covering over the damaged nuclear plant. In many respects the story of Chernobyl resembles a bad post-holocaust movie. For example, since robots could not work inside the damaged plant, ordinary Russian soldiers were simply nicknamed 'Bio-Robots' and sent inside. One message is clear: Chernobyl is forever.

These are the Damned. 1961. Dir: Joseph Losey
At a secret base in England, radioactive children are given lessons in how to survive nuclear war.

Threads. 1984. Dir: Mick Jackson. British TV Movie
A study of the aftermath of nuclear war in Sheffield, England.

The War Game. 1965. Dir: Peter Watkins
Originally done as a documentary on the effects of nuclear war for British television.

War of the Worlds. 1953. Dir: Byron Haskin
The earthling's high-tech weapons, including a flying wing and an atomic bomb, fail to stop the Martians. Interestingly, the movie substitutes religion for biological evolution as the cause of the Martian defeat.
. . At the end of the movie, the survivors give thanks to God for the sudden death of the Martians. The moral, which probably would have shocked H.G. Wells, is that our reason and science do not bring 'security' or redemption, our salvation rests solely in the hands of God. In Wells' story, the human race is saved because it had paid a steep price during centuries of biological evolution, and not because of

divine providence. Because the Martians have evolved on an alien planet, they are not immune to earthly germs and diseases.

We Will Never Forget That Night. 1962. Dir: Kozaburo Yoshimura. Japanese
Story of a young woman who survives Hiroshima and becomes a bar hostess.

The World, The Flesh and the Devil. 1959. Dir: Ranald McDougall
Harry Belafonte survives global thermonuclear war. The only other surviving male is a racist.

The Nuclear Web

These *Mega-Sites* contain hundreds of links to a variety of nuclear issues.

- *Nukefix* (www.nukefix.org/link.html#news) contains a huge number of links to different nuclear-related sites including search engines for nuclear news items in the United States, Russia, Pakistan, India, North Korea and Europe, as well as search engines dedicated to other important nuclear websites.
- *Proposition One Committee's Anti-Nuclear Web Site* (prop1.org/prop1/azantink.htm) has a very comprehensive list of nuclear links in alphabetical order.
- *The Big, Big List of Nuclear-Related Links* (www.fas.org/nuke/hew/News/Bigbig.html) is maintained by the Federal of American Scientists.
- *The Internet and the Bomb* (www.nrdc.org/nrdcpro/nuguide/guinx.html), published by the Natural Resources Defense Council, is available for free from their website. Of the hundreds of links listed, approximately 75% are devoted to US nuclear weapons including links to US government libraries, technical reports, publication repositories, government news sources, and government regulations. The international links include international government organisations, NGOs, and the United Nations. There are also links to specific documents.

- *The Nuclear Files* (www.nuclearfiles.org) provided by the Nuclear Age Peace Foundation, provides comprehensive historical and current information on ethical and policy problems related to nuclear weapons, nuclear energy, and nuclear waste.
- *CNN* (www.cnn.com/SPECIALS/cold.war/) produced a web-based interactive version of its multi-part documentary on the Cold War.

Technical Information about the effects of nuclear weapons and how these weapons work:

- *Nukefix* (www.nukefix.org/link.html#) has downloadable nuclear weapons computer programs for analyzing nuclear weapon blast effects, a nuclear power plant game, and other resources. The Nukefix homepage (www.nukefix.org) has information about blast effects and a computer simulation program so you try your hand at solving the nuclear weapons proliferation problem.
- The *Federation of American Scientists* (www.fas.org/nuke/hew/index.html) explains the basic principles of fission, fusion, and weapons design on its website, which also contains basic references on weapons physics.
- For specifics on plutonium and uranium, see The *Nuclear Control Institute* (www.nci.org) and The *Institute for Energy and Environmental Research (IEER)* (www.ieer.org/ieer/fctsheet/index.html). For inventories of plutonium in the civil-sector, go to The *Institute for Science and International Security (ISIS)* (www.isis-online.org/publications/puwatch/putext.html), and for a history of plutonium production, acquisition and utilisation in the United States, see *Plutonium: The First 50 Years* (www.doe.gov/html/osti/opennet/document/pu50yrs/pu50y.html).
- Information on the costs of nuclear weapons development in the United States can be found at The Brookings Institutions' *US Nuclear Weapons Costs Study Project* (www.brook.edu/FP/PROJECTS/NUCWCOST/WEAPONS.HTM).
- The *Trinity Atomic Website* (www.enviroweb.org/issues/nuketesting/) contains information about nuclear weapon physics and technology as well as the effects of nuclear weapons and war. This site also contains some of the text from *The Effects of Nuclear*.

Weapons, edited by Samuel Glasstone and Philip J. Dolan (US Department of Defense, 1977), a very useful book which is unfortunately out of print.

- Other US Department of Defense publications about nuclear weapons technology and effects can be found at the *Critical Military Technologies List* (www.dtic.mil/mctl/).
- For unclassified documents about the US nuclear weapons program from the Manhattan Project to the present, search the *Department of Energy OpenNet Database* (www.doe.gov/opennet).
- The *Query Nuclear Explosions Database* (www.agso.gov.au/information/structure/isd/database/nukexp_query.html) contains the location, time and size of explosions around the world since 1945.
- Publications from the now defunct US *Office of Technology Assessment* (http://www.wws.princeton.edu/%7Eota/) include documents on nuclear weapons technology, effects, and use.

For information about the *Nuclear Weapons Arsenals and Stockpiles* of various countries:

- For a history of the development of the atomic bomb by the United States, see *The Atomic Archive* (www.atomicarchive.com/main.shtml).
- The *Atomic Mirror Nuclear Atlas* (antenna.nl/nukeatlas/) contains information on the stockpiles and nuclear policies of various nations. This site also has a list of useful references about technical matters.
- *The Bulletin of the Atomic Scientists* (www.bullatomsci.org/issues/nukenotes/nukenote.html) regularly carries information about nuclear arsenals.
- The *Natural Resources Defense Council* (www.nrdc.org/nrdc/nrdcpro/tkstock/tssum.html) has a downloadable report that contains authoritative estimates of the sizes and locations of the nuclear arsenals of the US, Russia, Britain, France and China. The report contains detailed descriptions, including maps and tables.
- Information about the arsenals of both declared and suspected nuclear weapons states is maintained by the Federal of American Scientists at the *High Energy Weapons Archive* (www.fas.org/nuke/hew/).

- The latest on the US nuclear arsenal, including nuclear exercises, routine deployments and operations, nuclear planning, modernisation of nuclear warheads and weapons, procurement of nuclear weapons systems, and construction of nuclear facilities can be found with the *British American Security Information Council (BASIC)* (www.basicint.org/pulse.htm).
- Take a virtual tour of past components of the US nuclear arsenal at the *National Atomic Museum* (www.atomicmuseum.com).
- Information about US nuclear weapons and policies from official government websites can be found with:

    - The *Defense Special Weapons Agency* (www.dswa.mil/)
    - *Strategic Command* (www.stratcom.af.mil)
    - The *Department of Energy's Defense Programs* (www.dp.doe.gov)
    - *Lawrence Livermore National Laboratory* (www.llnl.gov)
    - *Los Alamos National Laboratory* (www.lanl.gov)
    - *Sandia National Laboratory* (www.sandia.gov)
    - The *Defense Nuclear Facilities Safety Board* (www.dnfsb.gov)

Medical Issues associated with the production and use of nuclear weapons:

- *Medicine and Global Survival* (www2.healthnet.org/MGS/MGS.html) is an international peer-reviewed journal devoted exclusively to the health and environmental consequences of war, weapons of mass destruction, environmental degradation, natural and human-caused disasters, human rights questions, and humanitarian intervention.
- The full text version of the *Journal of the American Medical Association's* (www.amaassn.org/scipubs/journals/archive/jama/vol_280/no_5/jsc80265.htm) August 5, 1998 article on Medicine and Nuclear War can be found on their website.
- Historical documents from the US government's research using human subjects are at the Department of Energy's *Office of Human Radiation Experiments* (tis.eh.doe.gov/ohre/).
- *The Radiation Effects Research Foundation* (www.rerf.or.jp/eigo/experhp/rerfhome.htm), a cooperative effort between Japan and the United States, provides information on the health effects of radiation.

For the *Nuclear Weapons Policies* of various countries, use *Nukefix's* country-specific *search engines* (www.nukefix.org/link.html#search).

Arms Control Treaties and *Verification* issues:

- The website of the *United Nations* (www.un.org/Depts/Treaty/) has the text of many treaties. Selected documents can be seen for free but many may, in the future, require a subscription fee.
- The *International Atomic Energy Agency* (www.iaea.or.at/worldatom/infcircs/) lists arms control treaties.
- For a searchable database of treaties, try *Tufts University's* Multilaterals Project (www.tufts.edu/fletcher/multilaterals.html).
- The text of many major arms control treaties can be found at the *Arms Control and Disarmament Agency* (www.acda.gov/treaties/).
- For the World Court decision on the legality of the use of nuclear weapons, as well as other international arms control initiatives, see the *International Association of Lawyers Against Nuclear Arms (IALANA)* (www.ddh.nl/org/ialana/wcpin.html).
- The *Stimson Center* maintains *The Internet Guide for Elimination Research (TIGER)* (www.stimson.org/zeronuke/tiger/) which provides a comprehensive listing of Internet documents and sites on eliminating WMD that can be searched by specific proposal, transition strategy, or key challenges faced.
- The *Cooperative Monitoring Center* (www.cmc.sandia.gov/index.html) at Sandia National Laboratories, has information and reports on verification technologies and promises virtual workshops and classes in the future.

Technical information about *Nuclear Power*, as well as radioactive waste transportation and storage:

- The *Atomic Mirror Nuclear Atlas* (antenna.nl/nukeatlas/) contains information on the types of nuclear reactors by country. It also has technical references about nuclear power in general.
- The *Nuclear Information and Resource Service* (www.nirs.org/nhome.htm) is an information and networking center for people and environmental organisations concerned about nuclear power, radioactive waste, radiation, and sustainable energy issues. It posts resources, including information about MOX, different types of reactors, and waste storage.

• For issues of nuclear power safety, see the US DOE's *International Nuclear Safety Center (INSC)* (resourcehelp.com/gov_secur.htm).

Disarmament, Abolition, and Peace Activism

Lists of groups and organisations working towards disarmament and/or the elimination of nuclear weapons can be found with The *Nuclear Age Peace Foundation* (www.napf.org/peacelinks.html) and also with *Proposition One* (prop1.org/prop1/azantink.htm). The *Alliance for Nuclear Accountability* (www.ananuclear.org) maintains a map of US nuclear sites with links to the government and grassroots groups that monitor the activities of these sites.

Organisations Working for Peace in South Asia

Coalition for Nuclear Disarmament and Peace (CNDP)
B-1, Second Floor, LSC, J Block
Saket, New Delhi 110017
Tel.: 91-11-9624323/ 6524324
Telefax: 91-11-6862716
Email: natcon2000@fnmail.com

Scientific Workers' Forum, West Bengal
LD/5 Kusthia Housing Estate
Calcutta 700039
Tel.: 91-33-3438374
Email: sm1@cucc.ernet.in
swfwb@hotmail.com

Anumukti
Sampoorna Kranti Vidyalaya
Vedchhi, Gujarat 394641
Email: admin@anumukti.ilbom.ernet.in
Website: http://members.tripod.com/~no_nukes_sa/anumukti.html

Journalists Against Nuclear Weapons:
G-2 Seashore Apartments
3, Jayaram Chetty Street
Thiruvanmiyur, Chennai 600041
Tel.: 91-44-4422670
Email: janw@hotmail.com
Website : http://www.pppindia.com/janw

Physicians for Peace
114J, Rostrevor Garden, Railway Colony
Chennai
Tel.: 91-44-4336296
Email: roshreh@eth.net

ISANW (Indian Scientists Against Nuclear Weapons)
c/o R. Shankar,
The Institute of Mathematical Sciences
C.I.T Campus, Chennai 600113
Tel.: 91-44-2351856
Fax : 91-44-2350586
Email: shankar@imsc.ernet.in
isanw@arbornet.org
Website: http://www.arbornet.org:81/~isanw/

Movement in India for Nuclear Disarmament (MIND)
1, Jaipur Estate
New Delhi 110013
Tel.: 91-11-6565036
Fax: 91-11-6862716
Email: mind123@angelfire.com
Website: www.angelfire.com/mi/MIND123/

Coalition for Nuclear Disarmament
71, 3rd Main Road
MLA Layout
RT Nagar
Bangalore 560032

Focus on the Global South
Flat No. 503, Bldg. No. 4
Sunshine Cooperative Housing Society
MHADA, New Link Road, Oshiwara
Andheri West, Mumbai 400053
Tel.: 91-22-6312889/ 6351271
Email: admin@focusweb.org

People's Initiative Against Nuclear Weapons
115A Rostrevor Colony
Teynampet, Chennai 600018
Email: PIANW@yahoo.com

Parmanu Bomb Virodhi Andolan
(Movement Against Nuclear Weapons)
302 Elite House, Zamrudpur Commercial Complex
New Delhi 110048

Pakistan Peace Coalition
c/o Pakistan Institute of Labour Education & Research (PILER)
St. 001, Sector X, Sub-sector V
Gulshan-e-Maymar, KDA Scheme 45
Karachi 75340
Tel.: 92-21-6351145-46-47 / 6350352
Fax: 92-21-6350354 / 4548115
Email: b.m.kutty@cyber.net.pk

Action Committee Against Arms Race
43/3-C, Shah Abdul Latif Road
Block-6, PECHS, Karachi

Citizens' Alliance in Reforms for Efficient and Equitable
Development (CREED)
44 Darulaman Society 7/8, Sharea Faisel
Karachi
Tel: 92-21-4530668
Fax: 92-21-4549219
Email: creed@awara.khi.sdnpk.undp.org
Website: http://sangat.org/creed

Pakistan Doctors for Peace and Development
PMA House, Garden Road
Karachi 74400
Tel.: 92-21-7214632
Fax: 92-21-7226433
Email: pdpd@pma.khi.sknpk.undp.org

Lahore Peace Forum
LPF 40 Abbot Road
Lahore
Email: lahore.peace@usa.net

Citizens' Peace Committee
PO Box 2342, Islamabad
Tel.: 92-51-270674
Fax: 92-51-278135
Email: Francisco87@hotmail.com

Sustainable Development Policy Institute
PO Box 2342, Islamabad
Tel.: 92-51-278134
Website: http://www.sdpi.org

Forum for Nuclear Disarmament South Asia
425/15, Thimbirigasyaya Road
Colombo 5
Tel: 94-1-501339
Fax: 94-1-595563
Email: pses-ssa@eureka.lk

South Asia Forum for Human Rights
G.P.O. Box 4906,
Kathmandu
Telefax: 977-1-527852
Email: South@safhr.wlink.com.np

TAJIKISTAN

AFGHANI-
STAN

Kashmir
(disputed)

CHINA

PAKISTAN

*Prithvi missile
storage facility*

▲ *Nangal*

Jullundur

Narora

New
Delhi ★ ■

*Narora 1 and 2, and Kakrapar 1
and 2 nuclear power reactors, not
subject to IAEA inspection and
therefore available to produce
plutonium for nuclear weapons.*

Nuclear test site

INDIA

NEPAL

BHUTAN

☀
Pokaran

Kota
■

Baroda
■
Hazira
■

Indore
■

Jaduguda
■

Uranium mining area

BANGLADESH

**Center for
Advanced
Technology
(CAT).**
*Development
of laser
enrichment
technology.*

Calcutta ●

Talcher
■

MYANMAR
(BURMA)

Kakrapar
Tarapur
Trombay
Bombay
(Mumbai)
Thal Vaishet

Chandipur

Missile test site

Bhabha Atomic Research Center (BARC).
*Primary location of India's nuclear weapons program,
including research laboratory, plutonium production
from Dhruva and Cirus research laboratory reactors,
and associated plutonium extraction plant (none
subject to IAEA inspection). Pilot scale uranium
enrichment plant, not subject to IAEA inspection.*

*Arabian
Sea*

Hyderabad
■
Kaiga

Manuguru

*Large plutonium
extraction plant, not
under IAEA inspection
when processing fuel
from Madras and
Narora reactors;
presumed to support
nuclear weapons
program. Two U.S.-
supplied electric power
reactors (under IAEA
inspection).*

Madras
Rattehalli

Kalpakkam
Tuticorin

Indira Gandhi Atomic Research Center. *Site
of Fast Breeder Test Reactor (FBTR) and pilot-
scale and large-scale plutonium extraction
plants. Also location of Madras 1 and 2 nuclear
power reactors—not subject to IAEA inspection
and therefore available to produce plutonium for
nuclear weapons.*

SRI
LANKA

*Pilot-scale uranium
enrichment plant, not
subject to IAEA
inspection.*

Koodankulam

*Indian
Ocean*

0   500

Miles

*Italicized names represent
nuclear-related sites. See chart.*

Carnegie Endowment for International Peace, *Tracking Nuclear Proliferation*, 1998

INDIA: Nuclear Infrastructure

Name/Location of Facility	Type and Capacity: Gross Design (Net) Output[a]	Completion or Target Date	IAEA Safeguards
POWER REACTORS: OPERATING			
Tarapur 1	Light-water, LEU and MOX 210 (150) MWe.	1969	Yes
Tarapur 2	Light-water, LEU[b] 210 (160) MWe.	1969	Yes
Rajasthan, RAPS-1, Kota	Heavy-water, natural U 220 (90) MWe.	1972	Yes
Rajasthan, RAPS-2, Kota	Heavy-water, natural U 220 (187) MWe.	1980	Yes
Madras, MAPS-1, Kalpakkam	Heavy-water, natural U 235 (170) MWe.	1983	No
Madras, MAPS-2, Kalpakkam	Heavy-water, natural U 235 (170) MWe.	1985	No
Narora 1	Heavy-water, natural U 235 (202) MWe.	1989	No
Narora 2	Heavy-water, natural U 235 (202) MWe.	1991	No
Kakrapar 1	Heavy-water, natural U 235 (170) MWe.	1992	No
Kakrapar 2	Heavy-water, natural U 235 (202) MWe.	1995	No
POWER REACTORS: UNDER CONSTRUCTION			
Kaiga 1	Heavy-water, natural U 235 (202) MWe.	1998	No
Kaiga 2	Heavy-water, natural U 235 (202) MWe.	1998	No
Rajasthan, RAPP-3 Kota	Heavy-water, natural U 235 (202) MWe.	1999	No
Rajasthan, RAPP-4 Kota	Heavy-water natural U 235 (202) MWe.	1999	No
POWER REACTORS: PLANNED AND PROPOSED			
Tarapur 3	Heavy-water, natural U 500 (450) MWe.	2004	No
Tarapur 4	Heavy-water, natural U 500 (450) MWe.	-	No
Kaiga 3	Heavy-water, natural U 235 (202) MWe.	-	No
Kaiga 4	Heavy-water, natural U 235 (202) M We.	-	No
Kaiga 5	Heavy-water natural U 235 (202) MWe.	-	No
Kaiga 6	Heavy-water natural U 235 (202) MWe.	-	No
Rajasthan, RAPP-5, Kota	Heavy-water, natural U 500 (450) MWe.	2004	No

INDIA

Name/Location of Facility	Type and Capacity: Gross Design (Net) Output[a]	Completion or Target Date	IAEA Safeguards
Rajasthan, RAPP-6, Kota	Heavy-water, natural U 500 (450) MWe.	–	No
Rajasthan, RAPP-7, Kota	Heavy-water, natural U 500 (450) MWe.	–	No
Rajasthan, RAPP-8, Kota	Heavy-water, natural U 500 (450) MWe.	–	No
Koodankulam 1	Russian VVER Light-water, LEU 1000 (953) MWe.[d]	–	Yes
Koodankulam 2	Russian VVER Light-water, LEU 1000 (953) MWe.	–	Yes
RESEARCH REACTORS			
Apsara BARC, Trombay	Light-water, medium-enriched Uranium, pool type, 1 MWt.	1956	No
Cirus BARC, Trombay	Heavy water, natural U 40 MWt.	1960	No
Dhruva BARC, Trombay	Heavy-water, natural U 100 MWt.	1985	No
Kamini, IGCAR, Kalpakkam	Uranium-233 30 KWt.	1996	No
Zerlina BARC, Trombay	Heavy-water, variable fuel, 100 Wt. decommissioned.	1961	No
Purnima 1 BARC, Trombay	Fast neutron, critical assembly, zero power, decommissioned.	1972	No
Purnima 2 BARC, Trombay	Uranium-233 .005 KWt, dismantled.	1984	No
Purnima 3 BARC, Trombay	Uranium-233[e]	–	No
BREEDER REACTORS			
Fast Breeder Test Reactor (FBTR) IGCAR, Kalpakkam	Plutonium and natural U 40 MWt.	1985	No
Prototype Fast Breeder Reactor (PFBR) IGCAR, Kalpakkam	Mixed-oxide fuel, 500 MWe, planned.	2008[f]	No
URANIUM ENRICHMENT			
Trombay	Pilot-scale ultracentrifuge plant; operating.	1985	No
Trombay	Laser enrichment research site.	early 1980s	No
Rattehalli (Mysore)	Pilot-scale ultracentrifuge plant; operating.g	1990	No
Center for Advanced Technology, Indore	Laser enrichment research site.	1993[h]	No

INDIA

Name/Location of Facility	Type and Capacity: Gross Design (Net) Output[a]	Completion or Target Date	IAEA Safeguards
REPROCESSING (PLUTONIUM EXTRACTION)			
Trombay	Medium-Scale, 50 tHM/y; operating.	1964/1985	No
Tarapur (Prefre)	Large-scale, 100 (25) tHM/y; operating.[i]	1977	Only when safeguarded fuel is present.
Kalpakkam	Laboratory-scale, operating.[j]	1985	No
Kalpakkam	Large-scale, two lines, 100 tHM/y each; under construction.[k]	1998/2008[l]	No
URANIUM PROCESSING			
Rakh, Surda, Mosaboni[m]	Uranium recovery plant at copper concentrator; operating.		N/A (Not Applicable)
Jaduguda, Narw-pahar, Bhatin[n]	Uranium mining and milling; operating.		N/A
Hyderabad	Uranium purification (UO_2); operating.		No
Hyderabad	Fuel fabrication; operating.		Partial
Trombay	Uranium conversion (UF_6); operating. Fuel fabrication.[o]		No
Tarapur	Mixed uranium-plutonium oxide (MOX) fuel fabrication; operating.		Only when safeguarded fuel is present.
HEAVY-WATER PRODUCTION			
Trombay	Pilot-scale; operational?[p]		–[q]
Nangal	14 t/y; operating.	1962	–
Baroda	67 t/y; intermittent operation.	1980	–
Tuticorin	71 t/y; operating.	1978	–
Talcher phase 1	62 t/y; operating.	1980	–
Talcher phase 2	62 t/y; operating.	1980	–
Kota	100 t/y; operating.	1981	–
Thal-Vaishet	110 t/y; operating.	1991	–
Manuguru	185 t/y; operating, under expansion.	1991	–
Hazira	110 t/y; operating.	1991	–

Abbreviations:

HEU	= highly enriched uranium
LEU	= low-enriched uranium
nat. U	= natural uranium
MWe	= millions of watts of electrical output
MWt	= millions of watts of thermal output
KWt	= thousands of watts of thermal output
tHM/y	= tons of heavy metal per year
MOX	= mixed natural U and plutonium oxide fuel

NOTES (India chart)

[a]The gross design capacity of the reactor is its original power rating, while the net operating capacity refers to *current* output as reported for the latest operational use. See *Nuclear Engineering International: 1997 World Nuclear Industry Handbook.*

[b]Up to 30 percent mixed oxide (MOX) fuel was planned for loading in late 1995, but no subsequent reporting has confirmed this. See Marks Hibbs, 'Tarapur-2 to join Twin BWR in Burning PHWR Plutonium,' *Nuclear Fuel,* September 25, 1995, p. 18f. Under contract, China supplied enough LEU to India to operate both units at Tarapur at 125 MWe until 2007. Mark Hibs, 'India to Equip Centrifuge Plant With Improved Rotor Assemblies,' *Nuclear Fuel,* December 1, 1997, p. 7f.

[c]RAPS-2 was shut down in 1994 for at least three years, and as of late 1997 had not been restarted. 'Rajasthan-2 Down for 3 Years to Replace All Pressure Tubes,' *Nucleonics Week,* May 25, 1995, p. 3.

[d]Based on a general agreement reached in October 1995, Russia plans to supply the two VVER reactors to India. The original provisions were for turnkey reactors, but India wants to change the sales terms so that it can build the reactors itself. This would amount to a technology-transfer, which Russia has not yet agreed to. Russia is reportedly under strong U.S. pressure to change the agreement to include a safeguards requirement, which would also cover spent fuel. See Mark Hibbs, 'India Seeks China-style Deal for Two VVERs. MINATOM Says,' *Nucleonics Week,* January 11, 1996, p. 4; and Jyoti Malhotra, 'U.S. Pressure Cited for Faltering Russian Nuclear Deal,' *Business Standard* [India], April 23, 1996, in *FBIS-NES-96-080,* April 24, 1996, p. 67.

[e]India listed Purnima 3 as an operating research reactor when it exchanged lists of nuclear facilities with Pakistan; no power rating was given. See 'India and Pakistan exchange lists of nuclear facilities,' *Nucleonics Week,* January 9, 1992.

[f]According to Indian Department of Atomic Energy Secretary Rajagopal Chidambaram, the design engineering for PFBR is complete, construction is expected to begin in 2000, and completion is expected in 2008. Mark Hibbs, 'Despite Chronic Delays, DAE Maintains Prototype Breeder to Be Built Soon,' *Nuclear Fuel,* December 1, 1997, p. 9.

[g]The Mysore plant, operated by India Rare Earths Ltd. (IRE), is intended to produce a small amount of HEU, enriched to 30-45 percent U-235, for use in a nuclear submarine reactor, which has thus far not been designed or built. Although the nuclear-powered submarine program has been under development since the 1980s, little progress has been made. India may also have requested centrifuge technology from Brazil based on a nuclear cooperation agreement signed between the two in 1996. In 1997 the U.S. Department of Commerce placed IRE on a list of companies that may not receive any U.S.-origin technology due to its procurement of unsafeguarded nuclear and ballistic missile equipment. Mark Hibbs, 'India to Equip Centrifuge Plant with Improved Rotor Assemblies,' *Nuclear Fuel,* December 1, 1997, p. 7; and Mark Hibbs and Mike Kanapik, 'U.S. Aims to Kill Our Program, India Says After Brazil Trade Cutoff,' *Nuclear Fuel,* November 3, 1997, p. 4f.

[h]Construction on the Indore research center continued in 1993, but some of the facilities, perhaps including the laser enrichment site, were operational. See 'India Funds Nuclear Construction, Operations, and Research in FY-92,' *Nucleonics Week,* March 19, 1992.

[i]The Power Reactor Reprocessing Plant (Prefre) has a nominal output capacity of 100 tHM/y, but has operated for more than a decade at about 25 tHM/y. Hibbs, 'Tarapur-2,' op. cit., p. 19.

[j]Reportedly built to reprocess spent fuel from the FTBR. Mark Hibbs. 'First Separation Line at Kalpakkam Salted to Begin Operations Next Year,' *Nuclear Fuel*, December 1, 1997, p. 8.

[k]According to a recent report, the first line is scheduled to begin hot operations in 1998, reprocessing spent fuel from the Madras heavy water power reactors. The second line, reportedly identical to the first but still under construction , is scheduled to begin operations when the first closes, in approximately 2008. While not fully clear on this point, this report may imply that a separate large-scale (1000 tHM/y) facility devoted to reprocessing fuel from India's first-breeder reactors, also planned for Kalpakkam according to the *1997 World Nuclear Industry Handbook*, P. 122, has been shelved due to financial constraints. Given this possibility, the second line could be adapted to separate this type of fuel. Mark Hibbs, 'First Separation Line,' op. cit., p. 8f.

[l]The initial target date for complention of the first line was 1990, but it was delayed bu subcontractors' failure to supply key equipment. See *1997 World Nuclear Industry Handbook*, op. cit., p. 122; Mark Hibbs, 'First Separation Line,' op. Cit., p. 8f.; and Hibbs, 'Tarapur-2,' op. cit., p. 18f.

[m]Sites listed in OECD Nuclear Energy Agency and International Atomic Energy Agency, *Uranium: 1991 Resources, Production, and Demand*, p. 197.

[n]These uranium milling sites are located in a 10-km area near Jaduguda. Listed in the Wisconsin Project *Risk Report*, March 1995, p. 9.

[o]This is a small plutonium fuel fabrication facility for Purnima II (5 Kwe) that was expanded to produce fuel for the FBTR. David Albright, Frans Berkhout and William Walker, *Plutonium and Highly Enriched Uranium 1996: World Inventories, Capabilities and Policies* (New York: Oxford University Press for Stockholm International Peace Research Institute, 1997), p. 206.

[p]See Andrew Koch, 'Nuclear Testing in South Asia and the CTBT,' *Nonproliferation Review*, Spring-Summer 1996, p. 99.

[q]The non-proliferation regime does not include the application of safeguards to heavy-water production facilities, but safeguards are required on the export of heavy water.

Khan Research Laboratory–Kahuta. *Large-scale uranium enrichment plant designed to produce enough weapons-grade uranium for a number of nuclear devices per year; not subject to IAEA inspection.*

UZBEKISTAN

TURKMENISTAN

Possible uranium enrichment R&D facility/pilot plant; not subject to IAEA inspection.

TAJIKI-STAN

CHINA

Kashmir (disputed)

Pakistani Institute of Nuclear Science and Technology (PINSTECH). *Laboratory and pilot-scale plant for plutonium extraction (the second not yet operating); neither subject to IAEA inspection. PARR-1 (10-MWt) and PARR-2 (30-KWt) research reactors, subject to IAEA safeguards.*

AFGHANISTAN

Wah *Golra*
Islamabad ★ *Kahuta*

Tarwanah ▲ *Sihala*
Missile production factory
Isa Khel *Rawalpindi*
Chasma ■ ■ *Khushab*
Sargodha ▲ *Lahore*

M-11 storage facility

Dera Ghazi Khan
Multan

☼ *Chagai Hills*

PAKISTAN

IRAN

Nuclear test site.

50-70-MWt research/ plutonium production reactor under construction; not under IAEA inspection. If completed, in conjunction with the nearby large plutonium extraction plant at Chasma and the pilot-scale plant at Rawalpindi, the reactor could be the source of a significant inventory of unsafeguarded weapons-usable plutonium.

Karachi

Canadian-supplied KANUPP nuclear power reactor; subject to IAEA inspection.

Large plutonium extraction plant; civil works complete; not subject to IAEA inspection. Chinese-supplied 300 MWe nuclear power reactor in early stages of construction, to be subject to IAEA inspection.

INDIA

0 ———— 250
Miles

Italicized names represent nuclear-related sites. See chart.

Carnegie Endowment for International Peace, *Tracking Nuclear Proliferation,* 1998

PAKISTAN: Nuclear Infrastructure

Name/Location of Facility	Type/Status	IAEA Safeguards
NUCLEAR WEAPONS R & D COMPLEX		
Khan Research Laboratories (KRL), Kahuta	Fabrication of HEU into nuclear weapon.	No
Chagai Hills	Nuclear test site.	No
Pakistan Ordnance Factory, Wah	Possible nuclear weapons assembly site.[a]	No
POWER REACTORS		
KANUPP, Karachi	Heavy-water, natural U, 137 MWe; operating.	Yes
Chasma -1	Light-water, LEU, 310 MWe; under construction.[b]	Planned
Chasma-2	Light-water, LEU, 310 MWe; planned[c]	Planned
RESEARCH REACTORS		
Pakistan Atomic Research Reactor 1 (PARR 1), Rawalpindi	Light-water, originally HEU, modified to use LEU, 9 MWt; operating.	Yes
PARR 2, Rawalpindi	Pool-type, light-water, HEU, 30 KWt; operating	Yes
Research/Plutonium Production Reactor, Khushab	Heavy-water, natural U, 50 MWt; under construction, expected completion 1998[d]	No
URANIUM ENRICHMENT		
Khan Research Laboratories (KRL), Kahuta	Large-scale ultracentrifuge facility; operating	No
Sihala	Experimental-scale ultracentrifuge facility; operating	No
Golra	Ultracentrifuge plant reportedly to be used as testing facility; operational status unknown.[e]	No
Wah	Enrichment plant possibly under consection.[f]	
REPROCESSING (PLUTONIUM EXTRACTION)[g]		
Chasma	Terminated by France (1978); indigenous construction of the building shell may be nearly complete; reportedly not equipped.[h]	No[i]
New Labs, PINSTECH, Rawalpindi	Pilot-scale, "hot cell" facility; design capacity up to 20 kg/y.[j]	No
PINSTECH, Rawalpindi	Experimental-scale lab for reseach on solvent extraction.[k]	No
URANIUM PROCESSING		
Baghalchar	Uranium mining; operating.	N/A (Not Applicable)

PAKISTAN

Name/Location of Facility	Type/Status	IAEA Safeguards
Dera Ghazi Khan	Uranium mining and milling; operating.	N/A
Isa Khel	Uranium ore processing; planned.	N/A
Qabul Khel, near Isa Khel	Uranium mining and milling; operating.	N/A
Lahore	Uranium milling; operating.	N/A
Dera Ghazi Khan	Uranium conversion (UF_6); operating.	No
Chasma/Kundian	Fuel fabrication; operating.[1]	No
HEAVY-WATER PRODUCTION		
Multan	Operating.	No
Karachi	Operating.	No

Abbreviation:

HEU	=	highly enriched uranium
LEU	=	low-enriched uranium
nat. U	=	natural uranium
MWe	=	millions of watts of electrical output
MWt	=	millions of watts of thermal output
KWt	=	thousands of watts of thermal output

Notes (Pakistan Chart)

[a]See 'India Denies Atom-Test but Then Turns Ambiguous,' *New York Times*, December 16, 1996.

[b]The civil works for the Chasma-1 power plant were completed by November 21, 1995, and the plant is expected to begin commercial operation by October 1998. See 'Chasma Milestone,' *Nuclear Engineering International*, February 1996, p. 9.

[c]Plans to build the second Chasma-2 reactor may have been shelved due to financial problems and pressure from the United States, although Pakistani officials have denied these reports. 'PAEC head denies report that U.S. money ills derail Chasma-2,' *Nucleonics Week*, July 6, 1995, p. 5.

[d]Some reporting suggests that the Khushab research reactor is already complete, but is awaiting unsafeguarded heavy water from China. Pakistani officials claimed in July 1997 that the plant was operational, but U.S. officials rejected this claim, noting that 'all the data at hand indicates that the reactor is still cold.' See 'U.S. believes Khushab still cold, no heavy water by China,' *Nucleonics Week*, July 3, 1997, p. 16; and Mark Hibbs, 'China accord would turn up U.S. heat on Pakistani reactor,' *Nucleonics Week*, August 14, 1997, p. 8.

[e]See David Albright, Frans Berkhout, and William Walker, *Plutonium and Highly Enriched Uranium 1996; World Inventories, Capabilities and Policies* (New York: Oxford University Press for Stockholm International Peace Research Institute, 1997), p. 269ff.

[f]A January 4, 1996 article in *The Muslim* reported that during a visit to Islamabad, U.S. official Robert Oakley accused Pakistan of constructing another enrichment facility at Wah with Chinese assistance. Pakistani officials confirmed the existence of

the project. As reported in 'Pakistan said to counter Indian nuclear test with its own,' *Nucleonics Week,* February 29, 1996, p. 14.

[g]It was suspected that Pakistan was also constructing a secondary facility to extract plutonium from spent reactor fuel at Khushab. In early August 1997, however, U.S. intelligence officials categorically declared that the secondary facility at Khushab is 'not a processing plant.' See Albright et al., *1996 World Inventories,* op. cit., p. 281; Hibbs, 'China Accord Would Turn Up U.S. Heat,' op. cit., p. 8.

[h]A 1996 report suggested that China was aiding Pakistan in the construction of the Chasma facility. See Bill Gertz, 'China aids Pakistan's plutonium plants,' *Washington Times,* April 3, 1996. Further reports from early August 1997, however indicate that Chinese and French assistance has stopped, and that U.S. officials believe the Chasma complex is 'an empty shell.' See Hibbs, 'China Accord Would Turn Up U.S. Heat,' op. cit., p. 8.

[i]Safeguards may be required because of the use of French technology supplied in the 1970's under the Franco-Pakistani bilateral supply agreement for the plant, which requires such monitoring. Because France refused to complete the facility, however, Pakistan has never acknowledged its obligation to place the facility under IAEA inspection, despite its incorporation of the French technology. If past reports of Chinese assistance to Pakistan to complete the reprocessing facility were true. China would be in violation of Article 3, Paragraph 2 of the NPT for failing to secure IAEA safeguards on the transfer of reprocessing technology to Pakistan.

[j]Contradictory reports have surfaced over the real plutonium output capacity of New Labs. Reports from the early 1980's before New Labs was operational suggested that it had a design output capacity of 10-20 kg/y. See Milton Benjamin. 'Pakistan Building Secret Nuclear Plant,' *Washington Post,* September 23, 1980; a secret U.S. Department of State report dated June 23, 1983, and titled 'The Pakistani Nuclear Program'– subsequently released in 1992 under the Freedom of Information Act – supports this claim. A 1997 report, however, suggests that New Labs can produce only about 1 kg/y. See Hibbs, 'China Accord Would Turn Up Heat, op. cit., p. 8.

[k]The secret 1983 Department of State report op. cit., notes that in the basement of the main PINSTECH building exists a small laboratory for research on solvent extraction. Solvent extraction in Pakistan should be subject to IAEA inspection pursuant to a trilateral safeguards agreement (France, Pakistan, IAEA – see INFCIRC/239).

[l]In parallel with efforts to manufacture fuel for its Canadian supplied KANUPP-1 PHWR, Pakistan has already developed the capability to manufacture the NATU [Natural Uranium] fuel for the production reactor [Khushab] on a pilot basis.' See Bhutto may finish Plutonium reactor without agreement on fissile stocks,' *Nucleonics Week,* October 6, 1994, p. 10. Under contract, China will supply fuel for the first three cores of the Chasma power reactor, and help Pakistan set up a fuel fabrication plant. See 'Chasma vessel manufacture said to be underway in China,' *Nucleonics Week,* November 30, 1995, p. 6.

CONTRIBUTORS

Contributors

Itty Abraham is an Indian historian and Program Director for South Asia and Southeast Asia at the Social Science Research Council, New York. He is author of *The Making of the Indian Atomic Bomb: Science, Secrecy and the Postcolonial State.*

Aijaz Ahmad is Senior Fellow, Centre for Contemporary Studies, Nehru Memorial Museum and Library, New Delhi. His book *In Theory: Classes, Nations, Literatures* marked a major critical intervention in the fields of literature, political science, cultural studies and Marxist theory. He is also the author of *Ghazals of Ghalib* and *Lineages of the Present: Political Essays.*

Eqbal Ahmad, who passed away in 1999, was one of the leading radical intellectuals of his generation. Born in India, brought up in Pakistan, he wrote and lectured extensively on imperialism, anti-colonial struggles, and issues of power and justice. He was one of the founders of the Transnational Institute and taught at Hampshire College, Cornell University and University of Chicago.

B. Baskar is a Chennai-based journalist with *Business Line*, an economic daily. He is also a member of the People's Union for Civil Liberties and of Journalists Against Nuclear Weapons.

Praful Bidwai is a columnist for over twenty newspapers and magazines in India. He was formerly Senior Fellow, Nehru Memorial Museum and Library, New Delhi. He is the co-author of *South Asia on a Short Fuse: Nuclear Politics and the Future of Global Disarmament.*

Sheba Chachhi is a Delhi-based photographer, writer and artist specialising in research and photo-documentation of the Women's Movement in India.

Surendra Gadekar is a physicist and pioneering anti-nuclear activist in South Asia. He is editor of *Anumukti*, a journal devoted to the struggle for a non-nuclear India. He is based at the Sampoorna Kranti Viidyalaya (School for Total Revolution), Vedchhi, Gujarat.

Pervez Hoodbhoy is professor of theoretical nuclear physics at Quaid-i-Azam

University, Islamabad, and one of Pakistan's leading public intellectuals. He is author of *Islam and Science: Religious Orthodoxy and the Battle for Rationality* and editor of *Education and the State: Fifty Years of Pakistan.*

T. Jayaraman is a theoretical physicist at the Institute of Mathematical Sciences, Chennai and an active member of Tamil Nadu Science Forum. He also writes regularly for *Frontline.*

Zafarullah Khan is a free-lance journalist and president of Green Press, Islamabad, a group of environmental journalists that also monitors press freedom in Pakistan.

Rajni Kothari is India's best-known political analyst. Founder of the Centre for the Study of Developing Societies, Delhi, he has been Chair of the Indian Council of Social Science Research, President of the People's Union for Civil Liberties and Programme Director of United Nations University's Programme on Peace and Global Transformation. He has written over twenty books, the most recent being, *Poverty. Human Consciousness and the Amnesia of Development* and *Communalism in Indian Politics.*

Smitu Kothari is a scholar-activist and founder-member of Lokayan, which seeks to bring together activists, concerned citizens and scholars working on a wide cross-section of political, cultural and ecological issues in India and South Asia. He also co-edits the *Lokayan Bulletin* and is on the editorial boards of *Development* and *Ecologist.* He has been a visiting professor at Cornell University and at Princeton University. He has co-edited *The Non-Party Political Process, Rethinking Human Rights* and *Voices from a Scarred City.*

Neeraj Malik is a reader in English at Indraprastha College for Women, Delhi University.

Matthew McKinzie is a physicist specialising in nuclear weapons development and effects with the Natural Resources Defense Council, a US-based environmental NGO.

Zia Mian is a physicist at Princeton University's Center for Energy and Environmental Studies and a Visiting Fellow at the Sustainable Development Policy Institute, Islamabad, working on nuclear energy and nuclear weapons issues in South Asia. He is editor of *Pakistan's Atomic Bomb and the Search for Security*, and *Making Enemies, Creating Conflict: Pakistan's Crises of State and Society.*

Ashis Nandy is one of India's most renowned social psychologists. He was Director of the Centre for the Study of Developing Societies, Delhi and is the author of numerous books including *Science, Hegemony and Violence, The Illegitimacy of Nationalism*, and *The Intimate Enemy: Loss and Recovery of Self Under Colonialism.*

A.H. Nayyar is Associate Professor of Physics at Quaid-i-Azam University, Islamabad. A leading activist, he has worked with human rights, labour and peace groups in Pakistan for several decades.

Anand Patwardhan is one of India's leading documentary film makers. His work, which has won numerous national and international awards, includes *Bombay Our City; In the Name of God; Father, Son and Holy War;* and *The Narmada Diary.* He is based in Mumbai.

J. Sri Raman is a Chennai-based Indian journalist and convenor of Journalists Against Nuclear Weapons and the Movement Against Nuclear Weapons (MANW).

M.V. Ramana is a physicist at Princeton University's Center for Energy and Environmental Studies working on nuclear weapons and nuclear energy in India. He is co-editor of the forthcoming book *Prisoners of the Nuclear Dream*.

Lalita Ramdas is an Indian teacher, writer and activist. She is a former President of the International Council for Adult Education. She lives in Alibag, Maharashtra.

Amulya Reddy is one of the world's leading authorities on energy policy and science and technology policy for developing countries. He is one of the co-authors of the pathbreaking books, *Energy for a Sustainable World*, and *Renewable Energy: Sources For Fuels and Electricity*. He is a Fellow of the Indian Academy of Sciences. He is based in Bangalore.

C. Rammanohar Reddy is senior editor with *The Hindu*, Chennai. He is co-editor of the forthcoming book *Prisoners of the Nuclear Dream*.

I.A. Rehman is a veteran journalist, formerly the chief editor of *The Pakistan Times*, and is currently Director of the Human Rights Commission of Pakistan, the leading independent national human rights organisation. He is based in Lahore.

Arundhati Roy, is the internationally celebrated author of *The God of Small Things* and *The Cost of Living*. She is also active with the campaign against the Narmada dam. She is based in Delhi.

Bittu Sahgal, based in Mumbai, is one of India's best-known conservationists. Editor of *Sanctuary* and co-editor *of Ecologist Asia*, he is a pioneering educator on the relationship of humankind with nature.

Kumkum Sangari teaches English at Indraprastha College, Delhi University, is Professorial Fellow, Nehru Memorial Library, New Delhi, and is the author of *The Politics of the Possible: Essays on Gender, History, Narratives and Colonial English*.

Tanika Sarkar teaches history at St. Stephen's College, Delhi and is a Research Fellow at the Nehru Memorial Museum and Library. A prolific writer on issues at the interface of gender, communalism and history, she has also co-edited *Women and Right-Wing Movements*.

Beena Sarwar is editor of *The News on Sunday*, Lahore. She is an activist with the Pakistani women's movement and on the board of the Human Rights Commission of Pakistan.

Amartya Sen is a Nobel Laureate economist, Master of Trinity College, Cambridge and Lamont University Professor Emeritus at Harvard University. He is the author of numerous books including, most recently, *Development as Freedom*.

Kalpana Sharma is a Mumbai-based journalist, columnist, and assistant editor with *The Hindu*.

R. Suresh is a Chennai-based journalist with *Business Line*, an economic daily. He is also a member of the People's Union for Civil Liberties and of Journalists Against Nuclear Weapons.

Achin Vanaik is a columnist, writer, and peace movement activist in Delhi. He is the author of *The Painful Transition: Bourgeois Democracy in India, The Furies of Indian Communalism: Religion, Modernity, and Secularization*, and co-author of *South Asia on a Short Fuse*.

K. Venkataramanan is a journalist based in Chennai and co-coordinator of Journalists Against Nuclear Weapons.

Shiv Visvanathan is a Senior Fellow at the Centre for the Study of Developing Societies, Delhi. He is the author of *A Carnival of Science*, and co-editor of *Foul Play: Chronicles of Corruption*.

Glossary

Ahimsa: The principle of non-violence; considered by Gandhi to be one of the highest values to live by

Akhada: A place for training people, usually in wrestling, or a place where sadhus (sages) meet

Barfi: A sweetmeat in a square or diamond shape, usually made from milk and sugar

Chakrayudha: Chakra: A circle or disc; *yudha:* War; the term is associated with Lord Vishnu

Chapati: Small, flat round piece of bread, usually rolled out and baked over a griddle

Haris: Anglicised version of Biharis; derogatory reference to people hailing from the state of Bihar

Jawan: An ordinary soldier

Khadi: Cotton cloth that is woven by hand, recommended for use by Gandhi at the time of the nationalist movement

Langur: A monkey native to the Indian subcontinent

Mahila Mandal: Group of women who meet, discuss and take action on common concerns

Neeti: Policies or principles

Panchayat: An elected village or local self-governing council

Rath-yatra: A religious journey, originally made on a chariot or *rath*

Samitis: Bodies or committees or panels

Shakha: A faction or a group; generally associated with the Rashtriya Swayamsevak Sangh, a mass organisation of the Hindu right

Shakti: The female principle of divine energy

Shanti: Peace

Swadeshi: The defence of indigenous production and indigeneity, including the boycott of goods manufactured abroad

Vidya: Knowledge

Index